Policing in France

The eminent contributors to a new collection, *Policing in France*, provide an updated and realistic picture of how the French police system really works in the 21st century. In most international comparisons, France typifies the "Napoleonic" model for policing, one featuring administrative and political centralization, a strong hierarchical structure, distance from local communities, and a high priority on political policing. France has undergone a process of pluralization in the last 30 years. French administrative and political decentralization has reemphasized the role of local authorities in public security policies; the private security industry has grown significantly; and new kinds of governing models (based on arrangements such as contracts for service provision) have emerged. In addition, during this period, police organizations have been driven toward central government control through the imposition of performance indicators, and a top-down decision was made to integrate the national *gendarmerie* into the Ministry of Interior.

The book addresses how police legitimacy differs across socioeconomic, generational, territorial, and ethnic lines. An analysis of the policing of *banlieues* (deprived neighborhoods) illustrates the convergence of contradictory police goals, police violence, the concentration of poverty, and entrenched opposition to the states' representatives, and questions policing strategies such as the use of identity checks. The collection also frames the scope of community policing initiatives required to deal with the public's security needs and delves into the security challenges presented by terrorist threats and the nuances of the relationship between policing and intelligence agencies. Identifying and explaining the diverse challenges facing French police organizations and how they have been responding to them, this book draws upon a flourishing French-language literature in history, sociology, political science, and law to produce this new English-language synthesis on policing in France.

This book is a valuable resource for researchers and practitioners working in and around French policing, as well as students of international law enforcement.

Jacques de Maillard is Professor of Political Science at the University of Versailles-Saint-Quentin and at Sciences Po Saint Germain en Laye, and Director of CESDIP (a research center affiliated to the CNRS, the French Ministry of Justice, the University of Versailles-Saint-Quentin, and the University of Cergy). He is a noted scholar in the area of police organization and management, local governance of crime, police reform, and private policing. He has conducted research in both France and the UK. He has been a visiting scholar at several American and British universities. His books on French policing include *Polices Comparées* (2017) and *Sociologie de la Police: Politiques, Organisations, Réformes* (2015).

Wesley G. Skogan is Emeritus Professor of Political Science and a Faculty Fellow of the Institute for Policy Research at Northwestern University in the USA. His research focuses on policing, community responses to crime, victimization, disorder, and fear of crime. He is a Fellow of the American Society of Criminology and was a Senior Fellow of the Center for Crime, Communities, and Culture of the Open Societies Institute. He organized the Committee on Police Policies and Practices for the National Research Council and served as its chairman. He is the co-author (with Kathleen Frydl) of the committee report, *Fairness and Effectiveness in Policing: The Evidence*. Earlier he spent two years at the National Institute of Justice as a visiting fellow. In 2015 he received the Distinguished Achievement Award in Evidence-Based Crime Policy from the Center for Evidence-Based Crime Policy.

Advances in Police Theory and Practice Series
Series Editor: Dilip K. Das

Policing Terrorism: Research Studies into Police Counterterrorism Investigations
David Lowe

Policing in Hong Kong: History and Reform
Kam C. Wong

Cold Cases: Evaluation Models with Follow-Up Strategies for Investigators, Second Edition
James M. Adcock and Sarah L. Stein

Crime Linkage: Theory, Research, and Practice
Jessica Woodhams and Craig Bennell

Police Investigative Interviews and Interpreting: Context, Challenges, and Strategies
Sedat Mulayim, Miranda Lai, and Caroline Norma

Policing White-Collar Crime: Characteristics of White-Collar Criminals
Petter Gottschalk

Honor-Based Violence: Policing and Prevention
Karl Anton Roberts, Gerry Campbell, and Glen Lloyd

Policing and the Mentally Ill: International Perspectives
Duncan Chappell

Security Governance, Policing, and Local Capacity
Jan Froestad and Clifford Shearing

Police Performance Appraisals: A Comparative Perspective
Serdar Kenan Gul and Paul O'Connell

Policing in France
Edited by Jacques de Maillard and Wesley G. Skogan

Policing in France

Edited by Jacques de Maillard and
Wesley G. Skogan

NEW YORK AND LONDON

First published 2021
by Routledge
52 Vanderbilt Avenue, New York, NY 10017

and by Routledge
2 Park Square, Milton Park, Abingdon, Oxon, OX14 4RN

Routledge is an imprint of the Taylor & Francis Group, an informa business

© 2021 Taylor & Francis

The right of Jacques de Maillard & Wesley G. Skogan to be identified as the authors of the editorial material, and of the authors for their individual chapters, has been asserted in accordance with sections 77 and 78 of the Copyright, Designs and Patents Act 1988.

All rights reserved. No part of this book may be reprinted or reproduced or utilised in any form or by any electronic, mechanical, or other means, now known or hereafter invented, including photocopying and recording, or in any information storage or retrieval system, without permission in writing from the publishers.

Trademark notice: Product or corporate names may be trademarks or registered trademarks, and are used only for identification and explanation without intent to infringe.

Library of Congress Cataloging-in-Publication Data
A catalog record for this title has been requested

ISBN: 978-0-367-13523-2 (hbk)
ISBN: 978-0-367-13524-9 (pbk)
ISBN: 978-0-429-02692-8 (ebk)

Typeset in Bembo
by Swales & Willis, Exeter, Devon, UK

Contents

List of Illustrations x
List of Contributors xi
Preface xiii
Series Editor's Preface xiv

1 Policing in France 1
JACQUES DE MAILLARD AND WESLEY G. SKOGAN

PART I
Historical Background 19

2 The Evolving Organization of Policing: From the Ancien Régime to De Gaulle and the *Police Nationale* 21
JEAN-MARC BERLIÈRE AND RENÉ LÉVY

3 The Colonial Legacy of French Policing 39
EMMANUEL BLANCHARD

4 The Dual French Police System: Centralization, Specialization, Competition 54
MALCOLM ANDERSON

PART II
Organizational Features and Reforms 69

5 Police Centralization and its Pathologies 71
CHRISTIAN MOUHANNA

viii Contents

  6 Intelligence-led Policing in Criminal Investigations: Implementing Reform   86
     CLÉMENT DE MAILLARD

  7 Specialization in Criminal Investigations   100
     ELODIE LEMAIRE

  8 Oversight of the French Police   116
     CÉDRIC MOREAU DE BELLAING

PART III
Changing Institutional and Political Context   131

  9 The Expansion of Private Policing in France   133
     FRÉDÉRIC OCQUETEAU

10 The Pluralization of Local Policing   147
     VIRGINIE MALOCHET

11 Security Partnerships in France   164
     THIERRY DELPEUCH AND JACQUELINE E. ROSS

PART IV
Police Problems and Strategies   185

12 Policing the *Banlieues*   187
     FABIEN JOBARD

13 Identity Checks as a Professional Repertoire   202
     FABIEN JOBARD AND JACQUES DE MAILLARD

14 A Social History of Protest Policing in France   219
     AURÉLIEN RESTELLI

15 Domestic Intelligence and Counterterrorism in France   234
     LAURENT BONELLI

16 Border Policing in France   253
     SARA CASELLA COLOMBEAU

17	Police and the Public in France SEBASTIAN ROCHÉ	269
18	Community Policing Initiatives in France JACQUES DE MAILLARD AND MATHIEU ZAGRODZKI	294
19	Policing and Gender in France MATHILDE DARLEY AND JÉRÉMIE GAUTHIER	310
20	The Police and Sexual Violence OCÉANE PERONA	326
	Index	342

Illustrations

Figures

2.1	The Organization of French Policing in the Modern Era	22
15.1	The Evolution of France's Domestic Intelligence Agencies	237
17.1	Trends in General Assessments of Police	271
17.2	Contextualized Assessments of Trust in Police	273
17.3	Performance of Local Policing	276
17.4	Trust in Police Fairness	278
17.5	Distributive Trust in Police	279
17.6	Judgements of Police Actions	282
17.7	Witnesses of Negative Police Behavior	284

Tables

9.1	Overview of Mission Activity by the CNAPS and CLACS	138
13.1	Stop Rates for Young Men Wearing Typical Youth Culture Clothing and Not Carrying a Bag (All Ethnicities)	206

Boxes

6.1	Case 1: Problem-solving Analysis of Organized Criminal Groups Involved in Heroin Trafficking – the *Police Nationale*, 2015	92
6.2	Case 2: Spatial Criminal Analysis of ATM Attacks – the *Gendarmerie*, 2015	94
6.3	Case 3: The Implementation of Criminal Intelligence within the DIPJ-*Police Nationale*, 2017	96

Contributors

Malcolm Anderson
Department of Politics
University of Edinburgh
Edinburgh, United Kingdom

Cédric Moreau de Bellaing
Department of Social Sciences
Interdisciplinary Center for the Study of Reflexivities
Ecole Normale Supérieure
Paris, France

Jean-Marc Berlière
Department of History
Centre for Sociological Research on Law and Criminal Justice
University of Burgundy
Dijon, France

Emmanuel Blanchard
Department of Political Science
Centre for Sociological Research on Law and Criminal Justice
University of Versailles-Saint-Quentin
Versailles, France

Laurent Bonelli
Department of Political Science
Social Sciences Institute on Politics
University of Paris X Nanterre
Nanterre, France

Sara Casella Colombeau
Researcher, Policy Department
French Collaborative Institute on Migration
Aubervilliers, France

Mathilde Darley
CNRS Research Fellow
Centre for Sociological Research on Law and Criminal Justice
Guyancourt, France

Thierry Delpeuch
CNRS Research Fellow
Pacte-Sciences Po Grenoble
University of Grenoble-Alpes
Grenoble, France

Clément de Maillard
Senior Officer
PhD graduate in Criminal Sciences
Gendarmerie nationale
Issy-Les-Moulineaux, France

Jacques de Maillard
Department of Political Science
Director, Centre for Sociological Research on Law and Criminal Justice
University of Versailles-Saint-Quentin
Versailles, France

Jérémie Gauthier
Department of Sociology
European Dynamics Center
University of Strasbourg, France
Strasbourg, France

Fabien Jobard
CNRS Research Director
Centre for Sociological Research on Law and Criminal Justice
Guyancourt, France

Elodie Lemaire
Department of Sociology
Academic Center for Research on Public Action, Politics, Epistemology and Social Sciences
University of Picardie Jules-Verne
Amiens, France

René Lévy
CNRS Research Director
Centre for Sociological Research on Law and Criminal Justice
Guyancourt, France

Virginie Malochet
Research Fellow
The Institute of the Paris Region
Paris, France

Christian Mouhanna
CNRS Research Fellow
Centre for Sociological Research on Law and Criminal Justice
Guyancourt, France

Frédéric Ocqueteau
CNRS Research Director
Centre for Sociological Research on Law and Criminal Justice
Guyancourt, France

Océane Perona
Department of Sociology
Mediterranean Laboratory of Sociology
University of Aix-Marseille
Aix en Provence, France

Aurélien Restelli
Doctoral student
Centre for Sociological Research on Law and Criminal Justice
Guyancourt, France

Sebastian Roché
CNRS Research Director
Pacte-Sciences Po Grenoble
University of Grenoble-Alpes
Grenoble, France

Jacqueline E. Ross
Professor, School of Law
University of Illinois
Urbana, IL, USA

Wesley G. Skogan
Institute for Policy Research
Northwestern University
Evanston, IL, USA

Mathieu Zagrodzki
Research Associate
Centre for Sociological Research on Law and Criminal Justice
Guyancourt, France

Preface

The vision for this book was to draw together a set of scholarly contributions that would provide a comprehensive view in English of contemporary policing issues in France. Planning for the book began while Jacques de Maillard was a Visiting Scholar at the Institute for Policy Research at Northwestern University. The authors of the chapters in this book are among the leading academic experts on their topics. Their chapters were written for an international audience, based on the latest scholarship. Each originally wrote their chapter in French and received comments on that draft by the first editor. The redrafted chapters were then professionally translated into English, with the collaboration of their original authors. We warmly thank the translators, in particular François-Xavier Priour, Camille Mather and Nathalie Plouchard-Engel. Next, the chapters were edited into final form by the second editor. The editors wish to thank the chapter authors for their timely and informative contributions, and for their responsiveness to editorial concerns. The support of our patient Criminal Justice and Criminology editors at the Taylor & Francis Group, and the editorial contributions of Elizabeth Riley, are also greatly appreciated.

Jacques de Maillard
Wesley G. Skogan

Series Editor's Preface

While the literature on police and allied subjects is growing exponentially, its impact upon day-to-day policing remains small. The two worlds of research and practice of policing remain disconnected, even though cooperation between the two is growing. A major reason is that the two groups speak in different languages. The research work is published in hard-to-access journals and presented in a manner that is difficult to comprehend for a lay person. On the other hand, the police practitioners tend not to mix with researchers and remain secretive about their work. Consequently, there is little dialogue between the two and almost no attempt to learn from one another. Dialog across the globe, amongst researchers and practitioners situated in different continents, is of course even more limited.

I attempted to address this problem by starting the International Police Executive Symposium (IPES), www.ipes.info, where a common platform has brought the two together. IPES is now in its 26th year. The annual meetings, which constitute the major annual event of the organization, have been hosted in all parts of the world. Several publications have come out of these deliberations and a new collaborative community of scholars and police officers has been created whose membership runs into several hundreds.

Another attempt was to begin a new journal, aptly called *Police Practice and Research: An International Journal* (PPR), which has opened the gate to practitioners to share their work and experiences. The journal has attempted to focus upon issues that help bring the two positions on to a single platform. PPR will be 20 years old in 2020. It is certainly evidence of a growing collaboration between police research and practice that PPR, which began with four issues a year and expanded into five issues in its fourth year, is now issued six times a year.

Clearly, these attempts, despite their success, remain limited. Conferences and journal publications do help create a body of knowledge and an association of police activists but cannot address substantial issues in depth. The limitations of time and space preclude larger discussions and more authoritative expositions that can provide stronger and broader linkages between the two worlds.

It is this realization of the increasing dialog between police research and practice that has encouraged many of us – my close colleagues and I connected closely with IPES and PPR across the world – to conceive and implement a new attempt in this direction. This led to the book series, Advances in Police Theory and Practice, which seeks to attract writers from all parts of the world. Further, the attempt is to find practitioner contributors. The objective is to make the series a serious contribution to our knowledge of the police as well as to improve police practices. The focus is not only in work that describes the best and most successful police practices but also one that challenges current paradigms and breaks new ground to prepare the police for the 21st century. The series seeks a comparative analysis that highlights achievements in distant parts of the world as well as one that encourages in-depth examination of specific problems confronting a particular police force.

In this contribution to the IPES Advances Series, it will be noted that while police research in the United States began to develop in the early 1960s, in France the start came later, in the 1980s. It was the work of pioneers in sociology, political science, and history. Forty years on, the situation is quite different. Research on policing is solidly established, and papers on many policing topics have been published in major French social science journals. Police research in France is very open to theories, concepts, and methods from around the world. However, much of it has not been translated into English, and in many places there is not a broad understanding of the breadth and significance of social science research on policing in France. Thus, the core mission of this book is to promote a broader understanding of the police system, police practices, and relations between police and the public in France, with a collection of original essays on key topics that are based on recent social science research. The authors of its chapters include some of those original research pioneers, plus many newly established scholars whose work in France touches on issues of interest to police researchers around the world.

It is hoped that through this series it will be possible to accelerate the process of building knowledge about policing and help bridge the gap between the two worlds – the world of police research and police practice. This is an invitation to police scholars and practitioners across the world to come and join in this venture.

Dilip K. Das Ph.D.
Founding President,
International Police Executive Symposium, IPES, www.ipes.info

Founding Editor-in-Chief,
*Police Practice and Research:
An International Journal*, PPR, www.tandf.co.uk/journals

Chapter 1

Policing in France

Jacques de Maillard and Wesley G. Skogan

Police Research in France

Until the early 1980s, social science research on policing issues was extremely rare in France. Most of what was written was essays by politicians, investigations by journalists or, more often, memoirs by former police officers. The rare academic works were dominated by narrowly legal approaches describing police powers and their legal framework, or philosophical texts discussing in the abstract what police powers should be. While these publications were of interest, they took little account of police practices in the field and the dynamic features of police organizational life. For many academics, policing in action was a "dirty subject," one associated with the mundane and sometimes unpleasant daily functions of the state (see Berlière and Lévy 2011, pp. 10–11). At the same time, the police saw their external observers as excessively critical, engaged in the needless airing of the organizational and political realities they struggled to deal with.

While police research in the United States began to develop in the early 1960s (Skogan and Frydl 2004), in France the start came later, in the 1980s. It was the work of a few pioneers who, in sociology, political science or history, invested in this field of research. Without the list being exhaustive, the research of René Lévy (1987) on the work of the judicial police, Jean-Marc Berlière (1992) on the professionalization of policing under the Third Republic, and Pierre Favre (1990) on the policing of political protests, were the among first social science inquiries in the field. But above all, the emergence of this field of research was led by the sociologist Dominique Monjardet. Coming from the sociology of occupations, where he had already carried out promising work, he stood at the origins of empirical research on public security and public order policing (see for a synthesis see Monjardet 1996 or 2008). It should be noted that the development of this field benefited from the creation of units such as the Institut des hautes études de la sécurité intérieure (IHESI) within the Ministry of the Interior in 1989. Research institutes brought together researchers and provided funding, and kindled forums for exchanges between academics and practitioners. The journal *Les Cahiers de la sécurité intérieure*, published by IHESI, provided an outlet for these activities.[1]

Almost forty years later, the situation is quite different. Research on policing seems solidly established (although see Ocqueteau and Monjardet (2005) on the complex relationship between research and the Ministry of the Interior). It is not possible in this short introduction to give a comprehensive overview of research conducted on French policing, but the variety of research fields that are being explored should be mentioned. These include the emergence of modern police forces, the history of colonial police forces, the professionalization of policing in the contemporary era, changing models of policing, policing during repressive periods in French history (for example, during the German occupation of the 1940s), the feminization of the police, stop and search practices, police relations with young people from minority backgrounds, efforts toward police reform, the introduction of neo-managerialism, the work of oversight bodies, the role of police in maintaining public order, the professional socialization of police officers, political surveillance, and police involvement in partnerships with other organizations and the community. Research on many of these topics have been published in major French social science journals, either generalist (*Revue française de sociologie, Revue française de science politique, Sociologie du travail,* and *Vingtième siècle*), or thematic (*Champ pénal, Déviance et Société,* and *Cultures et conflits*).

However, in this brief assessment one is struck by a paradox. On the one hand, this research has been very open to theories, concepts, and methods developed in other countries. This is illustrated by the work co-directed by Jean-Paul Brodeur and Dominique Monjardet (2003) that was devoted to the major texts of Anglo-Saxon research. Research in France has also internationalized and become involved in cross-national comparisons (Berlière et al. 2008; de Maillard 2017; de Maillard and Roché 2009; Fillieule and Della Porta 2006; Houte and Luc 2016). On the other hand, much of this work has not been translated into English, giving much of the world a restricted picture of police research in France.[2] Thus the core mission of this book is to promote a broader understanding of the police system, police practices, and relations between police and the public in France, with a collection of original essays on key topics that are based on recent social science research.

France: A Centralized Dualist System

In international typologies (see Bayley 1985), France is presented as a dualist, centralized system, consisting mainly of two national police forces, one civilian (the *police nationale*) and the other military (the *gendarmerie nationale*).[3] These two police forces are controlled by the central state and have distinct territories of action. The *police nationale* is active in urban areas, while the *gendarmerie* is traditionally responsible for rural and suburban areas. The *police nationale* is often described as responsible for 5% of the territory, 50% of the population, and 70% of delinquency, whereas the *gendarmerie* is responsible for 95% of the territory, 50% of the population, and 30% of delinquency. As we will see, these two institutions have distinct identities.

Police and *Gendarmerie*: Between Competition and Cooperation

The *gendarmerie* is an ancient institution, heir to the "Maréchaussée" of the Middle Ages. Malcolm Anderson, in his chapter, recalls the strong esprit de corps of the *gendarmerie*, marked by its military identity. The *gendarmerie* is considered an "arm of the state" (*une arme*), the *gendarmes* still define themselves today as "soldiers of the law." The national police is a more recent institution – the repository of the many transformations that have affected the police in urban areas since the 18th century. As Jean-Marc Berlière and René Lévy point out in their chapter, it is not one police force that France has experienced, but multiple and competing ones. Two dates are important for understanding the relatively late process of unification the *police nationale*. In 1941, under the Vichy regime, a decree-law was adopted nationalizing the municipal police forces of towns with more than 10,000 inhabitants, which resulted in the forces virtual disappearance as an independent entity. Second, in 1966, the General Directorate of the National Police was created, which integrated the previously autonomous Prefecture of Police (responsible for the policing of the national capital, Paris) into the national policing apparatus.

The identities of these institutions, shaped by history, are very distinctive. *Gendarmes* have military status and work in uniform in rural areas. They are often well integrated into local life. Until the 2000s they reported to the Ministry of Defense. The *police nationale* are stationed in cities, traditionally valuing criminal investigations and more often found working in civilian clothes. They report to the Ministry of the Interior, and they also have more tense relations with the public. The two bodies pursue somewhat different professional models, and they differ in unionization. The *gendarmerie* is not unionized (but since the 2000s they have a professional association), while the *police nationale* is represented by powerful trade unions.

This division between the police and the *gendarmerie* has resulted in notable cross-criticism, sharpened by implicit competition between them. As Malcolm Anderson's chapter describes, this rivalry has manifested itself in their duplication of functions. For example, the *gendarmerie* enhanced their investigative capacity during the 1980s by creating their own scientific and technical laboratories, doing so to the great displeasure of the *police nationale*, which traditionally did this work for them. Similarly, in the 1980s, the *police nationale* created an elite intervention unit based on the model of the Gendarmerie Intervention Group created in 1974.

In 2009, a potentially major change took place when the *gendarmerie* was moved under the authority of the Ministry of the Interior. This resulted in a greater harmonization of their organizational practices, pay schedules, adoption of a common code of ethics, and the creation of a joint directorate for international cooperation. But distinctions and rivalries between the two remain strong. The police and *gendarmerie* have different general directorates, different training schools, and separate operational doctrines. Inevitably, they compete for shares of the budget of the Ministry of the Interior.

Dualism thus remains a central facet of the French police system. The two branches have distinct organizational cultures, which are shaped in part by their respective professional training facilities. *Police national* leaders study at the Ecole nationale supérieure de la police, in Saint-Cyr near Lyon, while *gendarmerie* executives are trained at the Ecole des officiers de la gendarmerie nationale in Melun, near Paris. Many *gendarmerie* leaders are earlier graduates of Saint-Cyr, a prestigious military school. But these rivalries are also encouraged by the magistrates, as prosecutors may in some cases favor one branch or the other. Higher up, President François Mitterrand significantly entrusted his security to the *gendarmes* in 1981, whereas President Nicolas Sarkozy did the opposite in 2007. Dualism is a deeply institutionalized feature of the French police system.

Between Rationalization and the Pathologies of Centralization

Centralism is the second dominant aspect of the French system. France is one of the rare large countries where national police forces carry out local law enforcement, investigations, intelligence gathering, and the protection of daily public security. These activities are organized along extended hierarchical chains that run from the minister of the interior to the policeman in the field, a hierarchy comprising more than a dozen different levels. The pyramidal logic of police systems is fully in force here. Decisions are taken in Paris that are applied in Brittany, Alsace, and Corsica. As historians have clearly shown, this centralization is inseparable from the way the state was built in France, and from the logic of control by the center of the peripheries. The role played by the *gendarmerie* during the 19th century in the construction of the nation and consolidation of state control of rural areas was, for example, essential (Lignereux 2008). According to police and *gendarmerie* officials, senior civil servants, and principal political leaders, this historical centralization is an advantage of the French system as it faces contemporary challenges. These include action against cybercrime, the fight against terrorism, and international cooperation, all of which are facilitated by nationalized organizations that allow for an easier exchange of information as well as economies of scale through the pooling of resources. This centralization is thought to guarantee rational and effective action, and also greater equality of police protection throughout French territory.

However, as Christian Mouhanna shows in his chapter, the pathologies associated with centralization are numerous. It reinforces the bureaucratic and opaque character of police action. Accountability is seen as a vertical concept, imposed by central policies and hierarchical relationships, although in practice these are always discreetly counterbalanced by circumventions and adaptations on the part of subordinates faced with getting the work done. Centralization also contributes to downward management based solely on crime figures, which in turn favors political posturing featuring repressive action against (measures of) crime. Several chapters recount the role played by Nicolas Sarkozy as the ministry of the interior and president of the Republic in shaping an exaggerated version of police centralization during his administrations.

To say that the French police system is centralized and dualist does not mean that police action is totally controlled by the state and that vertical logics apply mechanically. Studies in the sociology of organizations have long shown the difficulties involved in making centralization work. The chains of command are long, it is hard to keep sensitive communications confidential, and policing often requires cooperation with other public agencies that is better managed at the local level. We have already stressed the competitive nature of relations between the *police nationale* and *gendarmerie*. The same is true for relations within the police. Although formally integrated within the general directorate of the national police force, the Paris Prefecture of Police enjoys a very high degree of autonomy, to the point that we can sometimes speak of three state police forces: the *gendarmerie*, the *police national*, and the prefecture.

Between Specialization and Attempts at Integration

A striking tension within French policing is that of the dialectic between the specialization of police techniques and organizations on the one hand and attempts to merge or create new units to facilitate information sharing on the other. Specialization is a classic feature of police organizations. As they develop, they are often marked by the internal multiplication of activities and units that are based on specialized interests and knowledge (see Maguire 2014). In the French national police, the logic of specialization has even been embodied in the structuring of national directorates organized by specific functions. There are central directorates for the border police, the judicial police, special protest and riot policing units and public safety. Specialization is usually seen as a way of creating elite units that focus on investigations and interventions and sit on top of the police prestige hierarchy. Elodie Lemaire's chapter documents how the process of specialization is also found within so-called ordinary police services. Based on field work within an investigative service in a *départment* (a French political and administrative territorial level), she shows how, in the space of a decade or so, specialized units multiplied. From a few brigades dealing with undifferentiated cases in the early 1990s, by the mid-2000s most of their work was successively subdivided into a dozen specialized units focusing of issues ranging from car thefts to phone thefts and payment fraud. Increased specialization was a response by police managers to political demands for improved results, and reorganization made it possible to achieve results in line with political and organizational expectations. They were also a way of affirming symbolically that the problem was being taken care of. Further, it was also a way of finding tasks of suitable status for graduate officers when actual opportunities for professional development within the organization were limited. But Lemaire shows the perverse effects of this strategy. It led to a reconcentration of managerial control in the hands of leadership, along with the standardization of practices, plus fragmentation through specialization led to reduced autonomy for police personnel.

Clément de Maillard's chapter compliments this analysis. It examines attempts to correct the limitations arising from excessive unit specialization by setting up new units responsible for collecting and analyzing data and promoting more global criminal approaches, in a manner similar to discussions of intelligence-led policing. Using the example of the gang war in Marseilles in the early 2010s, an event which resulted in a rapid rise in homicides in a context of increased competition in drug trafficking, it documents how various police units were not able to anticipate this phenomenon because they each had their own networks of informers and their own list of usual suspects. The ensuing reform effort involved the creation of units such as SIRASCO in the Central Directorate of the Judicial Police, which analyses organized crime groups based on their origin. There were also new training and analytic advances, such as the development of an application for criminal intelligence management in the *gendarmerie*. However, the reception of these new capabilities is still evolving. Their added value is difficult to determine, and many police officers question their lack of visible and measurable results. Organizational rivalries also continue. And Clément de Maillard emphasizes the extent to which the centralized French system remains primarily based on a reactive model of policing, one that is somewhat at odds with new thinking about policing in many other nations.

The Search for Control Mechanisms

Another development in French policing concerns the search for organizational control mechanisms that are external to the police. This is a longstanding question: "Who guards the guardians?" Cédric Moreau de Bellaing, in his chapter, identifies several actors likely to exercise this control. These include parliament, actors in the media and civil society, the judiciary, a body called the Defender of Rights, and internal control institutions such as the general inspectorates of the *police nationale* and the *gendarmerie*. Under the influence of its director, between 2014 and 2019 the General Inspectorate of the National Police underwent some modernization: this included the publication of a public report and setting up an online reporting platform. Nevertheless, this is an internal department within the Ministry of the Interior, which is regularly criticized for excessive protection of police officers. Recent investigations of controversial cases such the death of a young man, Steve Manico in Nantes in June 2019, or of the policing of the "yellow vests" movement of 2018–2019, have generated a great deal of controversy, drawing attention to the lack of independence of the investigators. The Rights Defender, created in 2011, is an external oversight body for the security forces. It replaced a National Commission on Security Ethics, created in 2000 as the first external oversight body. In recent years, the Rights Defender has published several reports making strong objections to abusive police practices, including the conduct of abusive identity checks, dismantling of migrant camps, racial profiling, and police practices while maintaining order during demonstrations. However, a major difficulty remains: the Rights Defender has little contact with the police and the *gendarmerie* and is not positioned to influence decisions taken internally by these institutions.

While these different mechanisms only allow for limited control of the police, Cédric Moreau de Bellaing emphasizes that what dominates is first and foremost their own, internal professional standards. Police behavior is importantly controlled by their professional identity and a set of norms that come with it that guide police practice. However, he stresses that this common identity is not enough to reliably ensure self-regulation on the part of police, especially when their practices are called into question externally.

In sum, many chapters in this volume highlight the lasting marks of a police system involving centralization, dualism, specialization, and weakness of external control, while underlining sources of instability in the system, including competition, fragmentation, lack of cooperation, and the failure of half-hearted organizational innovations to resolve systemic problems in policing. However, what we are going to see next is that the police system has been made more complex by the transformations undertaken since the 1970s, largely driven by dynamics external to the police.

State-controlled Police Pluralization

The logic of what we have dubbed "dualistic centralism" is based on the predominance of its national police forces when it comes to the production of security in France. It is a system that the sociologist Dominique Monjardet (1999) described as a "republican security administration." It is marked by its control by national authorities and the marginal role played by local governments, in a society where delinquency was traditionally not really on the political agenda. Nevertheless, as in other Western countries (see a vast literature summarized by Bayley and Shearing 2001), the French police system was to undergo a transformation beginning at the end of the 1970s. In the ensuing decades, the state monopoly over the production of security crumbled, and public police forces found themselves in competition with other types of actors, both public and private, and national and local, who contributed to the policing function. This development challenged the privileged position of the state itself, setting in motion a debate over the core principles of the republican tradition upon which it is based.

The Threefold Logic of Pluralization

It must be said from the outset that the state's monopoly over the police has never been total, even in France. At the beginning of the 1980s, Lascoumes et al. (1986) counted 177 bodies holding police powers in France, including those well beyond the *police nationale* and *gendarmerie*, or the municipal police forces that can be found in many cities. The changes initiated during the 1970s therefore amplify already-existing dynamics. Three trends, whose effects are combined, have been redefining the French police system: the rise of private security companies, the diversification of public police forces, and the spread of local partnerships.

First, as Frédéric Ocqueteau shows in his chapter, there has been a very large expansion in the number and scope of private security companies, the importance of which he documents. According to the National Institute of Statistics and Economic Studies, in 2017, there were 155,000 employees working in private security, of which 139,000 were in the human surveillance sector. The companies reported a total turnover of about 10 billion euros that year. Between 2010 and 2017, this turnover increased by 3.8% on average, a proportion that accelerated with the Euro 2016 championship, terrorist attacks in 2015 and 2016, and a strengthening of the Vigipirate plan for the prevention of terrorist attacks.

Second, within the public police there has been a growth in the number of personnel who do not depend on the central government but on municipalities, social housing estates, and transport companies. The first of these are, of course, municipal police forces, which have grown from around 5,000 agents in the early 1980s to over 22,000 today. Out of 125 cities with more than 50,000 inhabitants, only six have no municipal police. Even the City of Paris, despite its special status, established a municipal police force in early 2020. At the same time, their criminal investigation powers have been extended (municipal police officers are deputy judicial police officers), and municipal forces have upgraded their weaponry (37% of municipal police officers carried a firearm in 2014, compared to 53% in 2019). But the growth even of alternative public agencies has been notable. Transport companies, such as the SNCF (French railways) or the RATP (public transport operator), have set up their own security groups, as have some agencies managing social housing estates. In Paris this includes the employment of security personnel by the Groupement parisien inter-bailleurs de surveillance, which brings together 12 public and private social housing estates.

Finally, as Thierry Delpeuch and Jacqueline Ross show in their chapter, with the spread since the early 1980s of different forms of contractual arrangements, the police have become involved in regular exchanges with many partners, including municipalities, courts and prosecutors, landlords, and schools. Although these contracts and other agreements remain weakly binding, they imply a redistribution of relations with the community. Police managers need to regularly inform their partners, but also to diversify their sources of information on neighborhood security, including going beyond just recorded crime. In particular, the role of department heads at the local level (national police commissioners and *gendarmerie* company commanders) has been transformed: they must inform and exchange information with a wide range of parties, first and foremost being local mayors.

The Logic of Governance and the Role of the State

Taken as a whole, these transformations can be interpreted as a shift from a logic of government to a logic of governance (see de Maillard 2005; Roché 2004). This is a dynamic that international research on policing has long identified (Bayley and Shearing 2001; Crawford 2002; Dupont 2004). There is now a multiplicity of private and public actors in charge of policing, both from the point of view of providers and the jurisdictions in which they operate. Virginie Malochet's chapter gives an account of this growing diversification of policing, particularly in urban areas. On issues such as street peddling, homelessness, festive happenings in public spaces, and disorders in social estates, the state-controlled public police and other police and non-police bodies are now expected to act jointly. There are also new hybrid institutions that stand between the private and public spheres. One example is the National Council for Private Prevention and Security Activities, a body charged with regulating the private security sector. It is composed in part by private security companies that have gained powers previously reserved for public authorities, including the ability to regulate the security sector, authorize new private security companies, and license their employees.

The question of coordination and adjustment between these actors has become central. As noted by both Malochet and Delpeuch and Ross, the division of labor among them is a priority question. Are they engaged in the co-production of safety or do their efforts lie on different points of a security continuum? Analysing contemporary policing from a governance perspective is therefore a stimulating analytical perspective. It allows us to take into account a set of institutions and actors that are drawn from but also beyond government, ... the blurring of boundaries and responsibilities for tackling social and economic issues, ... the power dependence involved in the relationships between institutions involved in collective action, ... the autonomous self-governing networks of actors, ... the capacity to get things done which does not rest on the power of government to command or use its authority.

(Stoker 1998, p. 18)

However, it would be wrong to conclude that this pluralization means that the state is overwhelmed, or that it is just another player in security networks. The number of employees involved remains very much in favor of the state-controlled public police forces: most recently there were 145,000 officers serving in the *police nationale* and 100,000 *gendarmes*, compared with 22,000 municipal police officers. Their legal powers are also asymmetrical: municipal police officers are only deputy judicial police officers and have very limited investigative powers. We can also add that what is striking in the French situation is the importance of other public and semi-public actors, rather than purely private companies, in this domain, giving a continued public flavor to the governance of security.

Furthermore, the various policing actors that intervene in the public space do so largely employing traditional public policing models. Malochet clearly shows in her chapter how the model of the state police officer (that of the "cop" or "*le flic*") radiates beyond the *police nationale* and *gendarmerie*. For municipal police in search of legitimacy, it is necessary to develop units specialized in proactive policing and get involved in the fight against crime, imitating the units developed within the state police. There is pressure toward isomorphism, which leads municipal police forces (because they have fewer staff, less power, and less prestige) to try to resemble traditional state-controlled public police.

Maintaining the Boundaries of the State

The French police are directly involved in maintaining the stability of the state. Unlike their counterparts in North America and the United Kingdom, they are routinely engaged in what Jean-Paul Brodeur has dubbed "high policing" (Brodeur 2010). As a chapter by Laurent Bonelli highlights, in addition to protecting the rights and interests of individuals and local communities, they are charged with protecting the authority of the state itself. Since this inevitably gets bound up with protecting the interests of the incumbent officials who oversee them, this means that politics plays an important role in both their duty assignments and the manner in which they perform them. The police mission, organization, and operations are a by-product of government priorities, which in turn are partly influenced by the threat environment and in part by political concerns. Police do not just fight crime; they also contribute to defining the social order. Bonelli argues that they serve as a gatekeeper for the political arena, allowing some social movements to play a role in it, and disqualifying others. They work to neutralize social forces that might disrupt the political order, and thereby help define the limits of social and political change that the state will tolerate. As Bonelli puts it, they "take part in the closure of the political game."

Since the early 1960s, France has experienced repeated outbursts of political violence. In November 2015, the terrorist attacks in Paris and Saint-Denis that killed 130 persons and wounded more than 400 were among the most internationally visible episodes of violent terror, but the list of these events is a long one. Laurent Bonelli describes how the first line of defense against terrorism and other forms of political violence in France remains firmly in the hands of the police. Domestic intelligence services are an integral part of the national policing apparatus. Pressure on them to effectively contain terrorism has diverted attention from their other responsibilities, and police operations end up being justified largely by their effectiveness at counterterrorism. In turn, each major incident has led them to reassess their actions and make organizational and legislative changes. If trouble is contained, officialdom will defer to them and not ask too many questions. Many of these adaptations to the changing world of political violence are documented in this chapter. It offers an introduction to the world of domestic intelligence in France and examines its major transformations since the late 2000s.

Political disruption remains another, older, and seemingly constant, feature of French life. It too has challenged and stretched thin the resources of the police. Significant social issues often play themselves out in street protests and handing them effectively has severely tested the police. As this book was being prepared, the *gilets jaunes* (or "yellow jackets") stormed Paris, many of them traveling from their homes in small-town and rural France to protest rising fuel prices and the cost of living, and demand an increase in the minimum wage and the return of a special tax on wealth. By November 2018, hundreds of thousands of people were mobilizing across France, constructing barricades and blocking roads. Cars were burned in Paris and elsewhere. The yellow jacket movement subsided, aided by changes in government policy but also in the face of heavy-handed police tactics involving rubber bullets and crowd-dispersing hand grenades. At about that moment, new protests with a different social base and explicit policy goals broke out over the impending imposition of changes in national retirement policies. The marches that ensued took place in the context of widespread transit strikes and occasional electrical power cuts. The transit strike was the longest continuous stoppage France had seen in decades. By January 2020 investigations were already launched into the appropriateness of the police response to these protests as well.

In short, overt political street protests are common in France, and as a result protest policing is inevitably a highly salient issue. Aurélien Restelli reports that, for more than a decade, every significant social conflict in France has tested the police and led to new debates over the effectiveness of their response. In his view, protest policing strategies and tactics have not adapted well to new forms of political activism. The police have been seemingly incapable of containing the disorder that social conflicts engender. At the same time, they are been accused of being repressive and brutal. Restelli's chapter examines these parallel claims of harshness and ineffectiveness, to understand the political, social, and policy demands they place on contemporary policing.

Law enforcement officials representing a variety of agencies are both metaphorically and literally in charge of maintaining the boundaries of the state. Border control has not been a central focus of research on policing in France, but it has been addressed in numerous reports on border control practices and immigration policies. As a chapter by Sara Casella Colombeau reports, issues regarding who can enter and leave the country, and the movement and activities of resident foreigners, grew in importance with the emergence of a strong central state. In a more recent period, border control became linked to questions regarding the place of residents of its colonial empire in France itself. By the 2010s, these concerns were joined by the specter of large numbers of new migrants and refugees moving around and across the Mediterranean, and growing fear of the transnational activities of terrorist groups. The creation of the borderless Schengen Area by a 1995 treaty involving 26 European nations both simplified and made much more complicated the task of addressing all these responsibilities. Colombeau's chapter reviews the development of border policing in France, examining the operational practices involved and the organizations that are responsible for implementing them.

Maintaining the Social Hierarchy

Another role frequently played by the police is protecting the distribution of power and status in society. Criminal justice institutions are typically hierarchy-enhancing. That is, they operate in ways that reproduce social inequality and maintain existing power relations among groups, thus benefiting dominant groups. Policing is not just about crime. Conflict theory views crime control as an instrument used by powerful groups to regulate threats to their interests and to maintain the existing social structure (Turk 1976). Norm enforcement reminds those who are targeted of their place in the social hierarchy and the power of the police to keep them there. The most common policing tactic in France is to demand "*vos papiers*" (your papers). These identity checks may involve no offence or even any real suspicion. Often the police know full-well who their targets are, as they stop them repeatedly. Formally, these stops are described as being preventive, forestalling possible breaches of the public order by reinforcing police authority. They also remind subjects of their place in society.

Identity checks are controversial, as "public order" is vague enough to justify many and frequent police interventions. The police have a great deal of freedom when it comes to deciding what public order is or is not, and very wide discretionary power in choosing when and how to act. The distribution of these checks also has sparked concern over racial profiling. As the chapter by Fabien Jobard and Jacques de Maillard reports, police stops have also been implicated in sparking the longest and most striking round of riots in France's contemporary history. Identity checks offer an opportunity for aggressive behavior on the part of the police, especially towards youths from ethnic minorities, and have been documented as both discriminatory and highly discretionary. Since the 2000s, research has accumulated extensive quantitative and ethnographic evidence of the extent of these problems. This has helped drive identity checking onto the public agenda. There have been heated debates in France over the effectiveness and appropriateness of this policing tactic.

It is frequently in the poorest and most diverse urban areas of France where this conflict is carried out. "*Banlieues*" are urbanized areas lying on the outskirts of larger cities in France. Often, they are home to the poor, and frequently residents are migrants and their descendents. Troublesome *banlieues* (often referred to as "sensitive areas" in translations from French) concentrate a familiar range of social problems, including drug abuse and crime. Recently, issues like Islamic fundamentalism and violence against women have risen in visibility. However, these areas constitute a problem in part because of how police are deployed there. As a chapter by Fabien Jobard documents, policing in the *banlieues* is chronically understaffed, and as a result officers often resort to a militarized, defensive style of policing which encourages their use of preemptive violence. Further, transfers of officers from the *banlieues* in order to police large demonstrations in city centers have undercut staffing levels in poorer areas, and paramilitary units from elsewhere have been deployed to take up the slack. These trends interact with another French tradition: that of violent police control of racial minorities. In turn, *banlieue* residents are increasingly convinced that they are treated differently, unjustly, and unequally. There has been a visible rise in protests against violence by the police. The resulting violence aimed at police has further legitimized their continued militarization. In Jobard's analysis, behind this state of affairs lie large structural trends in French society. These include budgetary constraints imposed by the French state, geographical segregation by class and background, and deindustrialization of the economy.

One of the roots of routinized police violence against citizens of immigrant origin is the nation's colonial legacy. Emmanuel Blanchard's chapter in this volume traces the historical origins of a French policing style characterized by aggressive attempts to control racialized communities. He argues that this legacy of the colonial period has not received enough attention by scholars and social critics alike. The first to bring to the foreground the excesses of the colonial legacy were political activists. They highlighted contemporary continuities with policing practices shaped in the colonies, referring to "internal colonialism." Blanchard points out that domestic French policing was more directly impacted by its imperial legacy than was the case in Britain. The Algerian War (1954–1962) particularly affected police–public relationships, leading to organizational, institutional, and operational practices that emphasized tough anti-crime tactics, a heavy reliance on stop and search, and the militarization of civil policing.

Police and the People

In contrast to Brodeur's (2010) "high policing" or protecting the state, routine "low policing" is concerned with protecting communities and the general public. Traditionally, most low policing is reactive. Officers largely arrive on the scene because they have been called by victims, and their core mission is making arrests that survive review and lead to convictions and sentences via open legal processes. These features of routine policing promote transparency and can grant them a great deal of legitimacy, if they are accomplished effectively. However, many chapters in this volume speak to social and organizational factors that can get in the way. Bureaucratic, political, and cultural factors within police organizations can reduce their apparent effectiveness in the eyes of the public, who has developed different expectations. These expectations may have been influenced by the media, by political activists or critical politicians, or just by the experiences of friends and neighbors, but in the 21st century they have become an independent political fact. Further, surveys make it clear that public support for the police has fractured along race, class, and gender lines, and that creates an even more complex environment that the police must navigate.

An important domain of the everyday is sexual violence. As a chapter by Océane Perona documents, it is a contested one. Police treatment of victims of sexual violence in France has been denounced by women's movements for decades. Officers have been blamed for hostility towards the complainants themselves, and of not taking their complaints seriously or accepting their testimony with an open mind. To make sense of this apparent indifference to crime victims, research in social psychology and criminology has examined the attrition of rape cases as they proceed through the criminal justice system, identifying key decision points and the sources of case attrition along the way. Importantly, Perona's own study of units specializing in rape investigations finds that officers' decisions are the product of professional routines rather than simple gender stereotypes. Her work highlights the importance of organizational factors, in contrast to cultural ones. The general rules by which investigators classify and prioritize criminal cases lead them to value complex cases, those with an unknown suspect, and offenders who threaten to be a danger to society. Big cases are those that fit the police imagination regarding "real rape" – crimes by strangers that are rapidly reported and feature threats to life and limb. Solving violent assaults in public locations that demanded professional skill on the part of investigators gains them prestige within the organization. It is the use of these criteria to classify and prioritize cases that has led to a disjuncture between changing public expectations regarding the treatment of sexual assault cases and the apparent effectiveness of the police in dealing with them.

A chapter by Mathilde Darley and Jérémie Gauthier also dives deeply into the internal dynamics of police organizations in order to understand officers' views of their work and their relation to the community. It documents the role that gender norms play in officers' strategies for establishing their professional identity within the police. Key to this is a cultural resistance to the feminization of policing by many male officers. Masculinity in all its stereotypical aspects continues to mold their professional identity. In turn, the gendered structure of the policing profession affects interactions between officers, an issue of growing significance because of the growing feminization of the job. There is also evidence that it affects officers' views of the public and individual victims and offenders that they interact with. It may help sustain the warrior model frequently espoused by officers, that they need to be tough, they must be feared, and they must dominate encounters with the public.

There is also a growing body of research on how the traditions and practices of French policing have affected their support in the eyes of crime victims and the public, and the potential involvement of ordinary citizens in community safety. In a lengthy chapter, Sebastian Roché examines the current state of research in France on public trust and confidence in the police. He reports that things are not going well for them. In comparison to the countries that France would prefer to rank with, the public evidences relatively low levels of confidence in the police. Further, as in many places, there are important divisions within society over support for the police that overlay significant ethnic and social cleavages. Residents of the *banlieues* describe low levels of satisfaction and trust in the police and grant them little legitimacy. This is a finding that is consistent with many descriptions in this book of the police role in their communities.

Following a tradition in political science, Roché distinguishes between support for the police as an institution (diffuse support) and support for their activities (specific support). He finds that many respondents answer positively to general questions about the police role, but a lot less remain positive when asked to evaluate specific actions. He also documents a substantial uptick in trust in the police following terrorist attacks in France in late 2015.

Research comparing public opinion in France with other nations has become common, as new data from the European Commission's Eurojustis-France project, the European Social Survey, and the Police Youth Relations in Multi-Ethnic Cities projects have become available. The European Social Survey in particular included measures of perceived police fairness and procedural justice, which are topics that have been widely studied elsewhere. Overall, Roché concludes that ratings of police procedural justice, integrity, trust, and legitimacy are low in France, which is often ranked among nations it might not want to be compared to. Further sections of this chapter review popular evaluations of the use of violence in disadvantaged suburbs and police actions during riot control operations. Roché reports that people's most negative judgments concerned disrespectful and ethnically differential treatment by the police. Although these views were more common among residents of *banlieues*, the public in general did not have very positive opinions regarding these measures.

These empirical findings are linked to discussions of police reform, and particularly to the absence of policing policies designed to build trust and legitimacy and the failure to correct practices that undermine support for the police. Low public satisfaction and weak trust in the police in France when compared to many European Union countries illustrate a failure to treat problems that have been long diagnosed but not successfully addressed. The lack of reform moving police toward greater local accountability, the disproportionate use of violence against poor neighborhoods, and an absence of programs aiming at improving the quality of police services are the likely causes.

Then there is community policing. Based upon the features of French policing described in this book – beginning with its centralized character and extending through the role of national politics in its policies and operations, the urgency of its missions to gather domestic intelligence and thwart potential terrorism, its limited accountability to civil society, tension between youths and the police, and the primacy of its intrusive identity checks in maintaining control of the population – community policing has not gained a significant foothold. A chapter by Jacques de Maillard and Mathieu Zagrodzki details the emergence of community policing and the idea that community-oriented police forces would welcome public input and even active involvement in the business of their organizations. They describe the stages by which community policing advanced and then retreated on the reform agenda. During the 1980s and 1990s there were attempts to develop a more supportive relationship between police and underprivileged areas. Partnerships emerged involving municipal police and local bodies. A significant experiment in community policing was launched in the 1990s. Then, however, progress stalled. Terrorism, the politicization of security issues, and new managerial thinking pushed community-oriented policing off the reform agenda, where it has largely remained.

Notes

1 IHESI became the Institut national des hautes études de la sécurité et de la justice in 2009, and then was disbanded in 2020, a sign of the fragility of evaluative policy research.

2 It should be noted, however, that in addition to the publication in English of Didier Fassin's (2013) important work, authors as different in style as E. Blanchard, L. Bonelli, T. Delpeuch, J. de Maillard, J. Ferret, O. Fillieule, J. Gauthier, F. Jobard, R. Lévy, Ch. Mouhanna, F. Ocqueteau, G. Pruvost, S. Roché, V. Spenlehauer, and M. Zagrodzki (to name but a few) have published in English on French police.

3 Bayley (1985, p. 59) refers more specifically to a multiple coordinated centralized police structure, but we return to the issue of coordination below.

References

Bayley, D. H. 1985. *Patterns of policing: A comparative analysis.* New Brunswick: Rutgers University Press.

Bayley, D. H., and Shearing, C. 2001. *The new structure of policing: Description, conceptualization, and research agenda.* Washington, DC: National Institute of Justice.

Berlière, J. M. 1992. *La police des moeurs sous la IIIème République.* Paris: Seuil.

Berlière, J. M., Denys, C., Kalifa, D., and Milliot, V. (Eds.) 2008. *Métiers de police: être policier en Europe, xviiie-xxe siècle.* Rennes: Presses Universitaires de Rennes.

Berlière, J. M., and Lévy, R. 2011. *Histoire des polices en France: de l'ancien régime à nos jours.* Paris: Nouveau Monde Éditions.

Brodeur, J. P. 2010. *The policing web.* New York and London: Oxford University Press.

Brodeur, J. P., and Monjardet, D. (Eds.) 2003. *Connaître la police: grands textes de la recherche anglo-saxonne.* Paris: IHESI.

Crawford, A. 2002. Introduction: Governance and security. Pp. 1–23 in A. Crawford (Ed.) *Crime and insecurity. The governance of safety in Europe.* Cullompton: Willan Publishing.

de Maillard, J. 2005. The governance of safety in France: Is there anybody in charge? *Theoretical Criminology* 9: 325–343.

de Maillard, J. 2017. *Polices comparées.* Paris: LGDJ Lextenso éditions.

de Maillard, J., and Roché, S. (Eds.) 2009. Les chantiers de réforme de la police dans les états occidentaux. *Revue française de science politique* 59: 1093–1248.

Dupont, B. 2004. Security in the age of networks. *Policing & Society* 14: 76–91.

Fassin, D. 2013. *Enforcing order: An ethnography of urban policing.* Cambridge, UK: Polity Press.

Favre, P. (Ed.) 1990. *La manifestation.* Paris: Presses de la Fondation Nationale des Sciences Politiques.

Fillieule, O., and Della Porta, D. (Eds.) 2006. *Police et manifestants.* Paris: Presses de Sciences Po.

Houte, A. D., and Luc, J. N. (Eds.) 2016. *Les gendarmeries dans le monde, de la Révolution française à nos jours.* Paris: Presses Universitaires de Paris-Sorbonne.

Lascoumes, P., Barberger, C., Lambert, T., Maier, M. M., Prêtre, J. M., and Serverin, E. 1986. *Le droit pénal administratif instrument d'action étatique: incrimination-transaction.* Paris: Commissariat general au plan.

Lévy, R. 1987. *Du suspect au coupable: le travail de police judiciaire.* Paris: Librairie des Méridiens/Klincksieck.

Lignereux, A. 2008. *La France rébellionnaire: Les résistances à la gendarmerie (1800–1859).* Rennes: Presses Universitaires de Rennes.

Maguire, E. R. 2014. Police organizations and the iron cage of rationality. Pp. 68–98 in M. D. Reisig and R. J. Kane (Eds.) *The Oxford handbook of police and policing*. New York: Oxford University Press.

Monjardet, D. 1996. *Ce que fait la police: Sociologie de l'action policière*. Paris: La Découverte.

Monjardet, D. 1999. Réinventer la police urbaine: Le travail policier à la question dans les quartiers. *Les Annales de la recherche urbaine* 83: 14–22.

Monjardet, D. 2008. *Notes inédites sur les choses policières 1999–2006*. Paris: La Découverte.

Ocqueteau, F., and Monjardet, D. 2005. Insupportable et indispensable, la recherche au ministère de l'Intérieur. Pp. 229–247 in P. Bezes, M. Chauvière, J. Chevallier, N. de Montricher, and F. Ocqueteau (Eds.) *L'État à l'épreuve des sciences sociales: La fonction recherche dans les administrations sous la Ve République*. Paris: La Découverte .

Roché, S. 2004. Vers la Dé´monopolisation des Fonctions Ré´galiennes. *Revue française de science politique* 54: 43–70.

Skogan, W. G., and Frydl, K. 2004. *Fairness and effectiveness in policing: The evidence*. Washington, DC: National Academies Press.

Stoker, G. 1998. Governance as theory: Five propositions. *International Social Science Journal* 155: 17–28.

Turk, A. T. 1976. Law as a weapon in social conflict. *Social Problems* 23: 276–291.

Part I

Historical Background

Chapter 2

The Evolving Organization of Policing
From the Ancien Régime to De Gaulle and the *Police Nationale*

Jean-Marc Berlière and René Lévy

A belief often expressed in discussions of the sociology and history of policing is that there are two main, antagonistic models of policing: the British and the French. The "English versus French" controversy arose during the modernization of state policing systems in the 18th and 19th centuries. That is when the specter arose (among the British) of the "French model" – a centralized, state-controlled force whose main purpose was to spy on political foes. This was described as starkly contrasting with the decentralized British system, one based on popular consent (Levy 2012; Mawby 2008; Reiner 1991–1992).

Although long criticized, this dichotomous image remains vivid in the minds of many. This chapter argues that the often-painted picture of French policing as a highly centralized, strictly hierarchical system is far from a historical reality. This can be seen in the case of Britain in Clive Emsley's three-pronged typology of police systems. This classification is based not on police operations, but on links between the police and the central government and on their organizational structure. For example, in the 19th century the United Kingdom had the London Metropolitan Police, the provincial police, and the militarized Irish Constabulary. In other words, one force for the capital city, under the aegis of central authorities; a number of local (borough and county) forces, usually controlled by local government, though their management was often drawn from the ranks of the London police; and a militarized force established in a notoriously irredentist area (Emsley 1999).

Formulating it this way emphasizes how similar the British and the French contexts are. Paris, the capital city, has its own police headed by a government-appointed prefect (formerly *Lieutenant-général*); municipalities have local forces that, until 1941, were placed under their supervision, even though the commanding officers were also state-appointed; and rural areas are policed by a militarized *gendarmerie*.

France certainly has a history of centralization. This tradition is the heritage of absolute monarchy, Jacobinism, and the Napoleonic autocracy. However, France never had – either under the Old Regime, or during the 19th and 20th centuries – *one* police force. Rather, it had *several* forces that differed in terms of their status, jurisdiction, missions, and personnel. Policing under the Old

General Forces

The Sûreté générale
(The Sûreté Nationale from 1934)
- The police division at the Ministry of the Interior, heir to the Ministry of Police.
- Jurisdiction included the whole national territory.
- For a long time, its own (state-paid) staff only consisted of the railways police *(Police spéciale des chemins de fer)*. Became the "special" police in 1911, then the "RG-SN" = political police of the Third Rep. + ports and borders police + CE (since1899) + TSF (1923) + customs (1924). 1934 saw the creation of the *Contrôle général de la Surveillance du Territoire* (which took over the Customs and TSF in 1935).
In 1907, acquired a judicial police dimension with the creation of the "*Brigades mobiles régionales de police judiciaire*", a wide-remit criminal police force.
- Also in charge of recruitment and career management of the *commissaires de police* (superintendents) who headed the municipal forces (although their wages were paid by municipalities), and of the entire staff of various nationalised municipal forces (Lyon, Marseille...). The 1941 legislation both broadened its powers and increased its workforce.

The Gendarmerie
- Theoretical jurisdiction = whole country (including urban areas).
- A military corps attached to the Ministry of War, the *gendarmerie* was tasked with targeted policing missions and had a triple ministerial allegiance.
= the police *aux armées* (military police, Ministry of War).
= the judicial police of rural areas (Ministry of Justice), which remained its monopoly through its local squads until the *Brigades mobiles* were created in 1907.
= roads and thoroughfare policing.
= crowd policing (*Garde républicaine* in Paris. + the "*Gendarmerie mobile*," created in 1921), which remained its monopoly (except in Paris) until the advent of the GMR (1941) and the CRS (1944). For such missions, orders came from the Ministry of the Interior, via the prefects.

Territorial Forces

Municipal Forces
- Mandatory for all towns exceeding 5,000 residents, ever since the law of Vendémiaire year IV.
- Jurisdiction strictly confined to the municipality.
- Jointly led by the mayor and a *commissaire de police* recruited, appointed, and transferred by the *Sûreté générale*, yet paid by the municipality – resulting in frequent clashes.
- Staffing levels varied and could be very low. Staff included policemen, secretaries, *gardes champêtres*... paid by the municipality, recruited and potentially suspended by the mayor – although the prefect had the last word.
- All expenditures were mandatory but charged to the municipality.

Specific case of *département* capitals exceeding 40,000 residents
- Required to have one *commissaire* per 10,000 residents (still appointed and transferred by SG or SN, yet paid by municipalities). One of them acted as central superintendent.
- Rank-and-file staff were municipal, recruited and paid by the municipality. Staffing levels were decided through ordinances for executive authorities, based on proposals by the Ministry of the Interior, following a consultation with the city council and a ruling by the Council of State, and was proportional to the city's financial support, sometimes resulting in quite large forces that often featured specialized departments (uniformed law and order agents, and a "*sûreté*" unit in charge of criminal matters).
- Police spending, though mandatory, was taken from the municipal budget.

Nationalized Municipal Forces
- In Lyon (since 1851), Marseille (1908), Toulon and La Seyne (1918), Nice (1920), Strasbourg, Mulhouse, Metz (1925), 174 communes of S&O and 19 of S&M (1935) (+ Toulouse, XII-1940), the state took over from municipalities, which only kept a handful of functions (roads, street lighting, water).
- Jurisdiction strictly confined to the metropolis.
- Mayors' police powers and prerogatives transferred to the prefect and one general secretary, or the central superintendent.
- All police functions represented, from uniformed street policing to criminal police, at varying staffing levels.
- All agents recruited, paid, and transferred by the state.
- Budget voted by parliament (taken from "Expenditure" account of the Ministry of the Interior's budget), although some expenses reimbursed by municipalities ("Income" account of the Min. of Int.).
- The 1941 legislation nationalized all police forces in towns exceeding 10,000 residents.

The Préfecture de police
- A "Préfet de police" (the successor of *Lieutenants Généraux*), appointed by and reporting to the government, has been in charge of the Paris police since 1800.
- Jurisdiction confined to the Seine *département* (Paris + neighbouring towns).
- The most developed and best-funded of all forces, it boasted a larger workforce than the other cities and the *Sûreté Générale* combined.
- Organized in departments that specialized throughout the 19th century:
 - one uniformed "*Police municipale*" (since 1829) consisting of "*Sergents de ville*" (renamed "*gardiens de la paix publique*" in 1870) and acting as the public safety, street police.
 - The "*Sûreté*" was the judicial/criminal department of the PP, and the "*brigade criminelle*" (located *quai des Orfèvres*) its crown jewel.
 - The "*brigades de recherches*" (research squads) were the political arm of the force (the "*Direction des recherches*" was renamed "*Renseignements Généraux*" in 1913).
- "Sedentary" departments, including the commissariats, i.e. police stations (until 1914!), various offices (foreigners, "*filles publiques*" i.e. prostitution, etc.), as well as the *Identité Judiciaire*, the cradle of forensic police.
- The force was "municipal" insofar as its budget was voted by the city council and funded by the city (and Seine *département*), with the state chipping in.

Figure 2.1 The Organization of French Policing in the Modern Era
Source: prepared by the authors.

Regime featured both confusion between police and justice and profusion – one easily gets lost in the plethora of officers and institutions entrusted with policing tasks. The streamlining efforts of the revolutionary and Napoleonic eras failed to fully disentangle a complex, sprawling organizational architecture that has persisted, for the most part, well into the second half of the 20th century.[1] These developments emerged in a practical fashion and took shape very gradually, along the paths that were specific to each policy task. In addition, the many policing agencies charged with these tasks differed significantly in terms of their operational methods, status, staffing, and budgets, and in addition were each allocated their own portions of the country to oversee.

Figure 2.1 summarizes the structure of French policing prior to World War II. It describes the range of institutions that were involved in policing and the main trends in their evolution. These changes will be discussed in detail in this chapter. A breakpoint in this evolution came in 1941, when an authoritarian government that was established in the city of Vichy during the German occupation nationalized French policing.

Police Powers Under the Old Regime

The powers of police were always a bone of contention between the royal authority and a multitude of local ones (the *seigneurs*, municipalities, corporations, universities, churches, and other institutions) that vied for the power, authority, and revenue attached to police and the courts.

Rooted in Paris' legendary insecurity, the March 1667 Edict establishing the *lieutenance de police* epitomizes these struggles. The Edict is often described as signaling the birth of modern police. The Edict signaled a willingness of royalty to seize control of what used to be a municipal prerogative, one exercised in the capital city by a multiplicity of "*officiers*," whose posts had typically been purchased. By splitting the hitherto combined functions of police and the courts, the Edict brought a degree of orderliness to the Old Regime's policing organization. The *Lieutenant de police*, who "shall deal with the safety of the city," was the king's man, his post being both non-hereditary and revocable.

A subsequent (1699) attempt at extending this royal control over provincial towns was met with resistance from municipalities (Denys 2005, pp. 745–748). On the eve of the Revolution in 1789, the Parisian model in fact remained an exception.

From Revolutionary Decentralization to Napoleonic Centralism

The French Revolutionary period (1789–1799) was initially characterized by a decentralizing phase (1789–1793). It was directly inspired by "English liberties" and the young American democracy, both of which were hugely admired at the Age of Enlightenment. This initial phase was followed quickly by a take-over of policing by the central authorities during 1793–1799.

In the aftermath of the 1789 Revolution, the Declaration of Human and Civic Rights proclaimed that a "public force" was to be established "to guarantee the natural rights of man," and this was to be "for the benefit of all, and not for the particular use of those to whom it is entrusted." The new Constituent Assembly passed several pieces of legislation confirming that municipalities would continue to hold the policing rights that had been the prerogative of towns and *communes* for many centuries. This reaffirmed a highly decentralized – indeed, scattered – organizational structure, as illustrated by the fact that the *commissaires de police* were to be elected by the citizenry in all towns with a population in excess of 5,000. Paris experienced a similar trend. Policing was initially exercised at the neighborhood level by citizen committees, and subsequently (from 1790) this was entrusted to a municipal authority (Denis 2008). In rural areas, this structure was supplemented by the creation of the *gendarmerie* (ordinance of 16 January 1791), which took over from the Old Regime's *maréchaussée*.

As early as 1793, the domestic and foreign situation, the Jacobin dictatorship, and a drive toward the streamlining and efficiency of government rekindled a centralizing trend that then spread steadily. These developments are noticeable in policing legislation. In 1794, a Parisian "Comité de Sûreté Générale" was tasked with coordinating and centralizing all police surveillance, and appointing *commissaires*. Likewise, in the provinces, instead of being elected by the people, *commissaires* started being appointed by municipalities, which were under the growing influence of central authorities. Finally, in January 1796, the Directory (the newest national government) established a "ministry of the Police Générale de la République." This body was in charge of implementing all laws pertaining to policing as well as safety and public peace in the Republic. It was headed on four occasions between 1799 and 1815 by its most emblematic leader, Joseph Fouché.

Following the coup of 18 Brumaire, Year VIII (9 November 1799), Bonaparte established a personal, authoritarian regime. As first consul, he was of course never going to neglect a resource so essential to the surveillance and the repressive capabilities of his regime. Joseph Fouché served as Napoleon's minister of police. It comes as no surprise, therefore, that his work in this area was marked by a willingness to centralize – tempered, however, by a clever subdivision strategy to avoid concentrating too many of these formidable powers in the hands of one man. Up to the early 21st century, subsequent regimes, at least in part, remained faithful to this centralizing spirit.

As for municipal forces, although mayors were by no means stripped of their policing powers, they were however made utterly reliant upon central authorities. The law of 28 Pluviôse, Year VIII (17 February 1800) about the division and administration of the French territory laid the foundations for centralization by establishing the prefects and granting the head of state or the prefect, depending on town size, the right to appoint and replace mayors. To balance Fouché's power, Napoleon reinforced the imperial *gendarmerie*, headed by inspecteur Général Moncey (Lignereux 2002). In Paris, by creating the Préfecture de police, he reinstated the Old Regime model of the Lieutenance Générale.

The Préfecture of Police as a Successor to the Lieutenance générale

As the seat of authority and the home of constitutional bodies, diplomatic missions, assemblies, and ministries, the capital city required, in Napoleon's mind, a dedicated policing body. He envisioned a powerful, well-organized force that would be justified not only by Paris's demographic and economic weight, but also by the political role played by its residents, who had been instrumental in every upheaval during the Revolutionary era.

The law of 28 Pluviôse, Year VIII aimed at concentrating all policing powers in the capital city in the hands of one man by creating the – government-appointed – post of prefect of police. The prefect was to be assisted by several government-appointed *commissaires de police*. The extent of the prefect's powers was defined in the ordinance of consuls of 12 Messidor, Year VIII (1 July 1800), granting him a number of prerogatives. As a representative of the French state, the prefect held major administrative responsibilities. As a representative of the city of Paris (there would not be a mayor of the city for almost two centuries), the prefect commanded policing powers. In charge of all police-related matters, the prefect even held judicial powers (including the right of arrest and the power to conduct searches) (Berlière 2008a). This merging of powers was to be decried by generations of jurists. The prefect's territorial jurisdiction was limited to the Seine *département*, i.e. the city of Paris plus two dozen neighboring towns.

Though hated by all republicans, the "consular institution" created by Bonaparte with the dual objective of watching and reining in the people of Paris and countering the ominous power of the minister of general police, was nevertheless to survive – give or take a few reforms – all subsequent revolutions and regime changes. In fact, not only did the Préfecture de police (PP) survive its rival ministry of general police, but it even took control of its successor, the *Sûreté générale*, and eventually came to occupy an eminent position in the administrative pyramid and police hierarchy.

Yet in 1870, as the Republic was proclaimed, the days of the Préfecture of police appeared to be over. As early as September 4, the rise to power of its former victims seemed to presage nothing short of the dismantling of "this consular institution that is a disgrace to the Republic."[2] However, the Préfecture de police was eventually saved by the military defeat, the election of a monarchist majority at the Bordeaux assembly, and the Paris insurrection. In fact, its headcount actually increased following the Paris Commune events.[3]

The office of the Préfecture de police persisted into the 1960s. This was despite scandals, such as the one that shook the *service des mœurs* (vice squad). The prefect also survived a law of 1884 that reinstated the control of policing to elected municipal leaders, and it resisted the persistent demands of the Paris city council that it remain in control of its police force. Change did not come until 1966 (Berlière 1993a; Nivet 1994; Renaudie 2008, pp. 23–40). The Paris police was the largest in the country until World War II, superior in both numbers and financial resources to all other police forces in France *combined*. It remained so until the municipal forces of the provinces were nationalized by the Vichy regime in 1941.

Several specialized divisions that are taken for granted today actually appeared for the first time within the Préfecture de police, including:

- a *service de sûreté* – i.e. the crime squad, long placed under the leadership of former convict Eugène-François Vidocq,[4] until Prefect Gisquet decided in 1832 that the policing of thieves and murderers should henceforth be entrusted only to men boasting an unblemished criminal record (Berlière 1996);
- political units called *brigades de recherches* (investigation squads) that lasted quite a while;
- specialized units such as the vice squad (*mœurs*) and the hotels squad (*garnis*) (Berlière 1992);
- the municipal police division, which Prefect Debelleyme decided in 1829 should be uniformed in order to make their presence conspicuous, establish their formal authority, and to differentiate them from the tradition of Fouché's "*sbires*" and the Old Regime's "*mouches*" (literally "flies," but actually meaning "snitches" or "rats") (Deluermoz 2012).

The size of the uniformed units grew steadily, reaching 4,000 in 1870. By 1871, there were as many as 7,000 municipal police, almost 9,000 in 1913, and more than 17,000 in 1939. The budget of the Paris police – which, until 1939, dwarfed that of the *Sûreté générale* – was controlled by the Paris municipal council and was carried by the city's budget, although about half the cost of policing was reimbursed by the central government. The only state civil servant in the whole Préfecture de police was the prefect himself. The entire workforce, including and the *commissaires*, consisted of municipal functionaries recruited and paid by the City of Paris. Their pay was much better than in local municipal forces and even the *Sûreté générale*, they were the envy of colleagues in the provinces. As for the "*commissaires* of the Ville de Paris" – recruited on the basis of a highly selective competitive examination – they were notables in the city.

This abundance of men and resources can be explained by French centralization. Paris weighs heavily in the country and its history. However, this inequality in policing resources between the capital city and the rest of France has been repeatedly questioned.

It also explains why the Préfecture de police has long constituted a laboratory for modern policing. Their innovations have ranged from anthropometric identification methods and forensic police – both of which were undergoing decisive developments in Paris at the time – to vocational training and police academies. Their organizational innovations included the formation of the Renseignements généraux (general intelligence directorate) and the creation of a prestigious *brigade criminelle* at 36 quai des Orfèvres. The Paris force was also a hub for police innovation around the world. It drew the attention of capitals from Istanbul to Rio de Janeiro, and from Tokyo to Athens. These frequently mimicked what they saw in Paris, and along with the lessons of London's Metropolitan Police, it was considered a model police force at the turn of the century.[5]

Post-1815: Liberalization or Centralization?

Following the death of Napoleon I, the 19th century saw a series of modest liberal advances interspersed with authoritarian attempts at centralization. Regardless of the period, however, the constantly reasserted principle of municipal control of policing powers was largely hampered by two precautionary measures. One was the power of the prefect to overrule and even substitute for a mayor who would "refuse or neglect one of the actions prescribed unto him by law."[6] Second, mayors were, in any case, appointed by the government or the prefect. The role of the mayor, then, as far as policing was concerned, was that of an officer of national government.

Louis-Napoléon Bonaparte – president of the Republic (1848–1851), then prince-president (1851–1852), and finally emperor (1852–1870) – ushered in an era of authoritarianism, aiming to strip mayors of all independent authority in policing matters.

First came the law of 19 June 1851, which passed five months before the coup of December 1851 that brought a new Bonaparte to power. Despite vigorous opposition from both the Lyon municipal council and republicans at the Assemblée Nationale, this act granted the prefect of the Rhône *département*, covering all towns in the greater Lyon area, powers like those enjoyed by the Paris prefect of police over municipalities in the Seine *département*. The reasons given for this "preferential" treatment were twofold: the demographic and economic weight of the country's second-largest city, and the history of social unrest there. Then, from January 1852 to June 1853, a ministère de la police suddenly reappeared, under the leadership of Charlemagne Émile de Maupas. He was installed as the head of the Parisian police immediately after Napoleon III seized power in a coup. The formation of the ministry was accompanied by a series of ordinances that antagonized local authorities – particularly by imposing, in each *chef-lieu de canton* (county seat),[7] a "*commissaire de police cantonal*," defined as "a state functionary, who as such and as part of his remits, shall report directly to the prefect."[8]

Having seized power at last in 1870, would the republicans be true to their criticism of the Second Empire and, in the true spirit of 1789, reinstate mayors with their full and effective policing powers, or were they simply about to follow in the footsteps of the abhorred Empire?

The Law of 1884: The Ambiguous Republican Response

The situation, and the issue of municipal policing powers, was to be utterly disrupted by a now-forgotten, though still highly relevant law. The Goblet law of March 1882 restored the right of elected municipal councils to designate mayors in all towns, except for Paris. Mayors thus escaped the influence of central authorities, which meant that the issue of the policing powers attached to the function was reframed entirely. Conflict over this issue explains why, in the new municipal charter adopted in April 1884, the relevant articles took so long and were so difficult to draft.

The articles themselves seem clear. Except in Lyon and Paris, both of which retained their special status, the law reasserted the policing powers that had been granted to mayors in 1789 by the Constituent Assembly. However, the fact that the actual heads of municipal police forces were now elected officials meant that central authorities would be deprived of a "sovereign" device formerly used and enjoyed by every previous regime, and all subsequent governments were to lament this loss of power.

This effect had been clearly anticipated by parliament and senators, which goes a long way toward explaining why the matter was so disputed.[9] For some, it turned mayors – who first and foremost were concerned with wooing the electorate – into all-powerful yet irresponsible chiefs of police. Others, on the contrary, considered that the law continued to restrict the powers of municipalities and concede too much power to the state.

The Third Republic (1870–1940): Temptation to Centralize Again

The autonomy granted to police forces by the law of 1884 was problematic in more ways than one. First, urban forces differed wildly in terms of their size and financial means – as well as, incidentally, their uniforms. While cities such as Bordeaux, Lille and Nantes boasted well-equipped and well-staffed municipal forces, others had to make do with low police-to-resident ratios and scarce resources. Their budgets depended on the municipality's willingness to invest in policing. This inequality – and the proverbial penury of some municipal police forces – had a noticeable impact on the geography of crime.

Another weakness that municipal forces suffered from was the quality of their workforce. Staffing levels were a problem, as towns tried to keep their spending in check. Further, entrusting recruitment to mayors often resulted in cronyism, and electoral considerations could outweigh hiring criteria such as skills and abilities. Meager salaries and the job's low level of inherent attractiveness meant that typical applicants were of mediocre quality anyway. They were often retired or part-time workers with another occupation, or – worse still – shady individuals interested in gaining access to lucrative opportunities.

Finally, one can easily imagine how uncomfortable it was for *commissaires* to have their careers managed by a national agency – the *Sûreté générale* – while reporting on a daily basis to mayors who not only paid and fed them, but also recruited their staff. The situation was bound to become unmanageable in towns held by the opposition parties, resulting in the *commissaire* being caught in a double-bind between the mayor and the prefect, with no real say in the recruitment or assessment of a staff that could easily become hostile in pursuit of its own (and the mayor's) interests. Serious clashes were resolved by transferring the *commissaire*, a task an entire bureau of the *Sûreté* was devoted to.

The law of 1884 raised other issues for all subsequent cabinets, which found themselves deprived of a power carelessly left in the hands of elected, independent municipalities. The problem was political. Opposition municipalities – be they socialist or clerical in orientation – intended to leverage all their powers to pursue goals that may not have suited the government's priorities. The result was a permanent state of guerrilla warfare between the prefects, as representatives of the government responsible for ensuring that laws were complied with, and municipalities willing to use every trick in the book to locally hamper national measures and laws that their ideology, political positioning, or religious beliefs dictated they should reject.[10]

The problem was also technical, as this law led to policing being organized in such a way that police forces whose jurisdiction strictly stopped at the *commune*'s boundaries had no right of hot pursuit. This offered unhoped-for opportunities for crime. The advantages this gave organized crime, which was undergoing major changes at the time and which certainly benefited from such uneven police coverage, was lamented by both the police and the judiciary.

The situation was becoming politically untenable at a time when the issue of security was being raised daily in the press, and not only the government but also elected officials and the republic itself were being held responsible for police failures by public opinion. Some response was urgently needed. In the eyes of many, an obvious solution was to centralize, nationalize, and unify municipal police forces. As Louis Marin, chair of the Administrative Reform Committee of 1923 put it, "If one public service ought to be a state service, policing is undeniably it."[11] This option proved so difficult to implement that it had to be done in stages, in an excruciatingly slow incremental process.

Many felt that nationalization was the logical thing to do in order to regain control of police forces that had incautiously been turned over to independent-minded municipalities ready to fight for their rights. However, successive plans to accomplish this met with serious obstacles.

First, it was difficult for a self-professed democratic regime allegedly inspired by the principles of 1789 to act in a less liberal fashion than prior monarchist and autocratic regimes – even though power had been completely redistributed, since municipalities and mayors were now elected. Also, obtaining a majority in both chambers appeared impossible when dual-office holders – many members of parliament and senators were also mayors of municipalities – were intent on retaining "their" police forces. Opposition parliamentarians on both the right- and left-wings cared little for nurturing the police powers of a regime and government they were fighting, and thereby strengthening an institution whose job was to repress their supporters. Finally, there were financial issues. Nationalizing municipal forces required that expenditure hitherto taken on by municipalities be paid for by the state, which in turn necessarily implied raising taxes – a fearful prospect for members of parliament at a time when budget deficits were unimaginable.

This explains why the nationalization of municipal police forces under the Third Republic was an extremely slow, stop-and-go process. It started *at the request of the municipalities involved*, when the latter considered themselves unable to implement the recruitment and restructuring campaigns required by local circumstances. This was achieved by applying the same approach that had been resorted to in Lyon in 1851. After the Marseille police (1908), the forces of Toulon and La Seyne (1918) were thus nationalized, followed by Nice and then the towns of the Alsace-Lorraine region (Berlière and Lévy 2013). To manage these growing state police forces, a dedicated department called "Service des polices d'État" was created within the *Sûreté générale* (by the Ordinance of 23 July 1933).

The last and largest wave of nationalizations under the Third Republic occurred in the greater Paris area. In total, 174 *communes* of Seine & Oise, and 19 in Seine & Marne had their police forces nationalized by the ordinances of 30 October 1935 and 11 March 1936 respectively. This was an attempt to get rid of a "no police's land" that sprung up a mere 15 kilometers from the Eiffel tower. Prefects there had the same prerogatives as the Paris prefect of police and were assisted by high-ranking police officers. These "polices d'État de Seine & Marne et Seine & Oise," whose jurisdiction included the main towns of the two *départements*, had a right of hot pursuit. Their creation heralded the reform of 1941, which was largely inspired by them (Sicot 1959).

The *Gendarmerie*

Besides those municipal forces, nationalized or not, two general-purpose forces with an extended jurisdiction coexisted: the *gendarmerie* and the *Sûreté générale*. The *gendarmerie* is first and foremost a military unit. An elite body that was long – until 1920 – part of the Cavalry, it is the direct offspring of the Old Regime's *maréchaussée*, whose lineage, as the *gendarmerie* itself is delighted to declare, can be traced as far back as the 16th century, if not the Middle Ages.[12]

Gendarmes live in barracks, or *cantonnements*, and are organized in five-men squads called *brigades territoriales*. Theoretically there is at least one unit at each county seat. Until the 1970s, they were always required to be uniformed when on duty, so much so that *gendarmerie* reports begin with the following ritual statement: "Wearing our uniforms, and in accordance with orders from our leaders …." The gendarmes are military men and as such have long been subjected to strict discipline and hierarchy, which transpires in their *Règlements*, the house rules that, in the early 20th century, still explained in painstaking detail – in more detail, actually, than the actual technical and policing aspects of the job – how horses and saddlery should be taken care of.

Under a law of 28 Germinal, Year VI (1791), and ordinances of 1 March 1903 and 20 May 1903, the *gendarmerie* was placed in charge of specific policing missions. This was specified in article 1 of the ordinance:

> The *gendarmerie* is a force established to attend to public peace and see to it that order is maintained, and laws abided by. The essence of its service is an ongoing and repressive surveillance. Its action shall be exercised over the whole territory, as well as the armies. It is more specifically destined to improve the safety of the countryside and roads.

Gendarmes report to three different ministries – the Ministry of War (or Armies, the name varies), the Ministry of Justice for criminal police missions, and the Ministry of the Interior for order maintenance. They are tasked with four specific missions: they are military police; court guards (responsible for transferring prisoners); road and transport safety police; and criminal police in the countryside. The last of these was key, given that until 1932, most French citizens lived in rural areas. While the *gendarmerie*'s jurisdiction covers the whole country – including towns and cities – with a right of hot pursuit, it is the only body – along with the *gardes champêtres*, whose policing attributions have gradually waned – responsible for policing the countryside and towns with a population below 5,000. Finally, it is in charge, along with front line troops, of crowd control and riot policing – this is a monopoly mission, except in Paris, where the Préfecture of police has enough manpower and may additionally rely on a special body of *gendarmes*, the Garde républicaine. These order maintenance tasks are performed by removing one, two, sometimes up to three *gendarmes* per *brigade*. Order maintenance has made increasing demands on the corps ever since the late 19th century, given the growth of social unrest and workers' movements; confrontations triggered by serious political crises; and the rise of anti-republican, nationalist, and anti-Semite leagues. It is with these missions in mind that, in 1921, 111 "mobile *gendarmerie* platoons" were created, ultimately leading to the advent of the Gendarmerie mobile in 1927.

As far as policing is concerned, the *gendarmerie* has undeniable upsides. Its disciplined staff that always obey orders and have wide-ranging jurisdiction and hot pursuit rights makes it an asset in the eyes of magistrates, prefects, and elected officials alike. These qualities, however, have long been offset by weaknesses mostly due to a lack of manpower. The *gendarmerie* handles many tasks, including managing the military reserve, ensuring readiness for general war mobilizations, and especially incessant order maintenance task that has put huge amounts of pressure on many squads. In the area of criminal police, being forced to wear a uniform at all times has been a handicap. Also, many officers have long had a distaste for general police tasks. These were degrading and below their position, not to mention the fact that until 1903, no specific training was provided for this. Things have changed, of course. Police missions have now taken precedence, and the military character of *gendarmes* is receding as the policing side of the institution is taking over. Indeed, they now report directly to the Ministry of Interior.

The *Sûreté Générale*

The other general-purpose force, the *Sûreté générale*, is a far-removed avatar of the ministère de la Police générale de la République, which was established by the Directory on 12 Nivôse, Year IV (2 January 1796). The complex history of this ministry matches its infamous reputation. Several times dismantled and re-established, in 1853 it was eventually replaced by a "direction de la Sûreté générale" whose history was no less eventful before becoming for a while subordinate to the Préfecture of police.

Only on 31 March 1903 did it finally become an autonomous, permanent directorate in its own right, eventually named the "Sûreté nationale" in an ordinance of 28 March 1934. Following in the aftermath of the Stavisky affair[13] and the tragic riots of February 1934, this reform aimed to strike a new balance among police forces. It granted the *Sûreté* increased prestige in order to rectify the Préfecture of police's indifference toward its poor sibling from the rue des Saussaies.

This disdain and feeling of superiority are rooted in the past, of course, but also – in fact, mostly – in the resource gap that separated the branches. The well-endowed Préfecture commanded a large, specialized force. In contrast, the *Sûreté générale*, even though it was supposed to oversee all police forces in the country, was in a state of continual penury. Its premises on rue des Saussaies – a maze of unsuitable, inconvenient buildings – were a constant source of complaint by its directors. Its small number of actually active departments was simply bewildering to successive ministers of interior of the Third Republic, from Georges Clemenceau to Roger Salengro.

Among its nicknames were "an army of pen-pushers," and "a military staff with no troops."

Thus, apart from the *gendarmerie* and central departments of the Sûreté générale (or nationale), most French forces until 1941 were managed by local governments and operated on a municipal scale. The situation changed with the collapse of the Third Republic.

Vichy and the Legislation of Spring 1941

A new French state was born on 10 July 1940, after a massive vote of support by Third Republic members of parliament. It was designed to be a strong, authoritarian, and anti-democratic state. With an ideology rooted in the exclusion and repression of "anti-France" (i.e. foreigners, Jews, Freemasons, and Communists), it was never going to be content with the policing structure it inherited from the Republic. Police were expected to be efficient, numerous, professional, loyal to the government and regime, but most importantly compliant and easily led by the new authorities. Vichy officials, who obviously had no qualms about renouncing the principles of 1789, immediately proceeded to dismantle the "electoral police," as they called municipal police forces, and they re-established central state control (Berlière 2018).

From April to July 1941, a series of laws gave France a policing system whose influence can still be seen today.[14] It was effectively centralized under the leadership of a Secrétaire général pour la police, assisted by a *directeur de la police nationale*. Three major directorates – criminal police, public safety, and intelligence – were to oversee the various national departments. A fourth directorate was detached from the public safety branch in 1943 to manage the mobile paramilitary units separately.[15] The most spectacular feature of this reform – whose implementation in the occupied zone was long delayed by German forces in the area – was the nationalization of the forces of all towns with a population above 10,000, and the creation of police districts pooling together less populated yet strategic or sensitive areas. The new forces were modelled after Lyon and the police d'État de Seine & Oise, under a plan that had been pushed by the professional association of *commissaires* ever since the early years of the 20th century.

The Paris Préfecture of police – which had already avoided falling under the law of 1884 – was not impacted by the reform of 1941 either. Despite two attempts by Minister of Interior Pierre Pucheu, in late 1941 and early 1942, the Préfecture de police remained outside the realm of the *police nationale*. This isolation meant that it was thoroughly involved in the repression of Communists and Jews. When the Liberation came, the Paris police took an active part in the insurrection and was heavily involved in the *épuration*, a wave of purges that acted as a purification ritual, allowing the Préfecture to emerge unscathed and as powerful as ever.

To compensate for the loss of most of their control of policing, towns had seen most of their spending on police transferred to the state. Can this be considered a tipping point? Whatever the case may be, legislation by the "*de facto* authority calling itself 'the French government'" was considered null and void at the Liberation.[16] However, after the War very few towns expressed a desire to get "their" police back. As a result, Vichy nationalization of policing was retained. Under the Fourth Republic (1947–1958), only towns below 10,000 in population were not subjected to direct state control in police matters, and they were served by the *gendarmerie*.

As far as the Préfecture de police in Paris was concerned, there had been no shortage of attempts to reign in its independence since the late 1880s. However, neither the Third or the Fourth Republics, nor even the Vichy government, succeeded in ending the independence of the Paris police force. This was delayed until the late 1960s.

De Gaulle and the New *Police Nationale* 1966–1968

Governance reforms in the greater Paris area, driven by a law of 10 July 1964, triggered discussions among decision-makers about the status of the Préfecture of police and its staff. The pace of reform stepped up after the unbelievable fiasco dubbed "the Ben Barka affair."[17] This scandal illustrated – as the Stavisky affair had demonstrated earlier – just how disastrous the autonomous operation of the Paris police had become. As this scandal grew and wild rumors spread incessantly, General De Gaulle demanded change. Minister of the Interior Roger Frey was hostile to the idea of ending the dichotomy between the Paris police and the *Sûreté nationale* (as it was then called). The prefect of police, Maurice Papon, was also opposed. The ensuing Frey law (9 July 1966) required the creation by merger of a brand new national institution, the *police nationale* (PN) (Grimaud 2007, pp. 110–111 and 258–259; Renaudie 2008, pp. 154–158). The merger was in fact flawed. Of the two main objectives of the law – unifying the legal status of both forces and standardizing police administration – only the first was fully achieved through this reform. The Paris prefect of police was not required to report to the Direction Générale de la Police Nationale (DGPN), and thus could not receive orders from it. Thus, the Préfecture de police could not be considered to be some external department of the DGPN and was still independent. According to experts in these matters, the idiosyncrasies of the "*grande maison*" – which, in many respects, can be considered to constitute a form of deep state (in French, "*un État dans l'État*") – remain very much alive today, despite the statutory changes of 1966 (Renaudie 2008).

The result was that the Paris police continued to mark its own path. When the Jospin cabinet launched a French version of community policing in 1997, the Préfecture of police was keen to design its own variant. They were in general agreement with the Ministry, but kept to their own timeline and operational control. In another example, when the various domestic intelligence and counterespionage police departments were restructured in 2008, forming the Direction centrale du renseignement intérieur (DCRI), the Préfecture de police again had its way. It instead retained its former Direction des Renseignements Généraux, and simply renamed it Direction du Renseignement. In fact, the Préfecture de police had survived a whole series of other reforms, not least the most decisive reform of Paris institutions, namely the first ever mayoral election in 1977. Since then, the new mayor has done nothing to undermine the functions of the prefect of police in matters of public safety and order maintenance.

The formal integration of the Préfecture of police into the *police nationale* could be considered, in the early 1970s, as a finishing touch to the development of a dual policing structure: France now had two major, centralized, all-purpose police institutions, the civilian *police nationale* and the military *gendarmerie*. As for urban municipal forces, they had essentially ceased to exist in 1941. There remained only a few *gardes champêtres* – an archaic, if picturesque, form of rural police.

Still, a handful of specialized forces – reporting to other government agencies, with strictly limited competencies – still coexisted with the general-purpose police. Chief among these was the 20,000-strong customs authority (*douane*), which remained firmly established at the borders of the country (Clinquart 1990). There were also dozens of different types of enforcement agencies whose status varied considerably, and some bordered on being private regulators. Their highly specialized powers enabled them to identify and report a host of compliance violations of regulations in various sectors of industry. These included agents from the Office national interprofessionnel des vins de table (enforcing table-wine standards), the Commission des opérations de bourse (the French Securities and Exchange Commission), pharmacy inspectors, gamekeepers, and veterinary inspectors. There were a whopping 177 different types of regulatory offices established by the mid-1980s, as reported by a comprehensive survey (Barberger 1985).

The creation of the *police nationale* came in fact at the end of a cycle, which was followed by another – a "two-pronged" one this time. On the one hand, the ongoing streamlining of the state security forces kept going its merry way. The *police nationale* and *gendarmerie* were semi-consolidated in 2009, when both were placed under the authority of the Ministry of Interior. The customs and border agencies were reorganized, becoming the third-largest national police force, as the European Union's inner borders were scrapped. On the other hand, the government gradually offered increasing recognition to "security producers" such as municipal police forces – which had somehow reappeared in the 1970–1980s – and the private security industry.

Notes

1 To get an idea of how complex the "organization" of the only Parisian police was on the eve of the French Revolution, see the organizational chart in Kaplan and Milliot (2009, p. 115). In English, the most complete history of policing in France is Anderson (2011).
2 Comte de Kératry, new prefect of police, on 4th September 1870, quoted in Berlière (1996, p. 92).
3 For a practical approach to daily order and its actors in Paris at the time, see Deluermoz (2009).
4 On Vidocq, the best clarification is to be found in Kalifa (2007).
5 Examples and developments can be found in Berlière and Peschanski (1997) (e.g. Tipton on Tokyo police) and Berlière et al. (2008b).
6 Art. 15 of the municipal law of 1837.
7 The *canton* is a subdivision of the *département*, typically comprised of a dozen *communes* or so.
8 The surveillance and political espionage role the *commissaires cantonaux* were to specialize in brought them into such disrepute that getting rid of them was one of the first measures taken by the republican government of *Défense nationale* (ordinance of 10 September 1870).
9 For a detailed study of the inception of this law, as well as the discussions, debates, confrontations, and successive drafts, see Berlière (1998).
10 The hostility of Catholic circles to the Law of 1905 on the separation of church and state, workers and union demonstrations, the first Labor Days, and some episodes of social unrest saw sharp clashes between mayors who refused to repress or ban – as intimated by the prefects – demonstrations held by their own sympathizers or voters. In this case, prefects resorted to art. 99 and substituted for mayors. On this topic, see for instance Tanguy (2008); Tanguy (1987); Berlière (1998); Diaz (2007, pp. 27–50).
11 Louis Marin, *Rapport de la Commission de la réforme administrative*, 3 novembre 1923.
12 For more on the *gendarmerie* see Luc (2005, 2010), complete with maps, timetables, organizational charts, and information on staffing levels.
13 On the separation and age-old rivalry pitting the Préfecture of police against the *Sûreté générale*, and its harmful effects leading to the enduring impunity enjoyed by the embezzler, who was an informant for both forces, see Jankowski (2000). On the – largely aborted – 1934 reform of the *Sûreté*, see Goyard (1979, pp. 177–206).
14 Vichy France had no parliament or elected representatives of any kind.
15 The Groupes Mobiles de Réserve (GMR) were paramilitary units created by the Vichy regime in 1941. They were dissolved in 1944 and replaced by the Compagnies Républicaines de Sécurité (CRS).
16 "*l'autorité de fait se disant 'gouvernement de l'État français'*", Law of 9 August 1944 concerning the re-establishment of the legally constituted Republic on the French mainland.
17 An operation carried out by the secret service of Morocco to eliminate an opposition leader with involuntary complicity from two prefectures of police officers.

References

Anderson, M. 2011. *In thrall to political change. Police and gendarmerie in France*. Oxford: Oxford University Press.
Barberger, C. 1985. Justice pénale et administrations: Le droit de la discipline des codes administratifs. *L'Année sociologique* 35: 167–177.

Berlière, J. M. 1992. *La police des mœurs sous la IIIe République*. Paris: Le Seuil.
Berlière, J. M. 1993a. Du maintien de l'ordre républicain au maintien républicain de l'ordre? Réflexions sur la violence. *Genèses* 12: 6–29.
Berlière, J. M. 1993b. *Le préfet Lépine*. Paris: Denoël (2nd ed. : *Naissance de la police moderne*, Paris, Perrin, 2011).
Berlière, J. M. 1996. *Le Monde des polices en France*. Bruxelles: Complexe.
Berlière, J. M. 1998. Les pouvoirs de police: attributs du pouvoir municipal ou de l'État? *Jean Jaurès Cahiers trimestriels* 50: 73–104. [www.criminocorpus.cnrs.fr/article177.html].
Berlière, J. M. 2008a. Une menace pour la liberté individuelle sous la République: L'article 10 du code d'instruction criminelle. *Criminocorpus*. [http://journals.openedition.org/criminocorpus/262]
Berlière, J. M. 2018. *Polices des temps noirs (1939–1945)*. Paris: Perrin.
Berlière, J.M., and Lévy, R. 2013. *Histoire des polices en France : de l'Ancien régime à nos jours*. Paris: Nouveau-Monde éditions, (2nd ed.).
Berlière, J. M., Denys, C., Kalifa, D., and Milliot, V. 2008b. *Métiers de police. Être policier en Europe (XVIIIe-XXe siècles)*. Rennes: Presses Universitaires de Rennes.
Berlière, J. M. and Peschanski, D. (Eds.). 1997. *Pouvoirs et polices au XXe siècle: Europe, États-Unis, Japon*. Bruxelles: Éditions Complexe.
Clinquart, J. 1990. *La douane et les douaniers de l'Ancien Régime au Marché Commun*. Paris: Taillandier.
Deluermoz, Q. 2009. Présences d'État: Police et société à Paris 1854–1880. *Annales (HSS)* 64: 435–460.
Deluermoz, Q. 2012. *Policiers dans la ville. La construction d'un ordre public (1854–1913)*. Paris: Publications de la Sorbonne.
Denis, V. 2008. Une police sans policiers: la police du quartier du Palais Royal en 1789–1790. Pp. 475–486 in J. M. Berlière, C. Denys, D. Kalifa, and V. Milliot (Eds.), *Être policier: Métiers de police en Europe (XVIIIe-XXe siècles)*. Rennes: Presses Universitaires de Rennes.
Denys, C. 2005. Lieutenant général de police de province. Pp. 744–748 in M. Auboin, A. Teyssier, and J. Tulard (Eds.), *Histoire et dictionnaire de la police*. Paris: Robert Laffont.
Diaz, C. 2007. L'étrange attentat de Carmaux. *Cahiers Jaurès* 185: 27–50.
Emsley, C. 1999. A typology of nineteenth-century police. *Crime, Histoire & Sociétés/Crime, History & Societies* 3: 29–44.
Goyard, C. 1979. L'enquête sur le rôle de la Sûreté générale dans l'affaire Stavisky. Pp. 177–206 in J. Aubert, M. Eude, and C. Goyard (Eds.), *L'État et sa police en France (1789–1914)*. Genève: Droz.
Grimaud, M. 2007. *Je ne suis pas né en mai 68. Souvenirs et carnets 1934–1992*. Paris: Taillandier.
Jankowski, P. 2000. *Cette vilaine affaire Stavisky. Histoire d'un scandale politique* (trad. française). Paris: Fayard.
Kalifa, D. 2007. *Histoire des détectives privés en France (1832–1942)*. Paris: Nouveau Monde éditions.
Kaplan, S. and Milliot, V. 2009. La police de Paris: une 'révolution permanente'? Du commissaire Lemaire au lieutenant de police Lenoir, les tribulations du *Mémoire sur l'administration de la police* (1770–2792). Pp. 69–116 in C. Denys, B. Marin, and

V. Milliot (Eds.), *Réformer la police: les mémoires policiers en Europe au XVIIIe siècle*. Rennes: Presses Universitaires de Rennes.

Levy, R. 2012. About the proper use of policing "models". *Champ pénal/Penal field* IX. [http://champpenal.revues.org/8276; DOI: 10.4000/champpenal.8276].

Lignereux, A. 2002. *Gendarmes et policiers dans la France de Napoléon: Le duel Moncey-Fouché*. Maisons-Alfort: Service Historique de la Gendarmerie Nationale.

Luc, J. N. 2005. *Histoire de la Maréchaussée et de la Gendarmerie. Guide de recherche*. Maisons-Alfort: Service Historique de la Gendarmerie Nationale.

Luc, J. N. 2010. *Soldats de la loi: la gendarmerie au XXe siècle*. Paris: Presses de l'université Paris-Sorbonne.

Mawby, R. I. 2008. Models of policing. Pp. 17–46 in T. Newburn (Ed.), *Handbook of policing* (2nd ed.). Cullompton: Willan.

Nivet, P. 1994. *Le Conseil municipal de Paris de 1944 à 1977*. Paris: Publications de la Sorbonne.

Reiner, R. 1991–1992. La tradition policière britannique: Modèle ou mythe? *Les cahiers de la sécurité intérieure* 7: 29–39.

Renaudie, O. 2008. *La Préfecture de police*. Paris: LGDJ/Lextenso éditions.

Sicot, M. 1959. *Servitudes et grandeurs policières (40 ans à la Sûreté)*. Paris: Les Productions de Paris.

Tanguy, J. F. 1987. Autorité de l'État et libertés locales: Le commissaire central de Rennes face au maire et au préfet (1870–1914). Pp. 167–182 in Société d'histoire de 1848 (Ed.), *Maintien de l'ordre et polices en France et en Europe au XIXe siècle*. Paris: Créaphis.

Tanguy, J. F. 2008. Eugène Court, un commissaire de combat à Rennes au début de la IIIe République. Pp. 147–172 in D. Kalifa, and P. Karila-Cohen (Eds.), *Le commissaire de police au XIXe siècle*. Paris: Publications de la Sorbonne.

Chapter 3

The Colonial Legacy of French Policing

Emmanuel Blanchard

> No one commented on the militarization of the public order. No one seemed to notice that convoys of armored trucks could roll into troublesome neighborhoods at dawn. No one seemed surprised by the use of an armored column in France … It could be discussed from a practical standpoint: we are all familiar with the armored column; that explains why no one notices it … The police officers are young, very young. We dispatch young men in armored columns to retake control of no-go areas. They wreak havoc and leave again. Just as they did over there. The art of war does not change.
>
> (Jenni, 2011, p. 255)

From *The French Art of War*, his first novel published in 2011, to his latest book in the spring of 2019, Alexis Jenni has never ceased exploring the shadows cast and the hushed-up legacy of the Algerian War in contemporary France. He regularly discusses post-colonial policing practices in his work. He offers, for instance, some informative pages on facial discrimination in stop-and-search (Blanchard 2014), and, as in this chapter's opening epigraph, a recounting of early-morning police raids in so-called "sensitive" areas. By pointing out the militarization of public order in socially and racially differentiated areas, Jenni took on a widely discussed topic among sociologists of policing. For them, the phrase "militarization of the public order" encompasses such a variety of transformations of policing that one is hard-pressed to clearly define its conceptual and analytical scope in a way that it can meaningfully contribute to the examination of developments in public order maintenance in a variety of contexts (de Maillard 2017).

To the many commentators on Jenni's work, there is little doubt that colonial conflicts – and the Algerian War in particular – have produced contemporary conflicts that the novelist has been singularly apt at capturing (Stora and Jenni 2016). In fact, some scholars of post-coloniality have no qualms inferring direct links between the condition of the colonized and that of the residents of the underprivileged neighborhoods of French towns and cities today (Mbembe 2001; Stoler 2016). Crucially, even before Jenni began exploring these issues, several sociologists had penned noteworthy essays on the colonial origins of the militarization of public order in French suburbs (Rigouste 2009; Belmessous 2010). Nevertheless, colleagues who are most involved in the field of police studies tend to keep their distance from interpretations they are unlikely to resort to when it comes to explaining the idiosyncrasies of French-style policing.

Still, the idea that there is such a thing as a "French style of policing" is a common one (Lévy 2016; Gauthier 2017). Reputedly, French police operations are more aggressive than those of our British or German neighbors, the two guiding principles being intervention and arrests (Zagrodzki 2019). While these characteristics are especially noticeable in the disproportionate impact of stop-and-search (known in France as "ID checks") and police interventions in racialized communities, they are not limited to these targets. The repression of the "yellow vests" movement has shown that such developments in French-style public order maintenance can expand from suburbia to other "subversive" spaces and new social groups.

This chapter questions this analytical self-restraint in the study and use of colonial history. For policing experts, research on this topic raises the issues of distancing themselves from "activist" analytical traditions, and of overcoming the methodological obstacles that make it difficult to uncover correlations using the survey and other data methods widely recognized in the field of police studies. Socio-historical analysis, though, enables us to highlight continuities and legacies that may shed new light on some idiosyncrasies of the "French style of policing."

Politicization of Young Immigrants: Police Brutality and Colonial Racism

On 15 October 1983, several years of rallying against "racist crimes" culminated in a March for Equality and Against Racism. It departed from Marseille and reached Paris 50 days and 1500km later. This march followed several episodes of confrontational clashes pitting youths from the suburban areas of Lyon against police forces accused of misconduct. On this same day, protagonists involved in the event gathered by the Saint-Martin canal in Paris to pay tribute to the Algerian victims of the massacre of 17 October 1961 (Hajjat 2013).[1] These activists claimed that "Arab hunting," though it had assumed new shapes since the end of the Algerian War, was still very much present and "indicative of colonial racism and oppression" in contemporary France (Aissaoui 2006).

These reminders of historical continuities were voiced, among others, by the Movement of Arab Workers (Mouvement des travailleurs arabes – MTA). This group played a key role during the protests that followed the death of

Mohamed Diab on the premises of the Versailles police station in November 1972 (House and MacMaster 2006). Years before a connection between past and present was formulated by sociologist Abdelmalek Sayad, the MTA noted that there were "in France and in Europe colonized people, migrant workers" (Aissaoui 2006). Still, neither these hidden memories nor activist lines of reasoning were enough to turn the colonial legacy into the main analytical descriptor of the migrants' condition. True, some intellectuals engaged in these struggles. Félix Guattari warned that "a new, internal, colonial war was taking on former imperialist powers from the inside" (Guattari 1981). However, these early observations were unable to forestall the relative "occultation [obscuring] of colonial history" (Hajjat 2013, p. 166). Still, the appearance on the political stage of "young immigrants," as they dubbed themselves, was achieved by denouncing police violence and discrimination, current and past, and during the Algerian War of independence in particular.

After 1983, following especially the creation of the anti-racist organization SOS-Racisme, denunciation of colonial legacies disappeared from the agendas of the most institutionalized anti-racist movements (Juhem 2001). It remained, however, on the agenda of the organizations that took over the task of asserting the political autonomy of the communities living in the *banlieue* (underprivileged suburbs). One activist from the National Committee Against Double Jeopardy[2] (created in 1990) and subsequently from the Mouvement Immigration Banlieue (MIB, founded in 1995) put it this way: evoking his own militant journey and the centrality of struggles against police and judicial violence, he noted in 2000, "It's the post-colonial handling of housing projects that generates the troubles these neighborhoods go though" (Carrère 2000). The denunciation of "colonial justice"[3] was an increasingly popular reference at the time among the "Truth and Justice" committees (*Vérité et justice*). They highlighted police impunity in cases of – sometimes lethal – brutality against youths from the "*cités*" (housing projects or "hoods"), whom they portrayed as "victims of the colonial handling of the housing projects."[4] Therefore, when the "Call of the indigenous people of the Republic" (*Appel des indigènes de la République*) was published in January 2005, its searing denunciation of the "treatment of populations originating in colonization, [which] is furthering colonial policy" was in line with a long history of activism. In fact, political anti-racism agendas born in the French *banlieues* had been castigating the "coloniality of power" for about three decades (Quijano 2000). And though it couldn't be reduced solely to this, this attitude was considered to stem from in police practices rooted in the imperial past of France.

Internal Colonialism and the Silence of French Sociology

The early 2000s was an inflection point. Thereafter, references to the colonial past became increasingly central and more clearly drawn and were based on theoretical references shared by post-colonial and de-colonial studies (Grosfoguel 2011). The "rediscovery," both in the publishing and the academic worlds, of Frantz Fanon as a political reference point for a new form of political anti-racism is emblematic in this respect.[5] Throughout the 1960s, the author of *The Wretched of the Earth* was considered a key figure in the development of the concept of "internal colonialism" (Allen 2005). This emerged in Latin America to characterize the condition of indigenous people, but also in the United States to account for the multiple forms of dispossession endured in black ghettos (Blauner 1969; Gutiérrez 2004). The denunciations of "internal colonialism" focused particularly on the role of the police, and in the United States the Black Panthers set out to create armed protection groups with the goal of patrolling public spaces and illustrating that there was a possibility for self-organization that might allow for the expulsion of "occupation forces" from black neighborhoods.

The concept of "internal colonialism," however, was little used in France. There, spokespeople for the movements most heavily engaged in denouncing practices rooted in the imperial past sometimes resorted to the phrase "endo-colonial domination" instead (Abdallah 2012, p. 15). Yet the mobilization of black activists in the United States and the United Kingdom was not unheeded, and in fact directly inspired numerous initiatives. In the early 1980s, some British activists even provided concrete support and direct testimonies during several protests against police brutality in France. In the late 1970s, these exchanges were evidenced in slogans such as *"flics hors des cités"* ("cops out of the projects") and demonstrations like *Rock against police* with their denunciation of "police occupation" (Abdallah 2012, pp. 29–33). These shared practices were also noticeable during the summer of 1980 when, faced with a rise in racist attacks, self-defense groups started to crop up to ensure security in several housing projects in Seine-Saint-Denis, north of Paris (Abdallah 2010). In these areas, the police were perceived first and foremost as an institution that hampered their ability to act autonomously. Historical and current disputes were such that the police could hardly expect to be perceived as a public service capable of protecting residents against the crimes – especially the racist ones – these communities fell prey to.

While throughout the 1960–1980 period activist and academic circles in the United States were busy co-developing concepts such as "internal colonialism," the French intellectual tradition remained rather impervious to these theoretical exchanges. Although such eminent personalities as Jean-Paul Sartre and Michel Foucault did openly support mobilizations against racist crimes and police brutality, their denunciations of the racism endured by migrant workers did not draw upon this terminology. While Michel Foucault was already making occasional references to "internal colonialism" in his teaching at the Collège de France, these comments always referred to a distant past (from the 16th to the 19th century) that was not specifically linked to the present of the anti-racist protests he was contributing to at the time (Irrera 2015; Sorrentino 2017). Admittedly, Foucault already had the intuition – probably linked to his activist engagements – that "the boomerang effects of colonization on the mechanisms of power in the West" was a key issue (Foucault 2003, p. 103). Still, French academic circles remained generally unaffected by the passionate international discussions surrounding the concept of "internal colonialism" and its explanatory value. Its utility was in fact contested, and the concept was described by its critics as ill-defined, largely metaphoric, cut-off from historical knowledge, and a "catch-all" term that it ended up being used to describe any situation of dominance. As early as 1974, Michael Burawoy had described "internal colonialism" as a notion that brought little to the analysis of race relationships (an already popular field in US sociology) and one that may encompass class relationships that were by no means peculiar to colonial situations (Burawoy 1974).

Even though seldom explicitly quoted, Michael Burawoy's paper provides a good summary of the precautions, prejudices even, of many French sociologists when it comes to examining a present that is marked by past events and colonial domination. Ever since the early 2000s, these American debates have been re-enacted in a French context, where racial and the colonial questions are so closely intertwined that the late affirmation of the former was bound to bring about a resurgence of the latter (Fassin and Fassin 2006). Ethnicity and race did not appear at all in sociological studies on policing until the mid-1980s (Lévy 1987). They only became a regular feature of police practices analysis during the 2010s. Today, the point is no longer whether or not they should be discussed, but *how* they should be characterized and weighed against the significance of variables such as demographic factors (age, sex, occupation) or physical appearance (clothing, body) (Jobard et al. 2012; Gauthier 2015; Jounin 2015). The "colonial past" is a contextual variable that is harder than social factors to shoehorn into a statistical model, and more difficult to measure. As a result, it is usually just mentioned, if not simply ignored. Objectifying post-colonial continuities from both a historical and statistical point of view is a delicate task indeed, and assuming they are even invoked, such continuities tend to be asserted theoretically rather than proved empirically. In fact, whether they do add any heuristic value at all is a valid question. Does highlighting post-coloniality simply overlap the racialization of public order maintenance practices? Does it really contribute to stepping up from description (facial discrimination in stop-and-search for instance) to understanding and possibly explaining the racialized practices of police forces?

For advocates of the centrality of racial issues and their genealogy in the excesses of "the force of order" (Fassin 2011), these new paradigms can only be meaningfully taken into account if new research protocols are implemented. Room must be created for the representations and perceptions of the communities that are most impacted by the coercive dimensions of police work (Fassin 2016). This is why the ethnographic approach has been put forward as having the potential for rejuvenating police studies, whereas socio-historical analysis is somewhat hampered by the fact that policing in the French colonial empire only began to be studied quite recently (Blanchard et al. 2017). How could colonial continuities be asserted when the exploration of the specifics of police practices in a colonial situation has only just begun, and mainland events hardly seem to be considered relevant to research on the French empire?

On Colonial Policing

Police as an institution may have been considered as colonial in essence insofar as it was central in the processes used to civilize and discipline populations that resisted the dominant political and economic order. This type of approach was frequent in the 1970s, when the focus was on accounting how the salaried workforce of industrial European societies was effectively put to work and trained. Hence, the action of the police officers and *gendarmes* during the first decades of the 19th century has been described as that of "domestic missionaries" (Storch 1976). The gradual extension of political rights to peasants and workers, however, was accompanied by attempts to ensure consent to police authority by the people. This was especially true in the UK (Emsley 1996), but also in the French countryside and towns, where the model of a force serving exclusively the ruling class gradually waned (Lignereux 2008; Houte 2010; Deluermoz 2012).

These developments largely paralleled those of colonial expansion in Africa and Asia, where the question of consent to authority arose in very different terms. The native inhabitants of these territories were subject to conquest and extermination in the context of settler colonialism (Wolfe 1999; Elkins and Pedersen 2005). In daily life they were subjected to a logic of "penal surplus" and held prisoner by a particularly tight-knit coercive network (Brown 2002; Sherman 2009). The weight of the penal state and its despotic power could sometimes be measured in absolute terms – by the number of police officers, troops, and other "uniformed bodies" ("*corps habillés*") (Glasman 2015) – especially in some British penal colonies. However, looking at the size of the penal apparatus, the number of police, and the meagre findings of intelligence services, most colonized territories were far from police states. They eventually found themselves unable to account for political and social developments that were taking place there, especially in rural areas (Bayly 1993; Thomas 2008).

Their sometimes-low staffing levels notwithstanding, the primacy of repressive policies was nevertheless undeniable. This contrasted with the relative weakness of infrastructure (Mann 1984) and the embryonic agencies offering services such as education, health, and transport. Subtracting the forces of law and order, the administrative apparatus of colonial administrations was more than lean (Glasman 2015). This led to the appearance of the colonial state as poorly centralized and weak in terms of its staffing and effective authority. Remarkable, though, was its ability to inflict boundless violence on the population. This was usually the main response to attempted uprising or even mere protests. This could be justified by extensions of the right to punish provided by – and embodied in – the British Empire's Criminal Tribes Act and the French Code de l'indigénat (Merle and Muckle 2019). One reason why such state configurations now appear largely obsolete is precisely because these belittling, discriminatory legal statuses have gradually disappeared. Or have they? As far as the metropolitan territories of the French and British imperial powers are concerned, the point remains a debatable one for migrants and undocumented people (Mbembe 2016; Achiume 2019).

Whether one agrees or not with these views on the criminalization of immigration, the fact remains that post-colonial states are heirs to imperial settings in which the penal and the colonial questions were intertwined and contributed to one and the same social/racial configuration. The coloniality of power was not circumscribed by geographical borders so much as by limitations of the right to travel and other essentially penal restrictions on the general population. Students of comparative criminology argue that, at similar stages of economic development, the legacy of slavery and colonial expansion in the formation of states can account for variations in the intensity of police repression and influence of the penal system in Western countries (Tonry 2007, 2011). Still, these historical contexts are not easy to put into an equation, even though a decent statistical proxy can be found in the influence of ethnic and racial inequalities. For example, while the proper theoretical weighting of past events in analyses of contemporary discriminations is still being debated, it seems impossible to account for the current American penal state without integrating the legacy of slavery and segregation (Alexander 2010). In the French case, although the various forms of racial domination and arrangements obviously evolved in a different context, contemporary police practices certainly cannot be said to be color blind either.

The Colonial Legacy of the Algerian War

On the mainland, the police techniques and general punitiveness of overseas rule had spectacular "boomerang effects." From fingerprint records to the use of firearms against demonstrators, through the history of the death penalty and its late abolition, everything somehow stemmed from or transited through the colonies. The decolonization period – especially that following the Algerian War of independence – also left a mark on the police, including those who were never stationed in overseas territories. As early as the 1950s, for instance, ID checks and roundups targeting the "Muslim French" were denounced by Algerian nationalist demonstrators holding posters that read *"pas de rafles au faciès"* ("no facial discrimination-based roundups"). The policy of widespread ID checks became visible as early as the late 1940s in areas where numerous immigrants from Algeria tended to settle, and it did not stop with end of the Algerian War. From the mid-1960s onwards, these policies massively impacted young Arab men living in the *banlieues*, at a time when juvenile delinquency was increasingly being perceived along racialized lines (Mohammed and Mucchielli 2007).

Regarding identity checks, for instance, several colonial legacies may be pointed out. The national identity card was established in 1955 to help control travel during the Algerian War of independence (Piazza 2004). Even before this conflict, roundups and ID checks were a constant threat for some groups of "diminished citizens" ("*citoyens diminués*") such as prostitutes, homosexuals, vagrants, and gypsies (Blanchard 2011). Still, "*Vos papiers!*" ("Your papers!") had not yet become a routine announcement. Most residents of poor neighborhoods, including young men, were still spared this treatment by the "*gardiens de la paix*" ("peacekeepers," as the French constables were called). In the 1970s, however, as select neighborhoods were increasingly sealed off by riot police trucks, memories of the Algerian War inevitably resurfaced, generating protests against such "police occupation" (Zancarini-Fournel 2004, 2011; Abdallah 2012). These ID checks, which have been shown to proceed from professional logics that generate serious racial discrimination patterns, are now deeply entrenched in the routines of French policing. Any government initiative aiming to regulate their use would be perceived as a sure-fire sign of political defiance against the entire force. The sheer frequency of these "degradation ceremonies" (Garfinkel 1956; Blanchard 2014) is in fact a source of amazement among police from neighboring countries. They tend to rely much less on techniques that are known to be intrusive, humiliating, and also rather ineffective in terms of police performance (Gauthier and Lukas 2011; de Maillard et al. 2016; de Maillard 2019).

Identity checks are by no means the only legacy of the Algerian War in terms of police practices and institutions. An erosion of the quality of the police service offered to the public and the excessive focus of uniformed police on anti-crime issues (Mouhanna 2011) are an integral part of this picture as well. At the end of World War II, the French police attempted to rebuild their legitimacy by emphasizing that they meant to be "a force serving the citizens." They attempted to raise the profile of day-to-day policing tasks that pertained neither to surveillance nor to repression. The hegemonic trade union of Paris uniformed officers – Syndicat général de la police (SGP) – was instrumental in defending this perspective and promoting a renewed vision of the role of *constable* (Blanchard 2010). Starting in 1955, and especially 1957, the repercussions of the Algerian War in mainland France brought this trend to a stop. The weight of anti-terrorist measures was felt throughout the entire force, which was often targeted by Front de Libération Nationale (FLN) attacks and was engaged in massive surveillance and control actions against Algerian immigrants. Police stations were barricaded, armed jeeps and pick-up trucks patrolled the streets of Paris, beat police units were equipped with machine guns, and the rules of firearm engagement were relaxed. These extensions of routine policing powers came at a time when a state of emergency prevailed, and the media were heavily censored. During this period law and order was militarized, so much so that its long-run consequences were worrying even at the highest echelons of the force (Blanchard 2011).

As far as arms are concerned, the return of "peace" (France was not officially at war, but the state of emergency was lifted in 1963) promised to return things to normal, but transformations of the police persisted. For instance, it is at that time that the focus on crime reduction spread to fighting petty crime in order to justify the control of racialized populations. A Brigade des agressions et violences (BAV) had been created as early as 1953. It was purportedly formed to fight street delinquency. However, in fact mostly conducted an unheard-of spate of ID checks, punctuated by strong-arm raids in immigrant neighborhoods. The crime-control sham was so blatant – and had been since the unit's creation in a context of politicization of Algerian immigrants – that the BAV soon ended up openly specializing in the struggle against "North African terrorism." Although the *brigade* was discontinued at the end of the Algerian War, some of its duties and practices were reconstituted in other units, such as the Brigades anti-criminalité (BAC) (Gauthier 2004; Fassin 2011). Indeed, the BAC had little technical specialization that enabled it to deal with serious of crimes. Although not explicitly mentioned in their operational orders, they just happened to focus mainly on immigrant housing areas. They increasingly operated as public order maintenance squads, homing in on misbehaviors and incivilities of young residents from housing projects in the *banlieues*. Beyond the fact that the acronyms sound similar, the BAV and BAC shared more features linked to fault lines that occurred during the Algerian War. For example, the BAC was made up of constables or peace officers who viewed their specialization as an opportunity to do "real police work." In the end, from the 1960s to the 1980s, the SGP's repeated attempts to revive a broader, less aggressive definition of the peace officer's job were in vain. The aggressively repressive turn taken by police during the Algerian War had long-lasting consequences. Efforts to reimagine the role of policing in society died.

The history of the centralization of the French force is a long one. Historians and sociologists working on the distance separating the police from the communities they are supposed to protect are keen to remind us of this fact (see Chapter 2 in this volume). This is without even considering the decolonization era, even though that period further sets France apart from many other European countries, including other imperial powers. Ever since the early 2000s, for instance, several historians – and former police officers – have been reassessing the footprint of the colonial period on British forces (Whitfield 2004; Sinclair and Williams 2007). They have stressed Sir Robert Peel's double legacy. He was the founder of the Royal Irish Constabulary, a paramilitary police corps whose origins have been eclipsed by the prominence of Peel's other major legacy, the invention of the Bobby. Except for earlier struggles for Irish independence, followed by the extension of political conflicts within Northern Ireland to episodes of terrorism on the mainland, British police were spared wars of independence being waged in the homeland. Of all the African and Asian independence movements, only the Algerian FLN exported conflict to the heart of the imperial power. In particular, they targeted the police. Between 1957 and 1962, 80 officers were killed. In parallel, conflict-involved murders skyrocketed. As many as 5,000 Algerians were assassinated, mostly in the context of violence among nationalists. Most of these cases were dismissed without further action, fostering a general slackening of constraints on the criminal police services, which were literally overwhelmed by this flood of violence. In the absence of research on the topic, maintaining that memories of these outbreaks of violence still influence contemporary police perceptions would be a stretch, although their institutional effects clearly outlasted the period of the Algerian War of independence.

From Continuities to Resonances with the Past

The coloniality of power is embodied not only in its institutional, practical, and cognitive roots, but also in forms of governmentality that, though they cannot really be said to prolong the colonial experience, do sometimes look disturbingly similar. For lower-ranked officers, the colonial situation was characterized as much by an absence of policing as by the kind of "penal excess" that has generally been described in imperial history. Police forces were mostly expected to protect the colonizers' living spaces as well as areas where colonial products for export were being produced (Thomas 2012). Broadly speaking, day-to-day policing was rather underdeveloped, since police work centered on defending the pre-eminence of the political and economic interests of the colonial class. During the interwar period, local middle classes emerged. They began to vocally demand not just an expansion of individual and workers' rights, but also significant improvements in health care, education, and public safety services that had been promised (Cooper 1996). The question of "insecurity" became a central one, but not just in the sense of abstract dangers looming over colonial sovereignty. Every infraction against a colonizer was perceived as infringing upon their sovereignty. However, it was unlikely that the expectations of some with regard to the protection of their goods and persons could always be met (Bloembergen 2012). While security was paramount to colonized people as well, they most certainly had no role in defining security and public order priorities. Although the governed could be viewed as informants and were entitled to becoming police auxiliaries, they exercised no legitimate voice in determining the actions of the police, even within their own communities. An exception came when police powers were delegated to them as so-called "traditional authorities," but they were always in a subsidiary position as far as the hierarchy of police jobs and functions was concerned.

In contemporary times, places that feature the militarization of public order maintenance suffer not only from too much police control but also – concomitantly and paradoxically – from the weakness of certain forms of police presence. For instance, community policing – regardless of its modalities and institutional configurations – was never sustainably implemented in the poorest neighborhoods, those that were considered most impacted by crime (Skogan 2003). In France, a focus on "*reconquête républicaine*" – i.e. recapturing territories that are described as "lost" to crime by putting more police on the streets – was more prevalent. Neither was the general attitude of police towards such areas compatible with lending an attentive ear to the public's demands. Even when these demands are expressed in security terms, they are rarely considered; rather, they tend to be dismissed as potentially feeding crime.

Victimization surveys show that indifference or defiance towards the police is particularly high in the neighborhoods targeted by the most repressive units. One major reason for low crime reporting rates – that is, the share of victims who reach out to the police – is that the force is perceived as unprotective, inefficient, and generally not very good at listening to those who would like to be able to rely on them but do not want to slip into the shoes of being seen as an informant (Zauberman et al. 2013). A look at the channels and methods available for contacting the police demonstrates that these residents are perceived more as potential intelligence sources than as citizens with their own vision of order and the protection that they deserve. In this respect, their condition exhibits some characteristics in common with the colonial period. Can it be inferred that the police attitudes and practices are derived from colonial legacies, for instance in terms of racialized representations? Methodological rigor precludes any positive answer here. Still, certain congruences between the two periods in terms of the concerned territories or populations lend a "family resemblance" between their policing methods. This provides an invitation to conduct deeper historical analyses, not leaving a monopoly of thinking in terms of colonial legacies in the hands of novelists and non-experts of policing. Far from being a matter of theoretical paradigm, the coloniality of power resides in genealogies that need to be uncovered with the same rigor, but no more scruples, than other characteristic of the "French style of policing."

Notes

1 On 17 October 1961, the Algerian Front de libération national (FLN) exhorted Algerian immigrants to defy the curfew imposed by the prefecture of police and demonstrate on the streets of Paris. These massive protests were banned – as were

all street protests at the time – and repressed in bloody fashion. Although the final toll is not firmly established, several dozens of Algerians were killed that night; and according to the most careful estimates there were more than 100 conflict fatalities during September to October 1961 (House and MacMaster 2006).

2 In France, "double jeopardy" (*double peine*) refers to the possibility, for a non-national, to be incarcerated and subsequently deported for the same crime or offence.

3 "The trial of colonial justice" was particularly key in mobilizations surrounding the trial of the police officer (acquitted by the Versailles court in September 2001) who had killed Youssef Khaïf, a young resident from the Val-Fourré neighborhood in Mantes-la-Jolie on 9 June 1991 (Abdallah 2012, pp. 131–135).

4 In August 2003, the MIB's magazine, *L'écho des cités*, was headlined "Colonial management of neighborhood projects" (*Gestion coloniale des quartiers*) and illustrated with two photographs creating a parallel with the Battle of Algiers.

5 While Fanon did not particularly focus on forms of police and judicial repression, he was nevertheless keenly aware of how heavily policing issues weighed in on the political, social, and racial divisions of his time: "The colonized word is a world split in two. The dividing line, the border is marked by army barracks and police stations" (Fanon 1961, p. 47, author's translation).

References

Abdallah, M. H. 2010. La "Rumeur de Bondy". *Plein droit 85*: 35–39.

Abdallah, M. H. 2012. *Rengainez, on arrive! Chroniques des luttes contre les crimes racistes ou sécuritaires des années 1970 à nos jours*. Paris: Libertalia.

Achiume, T. E. 2019. Migration as decolonization. *Stanford Law Review* 71: 1509–1575.

Aissaoui, R. 2006. Political mobilization of North African migrants in 1970s France: The case of the mouvement des travailleurs arabes. *Journal of Muslim Minority Affairs* 26: 171–186.

Alexander, M. 2010. *The new jim crow: Mass incarceration in the age of colorblindness*. New York: The New Press.

Allen, R. L. 2005. Ressessing the internal (neo) colonial theory. *The Black Scholar* 35: 2–11.

Bayly, C. A. 1993. Knowing the country: Empire and information in India. *Modern Asian Studies* 27: 3–43.

Belmessous, H. 2010. *Opération banlieues. Comment l'État prépare la guerre urbaine dans les cités françaises*. Paris: La Découverte.

Blanchard, E. 2010. Les gardiens de la paix de la IVe République: Des policiers de proximité? Pp. 119–139 in J. M. Berlière and R. Lévy (Eds.) *L'historien, le sociologue et le témoin. Quand des policiers se mettent à table*. Paris: Nouveau Monde éd.

Blanchard, E. 2011. *La police parisienne et les Algériens, 1944–1962*. Paris: Nouveau monde.

Blanchard, E. 2014. Contrôles au faciès: Une cérémonie de dégradation. *Plein Droit* 103: 15–20.

Blanchard, E., Bloembergen, M., and Lauro, A. 2017. *Policing in colonial empires: Cases, connections, boundaries ca. 1850–1970*. Bruxelles: P. I. E. Peter Lang.

Blauner, R. 1969. Internal colonialism and ghetto revolt. *Social Problems* 16: 393–408.

Bloembergen, M. 2012. Vol, meurtre et action policière dans les villages javanais: Les dynamiques locales de la sécurité aux Indes néerlandaises orientales dans les années 1930. *Genèses* 86: 8–36.

Brown, M. 2002. The Politics of penal excess and the echo of colonial penalty. *Punishment & Society* 4: 403–423.

Burawoy, M. 1974. Race, class and colonialism. *Social and Economic Studies* 23: 521–550.

Carrère, V. 2000. Les bannis des banlieues. *Plein Droit* 45. [www.gisti.org/spip.php?article3650]

Cooper, F. 1996. *Decolonization and African society: The labor question in French and British Africa*. Cambridge: Cambridge University Press.

Deluermoz, Q. 2012. *Policiers dans la ville. La construction d'un ordre public à paris (1854–1914)*. Paris: PUPS.

de Maillard, J. 2017. *Polices comparées*. Paris: LGDJ.

de Maillard, J. 2019. Les contrôles d'identité, entre politiques policières, pratiques professionnelles et effets sociaux. Un état critique des connaissances. *Champ pénal/Penal field* 16. [https://doi.org/10.4000/champpenal.10318]

de Maillard, J., Hunold, D., Roché, S., Oberwittler, D., and Zagrodzki, M. 2016. Les logiques professionnelles et politiques du contrôle: Des styles de police différents en France et en Allemagne. *Revue française de science politique* 66: 271–293.

Elkins, C., and Pedersen, S. 2005. *Settler colonialism in the twentieth century: Projects, practices, legacies*. London: Routledge.

Emsley, C. 1996. *The English police: A political and social history*. Harlow: Longman.

Fanon, F. 1961. *Les damnés de la terre*. Paris: La Découverte.

Fassin, D. 2011. *La force de l'ordre. Une anthropologie de la police des quartiers*. Paris: Seuil.

Fassin, D. 2016. L'ethnographie retrouvée. Sur quelques approches contemporaines des pratiques policières. *L'Homme* 219–220: 287–310.

Fassin, D., and Fassin, É. 2006. *De la question sociale à la question raciale: Représenter la société française*. Paris: La Découverte.

Foucault, M. 2003. *Society must be defended*. New York: Picador.

Garfinkel, H. 1956. Conditions of successful degradation ceremonies. *American Journal of Sociology* 61: 420–424.

Gauthier, J. 2004. *D'un aspect des politiques publiques de sécurite interieure en France: Les brigades anti-criminalite (1973–2004)*. Paris: L'École des hautes études en sciences sociales.

Gauthier, J. 2015. Origines contrôlées: Police et minorités en France et en Allemagne. *Sociétés contemporaines* 97: 101–127.

Gauthier, J. 2017. L'art français de la déviance policière. *La Vie des idées*. [www.laviedesidees.fr/L-art-francais-de-la-deviance-policere.html]

Gauthier, J., and Lukas, T. 2011. Warum kontrolliert die Polizei (nicht)? Unterschiede im Handlungsrepertoire deutscher und französischer Polizisten. *Soziale Probleme* 2: 174–206.

Glasman, J. 2015. *Les corps habillés au Togo. Genèse coloniale des métiers de police*. Paris: Karthala.

Grosfoguel, R. 2011. Decolonizing post-colonial studies and paradigms of political economy: Transmodernity, decolonial thinking, and global coloniality. *TRANSMODERNITY: Journal of Peripheral Cultural Production of the Luso-Hispanic World*. [https://escholarship.org/uc/item/21k6t3fq]

Guattari, F. 2009. "Contre le racisme à la française", *Le Nouvel Observateur*, 4 mai 1981. Republished in Félix Guettari, *Les années d'hiver*, Paris: Les prairies ordinaires.

Gutiérrez, R. A. 2004. Internal colonialism: An American theory of race. *Du Bois Review: Social Science Research on Race* 1: 281–295.

Hajjat, A. 2013. *La marche pour l'égalité et contre le racisme*. Paris: éd. Amsterdam.

House, J., and MacMaster, N. 2006. *Paris 1961: Algerians, state terror, and memory*. Oxford: Oxford University Press.

Houte, A. D. 2010. *Le métier de gendarme au XIXe siècle*. Rennes: Presses Universitaires de Rennes.

Irrera, O. 2015. Racisme et colonialisme chez Michel Foucault. *Rue Descartes: La revue du collège internationale de philosophie*. [www.ruedescartes.org/recherches-en-cours/racisme-et-colonialisme-chez-michel-foucault/]

Jobard, F., Lévy, R., Lamberth, J., and Névanen, S. 2012. Mesurer les discriminations selon l'apparence: Une analyse des contrôles d'identité à Paris. *Population* 67: 423–451.

Jounin, N. 2015. Le faciès du contrôle. *Déviance et Société* 39: 3–29.

Juhem, P. 2001. Entreprendre en politique: Les carrières militantes des fondateurs de SOS-Racisme. *Revue française de science politique* 51: 131–153.

Lévy, R. 1987. *Du suspect au coupable: Le travail de police judiciaire*. Paris: Méridiens Klincksieck.

Lévy, R. 2016. La police française à la lumière de la théorie de la justice procédurale. *Déviance et Société* 40: 139–164.

Lignereux, A. 2008. *La France rébellionnaire: Les résistances à la gendarmerie, 1800–1859*. Rennes: Presses Universitaires de Rennes.

Mann, M. 1984. The autonomous power of the state: Its origins, mechanisms and results. *European Journal of Sociology* 25: 185–213.

Mbembe, A. 2001. *On the postcolony*. Berkeley: University of California Press.

Mbembe, A. 2016. *Politiques de l'inimitié*. Paris: La Découverte.

Merle, I., and Muckle, A. 2019. *L'Indigénat. Genèses dans l'Empire français. Pratiques en Nouvelle Calédonie*. Paris: Centre nationale de la recherche scientifique éd.

Mohammed, M., and Mucchielli, L. 2007. *Les bandes de jeunes. Des 'blousons noirs' à nos jours*. Paris: La Découverte.

Mouhanna, C. 2011. *La police contre les citoyens?* Nîmes: Champ social.

Piazza, P. 2004. *Histoire de la carte nationale d'identité*. Paris: Odile Jacob.

Quijano, A. 2000. Coloniality of power, eurocentrism, and Latin America. *Nepantla: Views from South* 1: 533–580.

Rigouste, M. 2009. *L'ennemi intérieur postcolonial. De la guerre coloniale au contrôle sécuritaire (1954–2007)*. Paris: La Découverte.

Sherman, T. C. 2009. Tensions of colonial punishment: Perspectives on recent developments in the study of coercive networks in Asia, Africa and the Caribbean. *History Compass* 7: 659–677.

Sinclair, G., and Williams, C. 2007. 'Home and away': The cross-fertilization between 'colonial' and 'British' policing. *Journal of Imperial and Commonwealth History* 35: 221–238.

Skogan, W. G. 2003. *Community policing: Can it work?* Belmont: Cengage Learning.

Sorrentino, V. 2017. Foucault et la question coloniale. *Cités* 72: 127–138.

Stoler, A. L. 2016. *Duress: Imperial durabilities in our times*. Durham: Duke University Press.

Stora, B., and Jenni, A. 2016. *Les mémoires dangereuses*. Paris: Albin Michel.
Storch, R. D. 1976. The policeman as domestic missionary: Urban discipline and popular culture in Northern England, 1850–1880. *Journal of Social History* 9: 481–509.
Thomas, M. 2008. *Empire of intelligence: Security services and colonial disorder after 1914*. Berkeley: University of California Press.
Thomas, M. 2012. *Violence and colonial order: Police, workers and protest in the European colonial empires, 1918–1940*. Cambridge: Cambridge University Press.
Tonry, M. H. 2007. Determinants of penal policies. *Crime and Justice* 36: 1–48.
Tonry, M. H. 2011. *Punishing race: A continuing American dilemma*. New York: Oxford University Press.
Whitfield, J. 2004. *Unhappy dialogue: The metropolitan police and black Londoners in post-war Britain*. Devon: Willan publishing.
Wolfe, P. 1999. *Settler colonialism and the transformation of anthropology*. London: A&C Black.
Zagrodzki, M. 2019. Les conditions de travail des policiers, déplorables, doivent être améliorées. *Le Monde* 2 août. [www.lemonde.fr/idees/article/2019/08/02/les-conditions-de-travail-des-policiers-deplorables-doivent-etre-ameliorees_5495729_3232.html]
Zancarini-Fournel, M. 2004. Généalogie des rébellions urbaines en temps de crise (1971–1981). *Vingtième Siècle Revue d'histoire* 84: 119–127.
Zancarini-Fournel, M. 2011. La destruction de la cité Olivier-de-Serres (1978–1984) à Villeurbanne: Charles Hernu précurseur de la politique de la ville? Pp. 115–123 in S. Béroud, B. Gobille, A. Hajjat, and M. Zancarini-Fournel (Eds.) *Engagements, rébellion et genre dans les quartiers populaires en Europe (1968–2005)*. Paris: éd. des archives contemporanes.
Zauberman, R., Robert, P., Névanen, S., and Bon, D. 2013. Victimation et insécurité en Île-de-France, Une analyse géo-sociale. *Revue française de sociologie* 54: 111–153.

Chapter 4

The Dual French Police System
Centralization, Specialization, Competition

Malcolm Anderson

Does France have a dual police system or is this a model which simplifies a complex reality or is it even a mirage, a distant reflection of an image constantly receding? There are two undoubted pillars of the French police system – the *police nationale* and the *gendarmerie nationale*. This form of dualism has been influential internationally. A national police force and a *gendarmerie* have been established in many countries, in societies often very different from France and not only in the French zone of influence. In these cases, the countries concerned are adopting a model and copying some practices, with variations to take account of local circumstances. But historical and sociological perspectives reveal a much more complex vision than this model of the various agencies which have powers of policing in France.

The police system is far from static. Important reforms have taken place in the last three decades, and their scope and nature should be seen in a historical context. These changes now appear to be advances on an unsatisfactory *status quo ante*. There is now better cooperation between police services, better communications systems, more professionalism, improved relations between police and *gendarmerie* and with most sections of the public. But changing circumstances produce new problems and old ones survive but survive in new and not immediately recognized forms. Only the passage of time reveals the full extent of these problems.

Although there are sometimes formidable obstacles to change, once decided, reforms can be affected reasonably quickly but perceptions of the police system can endure for many years. Three views of the system, especially tenacious outside France, require careful examination in order to assess whether France has in practice a dual police system. First, the *police nationale* and *gendarmerie* are distinctive institutions with clearly separate identities, they have different territorial competences, and they play a different role in French society. Second, police and *gendarmerie* are rival, competitive institutions. This rivalry has degenerated into a "war of the polices," the causes of which governments have been slow to address. Third, the French policing system is a highly centralized, hierarchically controlled, imposing a uniform system throughout the country. As with many socio-political stereotypes, all contain sufficiently accurate observations to be plausible but cannot encompass a complex historical and social reality.

Distinctive Identities?

The *police nationale* and *gendarmerie* have frequently been considered as distinct and separate organizations. Both have a venerable history and the *gendarmerie*, through the *maréchaussée*, traces its origins to the middle ages. The museum of the Prefecture of Police in the 5th *arrondissement* of Paris commences its chronology from the *prévôt de Paris* in 1032. This invented tradition of continuity through vast historical changes contributes to the *esprit de corps* of the *gendarmerie*, and a sense of having a well-entrenched distinctive identity. For this and other reasons, scholars have tended to study the *police nationale* and the *gendarmerie* separately, virtually never together as inter-dependent parts of one police system, although in the recent past this has changed (see for sociology Jobard and de Maillard 2015, and for history Berlière and Lévy 2011, and Anderson 2011). Most of the literature prior to 1990 on the two services was written by former police officers and *gendarmes* before the great explosion of scholarly work on the police and *gendarmerie*.

The *police nationale* and *gendarmerie* were under the authority of different ministries until 2009 when the *gendarmerie*, previously under the authority of the Ministry of National Defense, shifted to control by the Ministry of the Interior. This longstanding administrative division encouraged the development, for practical reasons, of a separate group of historians specializing in one or the other service. For historical research, the sources were distinct, and the locations of the archives made the task of studying the two institutions in parallel complicated. The national police archives are in the holdings of the National Archives but the important archive of the *Sûreté nationale* (the so-called "*fonds Moscou*") were in Fontainebleau, and the archive of the Prefecture of Police held separately in central Paris. For many years, the *gendarmerie* archives were held near Poitiers but are now in the archives of the historical service of the Ministry of Defense in Vincennes. Some are also held in Fontainebleau and others in Blanc (Indre). For different practical reasons, Dominique Monjardet pioneered the sociology of the police without taking account of the *gendarmerie*. The pioneering sociologist of the *gendarmerie*, François Dieu, deplored this situation, which he attempted to remedy, and he also criticized the paucity of research in the *gendarmerie* as a social phenomenon (Dieu and Mignon 1999).

The separate treatment of the *gendarmerie* was authoritatively defended by the leading historian in the field Jean-Noël Luc as, in the words of Napoleon 1, "*une force à part*" (Luc 2003, 2005). The main justification for considering it separately from the *police* is its military status, resulting in a different organization and outlook to the civilian police. The *gendarmerie* has been a corps (or *arme*) of the French army since the Revolution, sometimes called the first regiment of the army because it always parades in advance of regular army regiments. But the *gendarmerie* is unlike the rest of the French *armée de terre*. There is no regimental structure in the *gendarmerie*, with the partial exceptions of the *Gendarmerie mobile* and the *Garde Républicaine* (the main body of *gendarmes* was organized in brigades, companies, and legions). It did not have a commander-in-chief or even a titular head of the *gendarmerie* or a specialized directorate, for most of the Third Republic, to supervise a large corps of *gendarmes* with a complex role.

The head of the *gendarmerie* was a civilian, a practice continued for directors of the *gendarmerie* in the post-World War II period. In the immediate post-War period, the *gendarmerie* was administered by an inspector general whose correspondence files indicate that he was involved mainly in humdrum matters. These included entry examinations, rations, sickness, leave, rewarding creditable actions by *gendarmes*, decorations, establishments, and equipment (Archives du Service Historique de la Défense, hereafter SHD 1/PO). The role of the director was purely administrative in the Ministry of Defense. The director of the *gendarmerie* remained a civilian until 2004, when General Guy Parayre was appointed to the post. This was not the introduction of a commander-in-chief in the usual meaning of the term but a concession to the *amour-propre* of the *arme* and a signal that its military status would be continued after the envisaged transfer of the *gendarmerie* from the Ministry of Defense to the Ministry of the Interior took place. *Gendarmes* were often subject to authorities which were not their hierarchical superiors: magistrates when they were engaged in criminal investigations and civil authorities – minister of the interior, prefects, mayors, and police *commissaires* – when requisitioned in cases of threat to public order. In the absence of a real hierarchy headed by a *gendarmerie* commander-in-chief, commanders of legions (regional commanders) acted with independence and sometimes ill-discipline (SHD 9N332). There is less evidence of this after 1945 but *gendarmerie* commanders in the field retained a great deal of operational autonomy.

The military status of the *gendarmerie* has endured, despite criticisms, because it has been both useful to governments and valued by the *gendarmerie*. It was useful to governments because the *gendarmerie* is disciplined, units are easy to move to different locations, relatively immune to political pressures from parties and local notables, serving as a paramilitary force in cases of civil disorder, and with no troublesome unions and public displays of discontent, as with the police. This last characteristic changed after the 2002 great *malaise* in the *gendarmerie*, when for the first time the *gendarmes* demonstrated in public and subsequently were allowed to form associations that could suggest changes in policy.

During wars, the *gendarmerie* has rarely been mobilized as a fighting force. It was not involved in fighting in the Franco-Prussian War of 1870 or in World War I. This was very unpopular among ordinary soldiers because of its repressive role as a military police and also because they were non-combatants (although individual *gendarmes* volunteered to fight). The inadequacy of military knowledge and preparedness was adversely noted by inspections in the 1930s, although there were significant improvements later in the decade (SHD 4/PO 176). Conscious of the unpopularity caused by its non-combatant role, a regiment of *gendarmes* was mobilized and involved in fighting in 1940 (SHD, 1 A 312).

After World War II the *gendarmerie* took pride in its capacity to be a light fighting force with armored vehicles, helicopters, and aircraft. But it never engaged in military action and its semi-military role was confined to overseas. It was used in a paramilitary role in the Algerian War. The last times it was involved in a small-scale military action was against Kanuk (the indigenous population) militants in New Caledonia in 1989, and while participating in peacekeeping missions within the European Union framework, particularly in former Yugoslavia. There were nonetheless continuing military duties. The *arme* performed its traditional role as military police, protector of military installations, a counter-espionage agency, and organizer of mobilization for war. The Groupe d'Intervention de la Gendarmerie Nationale (GIGN), created in the early 1970s and favored by President Mitterrand over its police equivalent, could engage in military style assaults in hostage or hijacking incidents.

But the question remains, to what extent can the *gendarmes* be regarded as soldiers or is the military status mainly symbolic, indicating a difference with the *police nationale*? The military character of the *gendarmerie* was more evident in the past, but in recent decades decidedly less so. For the general public the *gendarmerie* is another police force and in ordinary speech national police officials are often called *gendarmes*. Until the end of conscription and the establishment of a specialized *gendarmerie* officer training school (both in the 1990s), all its officers and non-commissioned officers were trained with other soldiers. They were under military discipline (although the *gendarmerie* had its own special regulations), and they were housed in barracks or in married quarters. Yet conventional military discipline was hard to maintain, except on the surface, because brigades (the effective working units of the *gendarmerie*) were commanded by non-commissioned officers (NCOs) who were not in daily (or, in the past, even frequent) physical contact with their company commanding officers. The strictly military duties of the *gendarmerie* increased only marginally.

Yet the policing functions of the *gendarmerie* and the *police nationale* have for many years been identical – to preserve public peace, ensure public order, prevent and investigate criminal activity, provide emergency services, assist the public in many ways, and, when the use of force may be required, enforce decisions of the executive. The *gendarmerie* therefore became overwhelmingly a force engaged in ordinary policing and, in these activities, the *gendarmerie* tended to mimic the national police, strengthening *départemental* and regional organization and establishing specialized units for criminal investigation. They are seen as progressive and are treated by the government not as soldiers but simply as *gendarmes*, belonging to a police force with specific characteristics but not dissimilar to other police forces in terms of the roles they fulfil. Frédéric Péchenard, the director of the national police from 2007 to 2012, described the two services as parts of the same system. In an essay on how the police functions, the *gendarmerie* is in first place in his account (Péchenard 2007).

Between Hostility and Cooperation

An important reason why the *police nationale* and *gendarmerie* were considered as completely separate was the nature of the relations between them. These have often been poor. Poor coordination and competitive relations have sometimes degenerated into hostility. Although a very well-informed historian has written that the "war of the polices" belongs to the realm of myth rather than historical reality (Lopez 2014), since the 19th century there has been a litany of police services making allegations of incompetence (or worse) against other services. In certain areas evidence of non-communication of information was blatant, particularly in the sensitive areas of political intelligence and information on investigations. Police and *gendarmerie* conflicts occasionally became public, and the archives contain evidence of lengthy periods of poor relations. The reasons for this discord usually fell within certain categories: struggles over territory both geographical and functional, non-cooperation, and emulation that got out of hand.

While these tensions and hostilities have fascinated the press and the public, police leaders have minimized their importance. Maurice Grimaud, for example, wrote in 1966 shortly before he was appointed prefect of police, that relations between the four great services of police, *gendarmerie*, *Sûreté nationale*, and Prefecture of Police, were in general good and that the rules of good neighborliness, part written, part traditional, allowed cohabitation and avoided quarrels (Grimaud 1966). They did not, he said, promote cooperation; each carried out the requests of the other and quickly retired to their own territory. This emollient picture described relations in the most favorable terms. Certain kinds of disputes were recurrent. Since the division of territorial responsibility attributed the countryside and small towns to the *gendarmerie*, tension was exacerbated from the mid-19th century by rural emigration, leading to a shrinking population in *gendarmerie* territory and an increasing population in police territory, strengthening of the relative position of the latter. In the later 20th century, suburbanization and the growth of peripheral areas resulted in the *gendarmerie* having a greater proportion of urban population than before. Some modest redrawing of territorial responsibilities has taken place, but more radical proposals have been fiercely resisted by police unions, *gendarmes*, and by local mayors who wanted to keep "their" *gendarmes* or "their" police.

In public order policing, *gendarmerie*, police, and the army (until its gradual withdrawal after World War I) were used to working alongside one another. They developed an institutional memory of methods of cooperation and how to avoid mutual conflict. This was not the case for criminal investigations, where there was little experience of cooperation on cases (until 2002) and frictions were common. The criticisms made in the late 19th century were repeated in various forms until the end of the 20th century. The alleged defects were exploited for partisan purposes. Marie-François Goron, the head of the *Sûreté* of the Prefecture of Police in the late 19th century, was fiercely critical of the *gendarmerie* in order to strengthen his argument in favor of a national police. His memoirs and those of another member of the Paris *Sûreté*, Rossignol, contain caustic comments on the competence of *gendarmes* and on the nature of the institution (Goron 1897; Rossignol 1900).

Goron was disparaging about the effect of the military status of the *gendarmerie* on its effectiveness in investigating crime. The uniform, boots, sabre, *bandolier*, and hat meant that the *gendarme* could only act in an official capacity and in a highly visible manner. This form of dress prevented *gendarmes* from conducting criminal investigations as effectively as the judicial police. In 1907 the head of the *Sûreté générale*, Célestin Hennion, one of the most remarkable police officials of the Third Republic, was publicly scathing of the *gendarmerie* for its shortcomings in criminal investigations in order to promote the cause of mobile judicial police units to cover the whole of the national territory (*le Petit Parisien*, 22 April 1907; confidential note AN F7 13043). He criticized the lack of training of *gendarmes* in criminal investigation, the inappropriate military regulations governing the *gendarmerie*, and the distaste of *gendarmerie* officers for judicial police work. The effects of the introduction of the *police mobile* became fully apparent in the inter-war period and raised inevitable tensions.

Another long period of deteriorating relationships between the police and *gendarmerie* began in the 1960s and lasted for about three decades. The regional judicial police argued that they were specialized in criminal matters, and that serious cases such as hold-ups should always be reserved for them. From 1945, the judicial police developed specialized competence in prostitution, drugs, youth crime and in scientific policing techniques, which they argued the *gendarmerie* did not possess (although from the 1960s this was decreasingly the case). These advantages were used explicitly or implicitly to argue they should be the lead agency in criminal matters. They sometimes reached an agreement with the prosecutor about the kind of cases which should be assigned to them, but these were transitory since prosecutors moved on and, in any case, prosecutors had the right to choose with which service to work. Some prosecutors preferred to work with the *gendarmerie* or the judicial police units of the urban police, rather than the national judicial police.

Another cause of friction was that the *gendarmerie* seemed to be engaging in competitive mimicry with the *police nationale*. From the 1960s the *gendarmerie* developed specialized regional judicial police and criminal investigation units along the same lines as the police and police laboratories. One case in 1964 between the *gendarmerie* company based in Marseille and the *police* revealed the range of issues which could arise. The *gendarmerie brigades de recherches* (criminal investigation unit) had been revitalized in the early 1960s by Captain Pepin, who achieved exceptionally good results, receiving several letters of congratulation from the prefect and the public prosecutor. In this case, the judicial police made complaints against the *gendarmerie* for not communicating information and operating outside of their territory. The *gendarmerie* in turn complained that they communicated a lot of information to the judicial police without any reciprocity, even though a *gendarme* was posted as permanent liaison officer to the regional judicial police. According to the inspector general's report, despite public congratulations of the director of the regional services of the judicial police to the *gendarmerie*, "a climate not of emulation but of genuine rivalry has appeared and this has affected [the attitude of] ordinary investigators."

Meetings of judicial police chiefs contain reports of bitter complaints about problems and difficulties. One in June 1974 was a particularly comprehensive review of the difficulties by regional judicial police chiefs. They alleged they were being deliberately marginalized. The municipal police and the *gendarmerie* did not inform or delayed informing the prosecutor of criminal activities for fear of having the case removed from them and given to the national judicial police. The tone of the complaints made against the *gendarmerie* was particularly disdainful. They included, "This military organization behaves as if the other services do not exist, often conducting parallel enquiries improperly and in plainclothes on cases for which others have the legal responsibility" (Centre des Archives Contemporaines, hereafter CAC 19910697–6). The complaints of the police against the judicial police activities of the *gendarmerie* continued into the 1980s. One illustration is the weary cynicism of the police response to the reasonable suggestions of the Cabannes report (1988), designed to improve relations between the two institutions. The only recommendation (not implemented) which found favor was that unified scientific police laboratories should be under police management.

The nadir of poor relations was reached in Charles Pasqua's first term of office as minister of the interior. A 1987 study of the IGPN (Inspection Générale de la Police Nationale), ordered by Director Marcel Leclerc, condemned the expansionist policies of the *gendarmerie*, accusing them of systematic intrusion in *police nationale* territory. On 11 May 1987, the director of the *gendarmerie* issued a circular saying that the *gendarmes* engaged in criminal investigation could, for the purposes of reconnaissance and surveillance, wear civilian clothes (this was already an informal practice). This enraged the police and the police unions, for whom *gendarmes*, by definition, were uniformed, and the circular was seen as a symbolic intrusion on police territory. The *gendarmes* in turn attacked the moves by the uniformed police towards adopting military ranks, with similar titles to those of the *gendarmerie* but with different roles (Anderson 2011).

When the socialist Pierre Joxe arrived at the Ministry of the Interior in the 1980s, it was clear to him that something should be done about this unsatisfactory climate of relations. For Joxe, rather than being separate institutions, the *police nationale* and the *gendarmerie nationale* were two elements of the same law enforcement system. He developed a long-term strategy to rectify the problems.

Difficulties of Centralization

The degree of centralization, the third element in this review, is central to the question pf whether dualism is an accurate description of the French police system. Do two coherent organizations monopolize the field of internal security? Is authority within them exercised in a strictly hierarchical manner, or is it fragmented between quasi autonomous services? A considerable number of actors are actually engaged in policing and, from 1995, some of them have been legally recognized as co-producers of security. This includes municipal police, customs officers, and private security firms. Also, a range of regulatory agencies police special areas of social, economic, and political activity, and they have the right to impose penalties but with no powers of arrest. The legal and institutional landscape is thus complicated, but less so than that of the practice of policing.

In a formal constitutional sense, the executive and legislative branches of government establish general norms in the form of legislation and regulations which govern the activities of the police and *gendarmerie*. Ministers appoint directors of the *police nationale* and *gendarmerie* who have formal administrative authority over what, in legal and institutional terms, are hierarchical organizations. The center has the power to issue instructions, inspect, enquire, request information, and can intervene directly if something scandalous or embarrassing happens as a result of police action. But as René Lévy argues, the question of centralization or decentralization is complicated. It is not simply a matter of the relationship of the summit to the base of a hierarchy in a formal sense, which can be represented in an organization chart, but of the number of independent centers of command which exist (Lévy 1997).

There has always been a diversity of organizations in policing. During the Third Republic, describing the *police nationale* and *gendarmerie* as the instruments of a centralized and coordinated system would, according to certain authorities, have been seriously misleading. Until 1941, the dominant form of police was the municipal police forces. They were under the authority, for different purposes, of the mayor, the prefect, the Ministry of the Interior and (in criminal matters) the public prosecutor. Prime Minister Louis Barthou described "the police as a series of little anemic formations without cohesion and ignoring each other" (*La Tribune du commissaire de police*, July 1936) and one well-informed author suggested that decentralization was "the basic principle of the French police" (Allard 1934). The diversity has continued, although in different forms, since the formation of the national police by the Vichy regime. But this did not solve the question of strict hierarchical control.

In large hierarchical administrations there are common problems in exercising centralized control over the activities at the base of the hierarchy. These include long lines of communication, the necessity of keeping some communications confidential, the trade-off between control and efficacy of units whose tasks involve taking timely action in complex situations, the requirements of horizontal coordination with other services and administrations, and the difficulty of resisting the autonomy of units whose role requires a high level of expertise. The specialization of units brought benefits in terms of efficacy, but sometimes with problems when active units became too close to the milieu which they were supposed to police. This was the case in the areas of racing and gambling, until drastic action was taken in 2011 (sacking the director and reorganizing the service). A more general problem is the frequency of circumstances in which officials are responsible to an authority other than their own hierarchy. When all factors are considered, the police system can be represented as a balkanized, fragmented constellation in which the various parts are certainly interdependent but in whose activities the center provides a legal and regulatory framework but only rarely intervenes in operations.

Aspects of the legal and institutional arrangements of the national police also encourage the autonomy of subordinate units. The judicial police are an archetypical case of autonomy of units of lines of accountability as well as of operational efficiency. All criminal investigations are conducted under the authority and, in principle, the direction of the public prosecutor (or the examining magistrates they appoint). They in turn are responsible to the minister of justice. Thus, the control of the police hierarchy is absent except in one important respect: the resources allocated in each investigation are under its control. The detailed objectives, methods, and progress of each investigation remain confidential. The *parquet* (the public prosecution service) has the right to be closely informed and give instructions, but in practice they usually do not. Prosecutors handle many cases and preparing them for prosecution and presenting them in court is burdensome. In addition, prosecutors are often collaborating with police investigators who are older and more experienced (Mouhanna 2001). Prosecutors have as their working partners inspectors of the judicial police, normally without any intervention by the *commissaires* in charge or the senior prosecutors (*procureurs généraux*). Hierarchical controls are loosened, and police and magistrates operate in cooperative networks that escape hierarchical supervision or even notice.

According to Gatto and Thoenig (1993), cooperation or even connivance between magistrates and judicial police in reducing the control of their own hierarchies has increased in recent years, and they have come to regard each other as partners in a relatively equal relationship. Authoritarian magistrates, imbued with their own importance, are therefore in decline and there is mutual respect for the professionalism of other participants in the network. This gives great autonomy to individual judicial police officials and a strong partnership emerges with prosecutors when they are working on a case. The *Code de procedure pénale* remains the only basic element structuring relations between the various branches of the law enforcement system (police, *gendarmerie*, prosecution service, court officials, ministries).

Informal networks run in tandem with more formal systems of horizontal coordination established in order to improve the flow of information and engage in joint action. But this horizontal cooperation also weakens hierarchical control. Prefects have been, since their origins under Napoleon, responsible for public order, administrative policing, and until recently (though virtually never used in ordinary criminal cases) judicial police powers in their *départements*. They generally adopted a coordinating and supervisory rather than an executive role in policing, except in public order crises. "*Départementalisation*" of policing has been a politically controversial policy with a checkered history since the first attempt was made in 1924 to introduce *départemental* chiefs of police. In the early 1990s an abortive attempt was made to introduce *directeurs départementaux de police/sécurité publique* and in 1999 local security contracts were introduced which brought together the *police nationale* and municipal police, the *gendarmerie* and the various administrations with a role in policing and public order, such as social services. The first attempt was not a success, and this initiative was abandoned. In a modified form the second attempt, which includes *départemental* directors of security, remains in place, despite a difficult early phase including a temporarily successful opt-out of the *police judiciaire*. Although there is a directorate in the Ministry of the Interior to supervise these local coordinating arrangements, it cannot intervene frequently without destroying their purpose.

The fragility of central control of the base was a finding confirmed by the first major contribution to the sociology of the police. In the *police nationale*, Dominique Monjardet found an "inversion" of the police hierarchy. Effectively, the control of police work was located at the base, not at the policy-making summit of this hierarchy (Monjardet 1996). Since the *gendarmerie* has always had a military statute, it may be expected that the practices would be completely different. But this inversion of the hierarchy applied also to the *gendarmerie*. By force of circumstance, judicial police work, since the 19th century, was done by the other ranks who had no formal powers in the field (this slowly changed from 1950), and not by officers who were formally entrusted with these powers. The essential part of the work of most brigades was not, however, criminal investigation but surveillance, and this too was managed locally. This included activities such as patrolling the area, talking to people, and keeping watch on suspicious persons and happenings, supporting crime prevention initiatives, and the symbolic representation of the authority of the state. The lower ranks had considerable autonomy over their day-to-day work, because the officers, based in headquarters in the *départemental* or regional capital, were distant and, until recent years, few in numbers.

Modernization since the 1980s

The developments of the last three decades have been far reaching, particularly in the fields of police training, management, and coordination of services. Pierre Joxe, the socialist minister of the interior (1984–1986, 1988–1991) and minister of defense (1991–1993) conceived modernization of the police and *gendarmerie* as a process without any predetermined end. His proposals were set in the context of general aims – improved efficiency of criminal investigations for all types of crime, efforts in crime prevention, better deployment, and better coordination of policing. Police–public relations were to be improved by higher professional standards in police behavior by the adoption of a professional code.

His priorities were grouped under five headings: better integration of police into contemporary urban society; measurement and improvement of police performance; improved internal cohesion and coordination in the police services; adaptation to the requirements of further moves in European integration; and use of training as a source and motor of innovation (CAC 1989). The guiding theme was set out in a working paper presented at a meeting under the chairmanship of Joxe:

> In the past the National Police was based on the principle of specialisation, of impermeability ("*étanchéité*") between corps and services but the future priority will be the complementarity between specialists and generalists, the search for a simpler "architecture" closer relations between plain clothed and uniformed police, reduction in the number of corps, thinking in terms of necessary skills to define missions, constraints, tasks and career development.
>
> (Ocqueteau 2006, pp. 119–120)

This theme and its five headings were the basis of the 1995 general law on internal security and its two successors in 2003 and 2011 (LOPS, LOPSI, and LOPPSI). All three aimed at better coordination and cooperation between the *police nationale* and *gendarmerie*.

The great achievement of Joxe, ably assisted by others, was to change the intellectual climate concerning policing. National police training center courses, debates, and seminars were opened to outsiders in order to encourage new thinking regarding the problems of policing. A decisive step was taken in 1989, when IHESI (Institut des Hautes Etudes de la Sécurité Intérieure) was established with three ends in view: the education and training of senior police and *gendarmerie* officers, studies and research on the police, and exposing the police to other professional groups and a wider public. These three objectives were inter-connected and contributed to Joxe's other policy objectives. According to the results of an enquiry published in 1999, the three objectives were largely met. The training of *gendarmerie* officers separate from officers of other branches of the military was achieved in 1995 by the setting up of a *gendarmerie* training school with direct entry into the officer corps.

From the first initiatives of Joxe in the early 1990s and after his departure until 2009, measures were taken requiring that the *police nationale* and *gendarmerie* work together. The 2003 LOPSI contained a provision that police and *gendarmerie* cooperate closely in criminal investigation in regional intervention groups (GIR). LOPSI also contained the first legislation to integrate the *gendarmerie* into the Ministry of Interior. This was done in 2009, implicitly reviving the issue of civilianization of the *gendarmerie*, an idea never openly supported except at the political margins, for example by the Green member of parliament, Noël Mamère. Routine denials by ministers of any intention to do so were not wholly believed. *Gendarmerie* Commandant Jean-Hugues Matelly, an associate researcher in the National Council for Scientific Research, in public criticism of the move to the Ministry of the Interior, described it as "the death of the *gendarmerie*." He argued that it was a de facto merger with the national police and a prelude to civilianization of the *gendarmerie*.

Minor incidents continued to temporarily damage relationships between the *police nationale* and *gendarmerie*. In July 2009 a *gendarmerie* captain on detachment to the police wore a tee shirt on which was written "Fuck the Police." The police union, Synergie-officers, complained bitterly to the Ministry of the Interior that this was offensive and typical of a mentality in the *gendarmerie*. Although widely reported in the press, neither the police nor the *gendarmerie* took the matter further. Skirmishes continue such as the one immediately following the move of the *gendarmerie* to the Ministry of the Interior in 2009 over the gathering of domestic intelligence, apparently because *gendarmes* considered that the newly integrated police intelligence service (Direction centrale du renseignement intérieur – DCRI) overlapped with their traditional activities. This was scarcely a major incident but eagerly seized on by the press as a new expression of the "*guerre des polices*."

The situation had changed and the formerly poor relations between the *gendarmerie* and the *police nationale* could no longer be resolved in the traditional way of the two forces, supported by different *ministres de tutelle*, each defending "their people" in any argument. Fusions, new management systems, better management as a result of better training, and more efficient communication of information have limited the scope for serious conflicts.

Conclusion

The dualism of the system looks different depending on whether one considers the police as an institution or policing as an activity and social process (for this distinction see Jobard and de Maillard 2015). The broad outlines of the legal and institutional positions of the police in France are clear, even though opaque areas exist and even though since 1995 they have been modified. The *police nationale* and the *gendarmerie* are national institutions, both having legal competence covering the whole of the national territory. Since customs officers were granted judicial police powers in the 1990s (against the vociferous opposition of the *police nationale*), there is now a third national police force, with competence over the whole territory which overlaps with the other two in the repression of drug trafficking and counterfeit goods. There is a rough division of territorial competence between the *police nationale* and *gendarmerie*, with the former covering the large towns and the frontiers and the latter the small towns and the countryside. This division is by no means clear cut, with frequent presence of both in each other's territory.

Their responsibilities have been much the same in the fields of surveillance, maintenance of public order, prevention and investigation of crime, supporting public authority, and providing emergency services. Both are hierarchical institutions with the center having formal control over the intermediate levels and the base of their organizations. The internal rules of the *police nationale* and *gendarmerie* vary. Their disciplinary systems are different and the rules governing the use of firearms are more permissive for the *gendarmerie*. The municipal police and private security services, which have been described as "co-producers of security," have more limited competence (see Chapters 10 and 11 of this volume). All of the other agencies that "police" other areas, such as data protection, financial markets, environment, health and safety, usually have the power to conduct searches. However, for seizure and arrest, in the infrequent cases where these are necessary, they depend on the public prosecutor, *police nationale* and *gendarmerie*. The system in this sense is accurately described as a dual system with two dominant institutions plus a constellation of related organizations with limited competence but with authority to police importance social and economic activities.

When the actual practice of policing is considered, the apparent clarity of the legal and institutional landscape disappears. Policing is revealed to encompass a complex constellation of actors. The two dominant institutions into which corps and careers are structured, and in which formal controls and lines of responsibility exist, have a major presence in this world. But within and outside them, many actors have, with varying degrees depending on their activities and professional competence, de facto autonomy in selecting and controlling the work which they do. In both *police nationale* and *gendarmerie*, hierarchies are steep and geographical divisions (national, regional, *départemental* with sub-divisions within *départements*) mean that there can be as many as ten levels of bureaucracy between the top and the bottom. In this circumstance, systematic coordination and control is very difficult, and perhaps impossible. The apparent organizational tidiness and hierarchical clarity of policing in reality involves a high degree of autonomy of operational units, among which there are problems of efficient communication. Each organization exhibits its own *esprit de corps*. There has been a proliferation of specialized units, calling for horizontal coordination between different agencies inside and outside the *police nationale* and *gendarmerie*. There is territorial defensiveness and the tendency of criminal investigators, in both police and *gendarmerie*, and police intelligence services to hoard information. In areas of the specialized actors who police social, economic, and political activities, the intervention of the center is almost entirely restricted to setting them up and passing the laws and regulations which apply to their domain of competence. In the words of the ground-breaking sociological study in policing "one enters a world filled with autonomous administrative organizations too numerous to count" (Gatto and Thoenig 1993).

Institutional reform, both legislative and managerial, can affect the practice of policing, although it does not always do so (for a classic case study of when this did not happen after an exhaustive enquiry, legislation and managerial changes, see Wilson 1978). The Joxe reforms and subsequent initiatives from the 1990s changed practice, with new approaches to training and management. In 1995 there was reform of the corps and changes in career tracks which made the organization of the police clearer and more comprehensible. New communications and data-storage technologies provided the technical possibility of more coherence in *police nationale* and *gendarmerie* action, although this was delayed by the proliferation of databases (including some unauthorized ones). Common communications systems and common sources of information instantaneously available – impractical before the information revolution – are preconditions of improving the quality of coordination. Information overload can, however, create new problems. Technologies, such as artificial intelligence, will continue to change policing and to a limited extent, the institutional and legal framework of the police. Nonetheless the *gendarmerie nationale* and the *police nationale* will doubtless survive.

References

Allard, P. 1934. *L'Anarchie de la police*. Paris: Calman Levy.
Anderson, M. 2011. *In thrall to political change. Police and gendarmerie in France*. Oxford: Clarendon Press.
Archives du service historique de la défense. Paris.
Berlière, J. M., and Lévy, R. 2011. *Histoire des polices en France*. Paris: Nouveau Monde.
Cabannes, J. 1988. *Rapport de la mission de liaison et de prospective sur la gendarmerie et la police nationale*. Paris: Documentation Française.
Centre des archives contemporaines (CAC). 1989. *Contrat pluriannuel de formation de la police nationale*. Paris: CAC.
Dieu, F., and Mignon, P. 1999. *La force publique au travail: Deux études sur les conditions de travail des policiers et des gendarmes*. Paris: L'Harmattan.
Gatto, D., and Thoenig, J. C. 1993. *La Sécurité publique à l'épreuve du terrain. Le policier, le magistrat, le préfet*. Paris: L'Harmattan/IHESI.

Goron, M. F. 1897. *Les mémoires de Goron ancien chef de la Sûreté*. Flammarion, republished by Berlière, J. M. 2009, Versailles.
Grimaud, M. 1966. *Propositions en vue d'améliorer l'exercice de la police en France*. Paris: Ministère de l'Intérieur, Direction Générale de la Sûreté Nationale.
Jobard, F., and de Maillard, J. 2015. *Sociologie de la police*. Paris: Armand Colin.
Lévy, R. 1997. 'Qui détient le pouvoir de police?' Pp. 19–27. in J. M. Berlière and D. Peschanski (Eds.) *Pouvoirs et polices au XXe siècle: Europe, Etats-Unis, Japon*. Bruxelles: Complexe.
Lopez, L. 2014. *La guerre de polices n'a pas eu lieu*. Paris: Presses Universitaires de Paris Sorbonne.
LOPSI. 1995. *Loi d'orientation de programmation relative à la sécurité*. Journal Officiel de la République Française No. 0020 24 January.
LOPSI. 2003. *Loi d'orientation et de programmation pour la sécurité intérieure*. Journal Officiel de la République Française No. 66 du 19 March.
LOPSI. 2011. *Loi d'orientation et de programmation pour la performance de la sécurité intérieure*. Journal Officiel de la République Française. No. 0062 du 15 March.
Luc, J. N. 2003. *Figures de gendarmes*. CREDHESS 16.
Luc, J. N. 2005. *Histoire de la maréchaussée et de la gendarmerie: Guide de recherche*. Paris: Service historique de la *gendarmerie* nationale.
Monjardet, D. 1996. *Ce que fait la police: Sociologie de la force publique*. Paris: La Découverte.
Mouhanna, C. 2001. *Polices judiciaires et magistrats: une affaire de confiance*. Paris: Documentation Française.
Ocqueteau, F. 2006. *Mais qui donc dirige la police? Sociologie des commissaires*. Paris: Colin.
Péchenard, F. 2007. *Gardien de la paix*. Paris: Michel Lafon.
Rossignol, G. A. 1900. *Les mémoires de Rossignol, ex-inspecteur principal de la sûreté*. Paris: Editions littéraires et artistiques.
Wilson, J. Q. 1978. *The investigators: Managing FBI and narcotics agents*. New York: Basic Books.

Part II

Organizational Features and Reforms

Chapter 5

Police Centralization and its Pathologies

Christian Mouhanna

Among Western democracies, France represents the most extreme pole of intense political and administrative centralization, and the nation's police forces are no exception in that regard. Of course, many other countries also have a central police apparatus. Generally, it handles protection of the government or the most serious crimes, but in France, it is the day-to-day safety of every citizen which remains largely a state prerogative. The development of public safety policies is still for the most part in the hands of central government, and due to the distinctive structure of the French Republic, they are the responsibility of the president of the Republic and the minister of the interior.

Although France sits at one pole when it comes to police centralization, the local policing model that is prevalent in the English-speaking world – in the United States, England, and Wales – sits near the other end of the spectrum. A review of policing systems in Europe shows that many countries, far from engaging in a vast wave of decentralization, have opted for a more centralized organization (Fyfe, Terpstra and Tops 2013). This is particularly true of northern European countries, including the Netherlands (Terpstra 2018), Scandinavia (Holmberg 2014), Scotland (Fyfe 2013), and Ireland (Conway and Walsh 2011). In addition, centralization has traditionally been associated with southern Europe: Italy, France, and Spain, although Spain has also seen opposing currents, especially in Catalonia and the Basque Country (Martinez-Herrera 2002). France is the model for this group of centralizing countries, having experimented with the system the longest and likely the furthest.

Several arguments favor a centralized police force. We will examine four of these, returning to them later in this chapter. They pertain to the political, economic, organizational, and strategic dimensions of centralization. As such, they are of interest to different stakeholders: political leaders, managers of public funds, top-level chiefs of police, and supporters of a global approach to criminal phenomena. Many of them invoke the need to respond to the development of "new" forms of crime – terrorism, cybercrime, transnational economic and financial crime – in order to justify strengthening united forces under a single authority. Hence, the strong attraction of centralization comes as no surprise. In the case of France and several other countries that have adopted this trend, this centralized organization is to be found not only within the sections focusing on the national or transnational challenges above, but also those in charge of the protection of people and property, whose job it is to address the needs of the public.

The daily operation of a police force which is thus organized raises certain questions. Indeed, though there are in theory several advantages to a centralized, pyramidal structure, in practice this organizational form has several adverse effects. This is particularly true in a context like France, where citizens historically have a relationship with the state that borders on subjection. Under the French Republic, a paternalistic protective welfare state has replaced the traditional sovereign, and voters look to it to guarantee their safety. In such a framework, police officers are an essential tool for the implementation of national policies. But in return, they must also follow the rules those policies generate, thus putting national priorities ahead of the needs of the population (Monjardet 1996). The gap between police structures and the public, which has already been criticized in places with some less centralized police forces (Skogan 2006; Reiner 2010), is all the wider here.

This chapter describes the foundations of such centralized systems, first by reviewing the generic factors lying behind them – those that are hotly debated, including in countries tempted to move toward centralization – and then examining causes more specific to France. Second, it will examine the practical consequences and adverse effects engendered by the structure of the French policing system. Indeed, sociological research has long shown that the expected benefits of this type of organization do not necessarily outweigh their disadvantages. Next, it will show how the paradigm of centralization leads to policies that are not just irreversible, but that also systematically favor repression over prevention. We base this analysis on 30 years of sociological research into these topics. For various reasons (Mouhanna 2009; Jobard and de Maillard 2015), French police sociologists have been slower than their American and English counterparts to tackle police issues. This is particularly true regarding the adverse effects of a structure long described by its leaders as "the best in the world." Today, however, we have ample access to converging studies showing the limits of that structure.

The Presumed Benefits of Police Centralization

Though the description of the French policing system that follows may seem strange in some respects to the foreign observer, it is necessary to highlight that the ensuing portrait of a paradox-ridden organization does not reflect deliberate choices on the part of police administrators. Indeed, most of them are not blind to the oddities generated by the services they work in. When questioned face-to-face, they are aware of the contradictions they find themselves in and to which they contribute, whether they like it or not. Those that characterize the French *police nationale* and its rural counterpart, the *gendarmerie*, are founded both on each institution's specific history and on a general line of thought grounded in a rationality and a set of principles – particularly legal – that on the surface make perfect sense.

Greater Efficiency at Lower Cost

There is an essentially unanimous view among political and administrative leaders that the police services' present, centralized organization represents the height of efficiency. The first reason is to do with management. The idea of economies of scale has long been the norm in public organizations, including the police (Drake and Simper 2001). Multiple entities represent too great a cost for public finances; merging them avoids redundancy and saves on inter-departmental coordination. The spread in France after 2001 of the New Public Management philosophy and, concurrently, management by numbers (Matelly and Mouhanna 2007), only reinforced the already deep-seated idea that the centralization of forces and management could lead to budget savings, especially if supported by national management standards. Incidentally, this phenomenon could also be seen in countries with less centralized police forces, such as England and Wales (Hale et al. 2004). Budgetary constraints, which led governments to look for ways to save money, further strengthen the arguments of the proponents of centralization models. As we will see below, the existence of a national force provides the opportunity to rapidly achieve productivity gains, particularly by pooling support services between nearby cities, by closing a police station or *gendarmerie* posts, or by merging investigation units. Many police stations have been shut since the beginning of the 1990s and many *gendarmerie* units have seen their numbers dwindle in favor of pooled resources.

In practice, rural France is covered by a network of 3,500 *gendarmerie* brigades, each responsible for several villages. Since 2005, some have been grouped to form communities of brigades, ostensibly an interim measure and a prelude to mergers aiming to reduce the total number of brigades to 1,700 (Senat 2013). At the head of each brigade – the smallest ones comprising five to six gendarmes – is a non-commissioned officer or a lieutenant. At the next echelon, the company, led by a captain, heads several brigades. Above this is the *Groupement de Gendarmerie*, organized at the departmental level and under the command of a colonel assisted by a staff.[1] The pyramid continues, with a regional commander, usually a general.[2] All of these administrative units lie under the authority of the director-general of the *Gendarmerie Nationale*, who answers to the minister of the interior. About 62,000 *gendarmes* are organized in this way.

In urban areas, or cities with a population of more than 20,000, public safety is in the hands of the national police. The same militaristic hierarchical structure presides there as well, even though the *police nationale* – unlike the *gendarmerie* – is a civilian body. A central police station, or "commissariat" and its staff head each city's police force. The commissariats are placed under the responsibility of the *directeur départemental de la sécurité publique* (DDSP) or departmental director of public security. All the DDSPs are led by the Direction Centrale de la Sécurité Publique, or Central Directorate of Public Security, in Paris, under the authority of the *directeur général de la National Police* (DGPN), or director-general, himself also directly answerable to the minister of the interior.

The judicial or intelligence services of the national police or the *gendarmerie* are organized in a similar fashion. Their priorities and any structural reforms affecting them are decided by the Ministry of the Interior. Centralization and the pooling of resources have often led to greater unit specialization. Staff previously dedicated to traditional policing activities, when they are not made redundant, are redeployed to services highly specialized in dealing with one of the set priorities. The need to work on offenses considered "without borders," such as terrorism, large-scale economic and financial crime, cybercrime or the fight against illegal immigration, illustrates this movement particularly well, and has thus served to strengthen the centralization rhetoric.

More Effective Human Resource Management

The repercussions of such an organization on personnel management are significant. A leading feature of the national police force is its recruitment of candidates from across the nation, through competitive entrance exams that are common to all branches of the civil service. Once they have been selected and trained, new recruits are systematically posted far from their place of residence. This is attributable both to necessity and strategy. It is a necessity by virtue of the principle of territorial equality: all cities and villages must have national public safety officials. But the areas that put forward the most candidates are not those where there is the greatest need. This is particularly true of the very "sensitive" *banlieues* adjoining large cities. Few volunteers for entry into the police force come from the *banlieues*, and fewer still are ethnic minorities (Gautier 2017). By contrast, many officers are recruited from small, quiet provincial towns. In the national police, this unbalanced system leads to the constant placement of young recruits from other areas in problem areas and the Paris region, where their difficulties in adjusting to their new roles are compounded by the high cost of living. As soon as they have enough seniority to request a transfer, these officers typically move closer to their region of origin, or to areas considered less prone to crime. In the *gendarmerie*, the number of candidates is similar, but the system produces the opposite effect. The areas where there is a dearth of personnel are rural zones suffering from depopulation and rapid aging among those who remain there. These areas plot out a line across France known as the *diagonale du vide* (Oliveau and Doignon 2016), or low-density diagonal. Whereas in the past, *gendarmes* came from the rural world and remained attached to the region they grew up in, today, attracted by the advantages and services of large cities, they seek to join brigades close to urban areas, leading to the same vast tide of transfers (Mouhanna 2011b).

Centralization thus makes it possible to compensate for the lack of locally sourced police officers and *gendarmes*, be it from the difficult *banlieues*, the Paris region in general, or from the deserted countryside. The vast "bunny-hopping" career movement that ensues makes human resource management more complex. It is an essential issue that forces the authorities to engage in de facto co-management of these transfers with trade unions or staff representatives. The system thus manages to balance itself out, with young police officers and *gendarmes* in the neglected areas and senior officers in the more coveted postings.

The lack of grounding of personnel in the territories they police, as a result of this national movement, is not seen only as a disadvantage by the heads of police. There is a deep-seated idea in the French senior civil service that it is essential to avoid too much "collusion" between state employees and the public they serve, for fear this could lead to favoritism or corruption. In this framework, each person must be treated in accordance with instructions prescribed at national level, and not according to criteria that might be left to the discretion of a low-level official. This principle leads de facto to the predominance of a top-down logic in these national policing bodies.

Numerous examples illustrate the problems that have arisen from the resulting distance that exists between the public and police officers who are assigned to serve them. These have actually been exacerbated by national security policies instituted by senior Ministry of the Interior officials from the prefecture and by senior national police and *gendarmerie* officers. A 1998 order issued by the Gendarmerie Directorate set a limit on how long any *gendarmes* could remain in a posting. This rebuff of the *gendarmes*' traditional involvement with their local community was very poorly received and contributed to the birth of the *gendarmes*' protest movement in 2001 (Mouhanna 2011b). Chiefs of police or *gendarmes* cannot stay in a posting more than three years, if they do not wish to see their career advancement stalled.

The strategy regarding the deployment of forces for protest policing, i.e. preventing and controlling riots and demonstrations, is entirely in line with this approach. In addition to the public safety forces, those dedicated to judicial investigations or to intelligence, approximately 14,000 police officers (CRS) and 13,000 *gendarmes* (mobile *gendarmes*) constitute a reserve force to respond to outbursts that exceed the policing capacities of local units. This is a kind of "floating" force, insofar as they are not assigned to any given territory but are intended instead to operate in any location. Moreover, the doctrine states that these police officers and *gendarmes* should not intervene in the region where they are based but be assigned as far away as possible. And so, convoys are regularly to be seen crossing France's motorways, carrying police officers from southern companies to the north of the country, or western *gendarmes* to supervise demonstrations in Paris. In short, the state aims to ensure the loyalty of its servants by moving them from one place to another, in order to prevent them from developing excessive sympathy with local actors. Everything is done to make the police officer feel first and foremost answerable to the state.

Centralization as a Political Tool

As far as public safety is concerned, the practice of maintaining a distance between police and the population proves very useful for governments and the hierarchies of the police and *gendarmerie*. Indeed, the latter are relieved of the burden of responding to local concerns or heeding the warning bells of local officials tempted to enforce demagogical public safety policies. National police chiefs present in municipalities are expected to cooperate with local officials, and in particular with mayors, and this requirement is regularly reiterated in legislation encouraging its strengthening or its renewal. However, in reality, policing remains relatively impervious to outside influences, those that originate outside the chain of command (de Maillard and Mouhanna 2017). A *commissaire* might quite easily justify implementing policies that do not conform to what local decision-makers desire. Not respecting internal instructions, however, could cost him his career. In this framework, the main challenge for a section chief is to show his chain of command that he is following national policies and that he is doing his utmost to ensure that his subordinates do the same.

Regarding governments (and here we touch upon another, more political, dimension of French-style centralization), police and *gendarmerie* are not there only to guarantee the safety of citizens or respond to their needs. They are there, first and foremost, to implement national policies that are the fruit of complex political strategies and based on studies of crime, but they also respond to other considerations. In the French political system, where the president of the Republic holds a very central place and upon whom many decisions depend, citizens turn to him to guarantee their rights, regarding welfare (the national insurance system), health care (the hospital and social security systems), and public safety (the police). The last of these has long been at the heart of presidential election campaigns. The French state constantly seeks to strengthen its legitimacy as the sole protector of the people. In this context, the national police units are its armed wing. While municipal police units have developed since the 1980s and especially the 1990s, they are most often considered as auxiliary forces for the *police nationale*, which retains most of the powers of coercion and constraint.

In France, then, central government has a monopoly on the legitimate use of force. But it has also used this force to impose its views on citizens, often beyond the scope of public safety. As Clive Emsley shows (1999), in the 19th century, the *gendarmerie*, by building its fine-meshed territorial network, contributed – along with public schooling and military service – to the building of a homogenous French nation. Indeed, being part of a central administration designed to treat all citizens equally conferred on the *gendarmes* the legitimacy to intervene in the cultural, economic or political spheres, by repressing mayhem, traffic or hunting offenses and popular demonstrations. In doing so, they imposed uniform rules upon populations with very different traditions.

The links between centralization, authority, and nation-building are recurring themes in the history of France outside of the rural world. The nationalization of France's urban police occurred relatively late, in 1941, in a context of dictatorship in a country made fragile by the German invasion. Until then, urban police had for the most part been municipal, save in Paris. The decision to retain the centralized policing organization created in Vichy after the end of the war was taken by a weakened country seeking to rebuild its identity following the German occupation.

Thus thanks to a centralized police force – but also collective national social insurance and a national system of education – it was cultural values, shared common rules, and being part of one group under the protection of one authority, that made the nation, and not the fact of belonging to a community based on ethnicity, religion, or blood ties. The nation-state born of the French Revolution and indeed in a tradition that continues to this day, refuses any notion of community other than the national community (Schnapper 1991). In this sense, the preservation of a national police force, in the hands of a protective government, is part of a collective mindset, wherein centralization, equal rights, and standardization are blurred.

The Adverse Effects of Centralization

The above description of how the French police system operates, though it may correspond to a collective idea shared by the rulers and a segment of the population, is nevertheless more an ideal than a universal reality. We can easily see how it can be in the interest of government, who use the police for the purpose of social control, and of police officers or *gendarmes* entrenched behind their corporatism, to defend a model that is nonetheless problematic. Indeed, it is for this reason that we have emphasized aspects of centralization that are in theory rational, even though France's system is rooted in converging interests that has made it almost impervious to external influences and therefore extremely difficult to reform.

Not unexpectedly, even research on the police has been defined as one of those external influences and can run afoul of centralization. Applications to conduct field investigations require an authorization that almost invariably ends up in the minister's office. Unlike countries with a decentralized structure, where it is possible to approach another jurisdiction if one refuses to be involved in research, this makes it very difficult to conduct research.

The Tools of Rationalization Reinforce a Hierarchical Structure

The first consequence of this organizational design is that all the members of the hierarchy look toward the top of the pyramid in a "top-down" logic. Like their counterparts in other countries, officers working in the field seek a certain amount of freedom and to adapt their practices to their environment. Local *gendarmes*, despite serving in an ostensibly military organization, had historically acquired a very significant degree of independence from their chain of command. This could be explained (Mouhanna 2011b) by their dispersion into small units across a vast territory they knew perfectly well, compared to distant officers who were not in office very long. However, aware that their actual power was weak, at the end of the 1990s *gendarmerie* leaders reacted by adopting a strategy to break down the autonomy of the brigades. First, they placed command centers at the head of each community of brigades that were to handle emergency calls. They thereby they gained control of the decision to respond or not to events. In any case, officers on the ground had to submit a report as soon as they arrived at the scene. In addition, the command centers could summon patrols from other sectors. Second, three quarters of the brigades had been "pooled," meaning that several functions were shared between brigades from two or three sectors. It was no longer possible for each brigade to withdraw to its own territory. Third, departmental intervention and analysis units were created. The former making it even easier to bypass local brigades for patrol missions or traffic offenses, for example. Disconnected from the local social fabric, these "central" *gendarmes* were much less inclined than their colleagues to turn a blind eye or come to an agreement with offenders. Thus, the brigades "monopoly" on relations with the governed was broken.

As for the analysis units, the leadership pursued a similar goal by different means. They sought to capture the concentrated local knowledge previously in the hands of each brigade. To do this, they "imported" data held in their colleagues' computers, sent surveys or information requests to local decision-makers, and harassed the brigades for all manner of reports and statistics. Internal reports from the *gendarmerie* (Senate 2003) show an intensification of office work in the brigades since the early 1990s, at the expense of interaction with the public. The aim was that all this information could reinforce the authority of top managers to control the operational activities of employees whose independence was not to their commanding officers' taste. The strategy culminated in the enforcement, from 2001, of what police and *gendarmes* called "the number culture," whereby work plans were accompanied by quantified targets to be met (Matelly and Mouhanna 2007).

Naturally, as has been seen elsewhere (Eterno and Silverman 2012), such a policy generated a downward spiral of cheating on numbers and reports, biased readings of statistics, and non-recording of complaints. The information gathered at the central level was of a lesser quality than the analyses carried out by local brigades closer to the field, making the *gendarmerie* as a whole less sensitive to faint signals indicating changes in crime patterns, and less relevant in their responses to each individual situation. Digitalization and artificial intelligence are supposed to address these shortcomings. Be that as it may, the result is that the *gendarmes* feel disconnected from the field.

They feel "caught" by the demands of management, subjected to the plans and instructions of the command centers and thus deprived of control over their work. In this sense, while it has not necessarily produced an improvement in the service provided to the population, management by numbers has been used by the chain of command to reinforce the centralizing and bureaucratic nature of the *gendarmerie*.

This crisis of meaning is even more apparent in police stations. We began by explaining the situation in rural areas, where there was a strong tradition of the *gendarmerie* being close to the public. This tradition was almost annihilated by "modern" centralization, with its number culture and tight control exercised through digitalization and the monitoring of office computers. In the urban environment, the changes observed are similar, but more dramatic. Indeed, French police officers' interactions with the public were profoundly altered from as early as the 1970s.

Double Centralization of Urban Police

A study of police management policies over the past 50 years reveals a recurrent chain reaction mechanism at work. An observation that relations between police and the population have deteriorated leads to the promotion of a policy designed to address the issue, triggering a reaction by the policing organization and the government which contributes to minimizing this policy's actual impact (Mouhanna 2011a). In the mid-1970s, a commission was set up by the minister of justice, whose conservative positions, notably in favor of the death penalty, were common knowledge. The commission reported, among other things, a split between the French people and their police force (Peyrefitte et al. 1977). The police organization had shifted from an era during which beat officers patrolled the streets alone or in pairs, even outside of times of trouble, with no radio, to a new world in which motorized patrols respond to emergency calls and then speed off to the next intervention. Previously isolated police officers were grouped together in central commissariats, under the constant gaze of an ever-present hierarchy. Small neighborhood police stations were closed one after another, and officers were placed under the aegis of a command center demanding immediate reports. This "local" centralization, with one central city police station, can be seen in every police force in the world. However, in France this favored national-level centralization. The call centers were not merely forwarding the public's concerns to working officers; rather, they rapidly turned into a general staff responsible for the planning of actions or, more accurately, for the local implementation of national priorities.

Technological innovations – computerized offices and vehicles, GPS, CCTV – and the spread of police-work analyst-planners who can be found at headquarters and in other command centers, would repeatedly be used to keep tighter control of the work of police officers in the field. Far from supporting the latter, these "office" staff are a permanent constraint that working officers seek to avoid (Reuss-Ianni and Ianni 1983). Paradoxically, centralization leads not to increased solidarity within the force, but to a feeling of isolation among police officers in the field.

The effects of the national recruitment model described above deepen the divide between the police and the public. The nationwide transfer system means that new recruits, assigned to the most unmanageable neighborhoods, have no desire to invest personally in these areas where they will stay no more than a year or two. They continue to reside in their provincial town, only travelling to their posting to work four days a week at their assigned station. With no ties in the neighborhood where they work, they do not seek to form relationships with the local residents, whom are to them merely strangers and people to be managed. The elective nature of postings consequently does nothing to improve relations with the population, indeed quite the contrary. Finally, bureaucratic directives provide a further excuse for them to minimize their contact with the public.

In light of these observations, during the 1980s and 1990s, several plans were put forward promising to bridge the divide with the public, and at the same time to foster crime prevention (Bonnemaison 1983). Plans aiming to reinstate beat policing were implemented throughout the period. But it was at that time that opposition to the strategy of putting beat police officers in contact with their fellow citizens began to surface. When the beat police played by the rules and responded to citizens' needs, the priorities that arose were not in line with the instructions from the Ministry of the Interior. Local police chiefs then found themselves in a difficult position with respect to their own chain of command. In parallel, they witnessed the growing autonomy of the patrol officers. Stuck between a rock and a hard place, they began to campaign against the practice that had made citizens a pivot for police action (Mouhanna 2001). They would soon be joined by recalcitrant police officers who saw in practices aiming to bring officers closer to the population a division between preventive and repressive policing, and they favored the latter. Hence, as we see here, the principle of equality and standardization played against the reform.

The same scenario was to play out again during a major "proximity policing" reform from 1997 to 2001. This was an ambitious plan to revive beat policing on a nationwide scale, and to reopen small neighborhood police stations, especially in poor suburbs. This was a true paradox of French-style centralization, because this community policing initiative was developed inside the Ministry of the Interior, and it was to be applied in a standardized manner by police officers in the field everywhere. Clearly the Ministry was incapable of thinking other than in terms of centralization, including when it came to devolving government activity. For this reason, even the most fervent and committed community police officers were vulnerable. Not only did the chain of command resist relinquishing its control of the rank and file (in order to pander to the demands of the public, it was charged), but the political orders themselves were contradictory: get closer to the people while faithfully following only instructions from the center. At the central level, too, the minister of the interior refused to cede power to his community policing troops, although his control over other police, those in charge of repression, was weaker still (Roché 2005).

Centralization as synonymous with repression

As minister of the interior from 2002, Nicolas Sarkozy – who was close to the upper echelons of the police hierarchy – signed the end of this great reform effort. Despite support from local politicians and the public for community policing, it was permanently abolished in favor of an unbridled numbers-driven management culture. Quantitative targets were imposed on *gendarmerie* brigades and commissariats at the start of each year and they were to be met at any cost. To this was added a national competition between constituencies. A benchmarking process produced a ranking of all commissariats across France, based on those numbers. The poorest performers were penalized and had to answer to the Ministry. The pressure was tremendous.

This intensified centralization increased the volume of red tape and internal stonewalling more than ever. Nevertheless, it did have one saving grace for the minister: it confirmed his legitimacy as head of the French police. He laid claim to an old expression used by Georges Clémenceau[3], calling the minister of the interior *le premier flic de France* (France's first policeman), thereby cementing his image as protector-in-chief of the French people. This became one of the platforms on which he ran and won the ensuing presidential election.

Since then, each successive government has found itself engaged in the same strategy: to reassure the public, they take a stand as national chief of police, devise national plans to combat the most high-profile types of crime, and command the lower echelons to work in line with these policies. To do this, they must appear tough on crime and criminals, especially since police officers, distanced from the population, tend to forget their social or preventive role and demand ever tougher policing. Consequently, no subsequent government has suggested a return to real preventive policing. Indeed, it is easier to conduct, or claim to conduct, a centralized policy of repression than a central policy of prevention. The objectives of the former are simpler – or more simplistic – and make it possible to demand rapid results. The few police officers who would like to engage in preventive actions complain that their effectiveness cannot be demonstrated by the numbers gathered by management. Moreover, adapting policy to local needs requires a freedom of action which their chain of command is not ready to grant them.

The public policies that have followed since 2005 have all been marked by the same contradiction. Parliamentary reports or senior officials note that the gap between the police and the population has widened. The minister of the interior rolls out a pilot project to test a system like proximity policing,[4] thinking he can maintain that strategy while preserving the same centralized structure. Each time, a few police officers take part in the project, play by the rules, get closer to the public and start implementing responses to their demands, often by means of more preventive local strategies. And each time, the organization reacts by denouncing these practices as unequal, lax, and ineffective. Then it backtracks and revives authoritarian and repressive policies. It is not the minister alone who is responsible for this stonewalling. As we have shown, every actor in the police hierarchy, from the rank and file up to the minister – with the exception of the handful of police officers who believe that it is necessary to break the pattern – has an interest in returning to the *status quo ante*. This equilibrium sacrifices one essential victim, however: the public. The mass citizenry is the "absent third party" of public safety policies, to use Dominique Monjardet's words (1996). If they are not satisfied with the service provided, they can vote for another president who will be forced, as were his predecessors, to engage in a similar pattern again.

The centralized structure of police governance in France makes innovation and experimentation at the local level impossible because all districts must follow the standardized model. Thus, it is less and less likely a police chief will propose to diverge from this model: his hierarchy and the police unions are there to remind him that his career will suffer if he tries to change anything in a way that is too original. In 2018, a new policy, the Police de Sécurité du Quotidien (PSQ), or Daily Safety Police, was launched. At the time of this writing many details regarding how this will be organized have not yet emerged. But local police officers and chiefs, put off by years of backtracking, are wary about engaging in a movement that the government only barely pays lip service to, and that will probably fizzle out of its own accord, like the previous ones.

Conclusion: Centralization as an Irreversible Paradigm

Looking at the *police nationale* and *gendarmerie* through this centralization lens, we see that belief in the virtues of centralization are so strong, and the career stakes for the actors involved are so high, that it may be impossible to transform. For senior officials of the Ministry of the Interior as well as for the police hierarchy, and even for police officers in the field, the advantages of the centralized system do not bear criticism. The only major concession that was actually made was the formation, beginning in the late 1980s, of municipal police forces. These were expected to address the issue of contact with the population. As for the rest, matters that the state considers serious, including major criminal investigations, maintaining order, supervising demonstrations, and protecting state institutions and their monopoly on power, continue to be the predominate concern of government.

If a fault *is* detected in the functioning of the services, the reflex of the Ministry of the Interior and senior police officials is to centralize even more.

In 1965, when an opponent of the king of Morocco was kidnapped and murdered with the support of two police officers, the government decided to merge the state-run but autonomous Paris olice force and the *Sûreté nationale*,[5] which covered the rest of France. In 1999, to make the Paris police more effective, and because investigative services were considered too independent, they were attached to the public security police. In 2009, concluding that the pooling of resources would make them more effective, the Paris police annexed the forces of neighboring departments, placing them under the authority of the Paris police prefect.[6] In the same year, the *gendarmerie* was placed under the authority of the Ministry of the Interior, whereas before it had been under the authority of the Ministry of Defense[7].

These centralizing tendencies persist despite reports from government officials and parliamentarians, supported by research, of the depth of the police/public divide, particularly in disadvantaged neighborhoods. Attempts at reform in the end result in more centralization. There is an inability of administrators in the Ministry of the Interior to think otherwise. In this respect, it is interesting to compare the developments in police management policies in France and England. Without examining the effectiveness of either system, it is plain to see that England, unlike France, has made repeated attempts to devolve police management and democratize the development of local public security policies (Lister and Rowe 2015). Faced with problems like those encountered by the French, the English response has been the opposite of that of the French. A true change in the way French police organizations operate would require a *cultural* turnaround on the part of all the actors concerned, something they are not ready to do.

To conclude, we should add that this devolution to centralization is not without consequence for the general way of doing politics in France. Seeing the police as an ever-ready tool to control the population without needing to seek their cooperation – in other words, as a tool to "manage" the citizenry – the government, whatever its political leaning, tends to overuse it. When there is disagreement with a significant segment of the public on a matter of public policy that leads to public protest, the government increasingly responds by sending in the police to put an end to the debate. This is what we see today with the *gilets jaunes* (yellow vests) movement. The use of the police as a political tool is not without risk. It deepens the police/public divide, causing new social groups to see the police as an enemy. It also makes the police an essential player in public life, causing a backlash from police officers, who are standing up and making their views heard in the public debate.

Notes

1 France is divided into 100 departments, and at the head of each is a prefect, a *commandant de groupement pour la gendarmerie* and a *directeur départemental de la sécurité publique* (DDSP) for the national police.
2 France is divided into13 regions, each comprised of several departments.

3 Minister of the interior from 1906, he was one of the fathers of French policing doctrine.
4 UTEQ (*unités territoriales de quartier* or territorial neighborhood units), BST (*Brigades Spéciales de Terrain* or Special Field Brigades), and now the PSQ (*Police de Sécurité du Quotidien* or Daily Safety Police) are some of the successive community policing experiments led by the Ministry.
5 *Loi Frey* or Frey Bill of 9 July 1966.
6 Décret no 2009–898 of 24 July 2009 relative to the territorial competence of a number of managerial and other services of the Paris préfecture.
7 Law of 3 August 2009.

References

Bonnemaison, G. 1983. *Face à la délinquance: prévention, répression, solidarité: rapport au Premier ministre*. Paris: la Documentation française.
Conway, V., and Walsh, D. 2011. Current developments in police governance and accountability in Ireland. *Crime, Law and Social Change* 55: 241–257.
de Maillard, J., and Mouhanna, C. 2017. Governing metropolises: The false pretenses of metropolization. Pp. 77–94 in E. Devroe, A. Edwards and P. Ponsaers (Eds.) *Policing European metropolises: The politics of security in city-regions*. New York and London: Routledge.
Drake, L. and Simper, R. 2001. The economic evaluation of policing activity: an application of a hybrid methodology. *European Journal of Law and Economics* 12: 173–192.
Emsley, C. 1999. *Gendarmes and the state in nineteenth-century Europe*. Oxford: Oxford University Press.
Eterno, J. A., and Silverman, E. B. 2012. *The crime numbers game: Management by manipulation*. New York: CRC Press.
Fyfe, N. 2013. Making sense of a radically changing landscape: The key contours of police reform in Scotland. *Scottish Justice Matters* 1. 9–10.
Fyfe, N., Terpstra, J., and Tops, P. 2013. *Centralizing forces? Comparative perspectives on contemporary police reform in northern and western Europe*. The Hague: Eleven International Publishing.
Gautier, F. 2017. Une police 'à l'image de la population'? *Migrations Société* 3: 39–52.
Hale, C., Heaton, R., and Uglow, Steve. 2004. Uniform styles? Aspects of police centralization in England and Wales. *Policing & Society* 14: 291–312.
Holmberg, L. 2014. Scandinavian police reforms: Can you have your cake and eat it, too? *Police Practice and Research* 15: 447–460.
Jobard, F., and de Maillard, J. 2015. *Sociologie de la police*. Paris: Armand Colin.
Lévy, R. 2016. La police française à la lumière de la théorie de la justice procédurale. *Déviance et société* 40: 139–164.
Lister, S., and Rowe, M. 2015. Electing police and crime commissioners in England and Wales: Prospecting for the democratization of policing. *Police & Society* 25: 358–377.
Martinez-Herrera, E. 2002. From nation-building to building identification with political communities: Consequences of political decentralization in Spain, the Basque Country, Catalonia and Galicia, 1978–2001. *European Journal of Political Research* 41: 421–453.
Matelly, J. H., and Mouhanna, C. 2007. *Police: des chiffres et des doutes*. Paris: Michalon.

Monjardet, D. 1996. *Ce que fait la police: sociologie de la force publique*. Paris: La Decouvete.
Mouhanna, C. 2001. Faire le gendarme: de la souplesse informelle à la rigueur bureaucratique. *Revue française de sociologie* 42: 31–55.
Mouhanna, C. 2009. France: une lutte incessante autour de la recherche sur la police et le policing. Pp. 287–324 in P. Ponsaers, C. Tange and L. van Outrive (Eds.) *Regards sur la police: Un quart de siècle de recherche sur la police en Europe et dans le monde anglo-saxon*. Brussels: Editions Bruylant.
Mouhanna, C. 2011a. *La police contre les citoyens*. Nimes: Champ social éditions.
Mouhanna, C. 2011b. Rural policing in France: The end of genuine community policing. Pp. 45–57 in R. I. Mawby and R. Yarwood (Eds.) *Rural policing and policing the rural. A constable countryside?* Surrey: Ashgate.
Oliveau, S., and Doignon, Y. 2016. La diagonale se vide? Analyse spatiale exploratoire des décroissances démographiques en France métropolitaine depuis 50 ans. *Cybergeo: European Journal of Geography*. Espace, Société, Territoire, document 763 [Online 20 January http://journals.openedition.org/cybergeo/27439].
Peyrefitte, A., Schmelck, R., and Dumoulin, R. 1977. *Reponses à la violence: Rapport du Comité d'études présidé par Alain Peyrefitte*. Paris: La Documentation française.
Reiner, R. 2010. *The politics of the police*. Oxford and New York: Oxford University Press.
Reuss-Ianni, Elizabeth, and Ianni, Francis. 1983. Street cops and management cops: The two cultures of policing. Pp. 251–274 in Maurice Punch (Ed.) *Control in the police organization*. Cambridge, MA: MIT Press.
Roché, S. 2005. *Police de proximité. Nos politiques de sécurité*, Paris: Seuil.
Schnapper, D. 1991. *La France de l'intégration. Sociologie de la nation en 1990*. Paris: Gallimard, Coll Bibliothèque des sciences humaines.
Sénat. 2003. *L'organisation du temps de travail et des procédures d'information des forces de sécurité intérieure*. Rapport d'information n° 25 (2003–2004) de M. Aymeri de Montesquiou, fait au nom de la commission des finances, déposé le 15 octobre 2003.
Sénat, 2013. Projet de loi de finances pour 2014: Sécurités: gendarmerie nationale, Avis n° 158 (2013-2014) de MM. Michel BOUTANT et Gérard LARCHER, fait au nom de la commission des affaires étrangères, de la défense et des forces armées, déposé le 21 novembre 2013. https://www.senat.fr/rap/a13-158-11/a13-158-11_mono.html
Skogan, W. G. 2006. *Police and community in Chicago: A tale of three cities*. New York: Oxford University Press.
Terpstra, J. 2018. Local policing in a nationalized police force: A study on the local teams of the Netherlands' national police. *Policing: A Journal of Policy and Practice*. https://doi.org/10.1093/police/pay037.

Chapter 6

Intelligence-led Policing in Criminal Investigations

Implementing Reform

Clément de Maillard

In the early 2010s, a gang war broke out in Marseille that led to a skyrocketing number of homicides. Since the French Connection (an international drugs case linking Marseille to New York in the 1970s), Marseille has been known for its powerful and well-established organized crime groups. However, the murders of the 2010s were linked to the emergence of a new generation of young criminals from the city's underprivileged neighborhoods. They had not climbed the social ladder of crime as did their elders, yet they competed directly with long-established groups. Accustomed to keeping an eye on the actions of their "usual suspects," the police did not see the emergence this new generation of criminals and did not understand the gang wars that broke out between them and the old guard. When local authorities turned to the police to understand the resulting increase in homicides, they learned little and were unable to craft a response to it. Marseille's criminal police (*police judiciaire*) clung to the reactive approach of detecting and monitoring crime patterns and lacked a proactive policy response. They needed to better understand the criminal environment in order to better deal with this crisis. In response, a new criminal intelligence service was created, one dedicated to the detection of criminal groups and their interactions in the Marseille criminal landscape, with the aim of containing the bloody war that had broken out.

This example illustrates how the French police have turned to a method designed to better understand the criminal environment – problems that emerge, their causes, and their effects – based on developing criminal intelligence. Despite their lack of knowledge of new police techniques and doctrines elsewhere, they nevertheless confronted their own ineffectiveness. Recognizing their inability to understand criminal activities and therefore to respond to them effectively, a criminal intelligence strategy has been their response. But while this sudden awareness has led to significant organizational changes, it has not yet been accompanied by more broad-based reform.

Led by criminologist Jerry Ratcliffe (2016), the intelligence-led policing (ILP) model emerged in the mid-2000s. It is part of a trend among researchers and professionals to question the effectiveness of traditional policing strategies. Intelligence-led policing is a model of police organization that invites police forces to go beyond their reactive management of events and their iterative approach to problems, and instead adopt a proactive stance focused on the early detection of crime and disorder. The model is based on a methodology known as criminal intelligence. Criminal intelligence implements the intelligence cycle by applying it to crime and disorders issues. An intelligence-led police force is not defined only by the establishment of a criminal intelligence unit or adoption of a list of practices. It is also characterized by the ability to look at the big picture of crime in the community, and to shift from a reactive to a more proactive posture in response. The idea is to first better understand the crime environment and set policing priorities, then optimize police actions. Such an approach can only be achieved if the police service has three essential elements: a dedicated criminal intelligence organization, a criminal intelligence doctrine, and criminal intelligence practices. Thus, the creation of a criminal intelligence unit is not enough to consider that the police are applying the ILP model; however, an intelligence-led police force necessarily has a robust criminal intelligence system.

To be effective, criminal intelligence strategies must oversee events in three areas: the actions of prolific offenders and criminal groups, emerging crime patterns, and spatial crime analysis. Criminal intelligence supports key police functions. It engages at three organizational levels: the tactical level (support of investigations), the operational level (decision-making support), and the strategic level. To be considered as intelligence-led, a police force must therefore bring together these three subsets: a dedicated organization, an *ad hoc* doctrine, and effective criminal intelligence practices.

While originally developed in Anglo-Saxon countries (mainly the United States and the United Kingdom), intelligence-led policing has now been adopted by many countries with diverse cultures. However, for many reasons – including the indifference of French researchers to criminological issues and the resistance of the French police system – France has long remained out of these debates. These factors have also contributed to their resistance to police reform more generally. Fatally, when the ILP model began to become popular abroad in the 2000s, France remained out of the discussion. As described by other chapters in this volume, the French police organization is the heritage of the history of the state. It is composed of two police forces with national jurisdiction: the civilian *police nationale* and the militarized *gendarmerie nationale*. Beyond their labels, there are many differences between the *police* and the *gendarmerie*, and the way the two forces are structured plays a key role in the fight against crime. The *police nationale* is an urban force. It covers only 5% of the national territory but encompasses 50% of the population and 70% of recorded crime (Cour des Comptes 2011). The *gendarmerie* is primarily a rural police force. It covers 95% of the nation, 50% of the population, and about 30% of all recorded crimes (Cour des Comptes 2011). The problems faced by the police and the *gendarmerie* are different. The former serves areas of high population density, urban disorder, and organized criminal groups. The problems of the *gendarmerie* are more territorial. It covers a large jurisdiction and its resources are very dispersed. It must deal with the mobility of criminals and criminal activities. This is the context that determines their opportunities for action, and therefore the possible role that criminal intelligence can play. Regarding crime and disorder management, both police and *gendarmerie* have the same powers and enforce the same statutes. Their responsibilities (territorial, thematic, etc.) have developed historically and culturally. A distinction must be made between services that are charged with dealing with crime-solving (criminal investigations departments, the *police judiciaire*), those responsible for public order (public order and riot units), and those that ensure daily security and crime prevention (public safety).

The police and *gendarmerie* operate almost autonomously. They each have public order maintenance units, judicial police units, and public safety units; they are organized under the same legal authority, the Ministry of Interior. The organization of the national *gendarmerie* is pyramidal (Cour des Comptes 2011). In terms of investigations, the brigades (working out of 3,351 police stations) make up the base of the system. Brigades generally deal with public safety, crime prevention, and petty crimes. But one of the key principles the *gendarmerie* is based on is the concept of subsidiarity. Thus, each unit, from the most generalist – the brigade – to the most specialized, works in cooperation when it comes to crime fighting. In terms of investigations per se, the gendarmerie has *brigades de recherche* and *sections de recherches* that support the brigades, or even take over investigations when they require special expertise, long-term investigations, or national or international coordination.

Unlike the national *gendarmerie*, whose organization is organized along territorial lines model, the *police nationale* are organized in "silos" with different responsibilities. The Direction centrale de la police judiciaire (Central Directorate for Criminal Investigations DCPJ), which is responsible for serious and complex crimes (including organized crime), encompasses two service branches. One branch focuses on specific types of crimes, but with national jurisdiction. This involves eight central offices or *offices centraux* (drugs trafficking, prostitution, robbery, etc.), plus the SIRASCO:[1] – the national criminal intelligence service. The other branch is more generalist but covers a territorial jurisdiction (regional and interregional judicial police directorates DRPJ and DIPJ).

In 2013, the concept of criminal intelligence began to be explored in the two French police forces. Its appeal resonated with a requirement for collaboration and effectiveness in their actions, and this seemed to be the inexorable way in which law enforcement authorities were evolving. A commitment to intelligence resulted in the formalization of a doctrine within the *police nationale* and *gendarmerie*, and the creation of dedicated units within the services. New or strengthened criminal intelligence agencies have emerged. Yet, despite their seeming appetite for reform, criminal intelligence practices remain at the margins, and today still have little influence in terms of the fight against crime (de Maillard 2017).

New Interest in Criminal Intelligence

While the Marseille example described in the introduction may have played only a minor role in the emergence of criminal intelligence nationwide, it is symbolic of possible transformations of the French system. On the one hand, it highlighted the need to think about security issues differently. In the context of optimizing public security operations, it reflected a need to better understand organized crime and the need for an appropriate strategy for responding to it. But on the other hand, it demonstrated that knowledge of the criminal landscape could no longer be built on the traditional vision of the investigation departments. The slow and deep changes that have affected the judicial police (*police judiciaire*) have made this task more complex, revealing a new requirement: criminal intelligence.

Over the past 20 years, the French security context has undergone significant change linked to the transformation of crime and criminals (Perrot and de Maillard 2018), the evolution of individual rights in criminal procedures (Baume 2014), and the magnitude of information technologies in the commission of offences, and especially in the search for evidence (Jobard and de Maillard 2015). In parallel with these major changes, the French *police nationale* and *gendarmerie* have been under double pressure since 2008, both in terms of budget and security. The so-called *Révision générale des politiques publiques* (RGPP) – a wide public reform of French public institutions – has resulted in a reduction of government's resources allocated to the *police nationale* and *gendarmerie* (Cour des Comptes 2011, 2013). Because social and political pressure to reduce crime remained as strong as ever, the two forces were obliged to adapt accordingly. Between a decrease in budgetary resources on the one hand, and an ever-increasing demand for better performance on the other hand, the two administrations were stuck in the difficult situation of being called upon to "do better with less." And the problem faced by the Marseille police clearly illustrates the expression of this new requirement.

While optimizing police capacities necessarily required better knowledge of how crime works, one point became clear: the police already had the information in their hands they needed to understand criminality, but they had neither the organization nor the tools nor even the methods to act effectively. Without these capacities, they were restricted to reactive responses in terms of security management. And if the lack of method and organization had thus far been compensated for by the empirical knowledge accumulated by the traditional investigation services, they were now confronted with a major evolution that irremediably diluted this empirical knowledge: the hyper-division of investigation work. Police segmentation is not new, but so far it has been mainly described within the police organization itself, as a result of the proliferation of specialized "micro-services," each dealing with a particular issue. This vertical fragmentation should not be confused with horizontal fragmentation, corresponding to what is referred to here as hyper-specialization of investigation work. This one differs in shape and strength.

The work of the judicial police consists in seeking evidence in the context of three constraints. They are limited by the specific investigative methodology to be implemented according to the type of crime, by the management of evidence technologies, and by the legal rules of procedure. However, the cross-influence of the three factors previously described – proliferation of criminality, strengthening procedural rules, and an increase in the availability of scientific tools (Jobard and de Maillard 2015) – increases the burden of these constraints on the investigator. This new horizontal division of labor began in France in the 1980s and 1990s with the creation of specialized units to carry out tasks previously performed by the investigators themselves (Matelly 2000). It has generated new specialized police roles. Whereas in the past the investigator was versatile and participated in almost the entire investigation process – surveillance, wiretapping, questioning individuals, police custody, procedure drafting and management, arrests, confidential informant management, and even sometimes forensics – now each stage of the investigation work is specialized. Today the way investigations are carried out tends to specialize tasks and assign them to dedicated services: forensic experts search for traces with dedicated forensic methods, observation and surveillance require increasingly sophisticated operational and technical skills, assigned to special units. The complexity of criminal procedures (for long or complex investigations) requires the presence of a procedural expert ("*procédurier*") who ensures that each piece of procedure is compliant with the law. The amount of data collected during the investigation requires an analyst able to deal with and analyze it. Thus, several years ago, the *gendarmerie* developed a specialized role for of crime analysts. Crime analysts work along with the other investigators within the investigation departments. With their software (so-called ANACRIM), they support complex investigations and those with a large volume of data to be processed. Their role consists either in visually highlighting links that are otherwise difficult to perceive, or in developing new hypotheses for investigation. For example, the analyst visually builds up in matrix from the interactions between the protagonists of an organized crime group or a complex case, represents the chronology of events according to the witness and evidence (so as to reveal inconsistencies for example), and detects possible links in the big data collected by digital transmission firms.

However, this hyper-division of labor generates a hyper-distribution of knowledge. Each specific node within the investigation process develops its own knowledge, which is enriched as it becomes more specialized. This knowledge takes various forms: scientific or empirical, formal or informal, structural or cyclical, etc. While it contributes to a better understanding of criminality, by segmenting itself, this knowledge tends to feed an essentially endogenous know-how that certainly contributes to its further specialization, but also distances it from other nodes in the crime-solving network. This change therefore plays a detrimental role in terms of knowledge sharing within the investigation departments. Failing to harmonize all the collections of intelligence, the increasing technicality of the investigation departments has taken precedence over the development of a global understanding of crime. This change within the *police nationale* and *gendarmerie* has exacerbated their deep deficiencies in terms of criminal intelligence. And combined with a reactive model in which the understanding of security issues was neither prioritized nor even made explicit, this evolution has further widened the gap between the investigation departments and the criminal environment on which they operate.

Despite their disregard of innovative doctrines, the French police forces are like any others, undergoing several major developments in recent decades. And if in France this was not the result of the same philosophy as among ILP followers, criminal intelligence finally emerged because it met this two-fold internal requirement: the increasing demand for security performance on the one hand, and the inexorable need to manage its own capacities to better understand crime on the other hand. These two needs have led to the emergence of criminal intelligence alongside investigation departments.

Reform at the Margins

From 2013, attempts to improve the performance of the investigative departments led to the rise of criminal intelligence. Its definition remains rather vague and its contours are still poorly defined. But considering the exhaustion of traditional solutions, French police forces are enthusiastic about this concept, which aims to modernize traditional policing. They see in it an opportunity to reinvent themselves while responding to emerging requirements. This new approach gives meaning to security management (why?), by improving its action (how?), and without increasing resources (with what?). In this context, where efficiency is sought despite constraints in gathering intelligence, it therefore presents a major asset. Criminal intelligence has gradually emerged among decision-makers as an appropriate solution: by organizing information management differently, new perspectives were opened in terms of dealing with crime. It was set up with a top-down approach that first convinced decision-makers before convincing the grassroots.

The *police nationale* and the *gendarmerie* took on this mission. It is no secret that relations between the *police nationale* and the *gendarmerie* can in some respects be considered challenging, particularly in terms of the *police judiciaire* (Cour des Comptes 2014). In a context where the evolution of organizations is rare and codified, and where each reform is subject to intense discussion, the emergence of a new concept becomes an issue of power and influence. It attracted both branches of policing in France. Criminal intelligence became a new way to explore, as much as a new field to conquer. Within the *police nationale* and *gendarmerie*, the attraction of criminal intelligence has been most evident in investigation departments (*police judiciaire*); thus, they produce doctrines and develop new departments or strengthen existing ones.

While the first signs of change were noticeable as early as 2009, it was mainly from 2013 or 2014 that criminal intelligence became an operative strategy. Despite some common features, the *police nationale* and *gendarmerie* do not apply it in the same way, because the way they implement it responds first and foremost to their own internal culture and needs.

Within the *police nationale*, criminal intelligence is essentially perceived as a tool dedicated to attacking organized crime (Gayraud and Farcy 2011). It has developed mainly from human intelligence and ongoing investigations and focuses primarily on prolific offenders and criminal groups. In this respect, the SIRASCO network is symbolic: created in 2009, SIRASCO is a department attached to the Central Directorate of the Judicial Police (DCPJ). Positioned alongside the investigation departments, which are organized by type of criminal activity (in central offices) or by territory (DIPJ and DRPJ), SIRASCO addresses the issues of organized crime groups according to their origin: Asia, America (mainly Central and South America), Russian-speaking, Balkans, Italian mafia, motorcycle gangs, and local gangs. It draws most of its information from investigations (ongoing or closed), and from human intelligence that investigation departments agree to share. In 2013, SIRASCO bureaus were set up in all major French cities. They are local variations of the central SIRASCO. The police refer to the central SIRASCO and all of its local outposts as the "SIRASCO network." Each local SIRASCO works on its jurisdiction, then the information produced is centralized and harmonized by the central level.

Box 6.1 Case 1: Problem-solving Analysis of Organized Criminal Groups Involved in Heroin Trafficking – the *Police Nationale*, 2015

Following a series of disorders observed around a nightclub (noise, fights, repeated interventions by police patrols, complaints from local residents, etc.) that culminated in an attempted homicide of a security agent, several local security stakeholders met under the umbrella of the prefect to identify the problem and try to solve it. The local SIRASCO office coordinated intelligence gathering between both police patrol and criminal department crews. It analyzed all police interventions, retrieved testimonies, focused on financial aspects of the club, and cross-referenced all this data with that from other sources (criminal record files, ongoing investigations, human intelligence, etc.). SIRASCO determined that the club belonged to an important member of an international organized crime group. This group was reported to be particularly active in heroin trafficking. This group was being challenged and was in conflict with another local organized crime group that was attacking it through the club. Thus, SIRASCO highlighted that the disorders facing police and local residents on a daily basis were not the result of incivilities linked to night time activities but had their origins in conflict between two criminal groups. The nightclub had become a flash point for mounting tensions and a locale for settling scores. SIRASCO produced intelligence for decision-makers highlighting this issue and proposed recommended actions. By facilitating research and gathering of intelligence, SIRASCO proposed administrative closure of the nightclub, initiating separate criminal investigations into the two criminal groups involved, and disrupting heroin trafficking and putting a lasting end to disorders at the venue.

Case 1 in Box 6.1 illustrates, at the local level, the relevance of operational criminal intelligence, i.e., intelligence that directly supports decision-makers in their decision-making. However, and even if the SIRASCO denies it, its contribution is essentially strategic, i.e. more general and macroscopic (the purpose of strategic intelligence is less directly operative than tactical and operational intelligence). SIRASCO produces an annual report on organized crime in France. The report synthesizes elements provided by the investigation departments of the judicial police and its partners. Its main purpose is sometimes misused: most of its intelligence productions are used not by police officers, but by judges to inform them about how organized crime groups operate, and to help them contextualize court decisions.

In 2014, the *gendarmerie* displayed this new trend by renaming the Technical Service for Criminal Investigation and Documentation (Service technique de recherches judiciaires et de documentation – STRJD) the National Criminal Intelligence Service (Service central de renseignement criminel – SCRC). This change was not only symbolic: the STRJD was a service dedicated to the management of databases and various analytical files. With the SCRC, the *gendarmerie* retains this task, but pushes it forward with new analytical capacity. SCRC has national jurisdiction and relies on a judicial support brigade (*brigade d'appui judiciaire* – BAJ) and judicial support sections (*section d'appui judiciaire* – SAJ). These units deal with databases at the local level and coordinate judicial action. While they are now more prominent in the world of criminal intelligence, their capacity to analyze criminality still needs to be improved. In addition, unlike the police, which focuses on prolific offenders and groups, the *gendarmerie* focuses mainly on criminal activities and the detection of patterns of crime. Detection of crime patterns remains its primary mission. The *gendarmerie* detects crime patterns by focusing on the type of stolen objects (for example, agricultural GPS, construction vehicles). Commonalities can also be found in offender's *modus operandi* (attacks on ATMs with explosives, home burglaries in a specific area at a specific time, for example during daytime), and in physical evidence collected during investigations (shoe prints and the like). By linking multiple scattered facts together based on their common patterns, and then crossing these data with broader contextual information, criminal intelligence increases and contributes to solving cases. It mainly supports investigations (tactical criminal intelligence). It can also help decision-makers adapt their preventive actions, as in Case 2 in Box 6.2 below.

> **Box 6.2 Case 2: Spatial Criminal Analysis of ATM Attacks – the** *Gendarmerie*, **2015**
>
> In 2015, France was hit by a series of ATM attacks with explosives. In the middle of the night, the criminals blew up ATMs (using explosives or gas mixtures), seized the cash chest, and then disappeared in one or more powerful stolen cars. Their *modus operandi* was specific, and several teams of criminals were identified. The National Office for the Fight Against Mobile Organized Crime (Office central de lutte contre la délinquance itinérante – OCLDI) took over the case. After a calmer period thanks to the arrest of several criminal teams, an analysis was carried out on crime patterns. In addition to analyses focusing on criminal techniques (type of explosives, *modus operandi*, typology of offenders, typology of victims, etc.), a spatial analysis made it possible to highlight key elements of these crimes. The spatial analysis identified risk factors, and thus made it possible to define criteria determining which ATMs were at greater vulnerability to attacks. These criteria were considered, consciously or not, in the choice of targets by criminals. They evaluated potential targets by looking at the size of the city (generally small towns and villages), the absence of police or *gendarmerie* stations, and access to a highway. With the cooperation of French banks, this analysis enabled them to target the most vulnerable ATMs, identify the measures to be taken to thwart the possibility of an attack, and thus strengthen the passive security of these sites.

This example illustrates two aspects of criminal intelligence. On the one hand, spatial analysis – even if carried out *ex post* – is enlightening. Investigations alone could never have highlighted these points. On the other hand, it demonstrates that such an analysis can be crucial in terms of fighting organized crime. In this case, it has made it possible to take proactive preventive actions, focusing on future or potential victims and based on objective criteria that will help deal with crime in the future.

In 2015, the *gendarmerie* identified criminal intelligence as one of the six priorities of the judicial police. In the same year, it was the subject of an internal memorandum that formalized the concept and how criminal intelligence was to be managed. The *gendarmerie* is now seeking to develop other aspects of criminal intelligence, particularly operational (in support of decision-making) and strategic (as a support for analysis and planning).

To overcome their weaknesses, the *police nationale* and *gendarmerie* adopted measures to change their practices. In 2015, the National Police (DCPJ) issued an internal memorandum that laid the basis of criminal intelligence doctrine and confirmed its status at the national and local levels, with the creation of the Criminal Information Divisions (Division du traitement de l'information criminelle – DTIC). Positioned alongside the investigation services, these DTICs include local SIRASCO and CORAIL units, whose names were given to software developed by the *police nationale*. This software enables the *police nationale* to better detect crime series; the idea is to decompartmentalize intelligence on crimes and intelligence on criminals. The *gendarmerie* should soon have a similar tool, the Application for Criminal Intelligence Management (Application de traitement du renseignement criminel – ATRC). ATRC should facilitate the work of analysts in the field, giving them more time to produce an analysis. In addition, the *gendarmerie* under the umbrella of the SCRC has initiated training for criminal intelligence analysts to harmonize intelligence cultures and ensure dedicated resources, then build up an intelligence analyst community.

However, a look at the actual adoption of these initiatives reveals a contrasting reality. Despite the apparent willingness of decision-makers, and the allocation of resources to support reform, advances in criminal intelligence face resistance. Reversing the way a police system works, shifting it from a reactive to a proactive stance, confronts both structural and cultural challenges. Like other police forces that have initiated such reforms (Ribaux 2005), the French *police nationale* and *gendarmerie* have also to deal with vulnerability of the police services to constant distraction by pressing events. Whether they are in agreement or not with a proactive approach to policing, the proactive initiatives of the investigative services remain limited and their actions remain primarily dedicated to individually solving reported crimes (Cope 2004; Lemieux 2005; Walden and Ratcliffe 2010). Their difficulties in coping with change have been further compounded by the lowly status that criminal intelligence services hold in policing. These services – recently created and still finding their way – are struggling to gain a foothold within established police organizations. The reforms that were first promised proved to be symbolic rather than concrete. Criminal intelligence terms are now used to describe practices or services that existed before and have not fundamentally changed. While in theory a proactive approach should replace a reactive one, in reality the two approaches coexist and even push against one another. Most internal decisions and management processes favor investigation services, to the detriment of criminal intelligence efforts. The investigation services remain powerful and hold the upper hand. They do not allow the priorities of the criminal intelligence services to dictate guidelines and decisions. The criminal intelligence services have only marginal influence and struggle to exist. Their lack of status is reinforced by the distance that exists between operational units in the field and the analytical staff in the back office. The former often conclude that they have a better knowledge of the crime environment, while latter criticize their knowledge as simplistic. This point is not new, and has already been observed elsewhere (Cope 2004; Chermak, Carter, Carter, McGarell, and Drew 2013).

Further, unlike in many Anglo-Saxon police forces, the proportion of civilians working for these agencies is extremely low. Almost all criminal intelligence analysts are police and *gendarmerie* officers. This staffing pattern does allow for better coordination between services, since most officers are former investigators who know the capabilities of their peers (Cope 2004; Chermak et al. 2013). However, the utility of the intelligence services continues to be questioned, with some doubting their real added value. While the concept was praised for its promise to anticipate problems and optimize action, many decision-makers and investigation services now question the effectiveness of criminal intelligence. Some point to its lack of visible and quantifiable results. A similar observation was made by Adrian James in the United Kingdom. He pointed to the false formalism of the reforms, voiced the skepticism of decision-makers, and observed the predominance of investigative services at the expense of criminal intelligence services (James 2013). See Case 3 in Box 6.3.

Box 6.3 Case 3: The Implementation of Criminal Intelligence within the DIPJ-*Police Nationale*, 2017

In 2013, DTICs were created within the Interregional Judicial Police Directorates (Direction interrégionale de police judiciaire – DIPJ). This was decided at the national level (DCPJ). Here we examine their local implementation in two policing areas. Despite their origin in central government, the two DIPJs were not implemented it in the same way. The director of DIPJ "X" did not see the added value of criminal intelligence. Instead, he continued to rely on powerful investigation services, which had a solid reputation in the fight against organized crime. The context of DIPJ "Y" was different. There the director was sensitive to the possibilities of criminal intelligence and had already set up a prototype intelligence group within his unit before the national reform. In addition, DIPJ "Y" was facing competition with other investigative services (public safety investigation units normally dedicated to less important and complex crimes, but which are overlapping in their attributions), and indeed the investigation services of DIPJ "Y" sought to highlight their own added value. In these two DIPJs, the results of the reform differed. Within "X" the director did not make criminal intelligence a priority. The service was created in order to be in compliance with national policy, but without guidlines and the attention of management, the unit worked in a vacuum and without much supervision. Within "Y" the director appointed a renowned police officer who was respected by his peers, provided the unit with resources, and set some clear goals. As a result, this unit acquired a certain legitimacy among the investigative groups it works with. While its existence remains fragile, it can claim some added value.

Enthusiasm for the concept and resistance to the adoption of the ILP model are both not unique to the French police forces. Researchers have documented similar developments and offered explanations for them (Phillips and Carter 2015). These studies considered variables such as the size of the police force, its urban or rural profile, the degree of resistance to change, or the complexity of the socio-economic context (Mazerolle and Darroch 2015). There have been no studies of the effects of centralized versus decentralized institutional frameworks on ILP reform. Lack of interest in this point is probably due to the fact that Anglo-Saxon policing has been the focus of most researchers interested criminal investigations. By focusing on the study of their own police systems, they have mainly examined federal and decentralized systems, notably the American (Mazerolle and Darroch 2015; Phillips and Carter 2015; Walden and Ratcliffe 2010) and British policing (Cope 2004) scenes. Therefore they have not emphasized how the very structure of policing could also play a role in the adoption and successful implementation of a new policing model. However, as illustrated by the interest of French police in criminal intelligence that is described in this chapter, this is undoubtedly due in part to the centralized nature of its larger institutional arrangements.

It is no coincidence that intelligence-led policing has emerged and developed in federal and decentralized police systems. Indeed, in a federal or decentralized system, the local heads of police organizations have more flexibility. They are more independent; they are solely in charge of security for the jurisdiction and for the distribution of resources (human, logistical, financial); and they select their security strategy. In some cases, they are even directly elected by the public, as in the case of American county sheriffs. The disconnect between operational policing and any national policy gives them a large degree of autonomy and flexibility in action. Autonomy and flexibility undoubtedly play a key role in the development of reforms: heads of local police can reform their organization and monitor strategies, or experiment with innovative management.

On the other hand, this context, which is so favorable to the development of ILP reforms in a federal and decentralized system, cannot be directly transposed into a centralized French police system. The characteristics of the centralized police system are diametrically opposed: orders and strategies are driven by the central level and implemented at the local level (the local level can define its own strategy but only within the framework prescribed by the central level); police organizations have similar jurisdictions; and practices fit uniformly within standards shared with all the other similar services. Compared to a federal and decentralized model, the centralized system is subordinate (vs. autonomous), standardized (vs. flexible), and open (vs. isolated). But while it may now seem unfavorable (or even a hindrance) to innovation and the development of new strategies (such as intelligence-led policing), this centralization can also be a key asset in the implementation of global reform.

Indeed, the major difficulty faced by federal or decentralized systems is the lack of uniformity between the different police forces, either horizontally between forces at the same level, or vertically between national and regional forces (Ribaux 2005). They are isolated from one another; their legislative foundations vary and do not always coincide; they rarely share databases; their operational policies differ; and information exchanges can be difficult to work out. All these difficulties have been pointed out, for example, in the American and British systems. In contrast, the uniformity and openness of the French centralized system can be undeniable assets in the development of intelligence-led policing. These features theoretically make possible uniform information management through a single legal system, common and shared databases, and standards in terms of intelligence exchange and production. They also provide a horizontal continuity between geographical jurisdictions, and a vertical fluidity of police operational structures.

But another source of innovation in policing has been research focusing on strategies to improve police effectiveness. In other places, the academic world has become quite involved in security and policing issues. A collaboration between researchers and police has made it possible to define new strategies, to experiment with them, to criticize them, and thus to reform, adapt or even reinvent policing models. However, in France criminological research has not had this focus.

The emergence of ILP concept within the French police forces is recent. Totally ignored less than ten years ago, it is now essential that it is mentioned in official speeches, and in some respect has become part of the police lexicon. This adoption (at least on the surface) has been driven by particular decision-makers within the police establishment. Both the *police nationale* and *gendarmerie* have competed to adopt this new-sounding concept. However, they only became interested in it at a late stage and because it was driven, as in Marseille, by events on the ground. But despite the seduction by new ideas and the promise of new strategies, the intelligence-led policing model still struggles to gain acceptance. Indeed, although ambitious, the recent and sudden interest in the intelligence-led policing model does not reflect the reality of a system that is still largely dominated by reactive approaches and dominated by traditional investigative services. There are many reasons for this, not only because of a broad commitment to the professional model based on reactive investigations, but also because of the nature of the French police system itself, as well as the fact the initial experiments in ILP did not meet expectations.

Moreover, since 2016, and under the impetus of the government, a new strategy has been put forward: the *police de sécurité du quotidien* strategy (daily security police strategy). The *police de sécurité du quotidien* strategy lies somewhere between community policing and problem-oriented policing and aims to put police back in touch with and at the service of its population. The focus is on the work of the public security units. The existence – or even the rise of criminal intelligence services – is not threatened because in some ways they contribute to this strategy. However, criminal intelligence is still seeking its place in a system that is constantly reforming.

Note

1 SIRASCO: Service d'information, de renseignement et d'analyse stratégique sur le crime organisé (Information, Intelligence and Strategic Analysis Service on Organized Crime).

References

Baume, J. 2014. *Rapport sur la procédure pénale*. Paris: Ministère de la Justice.
Chermak, S., Carter, J. D., Carter, D., McGarell, E. F., and Drew, J. 2013. Law enforcement's information sharing infrastructure: A national assessment. *Police Quarterly* 16: 211–244.
Cope, N. 2004. Intelligence led policing or policing led intelligence? Integrating volume crime analysis into policing. *British Journal of Criminology* 44: 188–203.
Cour des Comptes. 2011. *Rapport sur la mutualisation entre la police et la gendarmerie nationales: rapport d'information*. Paris.
Cour des Comptes. 2013. *Police et gendarmerie nationales: Dépenses de rémunération et temps de travail: rapport public thématique*. Paris.
Cour des Comptes. 2014. *La fonction de police judiciaire dans la police et la gendarmerie nationales*. Paris.
de Maillard, C. 2017. *Le renseignement criminel dans les forces de police françaises: Une étude de l'absent et de l'existant au prisme du modèle de police guidée par le renseignement*. Thèse de doctorat. Lausanne: Université de Lausanne.
Gayraud, J. F., and Farcy, F. 2011. *Le renseignement criminel*. Paris: CNRS Éditions.
James, A. 2013. *Examining intelligence-led policing*. London: Palgrave Macmillan.
Jobard, F., and de Maillard, J. 2015. *Sociologie de la police: Politiques, organisations, réformes*. Paris: Armand Colin.
Lemieux, F. 2005. De la police guidée par le renseignement à la complexité des appareils policiers: Les limites de l'usage des renseignements dans la conduite des affaires policières. *Criminologie* 38: 65–89.
Matelly, J. H. 2000. *Gendarmerie et crimes de sang*. Paris: L'Harmattan.
Mazerolle, L., and Darroch, S. 2015. Intelligence-led policing: A comparative analysis of community context influencing innovation uptake. *Policing & Society* 25: 1–24.
Perrot, P., and de Maillard, C. 2018. From a priori to a posteriori approach: A new paradigm (in France) against crime. Pp. 21–36 in P. Carter and J. Johnston (Eds). *Applications in intelligence-led policing: Where theory meets reality*. Richmond, VA: CreateSpace Independent Publishing Platform.
Phillips, J. G., and Carter, S. W. 2015. Intelligence-led policing and forces of organizational changes in the USA. *Policing and Society* 25: 333–357.
Ratcliffe, J. H. 2016. *Intelligence-led policing*. Cullompton: William Publishing.
Ribaux, O. 2005. Le renseignement criminel pour le traitement de la délinquance sérielle dans un système fédéraliste: de l'idée à la mise en oeuvre. In *Actes du colloque international francophone: La police et le citoyen*. Nicolet: Ecole Nationale de Police.
Walden, J. H., and Ratcliffe, J. 2010. State police and the intelligence center: A study of intelligence flow to and from the street. *ALEIA Journal* 19: 1–19.

Chapter 7

Specialization in Criminal Investigations

Elodie Lemaire

The popular image of the French police includes two distinctive organizational traits. One is the specialization of services embodied by prestigious intervention units: the BRI,[1] the RAID,[2] and the BAC[3] ("anti-crime squad"). The second is the differentiation between the work of uniformed police officers (*gardiens de la paix*, or "peace guardians") in emergency interventions, versus that of plainclothes detectives in investigation units. This simplistic view never had any bearing in reality and departs significantly from the actual organization of police work, which has increased in complexity since the early 2000s. The analysis of police headquarters organizations reveals this. Central police stations have become "complex organizations made of directorates, units, divisions, services or brigades" (Jobard and de Maillard 2015, p. 51).[4] If we focus on judiciary services of *Sûreté départementale*, or ("departmental security"), these myths recede even more.[5] Officers (lieutenants, captains, majors) replaced the former inspectors in 1995, and do not lead investigations. Rather, the lead is taken by the *gardiens de la* paix and *gradés* (brigadiers and chief brigadiers) who work in plainclothes because of their specific missions.

In order to understand this evolution and its effect on police headquarters operations, we need to return to the genesis of these transformations in police work in the early 2000s. This era of police history has been poorly documented and is the topic of this chapter. At that point, an overspecialization of judicial policing services occurred, thanks to the proliferation of new, small, felony-specialized brigades. From four brigades dealing with undifferentiated cases in the early 1990s, most of *Sûretés départementales* judicial services were subdivided into a dozen specialized units in 2007 (car thefts, burglaries, phone theft, payment frauds, domestic violence, discrimination, and so on). At the same time, working groups were reorganized, and a stricter separation of functions followed a more pronounced chain of command. *Gradés*, whose number was dwindling, were removed from their private reserve, investigation work, and assigned administrative tasks.[6] They no longer shared office space with subordinates, and the management of the many units was allotted to higher ranked officers who led the investigation with police officers.

Why was this organizational strategy adopted? Broadly speaking, it reflected in part the adoption of "new public management." This movement (which could be seen across the Western world) stressed making public services more business-like and improving government efficiency by using private sector management techniques. In France, new public management met with a massive response during the early 2000s (Bezes 2009). Its methods and recipes inspired the "rationalized management" of public administration, which is essential to understanding this strategy. As much as any other public service, the administration of the police did not escape reform initiatives aiming for greater administrative performance (de Maillard 2009).

"Police accountability triggered by the LOLF ['Organic Law on Finance Acts'] will especially allow force police and *gendarmerie* services to produce a quantified assessment of their actions and results regarding their yearly budget allocation" (Ocqueteau 2005, p. 65). A clearer view of the distribution of tasks and functions thus is to produce increased control of everyday police work and agency outputs. What effects does a greater division of work have on professional practices? The question also arises because several tenets of the sociology of police work are challenged by this reform. In a context of "managerial division of work," is "discretion" for instance, still a "fundamental characteristic of police work?" (Monjardet 1985, p. 392) The paradigm of police culture (Gorgeon 1996; Boussard et al. 2006; Mouhanna 2011), which characterizes shared representations of police personnel regarding work definition and task distribution, is also called into question. What are the consequences for shared professional norms and collaborations between different services now that they are to perform distinct duties?

This chapter relies on materials gathered as a part of doctoral research in a *Sûreté départementale* (departmental security, a judicial police unit part of a Departmental Directorate of Public Security), located in a medium-sized French town of the provinces with a population of 134,000 inhabitants. The two-year ethnographic survey (2006–2007) included participant observations. Some 50 police officers of all ranks were interviewed, various institutional documents such as organization charts were collected, plus I retraced the career paths of a cohort of 147 police personnel. In order to confirm the trends observed in 2007, I regularly came back to the field (in 2010, 2012, and 2014), and I also carried out observations in precincts where officers I had interviewed earlier had been transferred.

In order to understand what is at stake in this police initiative toward specialization, we will examine two aspects of the matter. First, there appear to be three factors contributing to the weakening of police organization: the political orientations driving security; the *commissaires*' work reorganizations which adapt reforms in the field by creating specialized units; and the parallel effects of status reform, which transform and interfere with organizational changes. Then, we will show how the greater division of work is not to be reduced to a new work distribution, as it is from now on be driven by quantified performance targets.

The very structure of the organization was called into question in the early 2000s. Indeed, on the hierarchical axis, there has been a progressive change of social relationships between the services, as well as a reconfiguration of the forms of power within the institutions. Officers' ability to select and execute tasks as they wish has been reduced, while at the top of the hierarchy, the power to define and control operational practices has strengthened. Meanwhile, the horizontal division of work has been made more flexible through a process of professional specialization initiated by *commissaires*. But this, in turn, has shaken the implicit hierarchies of prestige within the police station. Contrary to what was expected by front-line police officers, this did not help in their quest for upward professional mobility.

The Organization and Evolution of Police Work

Organization charts provide useful data on trends in administrative organization in the early 2000s. However, they do not disclose the logic behind their reformulation but sources make it possible to shed light on the rationale behind the changing nature of police work. First, the study of the national corps and careers reform (1995 and 2004) and of the public security policies (community-based policing and the "repressive turning point") explain the changes in the hierarchical redistribution of labor and organization of judicial activities in policing. Also my own interviews with police personnel working in precincts in the late 1990s allow us to measure the reach of these reforms and impact of organizational decisions taken by *commissaires*.

Up until the 1990s, the organization of the police station that we studied featured a division between street policing and judicial work in two distinct services: a General Security Service and the Urban Safety Service. The first service was comprised of uniformed personnel (*officiers de paix*, or "peace officers"), *gardiens de la paix* ("peace guardians"), and the officer corps. It also included street crime units as well as an anti-crime squad. The second service included plainclothed officers (inspectors and investigators corps) in charge of judicial investigations. The latter did not merely execute orders or mechanically apply rules. Rather, they implemented an informal selection process in choosing their tasks. Senior officers provided their wisdom. As long as the number of cases for them to work (complaints, events, missions) surpassed the capacity of their personnel to handle them, they enjoyed some leeway in defining their tasks and organizing their work. Barbara Jankowski's research (1996) on plainclothed officers in 1994 confirms this. Inspectors had great autonomy as the hierarchy above them was in fact distant. They were free to record, triage, and file complaints or not, as long as they processed a steady flow of cases. The freedom offered to plainclothed officers existed to a lesser extent among their uniformed counterparts, to the extent that Dominique Monjardet defined the "selection principle" as a fundamental property of police work (Monjardet 1996). Their superiors' role was then reversed. They mainly justified decisions taken by subordinates. Indeed, management was widely dependent on the choices and initiatives taken by their subordinates and granted them great leeway in doing so.

In 1995, the first reform of the corps and the careers of officers changed the functions and distribution of tasks of various categories of officers. Introduced to improve police coordination and efficiency, the reform removed the distinction between uniformed and plainclothed corps, and divided officers into three corps (against five earlier[7]). These were the Control and Enforcement Corps (*gardiens de la paix*, chief-brigadier, brigadier-major), the Command and Supervision corps (lieutenant, captain, major), and the Planning and Management corps (*commissaire*, chief commissioner,[8] divisional commissioner). The goal was to separate management from operations. Although the corps reform deeply shook the police, it induced tighter relationships between subordinates and their superiors, as the work process remained cooperative. For instance, in judicial services, officers conducted inquiries with brigadiers and a few rare *gardiens de la paix* – with whom they also shared tricks of the trade. Superiors' professional authority still relied on a shared vision of what should be "real investigative work" and did not interfere with professional self-regulation.

Yet, the changes introduced in 1997, and even more in the early 2000s, created a more vertical hierarchy. The creation of community-based police units, described by the Lionel Jospin government as a social policy geared towards the destitute, led senior police leaders to urge their subordinates to prioritize small-time and medium-scale urban criminality (Proteau 2007). On July 10, 2002, the Framework Act on Internal Security (LOPSI 2002) was introduced by the minister of the interior, Nicolas Sarkozy, and marked a repressive turning point. The policy was followed by a reform of the corps' architecture,[9] which was supposed to improve police operational effectiveness. Even more clearly than the 1995 reform, the new corps and careers reform separated the functions and responsibilities of each corps, and ushered the norms of new public management into policing:

> The clarification of role and place of each corps will improve the Police efficiency through the development of its managerial competence at every level for the purpose of objectives-based management and result-oriented culture. Indeed, modern and dynamic management in public services requires everyone to optimize results in accordance with the resources allocated.[10]

Practically, the planning and management corps (*commissaires*) were tasked by the minister of the interior with increasing the planning, measurement, and control of police activity. The implementation of this policy was facilitated by the adoption of new indicators measuring activity, such as the number of arrests, custodies, offenses, and the clearance rate or the number of misdemeanors uncovered by the services (Ocqueteau 2007; Didier 2011).

The command corps (officers), in agreement with the *commissaires*, gave quantified performance targets to specialist brigades under their command, and later checked to see if their targets were actually reached. The relationships with the control and enforcement corps (*gardiens de la paix* and *gradés*) were thus less and less based on a "process of voluntary cooperation" (Thoenig 1994, p. 372). While they had a monopoly on investigations until 1995 (and were actively involved up until the late 1990s), they seldom stepped in. The redistribution of functions and responsibilities among the different police corps and the numbers of personnel meant that this time the police chiefs were able to change the organization of judicial work. In the middle of the first decade of this century, the Investigations and Research Service was renamed *Sûreté départementale* (departmental security) and divided into specialized brigades. This reorientation of judicial activities changed the job descriptions of line officers who, in 1994, had prioritized what they perceived to be more serious matters.

Although effecting the division of work is well within the intent of police administration reforms, the creation of specialized units is, however, the result of *commissaires* initiatives, as they have more leeway to organize their departments since the early 2000s.[11]

Commissaires at the Helm

Since 2004, the corps and career reforms formally defined *commissaires*' functions. They replaced "service heads" with "managers" (Ocqueteau 2006). Indeed, the planning and management corps is now tasked with "designing and implementing programs and projects related to the fight against crime," and encouraged to "develop its managerial competence for the purpose of objectives-based management in order to optimize results in accordance with the resources allocated."[12] Those committed to these transformations strive to create new specialized judicial units (Lemaire 2016a). How do they profit from it?

First, for *commissaires*, these "organizational innovations" were an opportunity to distinguish themselves from their competitors for higher positions, and from senior leaders who, according to *commissaires*, "do not try to prove they're able to adapt." Innovations can also promise more control over officers (Ocqueteau and Damien 2009). By being the sole driving force behind reform proposals, and by constraining officers to abide by their instructions and implement their policies, *commissaires* attempt to establish and maintain the legitimacy of their positions and to protect their associated benefits. To avoid being viewed as servile to the *commissaires*, or as "teacher's pet,"[13] some officers, such as Major Guillaume P., attempted to resist. He claimed to have fought for the recognition of his power over work organization in the service, once he became the assistant to a newly arrived *commissaire* of the local security service, "Mohamed R.":

> With Mohamed R., it was a bossy, uncompromising, unchallenged command office. I fought for crumbs of authority, and bit by bit, I managed to

obtain some autonomy. I didn't allot cases, but I supported, or I advised. Now he revokes any bit of autonomy the major had. Sometimes it's better to be active, to demand, to show we exist. If he has timid people under him, he will eat them up. To him, he's here, he's competent, and mid-management is useless.

("Guillaume P." a major, assistant to the *commissaire*,
Sûreté départementale in 2007, 42 years old)

However, the evolution of the *commissaires*' role is not enough to explain this organizational choice. The creation of new specialized units caters to the career strategies of *commissaires*, who convey their willingness to adapt to their oversight authorities by acting as a mouthpiece for public security-policy orientations, as is the case of "Dominique S.," a *commissaire* of the *Sûreté départementale*. During a speech at the Paris police prefecture on August 20, 2002, Minister of the Interior Nicolas Sarkozy indicated, "In particular, I intend to put a stop to the development of new types of criminal activity that are emerging, such as car, cell phones, or credit card theft." In 2005, Dominique S. adapted his service to these politics-led crime priorities by creating a brigade for reducing automobile-related offenses, especially car thefts; a robberies group specializing in tackling the theft of mobile phones; and, in 2007, a payment-methods fraud group that combated thefts of bank cards and checks.

Ultimately, the analysis of *commissaires*' organizational decisions cannot ignore the management priority to obtain quick results. Yet, these orders gathered approval from a number of *commissaires*. "You need to see the new units we created. I am very proud of them. These are specialized services bringing in very good numbers," as stated by the *Sûreté départementale commissaire* whose eagerness to relay managerial imperatives related or depended directly on his belief in the effectiveness of their strategy. This belief eventually turned into reality as clearance rates increased significantly a few months after the specialized units' creation.

Although the *commissaires*' motivations are decisive in understanding the forces at work behind changes in the horizontal division of police work, some officers have a special interest in the creation of new units, as the specialization of judicial activities creates new sources of recognition inside the institution.

New Prospects for Intra-organizational Mobility

In the mid-2000s, the corps and career reform and the continued subdivision of judicial services reconfigured the career path possibilities for officers. How does the new division of labor create career opportunities? Do police personnel eventually achieve their sought-after positions?

Up until the mid-1990s, horizontal advancement (between services) and vertical advancement (up their own hierarchy) were regulated. On the one hand, a *gardien de la paix* or a *gradés* willing to work in an investigation service would have had to change corps to join the police investigators corps. On the other hand, moving up toward a superior rank among a professional corps depended upon stringent rules of advancement (seniority and level of qualification). Since 1995 and the first reform of career advancement possibilities, the requirements for horizontal advancement were softened. For instance, *gardiens de la paix* are not limited to the uniformed street-crime assignments anymore. They can now change positions. They can, for example, work for an investigative service without having to change corps, unlike before 1995. However, the more limited number of sub-offices in the commissariat's services still restricts internal mobility. Furthermore, for a *gardien de la paix* to join a prestigious unit of the *Sûreté départementale* (such as any service with investigation prerogatives), they still require the rank of brigadier and/or the title of OPJ (officer of judiciary police),[14] as well as a stint at the *Service du Quart*.[15] Thus, the acquisition of skills and/or rank allows for accrued horizontal career opportunities and increases the chances of joining a prestigious service.

However, as the commissariat divided and specialized its activities, horizontal mobility increases the probability of joining a judicial service (whose access was once limited to *gradés* and officers).[16] Yet, unit specialization confers a symbolic benefit to those in charge. Specialized units are valued more in the institution because they allow officers to distinguish themselves from mere generalists. Simultaneously, the leeway gained by *commissaires* – thanks to the creation of "new" positions and their distribution – allows them to deal with the effects of the latest corps and career reforms on police personnel headcount and aspirations. When they create new specialties, *commissaires* indeed both widen the services area of expertise and deal with staff reductions. *Gardiens de la paix* redeployment is based on units rather than numbers of officers, and two officers are enough to create a specialized judicial brigade. In the early 2000s, a minimum of five was necessary for the same classification. The multiplication of specialized services thus constitutes a full-blown feature of personnel management. *Commissaires* now have a larger board at their disposal on which they can position their personnel. They also use the specialized units to deal with new ambitions among *gardiens de la paix* and *gradés*. Indeed, the former have more education credentials (Coulangeon et al. 2003) and are more skilled regarding judicial and procedural matters. Nonetheless, a stint in specialized units has become a one of the conditions for a *gardien de la paix* to be assigned to the commissariat's most sought-after units. The latter, whose headcount is rising, are placed at the head of small specialized units. Thus, *commissaires* turn the constraint of posting for *gradés* (who wish to join more valued investigation units) into an opportunity for command. Some *gradés* are thus retained in the units dealing with petty crimes, hoping to join more prestigious units later.

Three Sources of Police Unease

Is specialization a good strategy? Participant observation of day-to-day police work enables us to see its most salient effects. The reconcentration of (managerial) control tools in the hands of leadership, along with the standardization of practices, and fragmentation through specialization, led to reduced autonomy for police personnel. A professional bureaucracy leaving some leeway to its subordinates was soon replaced by a more classical hierarchical organization resting on the leadership's ability to define, impose, and control their subordinates' goals. The consequence was a greater organizational distance between leadership and subordinates. Moreover, strong specialization increased internal rivalries, competition, and differentiation, aggravating the vertical corridors (or silos) that plague police administration. Finally, in an over-specialized environment, the significance of career advancement becomes murky and eventually results in "*malaise de position*" (Bourdieu 1993).

Reorganization of the Hierarchy of Police Work

Until the early 2000s, the autonomy of police personnel rested on their ability to delineate and chose their tasks, as the essence of police activity was about "emergency processing of events characterized by uniqueness and unpredictability" (Monjardet 1994, p. 394). However, after 2006, their tasks became more and more prescribed. While investigators used to have leeway in processing, triaging, and filing complaints (or not), now *commissaires* select complaints themselves and divide them among judicial units under their command.[17] Moreover, the processing of allotted complaints is more tightly controlled. *Commissaires* and officers also follow up and inquire about investigation progress and expect results the same day or the day after. Unit specialization also weakens the leeway police personnel had regarding the choice of assignments they wish to complete. They are now exclusively restricted to the types of cases related to their unit's specialty: car theft, phone theft, burglaries, and the like. To put it differently, they can no longer avoid cases they are entrusted with in favor of nobler ones (such as armed robberies), which was possible in the previous regime.

That being said, police officers still have some leeway in how they do their day-to-day work. Indeed, they try to contend with oversight by using slowdown strategies, or "voluntary reduction of productivity strategies" (Purenne and Aust 2010, p. 19). However, they do not always have the same ability to do so. Moreover, their interest in circumventing these constraints decreases as working conditions and rules of rewards and sanction change. Indeed, personnel shortages and real-time case processing[18] dissuade police officers from personal initiative and urge them to ignore events that could hinder their ability to reach target goals – although these events can still be used as an excuse to reduce their workload. Favoring easy cases that can be dealt with quickly is now more beneficial, because more complex cases involving police technical work and generally require long-term involvement. Formerly valued know-how (such as how to conduct surveillance, working undercover, gathering neighborhood information, and working informants) is downgraded as command's conception of "efficient" police work demands other priorities. What matters now is closing cases, plus avoiding any breach of the law or procedure. This has become a route to being recognized as a true professional and to advance in the organization. The counterpart to new possible rewards is the sanctioning of police officers failing to meet performance requirements. *Commissaires* transfer those who do not comply with their expectations.

The greater proceduralism of police work is also enabled by turnover within the corps. *Gardiens de la paix* and *gradés* joining new judicial units and lacking the necessary skills to be perceived as true investigators can have a vested interest in overlooking aspects of an order that does not benefit them. To assert themselves in the face of more senior officers (who more often are reluctant to produce the required numbers), newcomers value the mastery of the process and the ability to swiftly reach the target goals assigned to them. Indeed, young *gardiens de la paix* are concerned with producing thorough, straightforward, well written, and legally flawless procedures. They would rather deal with smaller-scale cases requiring less investigative work and whose resolve is certain, especially as performance is measured according to the number of records and arrests are made, as well as their ability to deal swiftly with complaints. Furthermore, this growing bureaucratic formalism tends to correspond to the newcomers' social and cultural properties and their higher levels of qualification.

The Loss of Solidarity Within Organizations

The transformations of police work organization had significant effects on the relationships between police officers from upper and lower ranks, as well as on the way skill transfer occurs in commissariats. Officers of judiciary police (OPJ) now confer with *commissaires* to promote procedures to produce swift quantifiable results at the expense of more complicated cases. At first, this arouses suspicion and disbelief among more senior officers, whose day-to-day work now requires them to implement orders conflicting with their vision of the investigator's work. Indeed, officers trying to preserve earlier definitions of "good cases" feel like their superiors have ceased to value the honor and prestige that they used to have. They suspect they can no longer rely on officers to defend or promote their professional interests with *commissaires*. Observations of backstage activity reveal active tension within police organizations. During an informal gathering, older officers avoid their colleagues and command, and remain among themselves, while newcomers enjoy chatting in the *commissaire*. Newcomers and their superiors share similar views on work, and younger officers have committed to the production of quick results. Others do not view this kindly:

The major is a nice guy, but he is bad. He doesn't know the first thing about investigations. What strikes me is that officers aren't even able to follow due process or to operate in the field anymore. They're bogus and useless.
    (Stéphane, *gardien de la paix*, 31-year-old, street crime service, 2007)

Why so much resentment? Earlier, the valuing of officers' investigation skills enabled them to subordinate young *gardiens de la paix* and *gradés*. However, the newcomers' rising levels of educational qualifications and their new judicial and procedural skills undermine the chain of command's legitimacy. Bosses whose authority and know-how were once recognized are now treated as "incompetent suits" whose role is limited to controlling *gardiens*' performance. These tensions flare up as officers' roles in training and skill transfer decrease. In the commissariat's judicial services, and up until the 2000s, officers held a crucial role in training *gardiens de la paix* and *gradés*. Not only did they pass on their know-how, but they also shared professional norms (for example, in closing good cases and gathering evidence in the field). Many police officers claim to have been trained on the job by officers from investigative units at the end of the 1990s:

When I left the "outfit" and arrived in the judiciary, the officers taught me everything. How to conduct an interrogation, knowing to listen to people, how to adapt to the profile of the people you're facing, and how to find a weak spot. I was a go-getter, and officers were here to dampen, let things be when needed because sometimes you need to know when to stop and calm things down, especially when they are moving too fast. You need substantive elements to arrest someone or check on them. If it's about doing a check before they break a car, maybe it's best to wait, you need to observe, observe, and when you're out the academy, you lack hindsight. The officers had that.
    (Julien, 45-year-old, chief brigadier, street crime service, 2010)

Ever since officers were relieved of investigative work and assigned to subordinate work, members of the command and supervision corps (chief brigadier or former *gardiens de la paix*) now pass on the skills necessary to work as investigators. The reconfiguration of skill transfer fractures professional solidarities between the enforcement corps (*gradés* and *gardiens de la paix*) and the supervision corps (*officers*). Distrust is the basis of *gardiens de la paix* and brigadier behavior toward their hierarchic superiors, as well as the basis of the discourse they use with outsiders. For instance, *gardiens de la paix* avoid meeting their superiors in the hallways and prefer to work behind closed doors to escape surveillance. Some even question their authority in front of others, by rolling their eyes once their superiors leave the room. This highlights that not only has police unity decreased, but also that the authority of supervisors has been eroded.

Thus, the redistribution of functions changes "solidarity modes" (Durkheim 2004) inside the commissariat. A short while ago, working officers were the ones to train newly promoted *gardiens de la paix* in investigative services. Newer staff could seek advice, help, and support from them. Now, officers appear to be a simple agent of management requirements. The basis of professional representation and cohesion is at stake. All the more crucial is the fact that this institution actually functions thanks to information exchange and informal cooperation.

Change as a Fool's Bargain

The reconfiguration of the police hierarchy agreed, for a while, with subordinates' perceived professional interests. But soon, they understood it as a fool's bargain (Lemaire 2016b). At the end of the 1990s, the hierarchy of positions (and with it, opportunities for promotion) was clear. Staff were categorized and honored on a subtle prestige scale reflecting their type of assignment and client base. In the early 2000s, a break-up of the judicial service into special divisions strengthened horizontal mobility, but at the same time it blurred the reference points that previously marked a stable internal scale of prestige (Proteau and Pruvost 2008). Working officers could no longer define their position by referring to an informal but widely recognized prestige scale. As *commissaires* created specialization after specialization, some officers were continuously on the move, and did not feel like these moves were helping them rise in police hierarchy. Their career paths were diagonal rather than upwards. Compare this to climbing a flight of stairs. The commissariat structural transformations reduced the height of the steps, which made them easier to climb, but now they are more numerous. *Commissaires* added small steps to the stairs by creating new units that slow down officers' advancement. When mobility offers an opportunity to rest after a demanding posting, professional stakes quickly take over the advantages this diagonal move would have brought.

In addition, one goal of this new organization of police work is to combine specialization with flexibility. The fragmentation and specialization of the commissariat's many small units does not make for a stable organizational design. Units are not permanently established; their continuation is subject to several threats. The first threat is to their efficiency. The *in flagrante* unit, born in 2003, was disbanded in 2005 for lack of significant results. The transfer of the *commissaire* responsible for the unit creation is a second risk. In that case, the successor generally seeks to leave a mark in the commissariat by shutting down his predecessor's units. The configuration of positions became too shaky for police officers to be able to assess a position's value and to fit into it. They must contend with the unpredictability of another organizational change, which threatens their position. Thus, there is a permanent mismatch between a police officer's expectation of a new posting and what they encounter when they hold the position. Meanwhile, the advent of a new unit shakes up symbolic hierarchy, as todays newly promoted can be tomorrow's downgraded. The institution's timeframe, within which police officers operate, is indeed crucial to assess their advancement. Long-term structures used to provide a frame within which career paths could respond to the needs of a steady, predictable organization. Since the mid-2000s, a shorter timeframe is in place, and while it does not restrict mobility anymore, it does create confusion around career path meanings and orientation.

Finally, the corps and career reform measures increased *gardiens de la paix* opportunities for advancement. However, the growing number of contenders (especially through promotion) creates a relative devaluation of status, the same way a growing number of holders of a specific diploma diminishes its value (Bourdieu 1978). Furthermore, some *gradés* think they could objectively expect better positions, considering their level of formal education. They are indeed subjected to an arbitrary distribution by *commissaires*, who can keep them in units devoted to minor offenses with the prospect of later joining higher-scope units. As a consequence, newly promoted police officers at a new rank feel downgraded as their career path does not take them to more valued postings. This mismatch between, on the one hand, expectations aroused by new units and the opportunities they actually offer, and, on the other hand, the symbolic profit associated with a move up the ranks and its actual benefits produces discontent and frustration – in the most trivial sense of the words – as well as a more fundamental *"malaise de position."*

Conclusion

English-language research analyzing police organizational change points to an increasing specialization within organizations (Maguire 1997; Skogan and Frydl 2004), despite the difficulties in measuring the phenomena (Maguire et al. 2003). Comments on the rising number of specialized police units generally focus on the strengths and weaknesses of specialization, as well as efficiency, control, and liability issues raised by over-specialization (Gaines and Worrall 2012). For instance, specialized units can be associated with certain areas associated with corruption (Skogan and Frydl 2004). Other research reveals the logic behind specialization. This includes police management's belief in the effectiveness of this strategy as an answer to political demands, as shown by Skogan and Frydl, or to external pressure from politicians. Far from being a response to local crime, these organizational changes can be regarded as ceremonial (Crank and Langworthy 1992), in line with institutionalist sociology research. Katz' research on the creation of an anti-gang unit attests to this point. He notes,

> the gang unit was created as a consequence of pressures placed on the police department from various powerful elements within the community, and that once created, the gang unit's response to the community's

gang problem was largely driven by its need to achieve and maintain legitimacy among various sovereigns in their environment.

(Katz 2001, p. 65)

In France, the specialization dynamic at work in police headquarters in the early 2000s cannot be reduced to a simple cosmetic change. Its practical effects are stronger than suggested in institutionalist literature, and its causes, sometimes similar to those observed in the Anglo-Saxon world, are not limited to it; they also result from mid-level management initiatives. Above all, this specialization process exposes new stakes. The efficiency norms of the new public management movement have proven to have insidious effects on the division of police work, by increasing work specialization among units.

What assessment can be made from this organizational strategy? The effects of specialization are mixed. The commissariat's previous configuration (*ante* neo-management) was marked by the strong autonomy of agents and limited work specialization. The selection of cases to be worked tended to set aside those deemed too easy, due to lack of interest from investigators. As a result, some misdemeanors were underrepresented in official records. A relevant example: domestic violence used to be cast into the "unsorted" files by the judicial research brigade (*brigade de recherche judiciaire*). These cases aroused little interest from police officers, who considered them as less significant than other crimes. Domestic violence cases did not even require complex investigations, as the offender's name was often included in the complaint! There was no prestige to be gained with no mystery to be solved. Since the beginnings of the 2000s, unit specialization, along with a tendency towards hierarchic re-inversion of work, reduced police officers' leeway and, simultaneously, improved the processing of domestic violence cases. However, indicator-based management lead to the shelving of more complex cases with an unpredictable route to resolution. Consequently, the content of police work in investigation services was transformed significantly. It now focuses on simple tasks whose results are predictable; this has led to the dwindling of traditional investigative fieldwork.

According to the professionals, changes in the organization of police work have created some unprecedented career mobility. The stairs to be climbed were many but less steep, and some benefited from that. However, organizational target-setting (that is, the assessment of activities according to quantified objectives set by the command) has caused much disappointment. Joining small specialized judicial units "close to the *commissaire's* minions"[19] is not always attractive, and officers who are part of these units may withdraw in favor of devoting more energy to their family or social life – their place in the organization having been downgraded or their chances of advancement seeming uncertain, an ability to go home at a fixed time and have free weekends can appear more appealing. Yet, some specialization continues to be seen as positive and signaling a valued mission on what remains of the internal prestige scale. Stable work, collective effort, investigator autonomy, and the continued use of traditional policing skills remain attractive. Thus, when I returned to the commissariat some five years after my first research there, police officers posted to vice and narcotics squads had become defenders of the old values of investigation work that the new police efficiency does not seem to have dethroned (de Maillard and Savage 2017). For a period, they were performance-measurement enthusiasts who focused on swiftly solving small cases during their posting in devalued and often reorganized units. However, since the mid-2010s their organization charts have grown more stable. The commissariats still determine the tasks to be accomplished by specialized judicial brigades saddled with minor offenses, but quantifiable objectives are less and less associated with the brutal reorganization of work. They are now much more integrated into day-to-day policing. They have created new methods for distinguishing between peers, and they are in the fight over the legitimate definition of proper police work.

Notes

1 Research and Intervention Brigade (Brigade de recherche et d'intervention) commonly known as anti-gang brigade.
2 Research, Assistance, Intervention, Deterrence (Recherche, assistance, intervention, dissuasion) is an elite unit of the *police nationale*.
3 Anti-crime squad (*brigade anti-criminalité*).
4 In France, police headquarters (or central commissariat) is led by a divisional commissioner and also serves as a Departmental Directorate for Public Safety (Direction départementale de sécurité publique). Central commissariat notably includes a *Sûreté départementale* service in charge of investigations. This judicial investigative service differs from local commissariats (which can deal with "small" judicial investigations), as well as from the judicial police, which only deals with greater criminal offenses.
5 In *Sûretés départementales*, plainclothed personnel conduct inquiries regarding minor offenses as well as crimes. Units can be specialized in narcotics, burglaries, or street criminality.
6 Since 2004, French police have been structured into three police forces or corps: the planning and management corps (*commissaires* in charge of commissariats), the command and supervision corps (officers which constitute mid-level management), and the control and enforcement corps (*gradés*, small team chiefs, *gardiens de la paix* executing orders).
7 *Commissaires, officiers de paix* (peace officers), *gardiens de la paix* (peace guardians), inspectors and investigators.
8 This rank is no longer awarded.
9 See the statement made in Saint-Cyr-au-Mont-d'Or on June 24, 2003 by Nicolas Sarkozy, then interior minister, on the missions and competences of police *commissaires* and on the proposed reform of the architecture of the national police's different corps, available at www.discours.vie-publique.fr.
10 *On the corps and careers reform*, Memorandum, June 2004: 4
11 Since the beginning of the 2010s, *commissaires* leeway regarding local innovations (creation of specialized units) has been greatly reduced; they now must comply with Central Directorate instructions.

12 *On the corps and careers reform*, Memorandum, June 2004: 1
13 Phrasing used during interviews by *gardiens de la paix* and *gradés*.
14 In November 1998, a law defended by É. Guigou (then Ministry of Justice) granted members of the control and enforcement corps (*gardiens de la paix* and *gradés*) the ability to obtain the OPJ certification (under conditions including a successful training), while not being ranked (nor paid) as officers. The OPJ certification allows the ability to lead an investigation, to order identity checks, or to take people into custody (*garde à vue*).
15 Phrasing used during interviews by *gardiens de la paix* and *gradés*.
16 In 1999, the *Sûreté départementale* included ten *gardiens de la paix*. The creation of new specialized units allowed for 23 *gardiens de la paix* to access postings previously restricted to officers and *gradés*.
17 This practice might be a local specificity, as, generally, only "significant crime" cases attract the *commissaires*' attention.
18 The goal of real-time processing is to follow up on every file with a swift response. Practically, the public prosecutor is notified of every minor offense (by phone or by email) in order to shorten the decision-making time on prosecution, and to diversify judicial responses.
19 The phrasing comes from police officers posted in small specialized judicial units of the *Sûreté départementale*.

References

Bezes, P. 2009. *Réinventer l'État: Les réformes de l'administration française (1962–2008)*. Paris: Presses universitaires de France.

Bourdieu, P. 1978. Classement, déclassement, reclassement. *Actes de la recherche en sciences sociales* 24: 2–22.

Bourdieu, P. 1993. *La misère du monde*. Paris: Seuil.

Boussard, V., Loriol, M., and Caroly, S. 2006. Catégorisation des usagers et rhétorique professionnelle. Le cas des policiers sur la voie publique. *Droit et société* 48: 161–175.

Coulangeon, P., Pruvost, G., and Roharik, I. 2003. *1982-2003: enquête sociodémographique sur les conditions de vie et d'emploi de 5221 policiers*. Paris: INHES.

Crank, J. P., and Langworthy, R. 1992. An institutional perspective of policing. *The Journal of Criminal Law and Criminology* 83: 338–363.

de Maillard, J. 2009. Réforme des polices dans les pays occidentaux: Une perspective comparée. *Revue française de science politique* 59: 1197–1230.

de Maillard, J., and Savage, S. 2017. Les détectives dans la cage de fer néo-managériale? Une analyse de deux polices britanniques. *Sociologie du travail* 59 (en ligne).

Didier, E. 2011. Compstat à Paris: initiative et mise en responsabilité policière. *Champ pénal/Penal field* VIII (en ligne).

Durkheim, E. 2004. *De la division du travail social*. Paris: Presses universitaires de France.

Gaines, L. K., and Worrall, J.L. 2012. *Police administration* (3rd ed.). New York: McGraw-Hill.

Gorgeon, C. 1996. Socialisation professionnelle des policiers: le rôle de l'école. *Criminologie* 29: 141–163.

Jankowski, B. 1996. Les inspecteurs de police: contraintes organisationnelles et identité professionnelle. *Déviance et Société* 20: 17–36.

Jobard, F., and de Maillard, J. 2015. *Sociologie de la police. Politiques, organisations, réformes*. Paris: Armand Colin.

Katz, C. 2001. The establishment of a police gang unit: An examination of organizational and environmental factors. *Criminology* 39: 37–73.

Lemaire, E. 2016a. Les usages de la spécialisation dans la police: Les formes discrètes du management public policier. *Revue française de science politique* 66: 461–482.

Lemaire, E. 2016b. *Réforme des corps et carrières et illusion promotionnelle dans la police [Outiller les parcours professionnels. Quand les dispositifs publics se mettent en action].* Lausanne: Peter Lang: 127–142.

Maguire, E. R. 1997. Structural change in large municipal police organizations during the community policing era. *Justice Quarterly* 14: 701–730.

Maguire, E. R., Shin, Y., Zhao, J., and Hassell, K. 2003. Structural change in large police agencies during the 1990s. *Policing, An International Journal of Police Strategies and Management* 26: 251–275.

Monjardet, D. 1985. À la recherche du travail policier. *Sociologie du travail* 27: 391–407.

Monjardet, D. 1994. La culture professionnelle des policiers. *Revue française de sociologie* 35: 393–411.

Monjardet, D. 1996. *Ce que fait la police. Sociologie de la force publique.* Paris: La Découverte.

Mouhanna, C. 2011. *La police contre les citoyens.* Nîmes: Champ social.

Ocqueteau, F. 2005. Mutations sociales et transformations des contrôles policiers: Efficacité, résultat, performance. *Informations sociales* 126: 58–67.

Ocqueteau, F. 2006. *Mais qui donc dirige la police ? Sociologie des commissaires.* Paris : Armand Colin.

Ocqueteau, F. 2007. Les indicateurs de performance en sécurité publique. *Nouveaux regards* 39: 26–31.

Ocqueteau, F., and Damien, O. 2009. À propos de l'encadrement de la police nationale par les commissaires: Regards croisés entre un sociologue et un commissaire syndicaliste. *Champ pénal/Penalfield* V (en ligne).

Proteau, L. 2007. Vision doctrinale et divisions pratiques: de quelques contradictions structurelles entre proximité et police. *Journal des anthropologues* 108–109: 249–277.

Proteau, L., and Pruvost, G. 2008. Se distinguer dans les métiers d'ordre. *Sociétés contemporaines* 72: 7–14.

Purenne, A., and Aust, J. 2010. Piloter la police par les indicateurs? *Déviance et Société* 34: 7–28.

Skogan, W. G., and Frydl, K. 2004. *Fairness and effectiveness in policing. The evidence.* Washington: The National Academies Press.

Thoenig, J. C. 1994. La gestion systémique de la sécurité publique. *Revue française de sociologie* 35: 357–392.

Chapter 8

Oversight of the French Police

Cédric Moreau de Bellaing[1]

Questions about the oversight of police activity are as old as debates on the scope and nature of the mandate of the institution of the police. Thus, during the French Revolution, legislative discussions on the nature and remit of law enforcement kept stumbling over an inextricable issue: what control mechanisms could be implemented to prevent the police's mission, at the crossroads of law and facts, from becoming a source of authority autonomous from the state (Napoli 2003a)? In other words, what forms of oversight should be imposed on law enforcement to ensure that it does not become excessively autonomous? In a way, the dilemma faced by the revolutionaries was like that which arises today in public controversies, whenever people struggle to obtain the recognition of unlawful acts of violence committed by the police. Can police activity be subject to oversight, particularly legal oversight, or does it, by definition, escape monitoring, thus constituting itself as its own measure (Napoli 2003b)?

This chapter will examine this dilemma on an empirical basis and suggest a sociological interpretation of its various aspects. I provide an overview of the many forms of oversight of police activity that currently exist in France, and then discuss their respective strengths and weaknesses. I will show that, as the French revolutionaries feared, the oversight of police activity is hardly effective. Out of all possible forms of police misconduct, this chapter will delve into cases of unlawful violence in particular. I will show that in France police activity is primarily monitored through professional standards. However, this form of oversight is ambivalent. It is deeply entrenched, for it is constitutive of the professional identity of the police, but it is also likely to fail when professional standards are put to the test, as has been the case in France in recent years.

The Role of Parliamentary Oversight

As in most representative democracies, police activity in France is functionally subject to parliamentary oversight. This can take the form of parliamentary debates when a bill is introduced and of committees of inquiry (though this is rarer).[2] Parliamentary committees of inquiry are created by elected representatives and have broader prerogatives, especially regarding holding hearings. Nevertheless, the recommendations put forward in their reports are not binding, as the committees of inquiry have no power of enforcement. These committees can be set up routinely or as a result of special events. Paradoxically, their reports offer an assessment – at least partially critical – of the situation of law enforcement as well as proposals aimed at addressing the shortcomings and problems encountered. But at the same time, they also echo the demands of the heads of the institutions concerned, who use committees of inquiry to express their certainties, their doubts, and their own criticisms. For instance, this is the case of both the report issued by the recent parliamentary committee of inquiry on "the unease of the domestic security forces" (Senate 2018) and the report on "the situation, the missions, and the resources of the security forces, be it the national police, the *gendarmerie*, or the municipal police" issued on July 9, 2019 (National Assembly 2019).

However, when committees of inquiry are set up as a result of police actions deemed to be very serious, the public expects from them particularly strong oversight efforts. Since the beginning of the Fifth Republic, only three committees of inquiry have been launched under these circumstances. In all three cases, they were set up after deaths were directly caused by police or *gendarmerie* activity during social movements. The first two committees, one in the National Assembly, the other in the Senate, were formed in 1986. This followed the death of Malik Oussekine, who had been killed by two police officers from a brigade known as the *Voltigeurs*, and, more generally speaking, following numerous police abuses committed during demonstrations against the Devaquet Law (Senate 1987). The third parliamentary committee of inquiry was set up following the 2014 death of Rémi Fraisse, an environmental activist killed by an offensive grenade thrown by a *gendarme mobile* during night clashes on the sidelines of a protest against the construction of the Sivens dam in south-western France. The proceedings of this committee of inquiry were particularly hectic due to strong disagreements between the rapporteur and the president of the committee – disagreements reflected in the final report (National Assembly 2015). However, no committee of inquiry was set up following the deaths of nine communist activists at the Charonne metro station in February 1962 (Dewerpe 2006) or following the long clashes of May 1968 (Provenzano 2019).

The parliamentary oversight of police activity has thus produced mixed results. Though common and extensive, this oversight is – save in exceptional circumstances – akin to an improved form of audit, at the end of which proposals are formulated. However, only exceptionally does it spark a collective deliberation on the missions and activities of law enforcement agencies. This exceptional nature is evident when one compares this situation with that of Canada, for instance, where the number of parliamentary committees of inquiry (or their counterparts) is much higher, and the character of policing in Canada does not seem to account for this difference. For instance, over the last 40 years, the Canadian federal government has launched no less than 11 public inquiries into law enforcement activities in the province of Quebec alone.

The Role of Judicial Oversight

The judicial arena does not seem to be particularly conductive to monitoring police misconduct either, especially when it comes to police brutality. According to a recent report issued by ACAT (Christian Action for the Abolition of Torture), obtaining a court ruling in favor of the plaintiffs in matters of unlawful violence is akin to running an "obstacle course" (ACAT 2016) from the filing of the complaint to the actual conviction of the police officers involved. Indeed, research highlights the leniency of court rulings on such matters. Thus, in his work on the social and legal conditions conductive to the occurrence of police brutality, Fabien Jobard examines case law and shows that judges let officers assess what amount of "necessary force" they should use during police operations (Jobard 2002). In so doing, court rulings have helped reinforce the primacy of professional standards over basic legal norms, while also making it even more difficult to denounce police violence. According to Fabien Jobard, the consolidation by case law, if not by law, of the social arena marked by situational logic conducive to police brutality makes it possible to discern, within these areas, a highly distinctive form of police sovereignty.

This leniency could mainly be explained by the fact that, since the law remains relatively vague as to the conditions for the exercise of lawful violence (it establishes, in general, that the use of force must be necessary and proportionate), judges consider that police officers are in the best position to assess the amount of force to be used in a given situation. In addition, in preliminary investigations, acts of violence by police officers always become part of a situational dynamic supposed to help understand, if not justify, outbreaks of violence. Therefore, apart from situations of abuse clearly beyond the legal scope of the use of force, police officers are rarely convicted of unlawful violence. These court rulings unquestionably point to an oversight of police activity; but the latter is often criticized for its unilateralism. Nevertheless, the situation is quite different when it comes to facts other than unlawful violence, but data are incomplete on this issue (Maguer 2004). In this respect, however, it may be noted that the Open Society Foundation took legal action against the French state in 2012 for discriminatory identity checks, which resulted in the conviction of the French state by the Paris Court of Appeals – a conviction affirmed by the Court of Cassation on November 9, 2016.

Internal Oversight Mechanisms of the *Police Nationale* and the *Gendarmerie*

In France, an important part of the oversight of police and *gendarmerie* activity rests with the General Inspectorate of the National Police (IGPN) and the General

Inspectorate of the National Gendarmerie (IGGN), respectively. The two inspectorates bear a number of similarities. Both are composed of members of the institutions that they monitor (police officers in the case of the IGPN and *gendarmes* in the case of the IGGN); both carry out audits as well as investigations.[3] Finally, both conduct administrative as well as criminal investigations. However, they differ in the number of cases handled (the IGGN carries out significantly fewer investigations than the IGPN) and in the amount of exposure received (the IGPN is the most well-known and controversial oversight body in France). This asymmetry is also noticeable in public debates and in academic work. Public documents relating to IGGN activity are rare, and research on this inspectorate is lacking.[4]

The IGPN is, however, better known and more studied. This internal oversight division is authorized to carry out administrative investigations (290 in 2018) and criminal investigations (1180 in 2018) (IGPN 2018), which means that the oversight of police activity by the courts is largely dependent on the action of the IGPN. For a few years, the judicial authorities, the heads of the police, and private individuals have been able to refer cases to it on a dematerialized platform supposed to facilitate referral (and, incidentally, to exempt the IGPN from having a complaint department with a physical address). However, the IGPN is not a disciplinary division. Its members are not authorized to impose sanctions; rather, it *proposes* to the General Directorate of the National Police either to close the case, to issue minor sanctions (official warnings and reprimands), or to hold disciplinary hearings (Renaudie 1999). The IGPN is one of the directorates directly answerable to the General Directorate of the National Police (DGPN), and the appointment of its director results from a compromise between the minister of the interior and the director general of the *police nationale*. The IGPN thereby actively embodies a form of internal oversight, whose increasing transparency (encouraged, in particular, by its director, Marie-France Moneger Guyomarc'h, between 2012 and 2019) does not hide the fact that the body reports directly to the minister of the interior, and whose claim to independence is, at best, shaky.[5] Indeed, the IGPN is a police division, whose functioning and organization directly fall under the Ministry of the Interior, as does the career development of its officers.

For many years, the IGPN was not authorized to monitor police activity within the territory of Paris and its neighboring *départements*, which fell within the remit of the General Inspectorate of Services (IGS). While, in 1986, the Ministry of the Interior decreed that the two inspectorates had to come together, both in fact operated largely independently. It was not until a scandal directly involving IGS officers broke out that the final merger of the two inspectorates (and the *de facto* disappearance of the IGS) took place in 2013.

A Case Study in Policing and Political Corruption

In January 2012, the newspaper *Le Monde* published an investigative article reporting that, five years earlier, the IGS had deliberately rigged the preliminary investigation into the possible trafficking of residence permits within the division of the Paris Police Prefecture in charge of issuing such permits. In 2007, five police officers and administrative agents of the Prefecture, including Yannick Blanc, the then director of the General Police, were held in custody, suspended, and, for some, investigated for issuing – unduly and in exchange for payment – residence permits to people not supposed to obtain them. The police officers implicated tried to prove their innocence and had plenty of supporting evidence, but nothing undermined the investigators' conviction of their guilt. Yet charging these two agents was merely the first step of the process. The second step consisted in incriminating the head of their division, Yannick Blanc, for overseeing and authorizing the alleged trafficking. A month later, he was dismissed. Yet, very quickly, the preliminary investigation revealed many inconsistencies – including discrepancies between the statements attributed to the accused and the verbatim minutes of the hearings – pointed out by the judges handling the investigation. In March 2011, the Paris Court of Appeals found all these police officers innocent and questioned "the extent of the procedural means deployed" by the IGS in this investigation. In addition to their being found innocent, the accused obtained the replacement of the initial judge, so that the procedures of the IGS could be investigated. Many irregularities were then identified. These included censored minutes, doctored transcripts of tapped phone calls, and fabricated evidence with a view to incriminating Yannick Blanc. In 2011, the judges finally heard from the IGS director, who had already been working at the internal oversight division at the time of the incident, as third in command in the department. While the IGS director claimed to have been manipulated, the judges soon found out that the whole case was a setup orchestrated by the IGS. It appears that the police officers implicated were the target of these attacks because they were politically close to the Socialist Party and, therefore, visibly distanced themselves from Nicolas Sarkozy's supporters. The court case is still ongoing.

The status of the IGPN as an internal police division is a double-edged sword. According to IGPN officers, it constitutes a unique asset for the conduct of their investigations, as it ensures that they have intimate knowledge of both police procedures and the best ways to conceal wrongdoings. Conversely, they gladly use to their advantage their reputation of being relentless in hearings, which is why they are unanimously hated by a large majority of police officers. The latter view their own institution as a besieged fortress and consider that the investigative activity of IGPN officers undermines group solidarity – a consequence that they resolutely condemn.[6] IGPN investigators are thus commonly referred to as "beef-and-carrot stews" within the police institution, because they are known to let suspects "stew in their own juices."

However, the status of the IGPN as an internal oversight body remains highly controversial. Indeed, it is often considered that the fact that it is entirely composed of police officers and functionally integrated in the DGPN inevitably leads to collusion and therefore to leniency toward the police officers under investigation.[7] Strong accusations have been made against the IGPN in recent months, particularly after its highly questionable reports on "teenagers from

Mantes-la-Jolie,"[8] or following the death of Steve Maia Caniço.[9] These investigations were thus deemed biased because they were incomplete and tried – too openly – to exonerate the police officers involved. Though known to have spoken to the media, key witnesses were not heard, while the current IGPN director, Brigitte Jullien, said that she *"totally refutes the term 'police violence,'"* echoing a (very questionable) statement by President Emmanuel Macron.[10]

An examination of internal oversight in practice reveals two related phenomena. The first is that there is a very large gap between the number of complaints filed for alleged acts of unlawful violence (around 40% of complaints) and the number of sanctions imposed for such acts (around 17%) (Moreau de Bellaing 2015). This gap widens when one considers the nature of the alleged violence. While nearly 89% of the complaints are lodged for on-duty violence, 75% of the sanctions are imposed for violence committed by police officers in their private lives. In practice, this means that unlawful violence reported to the internal oversight body is punished relatively rarely. This is partly due to the difficulties encountered by IGPN officers in their investigations, as they often struggle to find conclusive evidence of unlawful violence. Moreover, these investigations tend to look for exonerating evidence. But to fully understand the previously mentioned gap, one should consider a second phenomenon. Unlike instances of violence, there is a category of police misconduct that is, proportionally, more punished when it is uncovered. This is abuse of police authority, or misconduct in the use of resources available to police officers, as law enforcement agents, for personal gain. This obviously includes corruption and personal use of police files, but the category extends well beyond that. It also refers to abuse of police authority in order to obtain small advantages (such as taking a forbidden second job); engaging in extra-administrative activities that might involve conflicts of interest (in particular when they relate to private security); theft facilitated by police duties; and the abuse of power for intimidation purposes. Each of these acts undermines the public-service nature of police activity; in this respect, these acts can be described as forms of the privatization of policing.

The same applies to the punishment of police officers who committed acts of private violence. It is less the use of violence that is punished than the fact that these acts do not fall within the scope of the use of *public* force. The emphasis put by the internal oversight body on the preservation of the public nature of the police mission – to the detriment of the more spectacular and media-oriented issue of unlawful violence – exposes the Inspectorate to criticism. Indeed, acts of unlawful violence are proportionally *less* punished when they are uncovered, which fuels accusations of collusion that denounce the excessive leniency of IGPN police officers toward their colleagues.

The National Commission on Security Ethics and the Rights Defender

International comparisons shed light on the French case most particularly in the area of the external oversight of police activity. Comparatively, we define this as any form of monitoring carried out by institutionalized commissions which are neither representative of advocacy groups nor internal to law enforcement. The English-language literature on this subject is abundant, which makes sense given the prevalence of external oversight bodies, particularly in the United States (Reiner 1996; Goldsmith and Colleen 2000; Ivković 2005; Walker 2005). In contrast, books and articles on external oversight mechanisms in France are rare, as are these mechanisms themselves.

In France, external oversight of police activities was first formalized on June 6, 2000, with the creation of the National Commission on Security Ethics (CNDS). Cases could be referred to this independent administrative authority by a parliamentarian, the prime minister, the Children's Ombudsman, the mediator of the Republic, or the president of the French Equal Opportunities and Anti-Discrimination Commission (HALDE). The CNDS was responsible for "ensuring that people carrying out security activities on the territory of the Republic comply with ethical standards." Their jurisdiction included members of the *police national* and *gendarmerie*, the prison administration, the customs administration, the municipal police, public transportation surveillance services, and private security services. Modeled on the experience of ombudsmen abroad (in Belgium, Northern Ireland, England, and Quebec), the CNDS was not meant to replace the internal disciplinary bodies of the security services. Rather, it provided an external remedy for citizens feeling mistreated by these services. As such, it was responsible for investigating the facts brought to its attention and, where appropriate, forwarding to the judicial authorities cases with facts suggesting the existence of a criminal offense.

From the outset, the CNDS was composed of elected representatives (two deputies and two senators), high-ranking officials from the most prestigious bodies (a state councilor, a magistrate of the Court of Cassation,[11] a member the Court of Auditors), and six "qualified persons" appointed by the other members of the Commission. Despite its symbolically powerful composition, from the beginning the CNDS suffered from a tight budget and limited investigative powers (Ocqueteau and Enderlin 2011). Yet the Commission gained influence after 2006; it boasted good results, inasmuch as the authorities have taken into account some of its general recommendations. The same cannot be said for the individual recommendations made by the CNDS following investigations that it has carried out, as these recommendations were rarely put into effect. For instance, this was the case in all the recommendations regarding the deportation of foreigners (CNDS 2005), police detention of minors (CNDS 2008), or the use of stun guns (CNDS 2009). Generally speaking, the growing conflict between law enforcement and the CNDS made the latter's work increasingly difficult.

The Commission was officially dissolved in early 2011, when it was integrated into a new institution, the Rights Defender (DDD). The new body's ability to supervise and monitor law enforcement activity has been questioned, in particular by former CNDS members (Renaudie 2011). But the intensive work that the DDD carried out on police issues, the resources put at the service of the oversight of law enforcement activity, as well as the effort to publicize the reports and decisions of the institution, have allayed these fears (Ocqueteau 2016, p. 367). In recent years, the external oversight body has thus taken well-documented stands on the national police's abusive identity check practices.[12] These have included defending the need to create receipts allowing the traceability of identity checks; on the dismantling of refugee camps (DDD 2016); on "racial and social profiling" carried out by the Paris Police Prefecture (DDD 2019); on the excessive use of force during specific police operations; and on the deaths attributed to police misconduct (DDD 2018). Jacques Toubon's rise to head the DDD coincided with the "rise in power of the institution and a clear politicization toward the protection of freedoms against [the government's] excessive security policy" (DDD 2018, p. 368). However, a major difficulty, which had already been encountered by the CNDS, remains: the lack of real dialog between the DDD and police and *gendarmerie* institutions, including the IGPN (DDD 2018, p. 369).

Tensions between the DDD and law enforcement are reflected in police unions' recurring reactions to the opinions and recommendations formulated by the DDD. For instance, a leaflet from one of the main French police unions, Alliance, strongly condemned the "sensationalist statement" that the DDD made on identity checks.[13] More recently, a press release delivered by the same union similarly accused the DDD of systematically looking for incriminating evidence when investigating police officers. The narrow channel of communication between the external oversight body and law enforcement thus reduces the internal impact of the stands taken by the DDD, whose repressive powers are non-existent and which, for the time being, must confine itself to using a strategy of public pressure and, sometimes, to submitting opinions to the legislative power.

Criticism from Civil Society and the Media

The weakness of external oversight of police activity could be counterbalanced by a signification mobilization of advocacy groups. Indeed, there has been a relatively extensive network of advocacy groups concerned with police issues in France since the 1960s. Anthony Pregnolato (2017) identifies five forms of police oversight within this maze of advocacy groups. The first is composed of human rights advocacy groups that do not specialize in police issues, although they investigate matters – looking into both individual acts of misconduct and more collective dysfunctions – which can receive significant media coverage, and which can sometimes accompany legal proceedings. The second is composed of collectives formed by relatives of a victim, who seek truth and justice for their loved one and use their specific case to denounce more widespread abusive police practices and techniques.

They draw their legitimacy from their close relation to the victim, whether as family members or friends. The third collection of groups encompasses initiatives by local actors directly aimed at producing institutional change and open to negotiations, including conflictual ones, with the authorities and law enforcement. Their efforts would be familiar to those following the North American model of community organizing. The fourth is composed of groups of so-called "first concerned persons." Theirs is a highly racialized discourse, denouncing the colonial continuum that they see in contemporary police action. And, lastly, a far-left, "anti-securitarian" group, which sometimes condemns excesses by the police – especially since President François Hollande proclaimed the state of emergency on November 14, 2015 – and sometimes essentializes police brutality by vilifying the very existence of law enforcement. Overall, there are more than 15 kinds of collectives criticizing police activity – not to mention the many groups corresponding to the first form of police oversight. Yet their audience is limited, and critical advocacy groups struggle to gain wide recognition.

Their difficulties lead to widespread public controversies, propagated by the media and potentially helping monitor police activity. Caution must be exercised when examining this topic, as research on this issue is limited. There is no major work written in French specifically focusing on media coverage of police misconduct. In his book on police blunders, Fabien Jobard devoted a chapter to the construction of accounts of police brutality in newspaper articles and compared accounts of alleged unlawful violence that he had collected with journalistic modes of recounting of similar acts (Jobard 2002). But he focused on analyzing the social conditions that validate allegations of violence and allow them to be visible in the public sphere. However, media coverage of unlawful violence committed by the police is not, strictly speaking, at the center of his study. There is a collective work on the relations between the police and the media, but it deals mainly with representations of the police institution in the media, including in fiction, and only secondarily with the issue of the media oversight of police activity (Meyer 2012). It is thus noteworthy that there is no work on the social and media construction of the public problem of police misconduct, as police–media relations are instead examined from the standpoint of police officers' relationship to journalistic news (Le Saulnier 2012). Yet it would be wrong to claim that the issue is of no interest to the media. Press coverage of events during May of 1968, the 2005 uprising in Clichy-sous-Bois, or the 2007 riots in Villiers-le-Bel was quite extensive. However, there are few long-term journalistic investigations on police misconduct, just as journalists (as opposed to activists) rarely publicize a case. There are some exceptions, though. Most importantly, in many editorial offices, investigative journalists tend to specialize in a particular field, which contributes to the development of a kind of journalism specifically dedicated to police issues. Thus, certain figures in the news world, familiar with the police institution, have recently been behind the revelation of scandals (for instance, Louise Fessard at Médiapart or Camille Pollini on the news website Les Jours). One can thus hypothesize that police misconduct will receive increasing media coverage.

Conclusion

Now that the bodies responsible, in one way or another, for monitoring police activity in France have been identified, we have a basis for drawing an overview of the situation.[14] Police activity in France is institutionally strictly regulated. But depending on the type of misconduct committed by police officers, the nature of the oversight differs, as do its resulting consequences. While abuse of police authority, understood in the broad sense, is subject to tight control by internal oversight bodies, this is not the case for the unlawful use of violence. The latter is subject to parliamentary scrutiny only on rare occasions. The DDD is more concerned with these, but it has neither the power to impose sanctions nor sufficient resources. Oversight of police conduct by the press focuses on the most spectacular cases. The (criminal) case-law applied by the judicial authorities transfers to the police the ultimate responsibility for determining the right amount of force to be used in each situation, limiting its effectiveness in controlling misconduct. As for internal oversight, the violence that it investigates and punishes concerns privatized acts of violence committed by police officers. Therefore, if one considers the whole chain of control, one can justifiably say that in France unlawful uses of violence are rarely – and not very severely – punished.

We could conclude with this statement, but to do so would overlook some important consequences of this observation. Based on the previous statement, it would be reasonable to consider that police officers can avoid running risks when being violent. But then another question arises. In view of the great leniency granted to police officers when they use violence in situations in which its lawfulness is far from obvious, one wonders why they do not resort to unlawful violence more often. Of course, this does not mean that one should minimize the number and seriousness of acts of violence. Nor should one deny the regularity of unlawful police behavior in certain social spaces (Jobard 2005). But we should examine what does limit them in practice, what disciplines their behavior most of the time, in order to get a better understanding of what sometimes causes formal safeguards to fail. Knowing more about the true constraints on police behavior could suggest ways of strengthening them.

Discipline within the national police has historically relied mainly on direct hierarchy. Its pyramidal organization grants the heads of divisions substantial disciplinary power. But distinctions must be made between police divisions. In a 1998 article on the oversight of police activity, Dominique Monjardet noted that "the severity of sanctions is strictly proportional to the relative importance of discipline within the management of the various divisions" (Monjardet 1998, p. 78). In this case, the line management of the Central Directorate of Public Security has long preferred to handle acts of unlawful violence committed by police officers under its authority in an informal way. Until the mid-1980s, it had relied heavily on the internal oversight bodies of its disciplinary missions, as the heads of police stations preferred to avoid the hostility triggered by these measures and transferred the potential resentment harbored by police officers to the General Inspectorates, which already had a very bad reputation among officers (Ancian 1988).

Today, the main source of oversight of police activity tends to be found in collectively validated professional standards. These professional standards – that is, norms collectively recognized by a specific social group and likely to set off either positive or negative sanctions (Durkheim 2013 [1893])[15] – are formulated as early as the initial training period and assume greater significance as experience is gained on the street (Monjardet 1996). These norms are collectively defined by, and integrated into, professional doctrines in the most disciplined police divisions, such as the CRS (Republican Security Companies), but they can be as collectively relevant within police divisions operating in small units. We must be careful not to reify these standards. The sociology of the police has long shown that, across all divisions and ranks, the existence of a homogeneous police work culture is very limited. There is heterogeneity in the stands taken by police officers within their professional spaces (Monjardet 1994). But the fact that police professional space is full of contradictions does not mean that there are no shared, tacit rules on which officers can rely to judge, validate, punish, or criticize their colleagues' behaviors. Yet these standards are now the main source of oversight of police activity in France.

This observation raises questions and, inevitably, causes concern. Is too much professional autonomy and too much endogenization of the oversight of police activity likely to allow behaviors to persist unpunished by the police, although they would be deemed harmful by society as a whole (and, incidentally, potentially reprehensible from a legal standpoint)? This is precisely the tricky situation in which the French police force has been for several years. Recent police mobilizations (Jobard 2016), as well as controversies over the use of force during the *gilets jaunes* movements during 2018–2019 are indicative of this. Tension is becoming increasingly palpable within the police institution. It is based on the certainty, widely shared among officers, that they are faced with a growing level of antagonism while performing their daily activities. The fact that police officers consider themselves isolated from the social world is nothing new. But examination of their situation in recent years suggests this is a growing concern. The point here is not to determine whether it is true that the police force serves as the first and last safeguard for society. Rather, it is to highlight an emerging social trend among some police officers, who demand that the government, the institutions, and, ultimately, the public give them free rein in the fight they believe they should lead in the name of the defense of society. This may involve demands for weaponry. These demands have included automatic weapons to tackle perpetrators of mass killings, "compliance" weapons to target certain demonstrators in the event of public disorder, and the reform of the self-defense regime regulating the use of firearms by public security police officers. However, more fundamentally, many police officers also demand that they be entrusted with the task of assessing the adequacy of the means to be used in the fight against offenders. This requires less criminal control, fewer court decisions contradicting police expectations, less media coverage, fewer video recordings of police operations, and fewer hierarchical constraints. In short, less control, except that exercised by peers. But there is a significant risk that such reforms would contribute to bypassing and, ultimately, rendering meaningless the professional standards that help maintain police self-monitoring.

Notes

1 Translated by Nathalie Plouchard-Engel.
2 It should be added that the parliament also exercises oversight by conducting fact-finding missions, which are nevertheless limited to issuing a report and holding a debate without a vote.
3 Although the audit mission is far from negligible in terms of energy and staff, it is not well known, as the focus of attention is the investigative mission. In addition to these audit and investigative missions, the IGPN is responsible for "risk management," and it handles police officers' requests for legal advice and assesses managerial practices.
4 An exception is the analysis by Ocqueteau (2016).
5 Sebastian Roché, "Affirmer que la 'police des polices' est indépendante est faux." *Le Monde*, June 27, 2019.
6 Internal grievances against general inspectorates may take another form: the latter may be accused of being potentially instrumentalized by the political authorities for personal gain. This was the case with the scandal that led to the disappearance of the IGS.
7 See for instance Zamponi (1994). Moreover, this criticism is not exclusive to advocacy groups; it is also sometimes expressed within the police institution (Roux 1988).
8 On December 6, 2018, 151 teenagers were taken in for questioning by the national police on the sidelines of a high-school protest in Mantes-la-Jolie. While waiting for their transfer to police stations, these young people were forced to kneel, hands on their heads or handcuffed behind their backs. Apprised of the case, the IGPN dismissed it, after the Nanterre prosecutor said that "the fact of forcing the people taken in for questioning to kneel or sit, in handcuffs for some, seem[ed] justified by the exceptional context of serious urban violence and the number of people to be taken to police stations, requiring an incompressible material organization" (*Libération*, July 26, 2019).
9 On Music Day, which, in France, takes place on June 21, a techno party was held on a quay in Nantes, near the Loire River. The party was supposed to end at 4 a.m., but a DJ refused to turn off the sound and played a classic French punk track from the 1980s. This resulted in a violent police charge, along with an extensive use of tear gas to stop the party. During that night, several people

fell into the Loire, in particular during the police charge. The same night, a man, Steve Maia Caniço, was reported missing. His body was found five weeks later at the bottom of the Loire. The very day his body was discovered, the IGPN issued a report stating that no link could be established between the police charge and Steve Maia Caniço's fall into the Loire.
10 At a meeting held as part of the national debate organized by the executive to respond to the political crisis sparked by the *gilets jaunes* movement, the president of the Republic declared: "Let's not speak of 'repression' or 'police violence.' These words are unacceptable in a state governed by the rule of law." "Gilets jaunes: pas de 'violences policières', selon Emmanuel Macron," *Le Monde*, March 7, 2019.
11 The Court of Cassation is the highest court of the French judicial system. It is a court of last resort in legal proceedings and, as its name suggests, it can overturn or annul rulings by lower courts (including courts of appeals), or, conversely, uphold these rulings, making them final.
12 On February 13, 2015, the Rights Defender (DDD) published a series of observations and then submitted them to the Paris Court of Appeals, at the request of 13 plaintiffs who considered themselves victims of discriminatory identity checks. The DDD report condemned, in particular, the lack of traceability of identity checks, as well as the inadequate oversight of police activity carried out *a priori* and *posteriori* by the judicial authorities. See de Maillard (2019).
13 "Défenseur des droits, le poids des mots, le choc des photos," *Alliance Police Nationale*, March 8, 2016.
14 One could have added to the list of forms of oversight of police activity presented here monitoring by unions or by administrative courts (Vigouroux 1996).
15 For a contemporary analysis of the Durkheimian perspective, see Lemieux 2009.

References

Ancian, J. M. 1988. *La police des polices*. Paris: Balland.
Association Chrétienne pour l'Abolition de la Torture [Christian Association for the Abolition of Torture]. 2016. *L'ordre et la force. Enquête sur l'usage de la force par les représentants de la loi en France [Order and force. Survey on the use of force by law enforcement officials in France]*. Paris.
Commission Nationale de Déontologie de la Sécurité [National Commission on Security Ethics]. 2005. *Rapport annuel d'activité*. Paris.
Commission Nationale de Déontologie de la Sécurité [National Commission on Security Ethics]. 2008. *Rapport annuel d'activité*. Paris.
Commission Nationale de Déontologie de la Sécurité [National Commission on Security Ethics]. 2009. *Rapport annuel d'activité*. Paris.
Défenseur des Droits [Rights Defender]. 2016. *Rapport d'observation: démantèlement des campements et prise en charge des exilés [Observation report: Dismantling of camps and care of exiles]*. Paris.
Défenseur des Droits [Rights Defender]. 2018. *Le maintien de l'ordre au regard des règles de déontologie [Regulating public order with regard to ethical rules]*. Paris.
Défenseur des Droits [Rights Defender]. 2019. Decision of April 2, 2019. Paris.
de Maillard, J. 2019. Les contrôles d'identité, entre politiques policières, pratiques professionnelles et effets sociaux: Un état critique des connaissances [Stop and search policies and their effects: A state of knowledge in western countries]. *Champ pénal/Penal field* 16. doi:10.4000/champpenal.10318.

Dewerpe, A. 2006. *Charonne, 8 février 1962: Anthropologie historique d'un massacre d'État [Charonne, February 8, 1962. Historical anthropology of a state massacre].* Paris: Callimard.

Durkheim, E. 2013 [1893]. *La division du travail social [The division of labor in society].* Paris: Quadrige.

Goldsmith, A., and Colleen, L. (Eds.). 2000. *Civilian oversight of policing: Governance, democracy and human rights.* Oxford: Hart Publishing.

Inspection Générale de la Police Nationale [The general inspectorate of the national police]. 2018. *Rapport annuel d'activité.* Paris.

Ivković, S. 2005. *Fallen blue knights: Controlling police corruption.* Oxford: Oxford University Press.

Jobard, F. 2002. *Bavures policières? La force publique et ses usages [Police blunders? The public force and its uses].* Paris: La Découverte.

Jobard, F. 2005. Le nouveau mandat policier: Faire la police dans les zones dites de "non-droit" [The new police mandate: Policing in so-called "lawless" areas]. *Criminologie* 38: 103–121.

Jobard, F. 2016. Colères policières [Police anger]. *Esprit* mars–avril: 64–73.

Le Saulnier, G. 2012. La police nationale au défi des relations presse: Une information sous contrôle? [The national police face the challenge of press relations: An information under control?]. *Mots. Les langages du politique* 99: 129–142.

Lemieux, C. 2009. *Le devoir et la grâce [Duty and grace].* Paris: Economica.

Maguer, A. 2004. French police corruption: "Actors," actions and issues. Pp. 422–464 in M. Amir and S. Einstein (Eds.) *Police corruption: Challenges for developed countries–comparative issues and commissions of inquiry.* Huntsville: Sam Houston State University.

Meyer, M. 2012. *Médiatiser la police, policer les médias [Mediatizing the police, policing the media].* Lausanne: Antipodes.

Monjardet, D. 1994. La culture professionnelle des policiers [The police work culture]. *Revue française de sociologie* 35: 393–411.

Monjardet, D. 1996. *Ce que fait la police: Sociologie de la force publique [What the police do: Sociology of the public force].* Paris: La Découverte.

Monjardet, D. 1998. Contrôler la police… [Controlling the police…]. *Panoramiques* 33: 74–82.

Moreau de Bellaing, C. 2015. *Force publique: Une sociologie de l'institution policière [Public force: A sociology of the police iInstitution].* Paris: Economica.

Napoli, P. 2003a. *La naissance de la police modern: Pouvoir, normes, société [The birth of modern police: Power, norms, society].* Paris: La Découverte.

Napoli, P. 2003b. Qu'est qu'une mesure de police? Considérations historiques après Gênes 2001 [What is a police measure? Historical considerations after Genoa 2001]. *Multitudes* 11: 49–56.

National Assembly. 2015. Report No. 2794. Paris.

National Assembly. 2019. Report No. 2111. Paris.

Ocqueteau, F. 2016. Qu'est-ce qu'une police déontologique? *Revue internationale de criminologie et de police technique et scientifique* 3: 349–383.

Ocqueteau, F., and Enderlin, S. 2011. La commission nationale de déontologie de la sécurité: Un pouvoir d'influence [The national commission on deontology of security: A power of influence]. *Revue française d'administration publique* 139: 381–396.

Pregnolato, A. 2017. L'espace des mobilisations contre les violences des forces de l'ordre en France depuis les années 1990 [The social space of mobilizations against police violence in France since the 1990s]. *Mouvements* 92: 38–47.

Provenzano, L. 2019. Beyond the matraque: State violence and its representation during the Parisian 1968 events. *The Journal of Modern History* 91: 586–624.
Reiner, R. 1996. *Policing, volume II – Controlling the controllers: Police discretion and accountability*. Aldershot: Dartmouth.
Renaudie, F. 1999. *L'inspection générale de la Police nationale IGPN/IGS [The general inspectorate of the national police IGPN/IGS]*. Master Thesis: Paris II University.
Renaudie, O. 2011. La genèse complexe du Défenseur des droits [The complex genesis of the rights defender]. *Revue française d'administration publique* 139: 397–408.
Roux, P. 1988. Contrôler la police? [Controlling the police?]. *Esprit* 135: 30–40.
Senate. 1987. Report No. 270. Paris.
Senate. 2018. Report No. 612. Paris.
Vigouroux, C. 1996. Le contrôle de la police [The control of the police]. Pp. 743–760 in M. Braibant (Ed.) *L'Etat de droit*. Paris: Dalloz.
Walker, S. 2005. *The new world of police accountability*. Thousand Oaks: Sage Publications.
Zamponi, F. 1994. *La police: Combien de divisions? [Police: How many divisions?]*. Paris: Dagorno.

Part III

Changing Institutional and Political Context

Chapter 9

The Expansion of Private Policing in France

Frédéric Ocqueteau

Research on the growth of security services industry in France has been largely informed by a macro-sociological phenomenon that has affected all post-industrial democracies. This is the seeming necessity for states to adjust to resource constraints, and their resulting inability to meet the seemingly insatiable demand for protection from both companies and individuals. Over the years, several sociological theories have been proposed to account for this phenomenon, and theoretical paradigms for explaining it have gradually clarified. In France, liberal and critical theories about the coexistence of public and private schemes on the market have become quite commonplace. From a practical perspective, two frequent questions center on how functional the complementarity of public and private agencies is when it comes to delivering security, and whether their respective contributions should be viewed as a continuum or as confrontational.

Our aim in this chapter is to bring clarity to the debate by discussing three issues that are among the most vexing in contemporary France. First, we draw a critical picture of quantitative data on the expansion of the private sector. Then, we analyze the impact of CNAPS, a regulatory body for the private sector that was established in 2012. Finally, we show the circumstances – a rise of security-related tensions within the French state when it was confronted by Islamic terrorism in 2015–2016 – that led to the hitherto taboo issue of allowing private security personnel to carry defensive and offensive weapons to enter the political agenda and eventually become a reality.

Growth Indicators: Diversification in Time and Space

Private security companies and the number of people they employ have grown to such an extent that they have become irreplaceable. This includes both in the French urban landscape (Ocqueteau 2004; Warfman and Ocqueteau 2011) and in their overlap with public security organizations (Brodeur 2010, pp. 17–41). As the phenomenon of policing pluralization in France was last reviewed in the English language 15 years ago (Ocqueteau 2006), this chapter includes new information on the scale and the services performed by these organizations.

In France, data on the private sector can usually be found in three distinct sources. Although they can offer sometimes contrasting portraits, these data sources can be considered reliable because their data collection criteria are well-known. Two of them are public or semi-public sources of limited scope, while the third is gathered by an economics journalist. This private source gives a much broader and more diversified, if somewhat less dependable, picture of the security market.

The first data source, the French National Institute for Statistics and Economic Studies (INSEE), draws a rather restricted quantitative picture of the private security industry (Robin and Mordier 2013; Fressoz-Martinez and Vucko 2016; Gallot 2018). It is based on mandatory annual statements made by legal economic entities belonging to three categories of activities, according to a stable and verifiable industry classification system (Nomenclature d'activités française, or NAF):

Category 1 – *Private security* as such (NAF code 8010Z), i.e. guard and patrol services, cash and valuables transport by staff specifically equipped to protect the goods during transport;

Category 2 – *Security systems* (NAF code 8020Z), i.e. site and area surveillance, and remote surveillance using electronic security and alarm systems (which comprises the installation, repair, maintenance, and adjustment of mechanical or electronic locking systems, strongboxes, safes, and vaults, including on-site or remote surveillance thereof);

Category 3 – *Private investigation activities* (NAF code 8030Z), private investigaotrs (PIs) and the like – an economic sector whose revenue is extremely modest, if not negligible.

According to INSEE's latest available consolidated statistics for the year 2017 (Gallot 2018), Category 1 (private security guards) involves 5,700 companies employing 139,000 full-time equivalent staff. The sector's sales in 2017 totaled EU€7 billion (52% from home and industrial site surveillance; 22% from the control and surveillance of business activities; 11% from cash transport; 15% from other activities). Category 2 (electronic security systems) is comprised of 2,500 companies employing 16,700, with total sales of €2.4 billion. That is a total of 155,700 employees, a number that can be compared to other service sectors in what INSEE considers adjoining fields of activity, temporary employment companies, and the cleaning industry. Both of which rely on a very similar workforce. Their revenues for 2017 were respectively four times (€32.4 billion) and twice (€22.4 billion) that of the private security industry.

In addition, it should be noted that 86% of the customer base of Category 1 private security companies consists of businesses, whereas those from Category 2 deal more frequently with individuals or households (33%). While the former creates less added value (subcontracting excepted), as more than half of their revenue is spent on overheads, they have bigger profit margins (22% vs. 4%). Since security-systems companies offer services requiring more skilled employees, they command higher hourly wages and are more likely to employ full-time staff, resulting in lower employee turnover rates.

In the medium term, from 2010 to 2017, INSEE data show a 4% yearly statistical growth of revenue over the entire industry. 2016 saw a very significant acceleration (+7%) in revenue growth owing to three types of events: terrorist attacks, an overhaul of the Vigipirate plan, and (most importantly) the European Championship hosted by France. These were major events that kept the entire industry on its toes monitoring fans and protecting businesses.

For Category 2, another biennial specialized survey, the Prevention and Security Industry Report by *Cabinet I+C* (Institut d'Informations et de Conjonctures Professionnelles 2017) offers a second set of quantitative data. They are just as reliable as INSEE's but are aligned with the services they provide. This firm breaks down its data into 10,650 companies that generate €6.6 billion in sales from four major sectors of activity: human surveillance (surveillance, guards, fire safety, distribution); transport security; remote surveillance; and airport safety. The breakdown is as follows, in decreasing number of employees: 7,122 self-owned businesses with no employees; 4,000 companies with one employee (30% in the Paris region and 11% in Provence-Alpes-Côte d'Azur); 2,400 companies with one to nine employees. Nine out of ten companies in the sector employ less than 20 staff, accounting for 11.5% of total revenue, while the 39 largest actors (0.36%) generate a whopping 43% of sales.[1]

To conclude, it should be noted that the global picture offered by the two organizations converges on several points. According to INSEE, micro-companies have the highest profit margins (or economic performance), something the I+C survey does not dispute. This can be explained by the fact that the remuneration of their unsalaried managers is considered part of their gross operating surplus, as opposed to personnel costs. Besides, companies in the electronic security sector pay higher wages to their higher-skilled workers (€17.4 per hour gross salary). Similarly, the two organizations agree on why profit margins are much smaller in other security companies. The rule is that purchasers invariably tend to choose contractors offering the lowest possible cost. Competition is fierce in a market that is not yet too concentrated, and customers can pick up the best offer from a lower limit of €13/hour (gross), not dwelling too much on the unwanted effects inevitably produced by the resulting wave of subcontracting – which according to French law is often downright illegal (*délit de marchandage*).

As far as professional qualifications are concerned in the security industry at large, 87% of jobs are manned by little-qualified personnel (as opposed to the cash escorts, bodyguards, PIs, and the like, who account for 4% of the workforce). Private security employees are overwhelmingly male (84%) and typically younger than in other support activities; and, most importantly, the ratio of managers to workers is extremely low (2%). Although most are employed full-time, employee turnover is higher (29%) than in other support activities (25%). Not only are the tasks rather unattractive, but staff are not incentivized by solid career perspectives involving internal promotion to the management level.

While data available for Category 3 (private investigators) partly overlap with the other two, it also considerably widens the spectrum of activities that are included (Haas 2018). Haas has been tracking the market's trends yearly for three decades, based on the revenues of companies from 23 different sectors of activity grouped in three broad categories.[2] While these organizations report their revenue and workforce, this cannot be independently verified, so the source simply compiles the data annually based on a standard procedure. The three categories are the following:

1. Electronic alarm security organizations. This sector is comprised of burglar alarms; anti-terrorist systems; access control systems; shoplifting control systems; surveillance drones.
2. Physical security companies, whose job consists in protecting workers against accidents; providing armored equipment; fire safety; perimeter security; locksmithing.
3. Service companies. This category includes guard services; alarm interventions; bodyguards and personal protection; training centers; private investigations; airport safety; body search; cash transport. The latest report (2017) mentions 230,000 staff including, in decreasing order: 130,000 in guard services; 22,000 in fire safety; 11,000 airport security workers; 9,200 cash and valuable escorts; and 7,800 employees in burglar alarm services.

Specialized sociologists have long believed that remote surveillance technologies (telemonitoring and CCTV) were bound to ultimately replace the proletarian workforce that was tasked with keeping watch over goods and performing surveillance patrols, a job that increasingly exposes them to violence. This prediction was based on 30-year observations and predicted that the growth in the number of private security employees relative to the *per capita* number of public police officers would slow down (De Waard 1999; Ocqueteau 2006). However – and notwithstanding the fact that many criminologists consider the ratio of public to private security officers per 100,000 residents in each European Union member state to be devoid of meaning due to their different respective powers – INSEE does not see any trend suggesting that human personnel today are being gradually replaced by technology. Philippe Gallot actually concludes his macro-economic study by noting that although the revenue of the "private security" sector is about half as dynamic as that of "security systems," the latter is typically meant to *complement* the former, as opposed to being a *substitute* for it (Gallot 2018).

New Supervision Over Private Security

Three decades after the first governmental regulatory system was created (1983 to 1986) to supervise organizations entering the market, reform was deemed necessary. The process was quite an eventful one (Ocqueteau 2013;

Paulin 2017), but a new scheme did ultimately appear in the country's institutional landscape. Why and how? Five year on, what can be said about its functioning and impact?

What is the CNAPS? There are, generally speaking, two types of private security regulation schemes in the Western world. On the one hand, there are systems with minimal state regulation in common law areas (White 2010), where the basic premise is that the principle of business freedom should not be infringed upon. On the other hand, there are systems in which public authorities regulate market access and monitor for potential violations of civil liberties. The United Kingdom and France have long been viewed as polar opposites in this respect, and experts have compared the nature and impact of national legislation within the European Union states and more broadly in the developed post-industrial world (Cools and Pashley 2012). In systems where public authorities do oversee the private market (southern Europe), two distinct methods exist. One is where the state considers private employees to be direct auxiliaries to the national force (Spain, Portugal), and the other is where the federal (Canada, Germany) or central (France) state delegates industry regulation to a joint body. In France, the situation has changed recently. Although supervision by prefects at the level of the *département* had been perceived as having failed as early as 1983, it took about 30 years for a new approach to be initiated – inspired by the Quebec experience (Mulone and Dupont 2008). Then France launched a new system called the National Council for Private Prevention and Security Activities (Conseil National des Activités Privées de Prévention et de Sécurité, or CNAPS).

Established by article 31 of the law of 14 March 2011 and the ordinance of 21 December 2011, CNAPS is a new administrative public body that took over from departmental prefectures the task of reforming the private sector as a regulated profession, following on founding legislation that was passed on 12 July 1983 (Ocqueteau 1991). The CNAPS's missions are set by a board of directors, the *Collège*. Half of this steering body is comprised of representatives of public security agencies, and the other half of business leaders from organizations belonging to the different activity sectors – plus four other, qualified members. They have three missions: granting prior approval to companies and their employees via reviewing and renewing their credentials; taking disciplinary action should any rules be breached and create a legal dispute; and monitoring, advising, and assisting, which are more difficult to quantify.

Since CNAPS employees may legally access the police and court records of private security personnel, they are responsible for granting permits and credentials to the employees and managers of the concerned organizations, based on their criminal records and police files. This is done at a central "one-stop-shop" (*guichet unique*) in Paris. In addition, the CNAPS is in charge of ruling on any disputes that may occur when controlling the permits and credentials that have been granted and deviations from security companies and staff, through local committees. These committees include eight CLACs (Commissions locales d'agrément et de contrôle) in metropolitan France and five in overseas territories, with same member parity as in the *Collège*.

How does the CNAPS measure the effectiveness of its own action? Table 9.1 summarizes the data needed to measure the impact of the CNAPS's missions. First, it should be noted that most of its activity has to do with delivering permits and credentials. Given the very high employee turnover rates of the industry, the necessary background checks and the issuance of the permits are the most intensive daily tasks at the CNAPS. Still, this is expected to stabilize at about 55,000 permits per year before spiking again in 2020–2021.

Further, it can be noted that as far as disciplinary action is concerned, over the past two years, controls performed in companies or on-site, in about equal measure, have generated less incriminations regarding the most common violations. However, improved targeting by CNAPS investigators is said to have produced

Table 9.1 Overview of Mission Activity by the CNAPS and CLACS

Mission	2012	2013	2014	2015	2016	2017
ADMINISTRATIVE POLICE						
Delivered professional cards	33,597	38,159	92, 809*	81,397	66,519	50,992
Pat-down certifications **	-	-	-	-	17,551	17,466
Management certifications	-	-	-	-	1,637	1,613
Valid professional cards	-	-	-	-	31,719	-
DISCIPLINARY CONTROLS						
Number of controls	604	1,488	1,435	1,359	1,881	1,868
Agents controlled	-	-	-	-	10,115	-
Recorded violations	-	-	-	-	12,431	10,910
File sent to public prosecutor (art. 40 CPP)	-	-	-	-	134	200
CNAC referral	-	-	-	-	110	130
Case sent to CLAC	-	-	-	-	1,521	2,302
Financial penalties (in €)	-	-	-	-	1.5m	3.7m
LITIGATION						
Applications on the merits Summary judgments	-	-	-	-	304	406
Judgments on the merits	-	-	-	-	287	271
Sanctions pronounced	12	333	580	1,504	1,521	2,302

* 2014 and 2015 were record years in terms of the number of cards delivered nationally, since a great many staff were reaching the expiration date of their five-year credentials. In 2009, a reform had introduced new rules for professional qualifications.

** Agents performing pat-downs/body searches must be certified, an innovation since articles 613–2 and 613–3 of the CSI were reformed in 2016 (specific circumstances linked to serious threats as ordained by the prefects as well as access to sports venues in case of major events).

Source: CNAPS Annual Reports (2018, 2017, 2016). Data aggregated and the table created by the author.

"better quality" cases in terms of the seriousness of the violations, since the public prosecutor was informed more often. Two quantitative indicators suggest that although the CNAPS has no intention of ignoring its role as public authorities' "cop," its empirical vocation might be to improve the targeting of its controls and deal with any uncovered violations by seeking transactions rather than hampering the sector's economic activity. This has spectacularly affected fines for negligence, which have more than doubled over this period. Minor administrative and criminal litigation has risen from 2012 to 2017 as well, owing to improved violation detection, thanks to enhanced targeting.

While the "start-up" version of the CNAPS, in its quest for legitimacy, remains mindful of its policing role on the market (however symbolic), whether it can be considered an effective regulator of the industry's key players remains debatable. The data on sanctions are not highly reliable, and in any case the policies regarding the publicity of reprimands against transgressors on professional sites still somewhat escape control by the CNAPS.

Arming Private Guards

The years 2016 and 2017 saw a silent revolution regarding private security in France, in a context that was made particularly difficult by the deadly terrorist attacks which brought about the "state of emergency." A number of "panic," ultra-securitarian, anti-terrorist pieces of legislation were passed during this period (Alix and Cahn 2017; Robert 2018; Gautron 2019; Ocqueteau 2019; Ocqueteau and Laurent 2019), including an initial ordinance in the area of private security, and implementation decrees about the arming of private security guards.

First, there was an unprecedented decree arming private security guards. The decree of 29 December 2017 altered the domestic security laws (*code de la sécurité intérieure* – CSI) in order to better regulate the exercising of a private security activity involving the carrying of a firearm.[3] It made it possible for private security guards to carry two categories of weapons. These are so-called D-class defensive weapons (batons; telescopic batons; pepper or incapacitating defense sprays), and B-class offensive firearms (.38 chambered revolvers or 9mm handguns). Controversies about the lethal or less-lethal character of such weapons notwithstanding, this was a substantial innovation. Not since 1983 had private security guards been allowed to carry offensive weapons, and in fact, none had asked to be armed (Ocqueteau 2018).

The new regime governing the granting of firearm permits to private guards is aligned with that of the municipal police (Malochet 2019). At the same time, background checks became much more rigorous, especially in terms of normative precisions regarding firearm use and safety training. The decree specifically mentions that firearms must be visible (there is no concealed carry) and "combined with a mandatory bulletproof vest" during "surveillance missions that must be accomplished by two-officer units." As for clients wishing to contract with armed private guards, they must prove that a "particularly dangerous situation [involving a] risk of aggression" may occur in the mission carried out in or near the premises to be surveilled or secured.

This means that in 2017, in the wake of the panic created by the terrorist attacks of 2015 and 2016, lawmakers convinced themselves that they had to pass some legislation making it possible for security guards to defend themselves (Codaccioni 2018, pp. 281–308). The government decided to do away with the age-old doctrine of the French state that the private sector ought not to be granted coercive powers. Now it is as if there is a fourth force of *auxiliary* agents, hitherto ill-trained and devoid of coercive powers, that are no longer passive participants in security networks. For this to have happened, the rather rigid understanding among senior officials that the monopoly of legitimate physical violence was confined to the state, must have been seriously undermined. The victimization of private guards on the front line had to be recognized by the authorities as a real concern[4] in order for the state to be convinced that armed response was legitimate, and to lift this symbolic taboo. This major turn cannot be explained by the whim of desperate lawmakers and understood as a purely practical response to a practical issue. To fully appreciate the magnitude of it, one has to scrutinize the underlying shifts that altered the power balance between private and public stakeholders at the top of the state apparatus, a process that was made easier by the disinterest of the general public, which tends to care more about security than about liberty.

Second, there was a (lost) fight by human rights advocates against a security-oriented anti-terrorist ideology. These events unfurled during 2016–2017. It was as if, for surveillance and security guards accustomed from time immemorial to providing passive protection of goods and alerting private and public actors (tele-surveillance and remote security), self-defense had always been a necessity and was bound to finally happen. This called for new legislation granting private security personnel the right to carry firearms for active and offensive responses to threatening individuals they encountered during their rounds. This changed their status. They became the potential targets of a very specific form of urban violence, rather than regulators of the private and public spaces they were meant to control. Beyond the idea of recognizing them as potential *a priori* victims, the government intended to increase the pressure on the clients of security companies, who typically favor arming contractual guards without accepting to share accountability for their missteps. Security customers were required to justify to the local prefect why they needed to contract for guards carrying lethal weapons, after formal clearance from CNAPS. This requirement was a decisive factor behind the decree being enacted. But the sheer weight of the "pro-arming" lobby clearly tipped the balance in that direction.

Among the supporters, the first to jump into action to support the left-wing government (the Valls cabinet) in its decision to establish a durable state of emergency were the right-wing, law-and-order political parties. Following a Senate amendment from the right-wing LR (Les Républicains) group, it was acknowledged that the seminal law of 1983 (now part of book VI of the *code de la sécurité intérieure*) had allowed the principle of arming private guards *under certain conditions*. However, no implementation decree had ever been enacted, except for cash escorts – an obligation – and a formal ban for private bodyguards involved in personal protection. The rhetoric of the legal loophole was all the more easily heard in this context as an amendment pushed by two presidential majority (Parti Socialiste) senators had been enacted in 2017 to arm protection guards aboard ships navigating territorial and inshore waters, "if and when there is an exceptionally high risk that the life of people aboard the ship might be endangered."[5] Based on this precedent, the LR parliamentary group suggested extending the practice to all private guards in the national territory, a right-wing amendment that was embraced by the left without too much ado. Nor did the industry's two employer organizations oppose the principle of arming their guards, although the respective positions of the USP (representing major companies) and the SNES did differ slightly.

Labor unions, though, were frankly hostile, and quite vocally so (*AEF* 8/1/2018).[6] The CGT pointed out that in the field of prevention and security, armed workers would become much more exposed to risk, precisely because of their conspicuous weaponry. Furthermore, they would have to deal with constant – if latent – suspicion from the public, who could suspect them of potentially being private armies. The SNEPS-CFTC, a more moderate union, also voiced reservations, arguing that the "industry was still immature" and not everyone was yet properly trained in their duties – in particular, how clients would be involved and how the guards' firearm training was to be regulated were not known (*AEF* 30/10/2017). Nicolas Le Saux, an influential consultant (*AEF* 30/11/2017), also voiced his skepticism. He tried to promote another, more realistic (i.e. less costly) training pathway for would-be armed guards. He pleaded instead for an alternative network of public officers who could be seconded to private organizations or recruited specifically for private missions to be invoiced in due form (in the spirit of the *gendarmerie* missions paid for by utility provider EDF to protect their nuclear sites). Although the suggestion was not accepted, it highlighted a little-known but common career path by former police and army officers, who joined private security companies. This is a taboo, and thus greatly underestimated, practice (Ocqueteau 2016, p. 291).

These reservations and suggestions went unheeded; nor was the avowed hostility of human rights advocates taken into account. As early as February 2017, the National Human Rights Committee (Commission nationale consultative des Droits de l'Homme – CNCDH) reminded the minister of the interior of the Cazeneuve cabinet (which was busy preparing a new law on public security) of a statement the prime minister had previously supported: "the issue of arming some [private security guards] [ought to] be studied seriously, taking into account not only operational issues, but also the consequences in terms of societal choices" (*Avis CNCDH*, 2017, p. 16). The CNCDH remarked that preparatory work for the proposed new legislation did not include an impact assessment or a ruling from the Council of State. Nor had the Strategic and Foresight Council (Conseil de la Stratégie et de la Prospective), established in October 2016, been consulted, even though its role was precisely to provide in-depth thinking about public security policies. As for the Ombudsman Jacques Toubon (*Défenseur des Droits*), he waited no later than the day after the ordinance was enacted to voice similar hostility, threatening to examine these matters on his own account and to seek out victims or witnesses of violations of the code of good conduct for armed private security guards. Finally, the CNAPS *Collège* itself adopted a prudent, neutral stance when faced with the determined attitude of Gérard Colomb, the new minister of the interior, and his team, starting in May 2017. For the *Collège*, recognizing the status of armed private guards would have far-reaching implications. It would be necessary to align the practices of prefects all over France and adopt common criteria for determining whether an area was dangerous enough to necessitate the use of weapons and thus be classified as "ZIV" (*zone d'importance vitale*) or "at-risk public-access building" (*ERP à risque*). Last but not least, other more technical worries were expressed. "D-class weapons, whether unrestricted or subject to registration (batons, knives, telescopic batons, tonfas)," the *Collège* said, "are easily called non-lethal, whereas they can quickly become lethal when put in the wrong hands" (*AEF* 24/2/2017; see also Martel 2019).

Once the dust had settled on the political turmoil of 2017, while the ordinance was being enacted, four implementation decrees on the arming of private guards were published a year later, on 7 October 2018. The first decree dealt with the purchase, possession, and retention of the weapons used during activities common to surveillance, transport, and personal protection, and the differences between D- and B-class firearms licenses. The second decree regulated the initial training required for being certified as a card-holding B-firearm carrying private guard (ASA B) or D-firearm carrying guard (ASA D). The third was about training, and required skill maintenance and upgrade courses. Finally, a final decree provided a technical baseline for how training organizations were to be certified.

When these decrees were enacted, the very nature of expectations had already shifted significantly. New concerns appeared. While the Ministry estimated that about 1% to 2% of guards would apply to be trained for carrying firearms (between 1,700 and 3,500 out of 170,000 guards),[7] the Préfet délégué aux coopérations de sécurité (as the DISP was now called) said he feared that the human surveillance sector might be reluctant to meet the Ministry's expectations by following suit (*AEF*, 23/11/2018). The president of Unafos (Union nationale des acteurs de la formation en sécurité), which federates certified training centers (*AEF* 28/11/2018), stated that he frankly doubted whether the private sector was actually willing to enroll large numbers of newly qualified employees. The employer organizations USP and SNES called a truce on these differences of opinion (and they were to merge in 2019). They praised the new official global security doctrine, in which the private security sector now featured prominently, which contributed to alleviating their fears regarding the feasibility of the certification process of training organizations.

Adopting a step-by-step diplomacy strategy, the representatives of the security industry's employer organizations were, crucially, shrewd enough to put further pressure on the government by reassuring the authorities that they would fully collaborate, "provided that their workforce may benefit, just as the national and municipal police did, from legal protection by the State for their own agents" (AEF 1/2/2019). Things had come full circle in 21st century security in France.

Conclusion

Armed or unarmed? This symbolic dimension no longer is the only one in which the French state's strategy regarding private guards ought to be interrogated. Since oversight of the industry has been, for practical purposes, delegated to the ad hoc body that is the CNAPS, the most important innovation in public action, from a researcher's perspective, is the greater visibility of the client's accountability for the actions of their contractors. Security clients may now be taken directly to court, at least as a co-defendant, when private security somehow goes awry.

A number of new elements now contribute to explaining the increasingly permanent nature of employment in the field of security, which had so far always been identified by the sociology of occupations as an industry based on a proletarian, or at least highly precarious, workforce (Péroumal 2008). The role of purchasing departments as well as their substitute, facility management – not to mention unofficial negotiations for the lowest possible hourly rates in calls for tenders for public procurement – all largely contributed to helping the industry start to professionalize. Except in some rare cases or niches, clients tend to negotiate the cheapest "bundled" hourly rates for support, cleaning, and security, completely disregarding the utterly different nature of these services and jobs.

As for the impact of the CNAPS's delegated regulatory responsibilities, which have been in a trial period for five years and are supposed to improve the professionalism of private guards, they will only be effective if French authorities set an example by emphasizing the necessity of truly professional management, and by demanding better-trained agents (Arroyo 2017).

In a 2018 report, Members of Parliament A. Thourot and J.-M. Fauvergue (2018) aimed to "improve trust between partnering actors" (public forces and private security) in progress toward global security by rethinking the notion of a continuum uniting various security forces and suggesting new avenues for cooperation among them. The reply they received from the minister of the interior mentioned that,

> operationally speaking, ensuring consistency between national security forces, municipal forces, the agents in charge of transport security, and private security professionals is key. Their considerable growth over the last fifteen years has turned them into inescapable actors of day-to-day security. Their development and rise to national forces must henceforth be part of a global strategy.

This report is likely to end up in a filing cabinet (Malochet and Ocqueteau 2020). It never fully considered the conditions under which trust between security companies and other stakeholders could develop, especially because it assumed a top-down process could alter already deep-rooted practices via a mere ordinance. If no one is interested in assessing the good practices required to achieve professionalism in the field of security, only meaningless talk will occur, and it will be impossible to actually create a professional industry. The first concern should be for both private contractors and in-house departments to recreate earlier middle management functions that have been wiped away because of cost-cutting.

Besides, can trust be decreed when private security staff have no hope of climbing a more stable career ladder in the first place? For example, this could be achieved by creating bridges between routine security responsibilities, such as preventing individually malicious acts, and a broader conceptualization of security as managing risk and promoting safety in its many aspects. And finally, can trust be maintained when the direct supervision of private guards in vulnerable organizations remains the preserve of redeployed police, *gendarmerie*, army officers, and former civil defense firefighters?

Notes

1 The reason INSEE produces a slightly different picture from that of Cabinet I+C's report on the prevention and security industry is that it uses a looser definition of what private security is. Also, INSEE only distinguishes among four types of company sizes (large, intermediate, small SMEs, and micro companies).
2 In alphabetical order: access control, airport security, alarm intervention, armored equipment, burglar alarm, business tele-surveillance, cash transport, CCTV, cyber-security, fight against shoplifting, fire safety, guard services, industrial security equipment, locksmithing, national security, personal protection, personal protective equipment, private investigations, remote assistance, residential tele-surveillance, security engineering and consulting, surveillance drones, and training.
3 The current wording is as follows: "any activities pertaining to human surveillance, or electronic-systems surveillance, or guarding of movable or immovable assets as well as the safety of persons occupying said building or in said persons' public transport vehicles."

4 This turnaround was hinted at when violence toward security guards became more closely monitored after 2011, under the aegis of an inter-ministerial representative. Its funding was discontinued in 2013, although sporadic attempts to reactivate it have been made since then (Martin 2017).
5 This act from 10 May 2017 regulating the private protection of ships leaves the decision in the hands of the maritime prefect, upon request from shipowners, in the context of the fight against maritime piracy.
6 To access AEF Info Sécurité Globale for the various dates citied here, see www.aefinfo.fr/securite-globale.
7 *Blog 83–629*, 22/10/2018.

References

Alix, J., and Cahn, O. 2017. *L'hypothèse de la guerre contre le terrorisme, implications juridiques*. Paris: Dalloz.

Arroyo, A. 2017. *Professionnalisation et développement professionnel. Cas des agents de sécurité privée de la branche surveillance humaine en France*. Thèse de doctorat en sciences de l'Education, Université de Rouen-Normandie.

Brodeur, J. P. 2010. *The policing web*. Oxford: Oxford University Press.

Codaccioni, V. 2018. *La légitime défense, Homicides sécuritaires, crimes racistes et violences policières*. Paris: CNRS.

Conseil National des Activités Privées de Sécurité. 2016. *Rapport annuel 2015*. [www.cnaps-securite.fr/actualites/le-rapport-annuel-2015-du-cnaps-souligne-un-besoin-tres-soutenu-de-securite]

Conseil National des Activités Privées de Sécurité. 2017. *Rapport annuel 2016*. [www.cnaps-securite.fr/actualites/rapport-dactivite-2016-du-cnaps]

Conseil National des Activités Privées de Sécurité. 2018. *Rapport annuel 2017*. [www.cnaps-securite.fr/publications/rapport-annuel-2017]

Cools, M., and Pashley, V. 2012. La sécurité privée en Europe: Une analyse de trois livres blancs. *Cahiers de la sécurité et de la justice* 19: 40–54.

De Waard, J. 1999. The private security industry in international perspective. *European Journal on Criminal Policy and Research* 7: 147–177.

Fressoz-Martinez, C., and Vucko, F. 2016. La sécurité: un secteur toujours en plein essor. *INSEE Focus*, n° 66.

Gallot, P. 2018. Les entreprises de sécurité privée: une faible rentabilité malgré une vive croissance. *INSEE Première*, n° 1720.

Gautron, V. 2019. Surveiller, sanctionner et prédire les risques: les secrets impénétrables du fichage policier. *Champ pénal/Penal field*, XVII. [http://journals.openedition.org/champpenal/10843; DOI: 10.4000/champpenal.10843]

Haas, P. 2018. *Atlas de la sécurité: Panorama économique du marché de la sécurité*. Paris: Technopresse.

Institut d'Informations et de Conjonctures Professionnelles (Cabinet I+C). 2017. *Enquête de branche Prévention-Sécurité*. Paris.

Malochet, V. 2019. L'armement des polices municipales en voie de généralisation. *Institut d'Aménagement et d'Urbanisme- Ile de France*, n° 796.

Malochet, V., and Ocqueteau, F. 2020. Le gouvernement de la sécurité publique par la pluralisation des forces et des ressources. *Gouvernement et action publique* (forthcoming).

Martel, E. 2019. Le armes non létales sont-elles létales … et vice-versa? *The Conversation*, 6 février, online.

Martin, G. 2017. *La violence à l'encontre des agents de sécurité privée: La place du CNAPS entre prise de conscience et déficit d'investissement des acteurs du secteur.* Toulouse: Universite Toulouse Capitole, Mémoire de Master 2, Politique et sécurité.

Mulone, M., and Dupont, B. 2008. Saisir la sécurité privée: Quand l'Etat, l'industrie et la police négocient un nouveau cadre de régulation. *Criminologie* 41: 103–131.

Ocqueteau, F. 1991. Surveillance et gardiennage: recensement et enjeux. *Questions pénales*, IV, 4. [www.cesdip.fr/IMG/pdf/QP_12_1991.pdf]

Ocqueteau, F. 2004. *Polices entre Etat et marché.* Paris: Presses de Science Po.

Ocqueteau, F. 2006. France. Pp. 55–76 in T. Jones and T. Newburn (Eds.) *Plural policing, a comparative perspective.* London: Routledge.

Ocqueteau, F. 2013. First steps of the National Council for Private Security Activities CNAPS. *Penal Issues* V: 1–5. [www.cesdip.fr/wp-content/uploads/PI_11_2013-2.pdf]

Ocqueteau, F. 2016. La privatisation du renseignement en *questions: convergences* européennes et singularités françaises. Pp. 283–296 in S. Y. Laurent and B. Warusfel (Eds.) *Transformations et réformes de la sécurité et du renseignement en Europe.* Pessac: Presses Universite de Bordeaux.

Ocqueteau, F. 2018. Pourquoi l'Etat français a-t-il armé les agents privés de sécurité? *Métropolitiques* 5 (March).

Ocqueteau, F. 2019. "Guerre au terrorisme": Une croisade morale sous le regard critique des sciences sociales. *Revue Française d'Administration Publique* 170: 475–492.

Ocqueteau, F., and Laurent, S. Y. 2019. Les acteurs régaliens du renseignement, retour à l'empirie. Introduction. *Champ pénal/Penal field*, 17. [https://journals.openedition.org/champpenal/10672]

Paulin, C. 2017. *Vers une politique publique de la sécurité privée?: Réguler la sécurité privée, 1983–2014.* Thèse pour le doctorat de science politique. Guyancourt: UVSQ.

Péroumal, F. 2008. Le monde précaire et illégitime des agents de sécurité. *Actes de la recherche en sciences sociales* 175: 4–17.

Robert, P. 2018. Une justice instrumentalisée. Pp. 335–357 in M. Cicchini and D. Vincent (Eds.) *Le nœud gordien. Police et justice, des Lumières à l'Etat liberal.* Genève: Georg.

Robin, M., and Mordier, B. 2013. La sécurité, un secteur en pleine expansion. *INSEE Première*, n° 1432.

Thourot, A., and Fauvergues, J. M. 2018. *D'un continuum de sécurité vers une sécurité globale.* [www.gouvernement.fr/sites/default/files/document/document/2018/09/rapport_de_mme_alice_thourot_et_m._jean-michel_fauvergue_deputes_dun_continuum_de_securite_vers_une_securite_globale_-_11.09.2018.pdf]

Warfman, D., and Ocqueteau, F. 2011. *La sécurité privée en France.* Paris: Presses Universitaires de France.

White, A. 2010. *The politics of private security: Regulation, reform and re-legitimation.* Basingstoke: Palgrave Mcmillan.

Chapter 10

The Pluralization of Local Policing

Virginie Malochet

In France, security management bears the mark of a political and administrative model based on a strong state. It is deemed to be part of a dual and centralized state apparatus made up, on the one hand, of the national civilian police force with jurisdiction over urban areas, and, on the other hand, of the national *gendarmerie*, a force with military status that has authority over suburban and rural areas. Developed in the 20th century, this police system has reinforced the accepted notion that security is the exclusive preserve of the state's centralized and overarching authority. It is this aspect of the French system which inevitably stands out when international comparisons are made (Monet 1993; Ferret 2004).

Yet, this deeply ingrained model is neither complete nor rigid, and it would be a mistake to push this point too far. Given local realities, it is necessary to provide a more finely tuned picture. In practice, dealing with security challenges is not the exclusive province of state forces. Many other actors are involved whose role has been increasing continually in recent years, as shown by the rhetoric of the "coproduction of security," which has spread to the top of the state, thereby testifying to institutional changes in the management of public order (Ocqueteau 2004).

In an official speech in early 2019, the French minister of the interior called for "greater engagement with overall security" and for "strengthening cooperation between the state, local authorities, municipal police forces, voluntary organizations and private security actors."[1] His speech was in line with the work of a parliamentary mission mandated a few months earlier to deliberate on "conceiving a security continuum" (Fauvergue and Thourot 2018, p. 15). The very purpose of this mission testifies to the ongoing pluralization of policing in France and in most other European and Western countries (Jones and Newburn 2006). This trend towards the pluralization of policing reveals "an end to state monopolization of sovereign governmental functions" (Roché 2004), greater sharing of policing duties, and the "multilateralization" of possible linkages between the central and local levels and the public and private sectors (Bayley and Shearing 2001). Thus, in addition to the police, other actors with varying legal statuses operate in the field of security, raising questions about training, regulation, coordination, and the potential risk of confusion (Boels and Verhage 2016).

By adopting a broader historical perspective, we can question the apparent novelty of this phenomenon. In fact, the contribution of non-state actors to policing is nothing new, be it in France or anywhere else. But the current dynamic of pluralization is all the more significant because it goes against the preceding sequence of monopolization by nation-states. Today it is enabled by the transformation of public action in the context of a fiscal crisis and increased security pressure in an ever more risk-aware control society (Beck 2001; Garland 2001). And, of course, there is particular importance attached to the role of responding to terrorist threats. However, this dynamic does not manifest itself everywhere in the same way. It takes different forms depending on the territories concerned, their history, and distinguishing features (Terpstra and Devroe 2015; O'Neill and Fyfe 2016; de Maillard 2017).

Regarding France, three main trends are noteworthy. The first concerns citizen participation, which has been encouraged by the development of networks generally referred to as neighborhood watch,[2] and by the strengthening of policing reserve units assembled as part of the National Guard, which President Hollande wanted to establish following a wave of deadly attacks in 2016. That said, compared with many other countries, the direct mobilization of inhabitants remains limited as far as policing is concerned, all the more so as the organizational model of French society enshrines the primacy of the state, and the mobilization of citizens is held in suspicion, particularly since the deep trauma of collaboration with the enemy during World War II (Malochet 2017a). By contrast, the second trend is very marked. It relates to the development and legitimization of the private security market in the face of exponential growth in demand for surveillance and access control in shopping centers, airports, and other spaces open to the public (Ocqueteau and Warfman 2011).

A third trend concerns the diversification of security providers in the public or semi-public domain, in addition to central government providers. First, there are the security services provided by mayors and local government authorities, but also by bodies in charge of sectors that are structurally important for the lives of local areas, notably transport operators and social landlords. These various actors are becoming more and more involved in day-to-day security policies, which notably involves the deployment of their own security units. This is the issue this chapter aims to highlight. This issue might seem very mundane in contexts in which security is seen as a local concern. However, it is far from commonplace in a country such as France with its centralized tradition, particularly in a field that the national imagination strongly identifies as one of the state's sovereign governmental functions. Yet, the facts show evidence of a renewed division of security tasks in the face of the refocusing of state forces on their so-called core activity, which takes them even further away from their missions to preserve public peace. Policing is being pluralized in towns and cities through the increasing use of private guarding and surveillance companies as well as the development of municipal police and hybrid security forces charged with securing transport facilities and social housing spaces.

How should we describe these rising actors in the field of policing, who are now establishing themselves as mandatory partners of the state? What role do they play locally alongside the national police and gendarmerie? To what extent are they helping to reshape the internal security structure? Building on a series of empirical studies, this chapter highlights the challenges in terms of governance, linkages, and positioning that are emerging in the pluralized landscape of French policing.

Diverse Public and Semi-public Local Security Actors

In the mixed economy (Crawford et al. 2005) that now governs the production of security, municipal police forces, in-house security departments of transport businesses and social housing bodies, as well as state forces and private service providers are all stakeholders. Let us briefly review them.

The Municipal Police

Although based on a strong centralized state, the French political and administrative system encompasses local government authorities organized in several layers. This system is often described as multi-layered because it is very fragmented, this despite attempts to simplify it in a series of reforms. In parallel with central and devolved government departments, in France there are several levels of decentralized local government bodies, featuring some 35,000 municipalities (*communes*), over 1,200 intermunicipal authorities (*intercommunalités*), around 100 counties (*départements*) and 18 regions. To varying extents, these different tiers are involved in local security policies. Indeed, their involvement has been growing visibly as the pressure of security concerns has increased in the face of the heightened terrorist threat (Malochet 2018).

Although all levels of local government are concerned to some degree, it is municipalities, which represent the lowest level of government but are closest to the people, that are by far the most involved in security. French mayors have broad police powers to ensure law and order in the community. Since the late 1970s, mayors have been reinvesting in this aspect of their role (Le Goff 2008) and, as a result, municipal police forces have been gaining momentum. Their existence is not legally mandatory; it is the mayor who decides whether they are necessary. However, it must be said that they have developed greatly and become commonplace in the French security landscape. And yet their resurgence in the 1980s gave rise to a great deal of controversy. True, their deployment was marked by some legal uncertainty and abuses, but since then they have structured, professionalized, and institutionalized themselves, and debate about their role has become much more muted (Malochet 2014).

Now municipal police forces have raised their profiles and enhanced their legitimacy to the extent that they are described as "the country's third security force." Over a period of four decades, their headcount has nearly tripled to around 22,000 police officers spread over some 4,000 municipalities at the end of 2017. Today, out of 125 French towns and cities with over 50,000 inhabitants, only six do not have a municipal police force. Only one city with over 100,000 inhabitants is without a municipal force[3] (Malochet 2019a). Even the capital city of Paris – which has special status, with security management entrusted to a high-profile representative of the state appointed by the prefect of police (Renaudie 2008) – has intensified its action in favor of maintaining public order (de Maillard et al. 2015; de Maillard and Zagrodzki 2017). Moreover, as this chapter was being written, the mayor of Paris announced the establishment of an official municipal police force. Beyond the special status of Paris as the capital city, this example shows the growing involvement of local elected officials in an area where the stakes are high. Security is one of the dimensions considered when judging the quality of life, and comparisons are important when it comes to national and international competition among cities in the global marketplace.

During this period of expansion, several laws have been passed to reinforce the status of municipal police officers, increase their powers, and guarantee their official recognition. Within the limits of their powers, they are responsible for carrying out the tasks entrusted to them by the mayor regarding the prevention of crime, the supervision of good order, the keeping of the peace, and the maintenance of public health. Judicially, however, their area of jurisdiction remains more limited than that of state security forces. In terms of the criminal procedure code, if offenses are committed *flagrante delicto* (i.e., if offenders are "caught red handed"), municipal police officers have the same right as any citizen to arrest and hand them over to a police officer or *gendarme*. However, they have no investigative powers and do not have any authority to record complaints, which relieves them of a heavy procedural burden and frees them to concentrate fully on policing the streets.

For this reason, and given that, at most, they intervene at municipal or intermunicipal level, the municipal police forces arguably have many strengths for practicing "genuine proximity policing" (*vraie police de proximité*). At least, this is the argument that underpins the reasoning used by most local elected officials and municipal employees to legitimize their security role. However, the consensus in favor of this model is so broad that, in the last analysis, it does not say much about the nature of the actions undertaken. Beyond the components of a common language, a closer examination of local situations reveals contrasting realities. The action priorities, working hours, headcounts, and levels of equipment vary greatly from one town or city to another, reflecting significant disparities between territories as well as policy options (Malochet 2007).

Nevertheless, beyond these differences, several common trends are identifiable. Basically, the municipal police forces occupy a field of activity abandoned by the other providers, namely providing day-to-day security. However, the greater the role played by municipal police forces, the more central government agencies are tempted to assign more responsibilities to them. As municipal police forces have become settled in their ways and have been gaining new powers, they have tended to engage in more punitive forms of action, such as ticketing and arresting. The recent spate of terrorist attacks has accelerated this trend and encouraged this change in security policy, which has had an impact on the nature of the relationship between municipal police and the public.

The issue of arming municipal police officers is indicative of these trends. Under the current legal framework, it is up to mayors to decide if their police officers should be armed or not. This is a question which has long divided local elected officials. But the wave of terrorist attacks in recent years has had a profound effect on public debate over this topic. One of the victims of the terrorist attacks of January 2015[4] was a young municipal policewoman who was shot dead only because she was wearing a uniform. As a result, today, the general trend is to equip municipal police forces with both lethal weapons (revolvers, semi-automatic pistols) and non-lethal weapons (electroshock weapons, riot guns), a change in their operating model. According to the statistics provided by the Ministry of the Interior, 37% of municipal police officers carried a firearm in 2014, compared with 53% in 2019.

Public transport and social housing policing

Like city mayors, other actors have become involved in day-to-day security issues, in order to compensate for what they consider as the shortcomings of the state. This is true in particular of public transport companies (Le Goff and Malochet 2013) and social housing bodies (Gosselin and Malochet 2016). Under pressure from their employees, users, and the public authorities, these bodies have become involved in security in order to meet their legal obligations (securing their sites) and to achieve their marketing policy goals (enhancing service quality). In the transport and social housing sectors, some organizations have their own internal security departments. Under French law, such departments are involved in private security activities, even though they are an arm of semi-public institutions. By virtue of their status, these hybrid organizations provide services that are different from traditional security work (which their employers also use). Theirs is closer to police work than to the mediation systems also implemented in public transport facilities and social housing neighborhoods.[5]

The French Railway (SNCF) and Paris Public Transport (RATP)

In the field of public transport, two large state-owned organizations – la Société nationale des chemins de fer français (SNCF or French Railways) and la Régie autonome des transports parisiens (RATP or Paris Public Transport Operator) – have their own internal security departments. This follows the Transport Code and is a result of historical legacies dating from 1845 regarding the policing of railways. The railway security arm (*sûreté ferroviaire*) of the SNCF now has 3,000 employees, which is three times more than in the mid-1990s. At the RATP, over the same period the headcount of the Groupement de protection et de sécurisation des réseaux (GPSR or Paris Transport Network Protection and Securing Group) has doubled, reaching 1,000 employees today. Governed by the same laws, these two bodies are organized on a territorialized basis (with local branches), each with its own command and control center operating round-the-clock. Their staff members are equipped with revolvers and wear dark blue uniforms. They are sworn law enforcement officers and have the power to apprehend and even detain suspects, as the transport police. They are legally responsible as part of their prevention mission "for ensuring the security of persons and property, protecting the organization's personnel and assets and securing the proper functioning of the transport services" (article L2251-1 of the Transport Code).

Historically speaking, the functions of these organizations have significantly changed. Originally, their staff wore civilian clothes and their work focused primarily on dealing with theft and internal staff problems. Today, however, they focus on missions conducted in uniform in order to ensure that travelers benefit from their reassuring presence and any deterrent effects of their visibility (Bonnet 2008). Nevertheless, their image remains very much that of a transport police force. They are not to be confused with the units of the national police specially dedicated to the public transport networks. As already mentioned with regard to municipal police forces, their distinct image is growing along with their accumulation of new powers and the strengthening of security measures in transport environments that are deemed to be particularly exposed to terrorist threats.

Social Housing in Paris and Toulouse

In the field of social housing, landlords may also monitor activities associated with their buildings. However, until recently, the only implementation of this legal provision took the form of a grouping of social landlords in Paris known as the Groupement parisien inter-bailleurs de surveillance (GPIS). Made up of 12 social landlords (from the public and private sectors, with a few having a mixed status), this body was established in 2004 with the political and financial support of the city of Paris. It has nearly 200 employees. They wear dark blue uniforms and are equipped with bulletproof vests, defensive batons, and tear gas grenades. Their job is to keep the peace in social housing properties during the night. They patrol from 7.30pm to 4.30am and intervene in response to calls from tenants. They may intervene only in the common areas of the 500 social housing properties under their surveillance. In practical terms, their job consists of removing the people who occupying entrance halls, staircases, and communal gardens. Legally, however, they have no right to force them to leave. To keep "unwanted" people away they must rely on their powers of persuasion, but rather than depending on engaging in a dialogue with those they encounter, their persuasiveness depends on a show of strength (physical size, posture, and numbers). Even though they have no formal sanctioning power, they project the image of the strong, repressive arm of the landlord charged with policing the social housing stock (Malochet 2015a, 2017c).

Late in 2018, the same type of security arrangement was inaugurated in Toulouse, under the name of le Groupement Interquartiers de Tranquillité et de Sûreté (GITeS or Inter-neighborhood Peace & Security Group). Set up on the initiative of two local social landlords, it distinguishes itself from the GPIS by its smaller size (only some 20 employees), its approach (more focused on contact with tenants), and its times of intervention (afternoons and evenings until 2am at the latest). The question is, will other systems of this kind emerge? It is difficult to answer this question because of the costs involved and the issues raised. Their security goal divides the social housing community. For some, the security arrangements described here are models to be emulated, whereas for others they are examples not to be followed because they go beyond the scope of social housing and encourage the disengagement of the state from security. Thus, these services raise two fundamental questions about social landlords' investment in security: how should their role be charted? And to what extent they should get involved (Gosselin and Malochet 2017)?

The Institutionalized Coproduction of Security

This emerging pluralized system raises questions about the French model of security management. Not only does it show the changes that are underway, but it also testifies to continuity in the midst of change, because the changes remain in the hands of the central government.

In security matters, the state remains the main actor and the master of the game. Nevertheless, against a background of serious budgetary constraints and increased security pressure, the state recognizes the current dynamics of the pluralization of policing and, to some extent, favors it. Basically, the state is trying to benefit from it in order to optimize the internal security system. As it is also concerned to retain its leadership in this regard, it is the state itself that organizes and supervises the coproduction of security.

On the one hand, the state seeks to stay ahead of actors in the security realm who are deployed independently of it and are therefore to a great extent beyond its control. This is notably reflected in the role of law and regulation. Regarding municipal police forces, several laws have been passed to control and professionalize their activity. For example, the law of 15 April 1999 was aimed at the municipal police. It legitimized their activity by establishing state control mechanisms (procedure for arming them, requiring coordination with other state forces, the creation of an inspection system, etc.). Another example concerns the supervision of real estate lessors. Six years after the creation of the GPIS (Supervisory Grouping of Paris

Landlords) under the law of 2 March 2010 that intensified the fight against collective violence, lawmakers added a provision to the act that standardized what was at that time a one-off experiment. This made it possible for social housing groups to adopt it in other places. In other words, by regulating the conditions under which the activities of other local policing actors can operate, the state has given them official recognition, thereby also supporting their development.

But at the same time, the state has extended the prerogatives of the other policing actors, which means in practice that it has transferred to them certain responsibilities that used to be performed by state employees. It has enhanced their powers, increasing their authority to play a more familiar policing role. This is particularly clear regarding municipal police officers, whose law enforcement mandate has continually been strengthened over the last two decades. They have been granted new powers to issue fines to offenders for infringing the highway code, for smoking in non-smoking public spaces, for travelling by bus or rail without a ticket, and for obstructing the closure of doors on public transport, for example. To a lesser extent, the powers of the internal security forces of French railways and the Paris transport operator were also been increased by the law of the 22 March 2016. It was intended to reinforce the fight against and the prevention of terrorism, delinquency, fraud, and incivilities on public transport. This law notably restored the right of law enforcement staff to work undercover, wear civilian clothes, and be armed, evidently for the purpose of arresting people.

In addition to broadening the scope of their missions, the process whereby the state has legitimized these additional security providers has also included sharing with them symbolic aspects of the police function. In this regard, the most significant point concerns weapons. Bear in mind that in France carrying a weapon is strictly supervised and subject to detailed regulation. That said, today the state openly favors the arming of all security professionals, which represents a major turning point. This does not apply to the staff of the security services employed by the two major transport organizations; they were already armed as a result of their history. But things are different regarding municipal police officers. The decision to arm them or not is left to the discretion of the mayor of each town or city. As noted above, municipal police officers carrying weapons is now commonplace and the state is encouraging this trend. Since 2015, several measures have been taken to this end. About 4,000 revolvers have been made available by the national police; 9mm semi-automatic pistols have been added to the list of authorized weapons; and the conditions governing the arming of municipal police officers have been relaxed under the 21 July 2016 law extending the state of emergency.[6] At the end of 2018, parliamentarians charged with ensuring the security continuum suggested taking a step further by defending the principle of *mandatory* arming of municipal police officers (unless otherwise chosen by the mayor). It remains to be seen if their recommendation will be adopted (Malochet 2019b) – and that is a very big "if," since the minister of the interior publicly expressed his opposition to this proposal in July 2019.

With regard to the security options of social landlords, their officers may be equipped with truncheons and tear-gas canisters (D category weapons according to the French classification). This is now the case in the cities of Paris and Toulouse. This policy was made possible at the end of 2011 with an exemption clause that authorized the GPIS grouping of Paris social landlords to arm their personnel in this way. Until recently other private security guards were not allowed to carry weapons during their missions (with a few exceptions such as cash-in-transit guards). But the 28 February 2017 law governing public security amended this by stipulating, without making it mandatory, that certain private security activities may be conducted with the carrying of a weapon (Ocqueteau 2018). This was also a very significant measure.

In short, in the French case, the legitimization of non-sovereign policing actors still requires the imprimatur of the central government. Faced with exponential growth in the demand for security, non-sovereign policing actors are asserting themselves as indispensable partners of the central government. However, they are still not sufficiently powerful to free themselves from the requirement of central government support for their role. To a large extent, it is from the central government that the recognition of their role as coproducers of security flows. In other words,

> the pluralization of policing in France is therefore not necessarily a sign of the future weakening of public authority. Rather, it seems to form the basis of a "strategic state" that is learning to manage a complex system without always being able to keep its many ramifications and challenges under control.
>
> (Malochet and Ocqueteau 2020, p. 11)

Governance and Linkage Challenges

As in all comparable countries (Shearing and Stenning 2016), in the face of the current realities of multifaceted policing, security governance challenges are a real issue in France. Measures have been taken to foster greater overall policy coherence. At the municipal and intermunicipal levels, local security and crime prevention councils have been set up. Chaired by the mayors, these councils provide a consultation framework for setting policy priorities. At the same time, on a more operational level, coordination agreements have been signed between municipal police forces and the *police nationale* or *gendarmerie*. Local cooperation agreements may also be signed between public and private security forces in specifically identified places, such as railway station neighborhoods or shopping malls. However, as such, these arrangements offer no guarantees of results or any assurances of effective cooperation. Their real impact depends on what the actors make of them. In fact, the partnership dynamics are never the same and often turn out to be less flexible than claimed in official speeches. Relations between state police departments and other security providers vary greatly from one territory to another. In addition to interpersonal frictions, they face recurring difficulties due to jurisdictional boundaries, transfers of responsibility and the impact their actions necessarily have on each other (Malochet et al. 2008).

For successful partnerships to form, it is not enough to set up a consultative body or to sign an agreement; these arrangements must be made to function well by giving them a practical effective content while respecting the autonomy and prerogatives of each actor, which is no easy matter. In this system, each participant's responsibilities remain linked with clearly delineated geographical areas. Thus, the question of linkages between actors covers that of connections between different scales. The areas of operation of state agencies, municipal police forces, and other security operatives overlap without necessarily intermingling, which does not make governance any easier and poses problems of coordination. This explains why some, such as the members of parliament in charge of the mission on the security continuum, recommend freeing the security function from established institutional boundaries in order to base planning on territories as they are actually experienced. To this end, they invoke the concept of the "living area" or more specifically of "delinquency area." Although this concept is now part of the day-to-day language of police officers, it remains without explicit definition. Nevertheless, it is imposing itself as a category of public action (Malochet 2015b) that justifies initiatives that ignore existing administrative boundaries. Examples of this include the mutual agreements between police forces of several neighboring municipalities; setting up a local security council covering a very busy stretch of a regional railway line; or the extension in 2009 of the Paris prefecture's jurisdiction to encompass three neighboring counties at a time when discussion of the governance of "Greater Paris" appeared to be high on the public's agenda (Malochet and Le Goff 2015).

The concept of "living area" is therefore very versatile, as it is used to designate a great variety of spaces and places. However, like institutional perimeters, it inadequately reflects issues of far greater scale and complexity. Traditional territorial patterns and spatial approaches are indeed challenged by the dynamic flow of problems and solutions that raise the question of the relevant scale of action yet make it challenging to answer (Vanier 2015). In the last analysis, the real challenge is not to define the right scale, but rather to link the scales with each other beyond the limits and inconsistencies of the various territorial divisions – once again, with a view to strengthening cooperative relationships.

In the French case, these relationships remain under the domination of the state. They highlight interlinkages and reveal a mutual interest in cooperating, but they hardly correspond to the standard models established by Adam Crawford or Jan Terpstra and their colleagues, based on research conducted mostly in English-speaking countries (Crawford 2008; Terpstra et al. 2013). The municipal police forces and hybrid security services discussed in this chapter owe nothing to the "market model," as they are subject to no competitive pressure. Nor do they owe anything to the "private government model," as the areas in which they are active are not their exclusive preserve, given that the *police nationale* and the *gendarmerie* continue to intervene in towns and cities, around transport facilities, and in social housing estates. Nor are the organizations concerned integrated into the regular central government forces ("integrationist model") or even directly coordinated by them (the "steering model"). Rather, they are autonomous entities set up and administered by the municipalities, the transport companies, or social housing landlords for their own purposes. However, it would be an exaggeration to say that these organizations and state forces operate on the basis of horizontal alliances as if they were equal partners (this would be a "network model"). The national *police* and *gendarmerie* represent national sovereignty, with much greater powers, which explains why they enjoy a form of moral ascendency over the other security providers. Their relationships remain undeniably very asymmetrical. In principle, local elected officials are supposed to implement local security and delinquency prevention policies, and indeed some of them claim to position themselves in this way in the spirit of the additional model identified by Terpstra et al. (2013) (a "local government as the coordinator" model). But in practice, within the various partnership bodies, the representatives of central government departments often keep control. The centralized state model continues to prevail. It deeply permeates security modes of governance and very often betrays an impulse to subordinate the other actors.

Forging an Alternative Policing Style?

The pluralization of policing in France raises the question of "who does what?" in the field of local security. It questions the respective positionings of the actors involved, the nature of their approaches to situations, and the construction of their occupational identities. Underlying the notions of "coproduction" and "security continuum" is the idea of a sharing of tasks and of a renewed division of labor between the various contributors. It remains to be seen how this redistribution of roles works itself out.

Are plural policing actors complementary, or are they a substitute for state action? In relation to state police forces, the municipal police, internal transport company security units, and those of social landlords, all explicitly claim to provide complementary security services. Each has their own prerogatives and areas of action. They mobilize to ensure peace and quiet in all locations, they monitor compliance with the rules of community life, and they put a stop to disturbances. In other words, they operate in neglected areas of day-to-day security, in order to offset what is often seen as the disengagement of central government policing. In any case, this is how most of the actors concerned experience the situation and explain it ("nature abhors a vacuum," they often say), giving credence to the idea of a transfer of duties at a time of state budgetary restrictions and of increasing demand for security services.

At first glance, the jurisdictional boundaries that constrain alternate policing actors, the role of the bodies (municipalities, transport, housing) they work for, and their limited scope of intervention could seem to indicate that they have a distinctive scope of activity and even approach to policing that is more focused on the quality of life and the needs of residents and passengers. In contrast, state forces often lack local anchorage (Mouhanna 2011) and suffer from a lack of trust (Lévy 2016; Roché 2016). In reality, beyond the statements of principle regarding the *complementarity* of the services concerned, their respective roles are not always as clearly defined in practice as people are led to think in the official speeches and agreements.

Apart from the fact that certain units are responsible for much tougher interventions,[7] field observation suggests a certain permeability of the boundaries that generally define their differing missions. These overlaps are due in part to the fact that state forces are sometimes tempted to use other security providers as auxiliaries. They also occur during work shifts when all the actors (municipal police forces, transport security services, social housing surveillance teams) are on the front line, facing situations that extend beyond the scope of their initial intervention. Pending the possible arrival of national police or *gendarme* reinforcements, they have to deal with the situations that confront them. For example, they may have to use force, including use of their weapons, and otherwise adopt a role different from their basic one.

However, beyond these situational occurrences, it is true that alternative security units generally focus on handling disorders and delinquency, taking a classic police view of law enforcement. However, in town and city streets, on public transport facilities, or in social housing estates, the surveillance and security duties these units carry out are not basically different from those carried out by the *police nationale* and *gendarmerie*. True, their law enforcement powers are more limited, or even out of bounds in the case of the security forces of landlords. But this does not mean that they are reimagining methods for managing the peace in local areas or that they have a distinctly different policing style. Some unarmed, professional urban mediators, or even private security officers, may propose solutions to a situation by stressing engaging in dialogue, which differs from the typical practice of the police. This leads us think that the pluralization of policing in France also implies a diversification of policing methods (Bonnet et al. 2015). But this is not really the case among the actors on which this chapter focuses, who see state forces as a powerful model with which they more or less identify.

Thus, the standard model of policing predominates among members of the municipal police and of the hybrid security services dedicated to transport and social housing. This is true even though the officers concerned do not fully enjoy existing police powers. Their own definition of their work and the way they do their job in practice show that they attach more value to "active missions," such as dealing with flagrant offences and making arrests, even though these represent only a small fraction of their ordinary activities. They position themselves as actors who have a role to play in maintaining urban order and belong to the extended policing family (Johnston 2003; Crawford and Lister 2004). This is the professional group they identify with and to which they claim to belong. Their proximity to security professions is of much greater importance to them than being representatives of local government or members of the railway worker or social housing communities, with which they do not identify. In terms of professional culture and lived work experience, they feel closest to the world of policing, notably because of having to manage difficult relationships with the public.

Like national police officers and *gendarmes*, alternate security actors represent a form of law enforcement authority. However, in the field, their authority is regularly called into question ("you are not the real police"). Given their more limited powers, they have to be all the more convincing when they take action. Nevertheless, as they wear a uniform and are armed, they represent public order, which causes some hostility towards them. Because of this, they adopt behavior patterns like those that police sociologists have highlighted for a long time (see Westley 1970). In the aftermath of confrontational episodes, they tend to feel threatened and to shut themselves off from the public. This withdrawal reflex helps to strengthen their own sense of unity but has the unintended effect of fueling a climate of mutual wariness and of increasing tension with the environment.

In short, the municipal police forces and security services of landlords and transport companies share numerous features symptomatic of the pluralization of local policing in France. They indicate the prevalence of a complicated relationship with the public and the adoption of defensive behavior patterns. They show how difficult it is to reimagine policing frames of reference (de Maillard 2013), promote another model of peace keeping, and emphasize the *preventive* dimension of public security work (Dupont and Ocqueteau 2013). As they expand, these actors seem to be moving further away from the ideal of a regenerated service, capable of preventive action, restoring confidence, and improving the quality of relations with the population, including the most unmanageable youth "clients" (Malochet 2017b). Fundamental elements of their legitimacy, including their role in maintaining the peace and their proximity to the community, lack credibility. These functions need to be made more meaningful by actually putting them into practice with action, not just words. What is at stake here is the value added by the alternative actors involved in the French security system. This is important because, in spite of reforms aimed at bringing them closer to the citizenry, the national police forces seem to have abandoned their duty to provide a preventive and regulating presence, which should be the very essence of police work.

Conclusion

In France, despite the pervasiveness of a dual, centralized state-controlled police system, other actors have joined in what is now referred to as "the coproduction of security." Beyond the rise in private service providers, the development of municipal police forces and, to a lesser extent, of hybrid services for securing collective spaces (in this chapter, public transport and social housing) confirms a trend towards the pluralization of policing. However, although indicative of a greater sharing of urban security responsibilities, this trend continues to bear the mark of a national policing model in that it is firmly under the control of the central government. Indeed, in this typically state-controlled area, the state continues to play a leading role. As it occupies a dominant position, it is the state that supervises, institutionalizes, and regulates this "coproduction" system. Nevertheless, under budgetary pressure and faced with security challenges, the state must come to terms with the other policing actors on whom it is gradually becoming more dependent. These actors respond to needs not met by the *police nationale* and *gendarmerie*, notably that of securing day-to-day peace and tranquility. However, they do not propose an alternative model and have not managed to become fully autonomous in relation to the state, from which they draw their legitimacy. Thus, their development raises not only governance and coordination issues, but also the question of positioning. Indeed, although policing in France has been pluralized by the diversification of the professional groups involved, it has not reinvented its approaches to maintaining order and responding to crime and disorder.

Notes

1 Speech by Christophe Castaner, the French minister of the interior, given in Dreux on Friday 8 February 2019 on the first anniversary of Day-to-Day Policing of Security (*Police de Sécurité du Quotidien*).
2 In fact, there are two distinctive types of neighborhood watch networks. The first are part of an official framework, supervised locally by the mayor and the representative of law enforcement forces. The second form of neighbourhood watch is informal. These bring together groups of inhabitants linked through a web platform managed by a private commercial company. Although the existence of these two types of network sometimes causes confusion, their members are supposed, at least in principle, to stick to the same role, i.e. watch over their residential neighbourhoods and inform the police of anything suspicious. In no case may they directly intervene, given that in France local self-defence groups are strictly forbidden.
3 The six towns/cities without a municipal police force are: Brest (140,000 inhabitants, the 25th largest city in France), Créteil (90,000 inhabitants), Champigny-sur-Marne (78,000 inhabitants), Issy-les-Moulineaux (68,000 inhabitants), Quimper (63,000 inhabitants), and Ivry-sur-Seine (61,000 inhabitants).
4 A series of terrorist attacks which occurred between 7 and 9 January 2015, aimed notably at the editorial team of the *Charlie Hebdo* newspaper and the customers of a kosher supermarket.
5 In its own way, social mediation also contributes to the pluralization of policing by helping to keep public order in communal spaces, but by adopting a different approach centered on dialogue and prevention (de Maillard 2013).
6 It is still up to the mayor to ask for his staff to have permission to carry weapons, but unlike in the past he or she now no longer needs to justify the request, which means the prefect no longer has the right to refuse it.

7 See, for example, the night brigades of certain municipal police forces whose *modus operandi* is similar to that of the anti-crime brigade of the national police or the anti-pickpocketing group of the railway police made up of personnel working exclusively in civilian clothes – in other words, units focused on arresting people and even on conducting investigations usually done by central government police.

References

Bayley, D., and Shearing, C. 2001. *The new structure of policing*. Washington: National Institute of Justice.

Beck, U. 2001. *La société du risque [Risk society]*. Paris: Aubier.

Boels, D., and Verhage, A. 2016. Plural policing: A state-of-the-art review. *Policing: An International Journal of Police Strategies and Management* 39: 2–18.

Bonnet, F. 2008. Les effets pervers du partage de la sécurité. Polices publiques et privées dans une gare et un centre commercial [The unintended effects of shared responsibility for security. Public and private sector police forces in a station and a shopping centre]. *Sociologie du travail* 50: 505–520.

Bonnet, F., de Maillard, J., and Roché, S. 2015. Plural policing of public places in France: Between private and local policing. *European Journal of Policing Studies* 2: 285–303.

Crawford, A. 2008. Plural policing in the UK: Policing beyond the police. Pp. 147–181 in T. Newburn (Ed). *Handbook of policing*. Cullompton: Willan Publishing.

Crawford, A., and Lister, S. 2004. *The extended policing family. Visible patrols in residential areas*. York: JR Foundation.

Crawford, A., Lister, S., Blackburn, S., and Burnett, J. 2005. *Plural policing. The mixed economy of visible patrols in England and Wales*. Bristol: The Policy Press.

de Maillard, J. 2013. Le difficile renouvellement des métiers de la sécurité publique. Le cas des correspondants de nuit parisiens [The difficult renewal of public security professions. The case of night correspondents in Paris]. *Criminologie* 46: 109–130.

de Maillard, J. 2017. *Polices comparées [Comparisons between police systems]*. Issy-les-Moulineaux: LGDJ.

de Maillard, J., and Zagrodzki, M. 2017. Plural policing in Paris: Variations and pitfalls of cooperation between national and municipal police forces. *Policing & Society* 27: 53–64.

de Maillard, J., Zagrodzki, M., Benazeth, V., and Zaslavsky, F. 2015. Des acteurs en quête de légitimité dans la production de l'ordre public urbain: L'exemple des inspecteurs de sécurité de la Ville de Paris [Players' quest for legitimacy in producing public law and order. The example of the security inspectors of the city of Paris]. *Déviance et Société* 39: 295–319.

Dupont, B., and Ocqueteau, F. 2013. Introduction au dossier "Nouveaux métiers de la sécurité" [Introduction to the file on "new security professions"]. *Criminologie* 46: 5–11.

Fauvergue, J. M., and Thourot, A. 2018. *D'un continuum de sécurité vers une sécurité globale [From a security continuum to overall security]*. Rapport de la mission parlementaire [Parliamentary commission report].

Ferret, J. 2004. The state, policing and 'old continental Europe': Managing the local/national tension. *Policing & Society* 14: 49–65.

Garland, D. 2001. *The culture of control*. Oxford: Oxford University Press.

Gosselin, C., and Malochet, V. 2016. Acteurs de la tranquillité, partenaires de la sécurité: Les bailleurs sociaux dans un rôle à dimension variable [Contributors to tranquillity, security partners. The multiple roles of social landlords]. Paris: IAU îdF.

Gosselin, C., and Malochet, V. 2017. "Jusqu'où ne pas aller trop loin?" Les bailleurs sociaux face aux enjeux de sécurité ["To what extent should we not go too far?" Social landlords and security challenges]. *Espaces et Sociétés* 171: 129–143.

Johnston, L. 2003. From "pluralisation" to the "police extended family": discourses on the governance of community policing in Britain, *International Journal of the Sociology of Law*, 31: 185–204.

Jones, T., and Newburn, T. (Eds). 2006. *Plural policing. A comparative perspective*. New York: Routledge.

Le Goff, T. 2008. *Les maires, nouveaux patrons de la sécurité? Étude sur la réactivation d'un rôle [Are mayors the new leaders of security? Study of the reactivation of their role]*. Rennes: Presses Universitaires de Rennes.

Le Goff, T., and Malochet, V. 2013. *Étude sur la sécurisation des transports publics franciliens. Rapport de synthèse [Study of making public transport safer in the Paris Region. Synthesis report]*. IAU Île-de-France.

Lévy, R. 2016. La police française à la lumière de la théorie de la justice procédurale [The French police in the light of the theory of procedural justice]. *Déviance et société* 40: 139–164.

Malochet, V. 2007. *Les policiers municipaux [Municipal police officers]*. Paris: PUF.

Malochet, V. 2014. Les polices municipales, les maires et les transformations du paysage français de la sécurité publique [Municipal police forces, mayors and the changing French public security landscape]. *Les Cahiers de la sécurité* 26: 30–40.

Malochet, V. 2015a. *Le Groupement Parisien Inter-bailleurs de Surveillance (GPIS), Sociographie d'une exception parisienne [GPIS, grouping of Paris social landlords, social analysis of an exception in Paris]*. Paris: IAU îdF.

Malochet, V. 2015b. Bassin de délinquance: une catégorie opérante pour le Grand Paris? [Delinquency area: An operative concept for Greater Paris?]. *Les Cahiers de l'IAU* 172: 138–139.

Malochet, V. 2017a. *La participation des citoyens en matière de sécurité locale. Diversité des regards et des modes d'implication [Participation of citizens in local security. Diversity of viewpoints and modes of involvement]*. Paris: IAU îdF.

Malochet, V. 2017b. Les relations police/population sous le prisme de la pluralisation du *policing* en France: Le cas des polices municipales et des services de sécurité interne de la SNCF, de la RATP et des bailleurs sociaux parisiens [Relationships between the police and the local population from the point of view of pluralization of policing in France. The cases of municipal police forces, internal security services at SNCF, RATP and social landlords in Paris]. *Les Cahiers de la Sécurité et de la Justice* 40: 13–22.

Malochet, V. 2017c. Contours et positionnement d'une forme hybride de policing résidentiel. Le cas du GPIS [Contours and positioning of a hybrid form of residential policing. The case of GPIS]. *Champ pénal/Penal Field* [online] XIV.

Malochet, V. 2018. *La gouvernance de la sécurité publique en Île-de-France: Implication et imbrication des collectivités locales et des intercommunalités [Governance of public security in the Paris Region. Involvement and interlocking of local and intermunicipal authorities]*. Paris: IAU îdF.

Malochet, V. 2019a. *Les polices municipales des plus grandes villes de France. Panorama factuel [Municipal police forces in the largest French cities. Current panorama].* Paris: L'Institut Paris Region.

Malochet, V. 2019b. L'armement des polices municipales en voie de généralisation [The arming of municipal police forces in the process of being generalised]. *Note rapide de l'IAU* 796.

Malochet, V., and Le Goff, T. 2015. Le Grand Paris de la sécurité [Security in Greater Paris]. *Note rapide de l'IAU* 702.

Malochet, V., and Ocqueteau, F. 2020. Gouverner la sécurité publique. Le mdèle français face à la pluralisation du policing [Govern public safety. The french model faced with the pluralization of policing]. *Gouvernement et action publique* 9(1): 10–31.

Malochet, V., Pouchadon, M.L., and Vérétout, A. 2008. *Les polices municipales. Institutionnalisation, logiques d'action et inscription dans les systèmes locaux de sécurité [Municipal police forces. Institutionalisation, logical course of action and integration in local security systems].* LAPSAC-Université Bordeaux 2 & IRTSA report for l'INHES.

Monet, J. C. 1993. *Polices et sociétés en Europe [Police forces and society in Europe].* Paris: La Documentation française.

Mouhanna, C. 2011. *La police contre les citoyens [The police against citizens].* Nîmes: Champ Social Editions.

Ocqueteau, F. 2004. *Polices entre État et marché [The police forces between the state and the market].* Paris: Presse de la Fondation nationale des sciences politiques.

Ocqueteau, F. 2018. Pourquoi l'Etat français a-t-il armé les agents privés de sécurité? [Why did the french state arm private security agents?] *Metropolitiques* [online].

Ocqueteau, F., and Warfman, D. 2011. *La sécurité privée en France [Private security in France].* Paris: Presses universitaires de France.

O'Neill, M., and Fyfe, N. R. 2016. Plural policing in Europe: Relationships and governance in contemporary security systems. *Policing & Society* 27: 1–5.

Renaudie, O. 2008. *La Préfecture de police [The prefecture of police].* Paris: LGDJ.

Roché, S. 2004. Vers la démonopolisation des fonctions régaliennes: contractualisation, territorialisation et européanisation de la sécurité intérieure [Towards the end of the monopolisation of sovereign governmental functions: Contractualisation, territorialisation and Europeanisation of internal security]. *Revue Française de Science Politique* 54: 43–70.

Roché, S. 2016. *De la police en démocratie [The police in a democracy].* Paris: Grasset.

Shearing, C., and Stenning, P. 2016. The privatization of policing: Implications for democracy. Pp. 140–148 in A. Leander and R. Abrahamsen (Eds). *Routledge handbook of private security studies.* London and New York: Routledge.

Terpstra, J., and Devroe, E. 2015. Plural policing in western Europe: A comparison. *European Journal of Policing Studies* 2: 235–244.

Terpstra, J., Van Stokkom, B., and Spreeuwers, R. 2013. *Who patrols the streets? An international comparative study of plural policing.* Chicago: Eleven International Publishing.

Vanier, M. 2015. Des bassins, encore des bassins, toujours des bassins … [Catchment areas, more catchment areas, catchment areas everywhere …]. *Les Cahiers de l'IAU* 172: 12–14.

Westley, W. A. 1970. *Violence and the police: A sociological study of law, custom and morality.* Cambridge: MIT Press.

Chapter 11

Security Partnerships in France

Thierry Delpeuch and Jacqueline E. Ross

In France, as elsewhere, the management of security problems involves a growing number of stakeholders with diverse institutional affiliations and professional backgrounds. They are called upon to work together within the framework of inter-organizational and inter-professional mechanisms known as "security partnerships" (Crawford 1999). These devices are intended to initiate, orchestrate, and support the "co-production" of responses to insecurity (Delpeuch and Ross 2018). They now play a very important role in the implementation of security policies at both the national and local level, particularly regarding crime prevention. It is now generally accepted that all agents who have the capacity to do something to address a security concern must take part in a collective effort to solve the problem, an effort that most often takes the form of "networking" within a more or less organized and more or less formalized collective action system.

In France, all areas of internal security now include partnership mechanisms: international cooperation, crime prevention, community policing, criminal investigation, national security (political extremism, religious radicalization, terrorism, etc.), peacekeeping, order maintenance, risk management, threat abatement, and the like. These mechanisms can provide governance functions for networked collaboration, such as the Inter-ministerial Committee for the Prevention of Delinquency and Radicalization (Comité interministérielle de prévention de la délinquance et de la radicalisation, CIPDR) or the Local Security and Crime Prevention Councils (Conseils locaux de sécurité et de prévention de la délinquance, CLSPD). They may advise public authorities and develop standards on a specific issue, working closely with institutions such as the Inter-ministerial Mission to Combat Drugs and Addictive Behaviors (Mission interministérielle de lutte contre les drogues et les conduites addictives, MILDECA) or the Inter-ministerial Mission for the Protection of Women (Mission interministérielle pour la protection des femmes, MIPROF). Finally, they can carry out operational missions, as is the case with the Regional Intervention Groups (RIGs) responsible for combating crime by combining criminal, customs, fiscal, and administrative resources.

This chapter deals more particularly with local partnerships between public entities (administrations, local authorities, public services, etc.) and semi-public ones (associations), mainly at the local level. These cooperative ventures correspond to the English-speaking countries' concepts of crime prevention partnerships and the multi-agency approach. Public–private collaborations – i.e. partnerships labelled plural policing or third party policing by the international criminology literature – are not being discussed here, as they are much less developed in France than in English-speaking communities and are rarely studied by French police specialists (Bonnet 2008); the partnerships analyzed here take the form mainly of consultation and co-management forums in which territorial actors have the opportunity to share information and set up joint initiatives.

As for France, the development of security partnerships has been promoted and supported since the mid-1990s by the establishment of a legislative and regulatory framework, as well as by the construction of a "devices and instruments directory" designed to structure and facilitate horizontal collaboration at local level. Despite the elaboration of national schemes meant to support local partnership institutions, local security partnerships are struggling due to a series of obstacles and impediments that hinder cooperation and coordination within current frameworks for putting what they decide into action. Nevertheless, there are some French localities – particularly in large urban areas – in which local security partnerships are becoming stronger, more deeply rooted, and more diverse, even though significant local variation persists, and even though significant obstacles to cooperation remain.

The Institutional Framework of Local Security Policies

The expansion of local security partnerships in France results from a historical dynamic that emerged during the 1980s and 1990s: the transformation of public policies through the adoption of English and American models for managing security problems involving a plurality of actors (de Maillard 2009). The stabilization of an institutional framework for the co-production of security took place at the beginning of the 2000s, after two decades of trial and error, during which the country experimented with a succession of partnership mechanisms.

Since 1983, and the submission of the report by the Commission des maires pour la sécurité dans la ville (Commission of Mayors for Security in the City) chaired by Gilbert Bonnemaison, local security partnerships have been gradually institutionalized. The main stages of that process included: the creation of the Municipal Crime Prevention Councils (Conseils communaux de prévention de la délinquance, CCPDs) in 1983; the establishment of the Local Security Contracts (Contrats locaux de sécurité, CLS) in 1997, and the launch of the Local Security and Crime Prevention Councils (Conseil locaux de sécurité et de prévention de la délinquance, CLSPD) in 2002. These institutions have been integrated into an overarching contractual scheme for urban policymaking at the local level. This is the national framework for the social and economic development of disadvantaged neighborhoods and for urban renewal (Epstein 2013).

This institutionalization is part of a whole series of transformations in the dynamics of governance: decentralization of administrative powers from state to local authorities (Thoenig 1992); recognition that quality of life issues need to be addressed at the level (known as "territorialization" in French); efforts to develop new venues for democratic participation and consultation in the elaboration of public policy; de-sectorization and contractualization of public activity (de Maillard 2000) and the state's gradual relinquishment of its erstwhile monopoly on sovereign functions (Roché 2004a).

The principles of local security co-production were defined when, at the end of the 1990s, the first mechanism was set up to enable local actors to formalize a partnership strategy for deliberation about security concerns. This mechanism was called the Local Security Contract. This was an innovative framework for policymaking: it forced stakeholders to adopt a structured and streamlined approach, such as "project management," for deliberation and decision-making. Indeed, when developing a CLS, participants in this partnership must collaborate on a diagnostic study of local security problems. The resulting inventory must take account of crime, petty nuisances, public safety, quality of life concerns, and fear of crime. It must assess the adequacy and effectiveness of current approaches as well as the problems with the way such issues are being addressed. And it must specify residents' security needs and expectations. Based on this diagnostic report, partners must define objectives and priorities. They must also set up an action plan informed by the targeted problems; and the action plan must include target dates for the attainment of interim benchmarks and describe how the plan should be implemented. The plan must also provide for a mechanism that allows the partners to monitor results, using performance indicators that are agreed on in advance (Gautron 2010). Subsequent frameworks for collaboration took the same basic form.

The partnership approach aims to inaugurate a dialogue between the various local actors, with a view to creating mutual understanding and improving trust, knowledge, and a climate of trust. The aim of these discussions and exchanges is to identify and analyze problems of mutual concern and to bring the actors' vision of the problems more closely into alignment, culminating, ideally, in agreement on what actions to take and how to divide up the labor between the stakeholders. This requires the partners to share information and expertise, pool resources, and assess the impact of joint actions. Champions of such partnerships advocate a global approach to security; strategic management (inspired by the SARA problem-solving policing approach); networked collaboration; decentralized management of local security concerns; and efforts to obtain buy-in from local residents.

In 2002, the local governance of partnership action was entrusted to local security and crime prevention councils, including municipal councils, called CLSPDs, and regional councils, called CISPDs, that bring together multiple municipalities under one administrative umbrella. Coordinated by the mayor or a regional administrator, these councils bring together representatives of the prefect, the prosecutor, mayor's offices, and security forces (national police, national *gendarmerie*, municipal police). They also include public housing officials, representatives of common carriers, school officials, social services, victims' aid societies, and non-profit urban development specialists, along with tenants' associations. These CLSPDs have now replaced the CLS, though that older system has not been entirely scrapped.

CLSPDs encourage the formation of breakout groups (*cellules de veille*) that deal with security issues in critical districts. These bring together ground-level actors to monitor the security situation and formulate an immediate response to events that mobilize public outrage and that might otherwise trigger a riot.

Another important security partnership is the local crime treatment group (Groupe local de traitement de la délinquance, GLTD), which, unlike the others, is organized and headed by a prosecutor. It brings together police and municipal security officials, along with a subgroup of the officials who take part in the CLSPD, depending on the nature of the crime problem at issue. This collaborative venture focuses specifically on criminal offenses, not quality of life issues loosely construed. The point of this venture is to fine-tune criminal investigations, charges, and sanctions to the nature of a crime problem that is confined to a particular location and involves a very small range of targets – sometimes only a single individual. The idea is to assemble everyone with expertise on one particular crime problem, to deal with it collaboratively. GLTDs are created for a limited period of time, as the imposition of sanctions on a particular individual or group of individuals usually ends its reason for being (Wyvekens 1999, 2000).

Thanks to these different mechanisms, the municipality has become the main platform for public action in local security policies. Nevertheless, some coordination mechanisms remain at the level of the county (*département*). In particular, a new partnership entity was set up in 2002: the County Council for Crime Prevention (Conseil départemental de prévention de la délinquance, CDPD). This structure brings together, under the prefect's chairmanship, the same range of operators as the CLSPDs. Its mission is to undertake annual review of a comprehensive report on the security situation of the county; to suggest solutions to actors in the field; and to support their initiatives and to draw up county-level crime fighting and crime prevention in various domains: victim assistance, road safety, drug interdiction, reduction and management of addictions, violence against women, hooliganism, sects, and radicalization.

In addition to these numerous committees, various conventional instruments have been created to encourage and organize bilateral cooperation between a state entity (police, *gendarmerie*, justice) and another security actor – municipal police, a low-income housing organization (known as HLM, *habitation à loyer modéré*), public transportation, etc. Examples include coordination agreements between national and municipal police forces; citizen participation protocols to facilitate self-monitoring of the neighborhood by residents (in conjunction with the city hall and the police); agreements spelling out the terms of information sharing between professionals who must protect the confidentiality of clients; and agreements between landlords and the police to allow access to stairways and carry out searches of common areas.

All these partnership mechanisms and tools are special in that they do not constitute mandatory frameworks for public security action in the territories. Participants have considerable margins of autonomy, which allow them to choose not to use these mechanisms, to limit their involvement to purely formal participation, or to withdraw from them if they so wish. These instruments function much more like resources that participants wishing to promote partnership policies can mobilize. They are then used in a flexible way, as frameworks to facilitate networking and coordinating action plans, in the service of collaboration whose form, scope, and objectives vary significantly from one place to another and wax and wane over time, reflecting changes in the participants' level of trust and their willingness to engage each other as partners.

The characteristics of French partnerships

In France, there is therefore a profusion of mechanisms that can serve as institutional support for local security partnerships. Despite this diversity, however, these mechanisms share several features.

First, they focus their energies on a limited number of infra-municipal sites, most of which are relatively small. As a rule, they encompass an area that ranges from a city block to a neighborhood. Their selection is often a contentious issue, as these areas benefit from site-specific subsidies and additional police resources. The selection criteria are somewhat vague and vary with the place and time when the choice is made and with the institutions involved in the process. Relevant criteria include crime rates, indicators of social dysfunction, or vulnerability based partly on incident reports compiled by social workers, housing officials, common carriers, and other institutional actors, and demographic data indicating a sizeable presence of at-risk groups (Bonelli 2008).

Second, partnership mechanisms are mainly oriented towards dealing with petty crime and minor disorders that affect residents' quality of life and generate a climate of fear or a sense of public disorder. Many of these disorders are linked to juvenile misconduct: occupying or damaging public spaces, violence in schools or on public transport, noise pollution, motorcycle rodeos, etc. Partnerships aim to contain these phenomena by doing something about so-called "no-go" areas in which public actors are unwilling to intervene to maintain the public peace (Roché 2002). Preferred tools for this are video surveillance, situational crime prevention, and conflict mediation. In recent years, the partnership approach has been extended to new security concerns centering on economic crime, with county operational committees in charge of developing policy and action plans in this area. Newer crime-specific committees include the county-wide operational anti-fraud committees (Comités opérationnels départementaux anti-fraude, CODAF), created in 2008, and a new committee tasked with fighting terrorism and radicalization (Comités départementaux de prévention de la radicalisation, CDPR), which was set up in 2016.

Finally, municipal actors play a central role in most local security partnerships. This predominant influence was recognized by the 2007 Crime Prevention Act, which makes the mayor the main driving force behind local security policies, but it above all results from the many assets cities have at their disposal to assert their leadership on public action in this field.

Indeed, mayors are the only elected authorities in partnership arrangements. They know their voters hold them responsible for the security situation in the borough. That is why they have a strong interest in ensuring security partnerships operate effectively from a problem-solving perspective (Le Goff 2008). In addition, large municipalities have more budgetary flexibility than state administrations. Vested interests among their electorate have led many mayors to acquire their own resources to address security concerns. Mayors have set up a municipal service to deal with security, safety, and crime prevention issues. Mayors have also strengthened the municipal police; deployed urban video surveillance systems; recruited conflict mediators; fostered urban development to enhance the safety of public spaces; acquired geo-localization equipment; and hired specialists to aggregate and analyze incident reports (Bonelli 2008). Cities therefore have more resources dedicated to developing partnership actions than other local governments. They are able to encourage the national police to participate in inter-institutional cooperation, as this is difficult for police officers to do without the help of municipalities to carry out some of their tasks (such as dealing with problem families and young troublemakers, launching roadside check operations, monitoring sports or cultural events, intervening to stop motorcycle rodeos, etc.).

Here is another advantage of municipalities: their in-depth knowledge of the security situation. This is linked to the organization of municipal services by city zones, to the connections that exist between city councils and neighborhood associations, but also to the fact that residents constantly challenge local elected officials to address their problems and fears (Douillet and de Maillard 2008). The mayor is the only generalist participant in local security policies, unlike the other partners whose action is limited to more or less specialized problem areas. Mayors are therefore particularly capable of providing a global vision of security concerns in the community, and of linking neighborhood specialists with city-wide actors to improve the flow of information among network participants (Le Goff 2008).

Challenges Facing Security Partnerships

Most research on security partnerships highlights the difficulties partners encounter on the ground in implementing national policies developing partnership institutions in the long-term. The creation of a partnership structure in a territory does not automatically lead to the establishment of effective collaboration between participants. Indeed, several factors prevent actors concerned from truly making the available tools and mechanisms their own.

Heterogeneity of Views

One obstacle lies in the divergence of perceptions, interests, and agendas of heterogeneous stakeholders (Rhodes 2006). Depending on their professional background and institutional affiliation, participants tend to uphold their own visions of what is problematic, what problems should be accorded priority, and what constitutes an acceptable and effective solution. Such disagreements can lead to mutual mistrust, conflict, reluctance, or avoidance attitudes (Gautron 2010; Douillet and de Maillard 2008; Crawford 1999). For example, social workers, teachers, and health professionals are often reticent to be associated with the punitive interventions of the police, the judiciary, and municipal actors faced with an increase in criminal behavior (de Maillard 2001). Prosecutors and judges, in turn, want to keep their distance from other institutional players, in the name of the judicial institution's duty of impartiality (Delpeuch et al. 2014).

Rejection of Collective Constraints

Another obstacle to partnerships is actors' reluctance to abide by constraints on joint initiatives that call for coordinated action. Indeed, taking part in a collective project requires that participants question their own way of seeing things, subordinate their freedom of action to common decisions even when that means changing how they do things, accept partners' right to have a say in what participants do, and shoulder their share of the financial burden for common projects. Some actors reject the interplay of reciprocal obligations, mutual interference, and the additional costs associated with networking. They are willing to share information, engage in dialogue, accept a certain amount of coordination, but not to change their objectives and modes of action to fit into a joint strategy (Gorgeon et al. 2000). Such reluctance can be deduced from the behavior of participants who may be willing to exchange views in formal meetings, but remain unwilling to take part in joint operations, or to contribute to them in some other way. It is also reflected in entrenchment behind professional secrecy, in requiring strict respect for each other's area of competence, and even in criticizing other participants' inadequacies (Donzelot et al. 2003).

Since the early 2000s, many partners have come to insist that their repertoire of interventions as institutional actors is bound by the rules and logic peculiar to their distinct organizations. This in turn fuels resistance to investment in common projects, as it encourages partnership participants to focus on their "core business" and prioritize their organizational interests at the expense of related partnership activities. State administrations are torn between their duty to implement government and ministerial policies and the need to respond to requests from their local partners, especially since they have only limited budgets to finance partnership actions.

Problematic Management

Managing the dynamics of partnerships is challenging in a number of ways. The coexistence of multiple ways of performing certain tasks, of conflicting interests, and different degrees of commitment to the partnership project makes partnerships difficult to govern. Power rivalries, struggles for precedence, competition for resources, ideological antagonisms, and partisan conflicts oppose the different actors within steering bodies, and especially those in a position to claim leadership, namely, prefects, prosecutors, and leaders of the different government entities at the township, inter-communal, and county levels (Mouhanna 2005; Roché 2004b; Le Goff 2002). In France, the combined authority of the prefect and mayor over CLSPDs has sometimes led to political deadlock, when the two leaders belong to opposing political parties.

On the other hand, there is no obligation for actors involved in a partnership mechanism to fulfil their joint commitments. Each partner retains a high degree of autonomy in deciding what resources to allocate to collective endeavors. Everyone retains the freedom to withdraw or defect if they consider it necessary to change their priorities or consider themselves prey to unacceptable criticism from other actors or disagree with the choices adopted by the steering body (Gautron 2010; Gatto and Thoenig 1993). As a result, few partnerships have implemented instruments designed to monitor their respective contributions to the joint policy.

The lack of management tools and the lack of training in how to manage the collective initiatives of heterogeneous partnerships also impede the governance of partnership activities. Though political actors call on partners to develop strategic plans to the wealth of security issues they encounter, many partnership arrangements operate without a sound diagnosis of the environment in which they operate, without precise objectives and action plans, and without feedback or shared performance indicators. Partnerships also lack well-established procedures for how to work together and dispute resolution mechanisms. There are two main reasons for the amorphous organization of partnerships and their difficulty in developing strategic visions and approaches that go beyond modest tactical innovation to deal with individual security issues in a piecemeal fashion. First, partnership participants lack managerial know-how and, second, their willingness to work together often hinges on tacit agreement on the need to avoid tensions within the public policy network and to search for common ground. It is of course easier to agree on non-binding procedures and vague objectives. Due to such vagueness, some agents, such as law enforcement officers, are tempted to use the system to obtain commitments (from others) about things that the actors themselves care about (like actionable intelligence about serious crimes), while unloading on others those tasks they don't consider central to their own professional identity (like crime prevention). To cite another example, it is common for inner-city retailers to ask security partnerships to take action against homeless people who harass the retailers' customers, principally by removing them from the vicinity of the retailers' businesses. Similarly, some local elected officials use partnership forums as a platform to ask the state for additional police resources.

Fragility of Action Plans

One constraint under which many partnerships labor is that their dynamism depends on a few key managers' personal involvement and on those managers' ability to win the trust and cooperation of other network participants. (Such nodal figures are referred to as "*intégrateurs inter-administratifs*" (inter-administrative integrators) by Gatto and Thoenig 1993.) The departure of one or more of these central personalities can disrupt the functioning of the network or even cause it to disintegrate. The sustainability of partnership collaborations is therefore destabilized periodically by the departure and replacement of key figures. These include prefects, sub-prefects, departmental chiefs of the Public Security Police, *gendarmerie* commanders, prosecutors, mayors, and leaders of inter-municipal or departmental councils.

The organizational dynamics of law enforcement agencies also inhibit their liaisons' role in local security partnerships (Fleming 2006). Police officials must bring their political, administrative, and judicial authorities' demands to local partners' attention. Many of them view criminal investigation as the "core responsibility" of law enforcement. That is why they are reluctant to engage in local collaborations that most often emphasize order maintenance and prevention. Police officers and *gendarmes* have other good reasons to limit their involvement. Many of them lack professional training in partnership cooperation. As a result, they have trouble with finding solutions to the difficulties that arise from networking and see it as one more challenge rather as a vehicle for innovation. In addition, their performance indicators and internal promotion systems hardly take into account this type of (partnership) activity. They therefore have few material rewards and little in the way of symbolic benefit to expect from involvement in partnership ventures (Ocqueteau 2006). Finally, they must always be able to respond to unpredictable order maintenance emergencies that may call on their operational resources. Consequently, they prefer to keep their available resources in reserve instead of committing them to partnership ventures, from which they find it difficult to disentangle themselves, for obvious reasons of inter-institutional diplomacy (Gatto and Thoenig 1993).

Due to these various uncertainties and centrifugal forces, some of the partnership mechanisms fail to generate much momentum, so that members rapidly lose interest, though other partnerships have thrived despite fractious relationships between political leaders. As we have noted elsewhere (Delpeuch and Ross 2018, 2017), ground-level actors within the police needed informal contacts with outside stakeholders when the abolition of community policing in 2003 reduced the flow of information to the police from neighborhood contacts. Consultation is therefore formal and limited in nature, does not address conflicting issues, and does not lead to any concrete decisions (Le Goff 2004). The system is maintained for display purposes, to meet legal obligations, and benefit from the resources attached to it (public funds from an inter-ministerial allocation for the prevention of crime[1] and urban policy, additional police staff, etc.). The proportion of such ineffective devices has been decreasing since the 1990s.

Recent Developments in Partnerships

Despite these various inhibiting factors, security partnerships have been developing for the past 30 years within three areas: they address an increasing variety of security issues; they involve increasingly sophisticated organizational methods; and they promote the production as well as the mobilization of a great deal of new expertise in the security field.

Diversification of Objectives and Participants

The purpose of partnership initiatives has diversified. At first, it focused on petty crime and quality of life issues, educational and preventive initiatives, and victim support. It now covers a wide range of phenomena: organized crime, economic crime, fraud, bullying in schools, violence against women, radicalization, etc.

At the same time, the range of operators willing to engage in security partnerships has broadened. Actors in the housing, public transport, and private security sectors have gradually assumed the role of full participants in the collective elaboration of security policies. The reluctance of social workers and school staff to engage with law enforcement has waned over the years, although it has lingered in some places – which are generally those less affected by crime.

Partnership efforts to do something about violence in schools provide a good example of cooperation between actors who previously did not plan to collaborate with each other, given that schools prefer to solve disciplinary problems internally. The integration of schools into partnership schemes dates back to the early 1990s (Dumoulin and Froment 2003) and is reflected in recent efforts by school administrators to inform police and judicial actors of all serious criminal offenses committed on school premises. There has also been increased cooperation between junior high schools, police (including youth leisure centers run by police personnel), and the *gendarmerie* (particularly their brigades for the prevention of juvenile delinquency) as part of a concerted effort to counteract truancy and to provide programming for students whom the schools have suspended for disciplinary infractions.

Finally, each police station or *gendarmerie* brigade has a *"correspondant scolaire"* (school liaison), responsible for improving communications between schools and law enforcement officials. These officers play an important role as intermediaries and as situational crime prevention experts, since they advise schools on how to better secure their premises. They offer to teach educational modules about addictive behaviors, digital harassment, gender-based violence, and so forth. And they update the school on the progress of ongoing legal proceedings. This type of networking has become the norm in many other specialized areas of security policy, such as domestic violence, juvenile delinquency, hooliganism, road safety, crimes against the environment, economic fraud, and so forth.

French partnerships increasingly involve residents. For a long time, public security action did not go beyond the administrative sphere. Only institutional actors had a voice in the conduct of security policies (Donzelot et al. 2003). Associations were viewed with suspicion, except when they served as a conduit for administrative initiatives. The latter excluded direct citizens' involvement in their work, except as sources of information. Public authorities did not go beyond the occasional consultation of residents, which was designed to help police leadership to better understand residents' expectations and to improve techniques for quantifying changes in residents' fear of crime. Even then, public authorities only marginally integrated the points of view thus collected (Le Goff 2004).

However, since the 2000s, partnership mechanisms have been evolving towards greater public participation. Inspired by American "neighborhood watches," the *gendarmerie* has put in places similar measures since 2007, with emphasis on combating burglaries (through so-called *"voisins vigilants"*, i.e. vigilant neighbors). These watches were renamed *"participation citoyenne"* (citizen participation) in 2011. Some CLSPDs involve citizens' advisory committees in the design and evaluation of the actions carried out (for example, in Lyon, see Germain 2012, or in Marseilles and Nantes). Numerous French cities now invite representatives of tenants' associations to participate in such partnerships, and some cities have begun to experiment with focus groups of "trusted citizens" (often nominated by the police or *gendarmerie* themselves) in partnership deliberations. Some cities have found it easier to include members of the public in discussion groups sponsored by the city itself rather than by the police. For example, some municipalities have organized citizen focus groups that fold security discussions into discussions about the beautification and redesign of public spaces (which must now take situational crime prevention into account.)

Formalization of Cooperation

In addition, there has been greater formalization of partnership procedures. In the 1980s and 1990s, the most effective security collaborations took place outside formal mechanisms, in informal networks of personalized relationships.

Institutional meetings had little influence on stakeholders' decisions and had even less impact on daily practices. Formal consultation and coordination procedures were subject to "ambivalent appropriation," aiming at developing an interconnection of organizational and professional cultures, and at introducing clarity and predictability about the actions planned by one or another of the partners (Gatto and Thoenig 1993).

Informal contacts between local actors allow them to share knowledge and information useful to each. Informal relationships with trusted interlocutors are now deemed the best way to obtain relevant and reliable information about how partners intend to handle situations of common interest. These informal relationships are the preferred channel for rapid exchanges of sensitive information, i.e. information relating to facts that may give rise to negative media comments (error or fault committed by an operator, increase in a criminal phenomenon, or an initiative getting poor results).

In short, whatever its degree of formalization, the partnership is first and foremost seen as a source of useful information. Stakeholders commit not so much to initiate joint actions, but to increase their capacity to anticipate sensitive events falling within their own prerogatives. Collaboration is accepted insofar as each partner retains full autonomy with regard to others and can make use of the partnership as a means of "fully controlling and occupying its own legal and regulatory areas of intervention with regard to those of others" (Gatto and Thoenig 1993, p. 73). For example, police organizations use their external partners to know whether their street staff actually carry out their work. This form of indirect control of daily activity allows managers to assess the quality of the services provided by their subordinates while giving the impression of upholding field staff professional autonomy (Gatto and Thoenig 1993, p. 37).

Attitude towards formal arrangements changed during the 2000s. Stakeholders have learned to view them beyond simply ways of sharing information, as places to initiate and implement operational collaborations. In a growing number of places, cooperation has been strengthened, although the extent of rapprochement between partners remains very uneven from one place to another. Three levels of coordination and integration of security partnerships continue to coexist across the country (Douillet and de Maillard 2008).

At the most limited cooperation level, actors simply recognize and encourage each other, as well as exchange non-sensitive information. At an intermediate level, partners agree on a small number of common objectives and allow for limited coordination of the resources for reaching them. They agree to some extent to adjust their activities according to collective consultations and choices but avoid intervening outside their usual sphere of action. They do not question their own definitions of problems and do not plan substantially to change the way they respond. Finally, at the highest level of integration, participants consent to the steering exercised by the partnership official governance body. They are willing to engage in long-term joint actions involving pooling their resources and systematically sharing sensitive information. They settle for a distribution of roles and tasks that can lead them to adopt new forms and modalities of action. This can also involve a willingness to integrate incident reports from different sources (police, fire fighters, hospitals), to consider new explanations for familiar phenomena that might call for a new approach (such as partnership with mental health experts as a way of conducting a triage of emergency situations), and to bring new forms of expertise (and new stakeholders) into partnership deliberations. (In Grenoble, this involved non-profit organizations with expertise in survey research and mediation.)

How Partnerships Deepen

Only a fraction of local collaborations have a dynamic that leads to a significant degree of integration. In other cases, cooperation is not so strong, remains at a standstill or falters. In France, no national study has been conducted to evaluate and rank security partnerships by their degree of cohesiveness and integration. Nevertheless, various studies, as well as our own empirical research (Delpeuch and Ross 2018, 2017), make it possible to reconstruct the process of developing a highly integrated partnership. Such a process involves a series of steps.

Initially, cooperation is limited to sharing information. It promotes dialogue between participants, who learn to talk and to listen to each other. In doing so, actors get to know and understand each other better. They will no longer blame each other for the persistence or aggravation of security problems. As their exchanges increase, they become more aware of their interdependence and embrace a norm of reciprocity. As trust grows, they accept giving others a say in what they do, which encourages them to invest themselves more in their own field of expertise (Fleming 2006; Donzelot et al. 2003).

Second, actors find it less and less difficult to agree on how to interpret and address problems. They begin to see the potential benefits of breaking down the barriers between their initiatives. The more everyone knows about each other's resources and constraints, the more they appreciate what it is realistic to ask and to expect of the others, and the more obvious the benefits and opportunities of cooperation become. For example, schools realize that law enforcement can help them better protect their students and staff; the national police understand that quick and easy access to video surveillance tapes managed by the municipal police is an asset for clarifying facts; the prosecutor realizes she needs regular updates with the town hall CLSPD coordinator to adjust or explain her enforcement policy with regard to sensitive matters (Bonelli 2008).

Bringing participants' perspectives more closely into alignment, and making them aware of shared interests, can facilitate a more active form of cooperation. The first close collaborations to emerge are usually bilateral, for example between the national and municipal police, between schools and the police, etc. Under suitable conditions (accumulation of positive experiences, heavy pressure due to the gravity of the underlying crime problems, the presence of partnership entrepreneurs, etc.), broader collaborations can be achieved, typically in the form of site-specific working groups. Most often, these ad hoc partnerships bring together a limited number of participants, who are more familiar with local problems, trust each other, and already have common working habits. Such collaborations have limited objectives, such as following up a targeted audience, monitoring a priority area, working to solve a specific problem, or engaging in a particular project (Douillet and de Maillard 2008). The partners attempt to transcend the individual institutional interests of the participants; to divide tasks among the partners; to pool resources; and to enlarge the repertoire of interventions. These efforts are often accompanied by a willingness to experiment with new approaches, to create synergies, and to lend reciprocal support in ways that enhance the legitimacy of each partner's approach to a problem.

Often there is no pre-established protocol for how to deal with certain problems, since cross-cutting problems that can be viewed through multiple interpretive lenses can call forth a wide range of responses from diverse sets of actors. In some cases, however, a coherent and coordinated system of action involving most local stakeholders manages to crystallize. All professionals concerned then collaborate daily and succeed in setting up collective strategies. The development of such generalized cooperation does not exclude keeping up bilateral or restricted cooperation. It is important to stress that these effective partnerships are, to a large extent, decoupled from the partnership arrangements that national policies have put in place. Operational coalitions built from the bottom up at local level, as well as institutional arenas established by central authorities, do not follow the same logic and do not apply the same rationale towards the same issues, even though the functioning of one may affect that of the other (De Maillard 2005).

The Effects of Partnerships on Police Organizations

Few local police departments or *gendarmerie* brigades today are not engaged in partnership cooperation in one form or another. One can rightly question the impact that the generalization of the partnership model has on police organizations. This can be described as limited organizational learning.

Participation in networking leads to changes in the way police liaisons think about security concerns, as a result of their integration into "*communautés de pratique*" (practice communities) that intersect several professional worlds. However, changing mindsets and the acquisition of new knowledge do not always inspire significant changes in approaches and modes of intervention of other actors within the police.

The most common and perhaps the most effective way of involving police in a partnership arrangement is to create a unit dedicated to the implementation of related activities. At best, this unit is well integrated into the overall organization, has adequately trained staff, and is equipped with appropriate means of action and management instruments. In the worst cases, it is decoupled or marginalized from the rest of the organization. Its members must learn all the tricks of partnership on the job and have to develop their own management tools. There is of course a diversity of intermediate situations between these two extremes, but in all cases, learning and changes are mainly located in the specialized unit and have little impact on the other components of the police organization. In short, the institutionalization of security partnerships causes increasing segmentation within the participating institutions, rather than bringing about generalized change in practices.

The effects of networked work on those who participate are well known: convergence of views; emergence of a sense of belonging and loyalty to the collective; clarification of roles and division of tasks; exchange of resources; and agreement on rules of the game, coordination mechanisms, and the like (Rhodes 2006). Security partnerships are no exception, but these dynamics are most often confined to the units and staff directly involved, so that the development of collaborations is not incompatible with enduring institutional identities together with entrenched administrative cultures and professional corporatism (all of which weaken partnership ventures).

Better Knowledge of the Security Environment Through Partnerships

Effective governance of partnerships requires procedures for collective consultation and decision-making by consensus. This in turn requires each participant to produce arguments designed to persuade the others. Among professionals, the most convincing arguments are evidence-based claims supported by expertise and systematic analysis (Fischer 2000). Viewed as systematic, rigorous, and objective, expert discourse is a language partners can identify with, beyond the diversity of their institutional, organizational, and professional cultures (Callon et al. 2001). It can provide a focal point for analysis of a problem and agreement on how to address it (Fleming and Wood 2006). In France, increasing integration into security partnerships motivates the police participants to develop their own expertise in matters like situational crime prevention. Indeed, this capacity is one of the main determinants as to the political weight and negotiating power of the police in the partnership processes for the development of local security policies.

In some French cities, public authorities have initiated new forms of intervention in consultation with experts, for example by working closely with child psychiatrists to put together a multi-disciplinary crisis intervention team to treat children exposed to domestic violence, child abuse, or suicide. Other cities have used the partnership framework to set up a local observatory and to cross-reference incident reports of hospitals and fire departments, as a check on police crime statistics; yet other cities have drawn on the expertise of urban design experts, sociologists, and consulting firms to assess security risks and identify gaps in public action. Studies that link crime to demographic data and truancy statistics contribute to better understanding of the security environment (Gautron 2010). These studies draw on the methods and tools of the social sciences – survey questionnaires, statistical analysis, fact mapping – to provide support for strategic or operational decision-making. Some municipalities (such as Nantes) have hired former members of French intelligence agencies to conduct their own security analysis on behalf of the city, in order to better triage complaints about "loitering juveniles." The aim is to fine-tune the city's response, depending on whether the problem involves truancy, drug dealing, or juveniles who lack recreational outlets.

Until now, the institutional response to the need for more specialized expertise within the police has been to set up national structures such as the National Institute for Advanced Security and Justice Studies (Institut national des hautes études de la sécurité et de la justice, INHESJ), heir to the Institut des hautes études de sécurité intérieure (Institute for Advanced Studies on Internal Security) created in 1989, or the Central Service for Territorial Intelligence (Service central du renseignement territorial, SCRT). These centralized responses are out of step with the expertise needs of county-level police and *gendarmerie* services. These structures do not have the means to conduct sophisticated diagnostics of the local security environment at the request of local law enforcement officials, who tinker with their own instruments for measuring local phenomena, and their own performance indicators. Accordingly, many departments draw on external partners' expertise or on a knowledge-poor decision-making environment.

Where do things stand today in France?

In various parts of France, the partnerships that emerged in the 2000s and 2010s were characterized by a high degree of inter-organizational integration, joint governance, and collective management. Although these partnerships represent "the very best France has to offer" in terms of partnership, they nevertheless have several weaknesses.

Despite progress in opening up partnership governance (to a wider range of institutions and citizens), three sets of authorities still carry predominant weight in the management of security partnerships: the mayors (along with the head of the inter-municipal structure, the deputy in charge of security matters, the CLSPD coordinator, the head of the municipal police); the administrative authority (prefect, sub-prefect, head of the municipal police or *gendarmerie*) and prosecutors. The dynamism of cooperation depends on agreement between these three groups of stakeholders, and on their skills as inter-administrative integrators.

Non-sovereign partners and residents are consulted but they have little say in the repressive dimension of local security policies. This still is the preserve of the police, prosecutors, and political authorities. For other forms of intervention, consultation has widened at multiple geographic levels, from the infra-urban to the inter-communal and regional realms. Each level has its own participatory bodies and partnership mechanisms.

In larger geographic units, partnership committees are generally said to be engaged in strategic management, while infra-municipal committees are said to only have an operational role implementing policy. But in practice, concrete responses to security problems are often defined by the actors closest to the field, i.e. by participants in neighborhood watch cells or other groups working at the neighborhood level or even below. The pitfalls and risks attached to multi-level security governance include tensions or decoupling between the different decision-making levels, fragmented and inconsistent actions carried out by the various devices, lack of transparency, and dilution of responsibilities. The participation of associations (and, through them, of citizens) has become the norm, but the complexity of the layered system makes it difficult to assess the impact of the public partners' daily work.

Today in France, the main partnership issues are no longer reluctance to cooperate and the "democratic deficit" – two pitfalls that have yet to disappear – but the difficulty in coordinating and controlling the multi-layered partnership mechanisms that have emerged over the past 20 years. In response to this problem, the multiple authorities have sometimes set up additional coordination bodies, which have been superimposed on the old ones without replacing them.

Here is a second current weakness: insufficient progress has been made to develop techniques and instruments for piloting security partnerships and managing their work. It is now widely accepted that partnership action requires investment in territorial expertise and decision-making tools. While local actors have, on the whole, been able to modernize their information systems to meet their partnership needs, this may not be said of their analytical capacities: these remain rudimentary in France compared with what exists in English- speaking countries. There, many police forces employ professional "strategic analysts" (i.e. specialists in local security policy design) and conduct problem-oriented policing or evidence-based policing schemes in collaboration with the local academic community.

French partnerships have gotten used to setting local goals and priorities and to evaluating the results of their interventions, but their expertise in doing this remains very limited. Some partnership bodies are certainly capable of producing accurate, insightful, and relevant analyses, but the driving forces behind such a high-quality diagnosis are primarily the participants' ability to share information and engage in collective deliberation than expertise in the management of partnerships. Security engineering capabilities are not evenly distributed throughout the country but concentrated in a few large cities that have chosen to engage in the security field. A large proportion of local authorities lack such capacities, particularly in outlying areas (rural regions, as well as small and medium-sized towns far from large cities, etc.). Most of the means of diagnosing and analyzing security problems are located outside the police, *gendarmerie*, and prefectures – i.e. outside institutions covering the whole of France: this is a major factor in the unequal distribution of effective partnerships across the national territory.

A third limitation lies in the dynamics of professionalization that accompany the institutionalization of security partnerships. To work well, studies show participants in positions of responsibility must learn specific skills from their partners. Participants must acquire knowledge and know-how related to information sharing; to inter-institutional diplomacy; and to inter-professional dialogue. They must learn to translate discourses from beyond the disciplinary boundaries that separate professions from each other and must be able to persuade by marshalling expertise. While local authorities have largely relied on the development of new professionals to carry out the tasks linked to partnerships (municipal police officers, CLSPD coordinators, or prevention and security officers, mediators, specialized consultants, etc.), national authorities have generally been content to provide (some) staff with supplemental training of limited scope. There is therefore a skills gap in partnership work that is sometimes considerable between highly professionalized municipal actors and other state actors (police, prosecutors, and prefects) who are much less professionalized. However, the police have been able to develop professional specializations in a small number of specific areas, namely, in situational prevention; in cooperating with schools (through anti-drug speakers and school liaisons); in preventing juvenile delinquency (through the CLJ and BPDJ); and in addressing domestic violence (through investigators from the family protection brigades and domestic violence liaisons).

Note

1 The Inter-ministerial Fund for the Prevention of Delinquency (FIPD) is a national mechanism designed to finance actions carried out by local authorities or associations to address a variety of security problems, such as the development of urban video surveillance systems, the prevention of violence against women or of juvenile delinquency, the fight against recidivism, assistance to victims, etc. The CIPDR's mission is also to promote local partnership initiatives (Dieu 2016, pp. 84–85).

References

Bonelli, L. 2008. *La France a peur*. Paris: La Découverte.

Bonnet, F. 2008. Les effets pervers du partage de la sécurité: Polices publiques et privées dans une gare et un centre commercial. *Sociologie du Travail* 50: 505–520.

Callon, M., Lascoumes, P., and Barthes, Y. 2001. *Agir dans un monde incertain: Essai sur la démocratie technique*. Paris: Seuil.

Crawford, A. 1999. *The local governance of crime: Appeals to community and partnerships.* Oxford: Oxford University Press.

Delpeuch, T., de Dumoulin, G., and Claire, L. 2014. *Sociologie du droit et de la justice.* Paris: Armand Colin.

Delpeuch, T., and Ross, J. E. 2017. The co-production of security in the United States and France. *American Journal of Criminal Law* 44: 187–216.

Delpeuch, T., and Ross, J. E. 2018. Crime-fighting and prevention as competing approaches to collective juvenile violence: A comparative study of the United States and France. Pp. 77–88 in U. Sieber, V. Mitsilegas, C. Mylonopoulos, E. Billis, and N. Knust (Eds.) *Alternative systems of crime control national: Transnational, and international dimensions.* Berlin: Duncker & Humblot.

de Maillard, J. 2000. Le partenariat en représentations: contribution à l'analyse des nouvelles politiques sociales territorialisées. *Politiques et management public* 18: 21–41.

de Maillard, J. 2001. Les travailleurs sociaux en interaction: Politiques sociales urbaines, mobilisation des professionnels et fragmentations. *Sociologie du travail* 44: 215–232.

de Maillard J. 2005. Les politiques de sécurité. Réorientations politiques et différenciations locales. *Sciences de la Société* 65: 105–122.

de Maillard, J. 2009. Réformes des polices dans les pays occidentaux: Une perspective compare. *Revue Française de Science Politique* 59: 1197–1230.

Dieu, F. 2016. *Réponses à la délinquance.* Paris: L'Harmattan.

Donzelot, J., Mével, C., and Wyvekens, A. 2003. *Faire société: La politique de la ville aux États-Unis et en France.* Paris: Le Seuil.

Douillet, A. C., and de Maillard, J. 2008. Le magistrat, le maire et la sécurité publique: action publique partenariale et dynamiques professionnelles. *Revue française de sociologie* 49: 793–818.

Dumoulin, L., and Froment, J. C. 2003. Ecole et sécurité: les politiques de lutte contre la violence à l'école. Pp. 62–82 in J. C. Froment, J. J. Gleizal, and M. Kaluszynski (Eds.) *Les Etats à l'épreuve de la sécurité.* Grenoble: Presses Universitaires de Grenoble.

Epstein, R. 2013. *La rénovation urbaine: Démolition-reconstruction de l'Etat.* Paris: Les Presses de Sciences Po.

Fischer, F. 2000. *Citizens, experts and the environment: The politics of local knowledge.* Durham: Duke University Press.

Fleming, J. 2006. Working through networks: The challenge of partnership policing. Pp. 87–115 in J. Fleming and J. Wood (Eds.) *Fighting crime together: The challenges of policing and security networks.* Sydney: University of New South Wales Press.

Fleming, J., and Wood, J. 2006. New ways of doing business: Networks of policing and security. Pp. 1–14 in J. Fleming and J. Wood (Eds.) *Fighting crime together: The challenges of policing and security networks.* Sydney: University of New South Wales Press.

Gatto D., and Thoenig J. C. 1993. *La sécurité publique à l'épreuce du terrain. le policier, le magistrat, le préfet.* Paris: L'Harmattan, IHESI.

Gautron, V. 2010. La coproduction locale de la sécurité en France: Un partenariat interinstitutionnel deficient. *Champ pénal/Penal field* VII.

Germain, S. 2012. Le retour des villes dans la gestion de la sécurité en France et en Italie. *Déviance et Société* 36: 61–84.

Gorgeon, C., Estebe, P., and Leon, H. 2000. De la prévention sociale à la tranquillité publique: Glissement sémantique et renouveau de l'action publique. *Les Cahiers de la sécurité intérieure* 39: 223–241.

Le Goff, T. 2002. Les contrats locaux de sécurité à l'épreuve du terrain: Réflexions sur l'action publique locale en matière de sécurité. *Politiques et management public* 20: 105–119.

Le Goff, T. 2004. Réformer la sécurité par la coproduction: action ou rhétorique? Pp. 81–104 in S. Roché (Ed.) *Réformer la police et la sécurité: Les nouvelles tendances en Europe et aux Etats-Unis*. Paris: Odile Jacob.

Le Goff, T. 2008. *Les maires, nouveaux patrons de la sécurité?* Rennes: Presses Universitaires de Rennes.

Mouhanna, C. 2005. Coproduction, cohérence ou concurrence? Réflexion sur la coopération élus-policiers en matière de sécurité. Pp. 103–120 in J. F. Jérôme and C. Mouhanna (Eds.) *Peurs sur les villes*. Paris: Presses Universitaires de France.

Ocqueteau, F. 2006. France. Pp. 55–76 in T. Jones and T. Newburn (Eds.) *Plural policing: A comparative perspective*. London: Routledge.

Rhodes, R. A. W. 2006. The sour laws of network governance. Pp. 15–34 in J. Fleming and J. Wood (Eds.) *Fighting crime together: The challenges of policing and security networks*. Sydney: University of New South Wales Press.

Roché, S. 2002. *Tolérance zéro? Incivilité et insécurit*. Paris: Odile Jacob.

Roché, S. 2004a. Vers la démonopolisation des fonctions régaliennes: contractualisation, territorialisation et européanisation de la sécurité intérieure. *Revue française de science politique* 54: 43–70.

Roché, S. 2004b. Réformes dans la police et formes de gouvernement. Pp. 9–37 in S. Roché (Ed.) *Réformer la police et la sécurité: Les nouvelles tendances en Europe et aux Etats-Unis*. Paris: Odile Jacob.

Thoenig, J. C. 1992. La gestion systémique de la sécurité publique. *Revue française de sociologie* 35: 357–392.

Wyvekens, A. 1999. Le souci du territoire, les groupes locaux de traitement de la délinquance. *Les Annales de la recherche urbaine* 83–84: 81–88.

Wyvekens, A. 2000. Les politiques de sécurité: une magistrature sociale, pour quelle proximité? *Droit et société* 44–45: 127–142.

Part IV

Police Problems and Strategies

Chapter 12

Policing the *Banlieues*

Fabien Jobard

For American audiences, French *banlieues* often evoke images inspired by the ghettos of North American cities. The differences between *banlieues* and American ghettos are, however, numerous. Some 20 years ago, Loïc Wacquant (1993) demonstrated that the two social geographies are not really comparable. In order to minimize the risks of confusion and ethnocentrism (equally widespread on both sides of the Atlantic), we begin by clarifying what is meant by "policing the *banlieues*." Next, we will examine the security policies that have been developed there, emphasizing the consequences of the riots of 2005 in Paris and elsewhere around the country.

Violence and Insecurity in the *Banlieues*

For over a century the term *banlieue* has carried a strong meaning, incorporating all the fears associated with the city. These have included otherness, deviance, and disadvantage (Hargreaves 1996, p. 607). However, it is essential to understand what it is like to live in these places before turning our attention to the crime and insecurity that they are associated with.

"*Banlieue* literally means suburb, but it carries different connotations from the British or North American suburb" (Dikeç 2007, p. 7).[1] *Banlieue* is in contrast the widely used term designating an urbanized area on the outskirts of a large town. Literally, *banlieue* means "banned location": in the Middle Ages, such areas were under the control of the main town and did not enjoy the rights and freedoms that local authorities in other towns had. From the end of the 19th century, industry and its workers gravitated to the *banlieues* in response to the low land and property rentals there. French economic growth during the 1950s and 1960s, the need for a foreign workforce, and the expulsion of French citizens and pro-French Algerians following Algeria's declaration of independence in 1962, led to a massive increase in the numbers residing in the *banlieues*. Huge social housing estates (in French, *cités*) were built to accommodate this influx of new residents. These areas were placed firmly in the spotlight by the first wave of rioting that occurred at the end of the 1970s. Progressively, the word *banlieue* has become synonymous in the public imagination with a range of social problems, including deprivation and degeneration, illiteracy, drug abuse, criminality, and violence. Among the more recent issues associated with these areas are inter-racial conflict, Islamic fundamentalism, violence against women, police brutality, and, of course, riots or urban disorder.

Focusing on the poorest neighborhoods of French cities, three elements mark the profound difference between *banlieues* and inner cities in the United States. The first is the rarity of firearm use. Though increasingly associated with drug trafficking, firearms are still not widely available. Victims of firearms-related crime are rare, and the police, for their part, use them as infrequently as elsewhere in Western Europe.[2] As a result, regardless of how deep concern about violence in the French *banlieues* is, shootings are unlikely except when drug traffickers are involved. The second difference from the United States is the small impact of changes in the penal system in French politics. France is among the list of countries that have experienced a significant increase in the severity of punitive sanctions, particularly in detentions, since the 2000s. But the French situation remains light years away from that of the United States, and, to a certain extent, Great Britain. The detention rate in the USA is about 700 for every 100,000 inhabitants, while it is 150 in Great Britain, and in France's between 100 and 110. This difference is not only arithmetic. Judges on one side and the European Court of Human Rights on the other have always been careful to limit the discriminatory and irreversible effects of penal policies, so that in France there is no mandatory sentencing nor a three-strikes provision or whole life sentences without parole. Contrary to the USA, where "high incarceration rates led researchers to claim that prison time had become a normal part of early adulthood for black men in poor urban neighborhoods" (Pettit and Western 2004, p. 151), young criminals in France do not necessarily see a life behind bars on their horizon. We join David Garland (2019) in observing that the United States is the "exception" in the West. Lastly, since at least 1945, France has boasted a health and welfare system that provides (including for illegal migrants) a safety net that run-down North American neighborhoods do not enjoy. Thanks to a conservative welfare regime that is still almost intact (Esping-Andersen 1999), living conditions for unemployed, unqualified young men in France's run-down urban areas, however deplorable, are still more enviable than that of their peers in the United States. Though these features of the two countries are general ones, calling attention to them helps clarify the context in which we place this discussion of crime and policing in France's *banlieues*.

To return to the ghetto metaphor, sociological research of the last two decades has shown that a very high concentration of wealth in large urban areas (perhaps "rich ghettos") has been driven by the financializaton of the economy. One effect of this is that it has become increasingly difficult for even the better-off middle classes (including young university professors) to live in city centers, and many therefore settle in the nearby *banlieues*. Further, since the early 2000s, the state's response to urban disorder has very often been massive urban renovation involving the destruction of high rises and their replacement by small, affordable, individual housing. The French *banlieues*, then, are territories undergoing a profound upheaval, home in many cases to a diverse population sharing a relatively small territory. The further you go from the city-proper, however, the more visible are the former tower blocks. These are shunned by the middle class, but they are also being abandoned by lower-middle or working-class residents, often of North African (formerly Spanish and Portuguese) descent. They also seek accommodation closer to the city-proper, for example in Paris, Lyon, Lille, and Strasbourg, by purchasing property. Thus, the French *banlieues* are in perpetual flux. Despite the fact that within the greater Paris urban area (seven million inhabitants and about 1,000 square kilometers), the towns marked by serious social issues are the same as 30 or 40 years ago, while the city of Paris itself (two million inhabitants per 100 square kilometers) has become ever richer. In the poor *banlieues*, several phenomena seem constant: high exposure of residents to crime, heightened feeling of insecurity, high demand for policing, and the militarization and brutalization of the police.

Delinquency remains very significant in the disadvantaged urban areas of large cities. For example, in the greater Paris area (12 million inhabitants over 12,000 square kilometers), victimization surveys have shown consistent results for the past 30 years (Zauberman et al. 2013). First, in this vast and contrasting space, all crimes are about twice as frequent as the national average. This includes assault, but also robberies without violence, burglaries and attempted burglaries, and theft of and from cars. The latter, however, is the only crime that has actually seen a significant decline in 20 years. In this territory, then, where rich and poor, people of migrant descent, and those that have been French for generations all live together, just under a quarter of those questioned in the survey reported being afraid to go out in the neighborhood at night, compared with just under a third 30 years ago. But fears about safety have fallen, particularly when compared to concern about economic issues such as unemployment and poverty. Only 15% of those surveyed considered safety to be one of the "problems that should be treated as a priority by the government" in 2013, versus 40% in 2001.[3] Seine-St-Denis is a well-known region located north of Paris and south of Charles de Gaulle airport, and it includes some of the poorest towns in France. There, 34% of residents claimed to be afraid to go out at night in their neighborhood, while this figure stood at 22% among Parisians. Nearly three-quarters of all parents in Seine-Saint-Denis declared that they feared for their children's safety while outside (70%), whereas this concern affected only half of Parisian parents. These residents of poor *banlieues* feel that their environment is undignified (loitering youth, substance abuse, and damage to property) and are much more inclined than others to want to leave. In the Ile-de-France department, it is among these inhabitants that the demand for police presence is the highest.

But we have so far only talked about Paris and its surrounding area. When we look at all poor neighborhoods of French cities,[4] everything points to higher levels of insecurity than elsewhere (de Maillard et al. 2020). First, the level of fear (the percentage of respondents who sometimes or often feel unsafe in their neighbourhood) was 26% in 2018. This was significantly higher than the level of fear among the remainder of the population, which stood at 13% in other neighborhoods in wider urban areas. When it came to avoiding going out alone for safety reasons, 19% of the residents of poor city neighborhoods said they did this sometimes or often. The comparable figure was 10% for residents of non-poor areas and 14% for the entire population of urban areas of over 100,000 inhabitants. Further, residents of poor neighborhoods were much more likely to have witnessed drug use or drug dealing in the past 12 months (30% in 2018 versus 10% in the surrounding urban areas) (Rémila 2018, pp. 204–205).

Policing in Poor *Banlieues*

What is the state's response in terms of the fight against crime in the *banlieues*? Paradoxically, the state provides a police response that is both notoriously insufficient and particularly brutal, militarized, and distant. The concentration in the city of Paris of all the centers of state power and most of the country's wealthy – in addition to tourists essential to the economy – makes Paris one of the European cities with the highest number of police per capita (one police officer per 100 inhabitants). But beyond the very inner city, the *banlieues* paint a different picture. Theirs is an urban landscape of social high-rises where police presence is rare. One is reminded of the nationwide wave of riots in 2005, which began in Clichy-sous-Bois, a poor town in Seine-St-Denis about 20 kilometers from Paris. There, two children died in what started as a simple identity check (Waddington et al. 2009). The officers carrying out the check were from a mobile riot-control police unit (Compagnie Républicaine de Sécurité, or CRS) because the city of Clichy (with 30,000 residents) did not have a police station at the time. It is a tragically paradoxical effect of the riots that they focused attention on the town's situation and led to a police station being opened there in 2010. The mayor of the town recalled often how, when he had first arrived there in 1978 to open a pediatrics surgery, the town hall (then under communist leadership) displayed a banner on its façade that read, "We demand a police station for our town" (Dilain 2006). With its riot police, under-staffing, identity checks, and riots, Clichy epitomizes the current policing situation in the *banlieues* today.

In poor towns, schools are under-funded and so are the police. The state attempts within its means to remedy the situation, but France's financial balance (subjected to public spending checks by the European Union) does not allow much leeway. In Seine-St-Denis, teachers are absent more often than in the rest of France and, more importantly, there are 1.5 times fewer chances of finding substitute teachers than elsewhere. Yet, educational needs are far higher than elsewhere. By the end of primary school, two-thirds of pupils in poor neighborhoods cannot read, and in the department the percentage of students making 25 or more mistakes in a dictation increased from 6% in 1987 to 20% in 2015 (Cornut-Gentille and Kokouendo 2018, pp. 12, 14 and 25). The difficulty of teaching in this department is undeniable: 36% of primary school teachers stay in their school for less than two years (versus 26% nationwide) and this figure rises to 50% in middle schools or *collèges*, which educate children aged 11 to 15 (Cornut-Gentille and Kokouendo 2018).

These observations highlight what France's fascination with the most spectacular features of policing in the *banlieues* (violence, militarization, etc.) too often relegates to the background: policing is a public service, so its budget tracks the extremely inequitable distribution of public services as a whole.

Since policing is a nationwide service, when a police officer is assigned to a suburban town, they do their utmost to escape that posting and move closer to their hometown, which is often a medium-sized city or provincial town. National spending policies initiated in 2008 drastically reduced the number of police and gendarmes nationwide (Cour des comptes 2011, p. 47). Yet the state, because it has the authority to do so, first assigns new recruits to *banlieue*. Paris and its three surrounding departments account for 60 to 70% of postings of police academy graduates. Before 2012, due to budget cuts, the number of positions open for new police officers became scarcer. Fully 4,700 law enforcement positions were opened in 2007, compared to just over 500 in 2011 and 2012. Fewer police officers are posted in the *banlieues*, but just as many still want to get out. Poor and violent *banlieues* continue to have less police protection than elsewhere.

Some municipalities with high crime rates (for example, Bondy, Sarcelles, and Stains) have a police per capita rate of 1 for every 400 or 500 inhabitants.[5] At the departmental level, in 2012 there was one police officer for 95 inhabitants in Paris, one for 350 in Seine-St-Denis and Val-de-Marne (the two poor suburban departments bordering Paris), and one for 240 in Hauts -de-Seine (a rich suburban department) (Ocqueteau 2017, p. 22). When related not to departmental population but to the number of reported offences, the inequalities between poor municipalities strongly affected by crime and rich municipalities are even more obvious, a fact that the press has not failed to pick up on (Mandraud 2009). At the end of the first decade of the 21st century, there were almost as many police officers (5,000) in the

Hauts-de-Seine (a rich suburb west of Paris) as in Seine-Saint-Denis (an emblematic poor suburb north of Paris and France's poorest *banlieue*), yet the latter department's victimization rate is more than twice as high.

The system also results in the poor *banlieues* being the areas where there is the greatest proportion of inexperienced police officers: 20% of police in Paris and the three surrounding departments are still in training. While the average tenure in a constituency is 16 years, it is half as long in Seine-Saint-Denis, where 70% of the workforce has less than five years of seniority in the postings where they are assigned. Yet, to offset their inexperience, these young recruits prefer a more "thin blue line" vision of their institution than do their elders, believing themselves less accountable to the chain of command (Roché 2016, p. 311). What you get are police officers who are young, "ill-experienced beginners" (Cour des comptes 2011), and outsiders with precious little preparation for facing very harsh working conditions. Sociologist Jérémie Gauthier, during his observations of the police in the *banlieues*, heard the town's police commissioner remark "Policing here is pitting immigrants from the inside against immigrants from the outside" (Gauthier 2010, p. 267), underlining that the officers in the *banlieues* are immigrants from quiet provincial towns, faced with ethnic minority residents (Fassin 2013, p. 239). The commissioner's observation reveals a sense of superiority within management and their lack of support from the chain of command, reflected in the particularly high suicide rate of police officers in France (approximately 1.3 times higher when age and sex are considered) (Pelletier 2019). Those who remain are often disillusioned with their institution and mistrustful of outsiders.

While wealthy cities and suburbs can afford to run a municipal police force (albeit with far fewer powers than the national police),[6] poor municipalities cannot compensate for the state's failings in this regard. Neither has the political situation helped to improve this. The terrorist attacks of 2015 (which left 238 dead) struck the hearts of cities and prompted the government to assign even more police officers to city centers, in particular on permanent guard at official buildings, Jewish places of worship, and major sports events or celebrations. Social movements, such as the protests against the labor law reform in 2016 or the yellow vests in 2018–2019, have also increased the need for additional units of the *police nationale* or the *gendarmerie* in city centers. As always, it is the forces stationed in the *banlieues* that are drained to swell the ranks for these large-scale operations in city centers.

Consequently, having failed to increase everyday police presence, the state has instead favored the militarization of police in the *banlieues*.

The Militarization of Policing in the *Banlieues*

To compensate for not having a stable, confident, professional police force, the state has instead been tempted to resort to various militarized units. Two of these are the riot police units of the *police nationale* (CRS) or the *gendarmerie* (EGM or Esquadron de géndarmerie mobile). These are typically dispatched for a few weeks to a neighborhood, and then they leave. There are other, smaller units attached to the local commissariat, but they also are armed, equipped, and uniformed to resemble the paramilitary units described by Peter Kraska and Victor Kappele (1997), even though, unlike in the United States, these units do not usually make use of firearms.

The state attempts to fill the policing gap that has emerged by sending in large riot police units such as the CRS or EGM, which are stationed in barracks elsewhere in France. They are dispatched as necessary to areas like *banlieues* when they are not assigned to protest policing operations in city centers. There they are used for large demonstrations or the prevention of terrorist attacks at sporting events or celebrations. Assigned to a neighborhood in an unknown *banlieue* for a few hours or a few days, these units know neither the residents nor the environment. So, they resort to standardized reponse: restoring order in critical situations and carrying out identity checks when there are no emergencies. From my own ethnographic observations of police teams in the Paris *banlieues* in the 2000s, I found that when these mobile units are assigned, the town's regular officers complain because the outsiders do virtually nothing but identity checks and thus monopolize local police radio channels (identity details are sent to the central commissariat to check if the person is wanted or has a record, etc.). This temporary, distant police force does little to address the need for police presence that is felt by the residents themselves. Their mode of action demonstrates the distance and contempt of state employees, rather than a closeness to the population and an ability to listen to community concerns. This behavior is exacerbated by the fact that these officers will never have to answer to those residents, since they will depart at the end of their assignment. There have been numerous ethnographic observations of these demonstrations of contempt, ranging from unwarranted ID checks to outright displays of violence which are rarely ever punished (Jobard 2005; Fassin 2013; Gauthier and Lévy 2015).

In 2012, the government created *zones de sécurité prioritaires* (high-priority safety areas, or ZSPs), in order to focus police resources in specific areas and encourage greater involvement of police in local life, be it at the political, administration, or civil society level. But the ZSPs were never able to resist budget cuts or their inevitable redeployment to counterterrorism or other newsworthy operations. The police are inevitably at the mercy of crime news reporting, to which they are quite rightly expected to respond. A commissaire in Seine-Saint-Denis might delight in seeing the recruits he had requested for so many years finally joining his ranks, only to have them leave his command a few weeks later for an emergency posting in Marseille following a shooting. When three police officers were attacked with a Molotov cocktail in their patrol car in October 2016, the ministry decided to send 103 officers to the Essonne department. However, in the face of the police protests generated by the attack, the ministry announced that in *all* ZSPs officers should thereafter patrol in threes, effectively reducing the sought-after police coverage in these urban areas. Examples abound of organizational changes which undercut moves to increase police presence. Empirical observation of policing in the ZSPs seems to show little change in the tactics of local police (Darley and Gauthier 2018). Riot police can be posted in a given neighborhood for longer than before (a few weeks), though still temporarily, particularly when current events call them once again to their initial vocation, which is patrolling terrorist target sites or supervising demonstrations in city centers.

In 2018, a new national measure, the creation of the *police de sécurité du quotidien* (the daily safety police), was announced by the government. It was apparently based on experience in the ZSPs, which were never the subject of a serious evaluation. The plan, launched with great media hype, illustrates just about every inadequacy of policing policy in the *banlieues*. First, the purpose was to roll out a police force that is close to people's needs. However, from the start the government's choice of wording was militaristic. The project's target urban areas were labeled "Republican recapture zones," with the attending understanding that these were dangerous, "no-go" areas where the rule of law was not guaranteed. This image of the problem is delusional, as we saw in the first section of this chapter. Second, it was clearly a communication exercise actually targeting a public that lives far from these neighborhoods (where electoral turnout is very low), putting on a show of toughness. France's budgetary situation makes a mockery of the plan. The 7,500 officers assigned to the plan will at best make up for the staffing losses recorded between 2007 and 2012. In the whole of France, the measure has been rolled out in only 15 neighborhoods, each of which benefitted from a net increase of 100 police officers and *gendarmes*.

The government no longer knows how to carry out urban policing (foot patrols, dealing with the public, intervening in domestic disputes) and even if they did, they would not have the means to do so. This furthers the tendency towards militarization of the police in the *banlieues*, since it is always easier for the authorities to have a police force at their command, responding to their every order, than it is to empower police units to decide locally how to respond to what residents want. This style of policing is never easy anywhere but is even less so in poor areas concentrating social issues.

Paris and its *banlieues* have experienced a clear process of centralization and militarization since a bill was adopted in 2009. The bill created a city police force, the *police d'agglomération,* and gave the police prefect command of all 30,000 public safety officers in Paris and its three surrounding departments. This centralization goes hand in hand with the militarization of a good deal of the police force. They are organized to be "propelled" into areas of unrest from the safe distance of command centers that are under the authority of the Paris Prefecture. The extreme unease of certain police departments, incapable of responding to the simultaneous urban riots of 2005 due to a lack of manpower and coordination (Dufresne 2013, pp. 55–66), reinforced the priority now given to having reserve forces to dispatch to events anytime, with the unfortunate consequence of a much diluted every-day police presence.

This tendency towards centralization has also been seen on a smaller scale. Budget cuts increasingly led to anti-crime brigades (*brigades anti-criminalité*, or BACs) within police stations being pooled, along with mergers of several or sometimes all the police stations in the department. These units were made up of police officers with a knowledge of their territory (or at the very least its criminology, or its "clientele"). They have subsequently become part of increasingly large units crisscrossing ever vaster territories, ready to be dispatched by a command center to deal with a case of unrest in some location in the district or department. Occasionally, even, the departmental BAC units have merged with the departmental protest policing units (known as the *compagnies de sécurisation*, or security companies).

Of course, this trend towards savings, centralization, and militarization has a strong impact on police practices and on the equipment used by the police. Public safety forces in the *banlieues* face two types of crime. The first are petty offenses, which are a burden on residents' day-to-day activities in the neighborhood. These include low-level violence, assault, or rowdiness in public spaces or on public transport, occupation of hallways and entrances of buildings, and other annoyances. Didier Fassin (2013) and Fabien Jobard (2005) have documented, at intervals of several years, the responses of the anti-crime brigades. A small gathering of young men at the foot of a building, listening to music or simply drinking and chatting loudly together, prompts an intervention by this police squad, which rapidly turns into a degrading ceremony or a humiliation ritual for the young people involved, sometimes accompanied by physical violence. There is also organized crime such as drug trafficking and its attendant violence, including gun crime. Drug-related crime accounts for a good deal of police time, due to the particularly high demand for cannabis in France, which is among the highest in Europe.

In addition, over the years, tension between residents and police has created a third type of crime that has become a priority for the authorities: crimes targeting the police. Stone-throwing, insults, and ambushes are among the drivers behind new public safety policies targeting what has become known in policing terms as "urban violence." As a consequence, in a context where victimization and concern for safety is high, one of the defining characteristics of the police in the poor *banlieues* is their preoccupation with their own safety. This paradox could be almost comical, if it were not for its dire consequences for the lives of the residents, and for the police, themselves.

The most visible consequence of this heightened concern by police for their own protection is the widespread adoption rubber-bullet weapons. In Europe, such weapons were used by forces deployed in Northern Ireland. In France, they were introduced in small numbers in July 1995, an initiative of the general director of the national police. At the time, their use was strictly limited to cases of self-defense when intervening in situations where officers were at risk (these included threats by knife, public brawls, and ignoring roadblocks). A single gun was kept at officers' disposal in patrol vehicles and could be used only with the authorization of the patrol chief. When Nicolas Sarkozy, the future president, became minister of the interior in 2002, he instigated a wave of purchases of these weapons to, in his own words, "impress the thugs." Following the 2005 riots, he declared "The past events have led us to reinforce and adapt equipment and uniforms. As an example, I have ordered the purchase of nearly 460 Flashballs." This was the name of a brand of riot gun then produced in France. In 2007, following riots and very violent clashes triggered by the death of two youths during a police chase in the Paris *banlieue* Villiers-le-Bel, the newly elected Nicolas Sarkozy ordered the purchase of a new type of riot gun, the LBD, with greater fire power. An instruction from the director of the police in August 2009 stated "Destined initially to equip certain specialized units, the use of this rifle has progressively been extended to all units operating in difficult neighborhoods. From now on, it is intended to be used by all units faced with violent situations." Note that this weapon (according to the wording of the 1995 instruction) "cannot be qualified as non-lethal because of the serious injuries it is likely to cause." So, a weapon designated for use in self-defense by officers operating in the *banlieues* became widely deployed in situations likely to be violent. This proviso covers almost every policing situation in places where violence is always a risk. The results of the widespread distribution of this weapon are unequivocal: around 20 people have lost an eye in *banlieue* areas since 1995, not to mention the consequences of its addition to the arsenal of protest policing equipment.

Rubber-bullet guns are not the only gear to have been introduced in reaction to the 2005 riots: 2,800 tear gas canisters and 6,700 "bliniz"-type rubber-bullet projectiles were also purchased in the weeks that followed, not to mention 875 bullet-proof helmets and 5,500 more of the helmets usually used by the CRS and EGM riot police. Though certain weapons were withdrawn from police storage lockers, including hand grenades, their new arsenal contributed to the militarization of police operating in the *banlieues*. Already the protective gear they used – helmets, shin-guards, hard-shell gloves, leg-guards, and chest and shoulder pads – gave residents the impression of a Ninja-like police force, impervious to dialog. The minister of the interior actually boasted of this in 2010. On launching yet another police unit for the *banlieues*, he stated that he did not want "social-worker-cum-big-brother-type police officers in shirtsleeves," but rather officers in "combat gear." Of course, their intervention tactics are not to be compared with those of the SWAT teams described by Kraska (2007). They differ greatly in their use of firearms, which French officers resort to far less pre-emptively. But the proliferation of such units contributes to building a police force that is hemmed in on itself and feels besieged by a local population that it needs to maintain at safe distance.

Police Practices in the *Banlieues*

One should never underestimate the impact of the word "*banlieue*" on the collective imagination, because the term itself truly has the effect of a self-fulfilling prophecy. As the chapter on identity checks in this volume demonstrates, France's highest court of law, the Court of Cassation, has very clearly ruled that anti-discrimination laws are not to be applied in the same manner in areas renowned for a high crime rate. This indicts all of the *cités* of the *banlieues*, particularly those whose names have been associated for decades with urban violence. In these territories, the police can carry out identity checks on any individual, whatever their behavior and by virtue of the place where the check occurred, and their targets will never be able to prove the discriminatory nature of the check before a judge.

This decision by the High Court highlights the extent to which informal norms, but also jurisdictional norms, paint a picture of a very different police in the *banlieues*. A police force whose officers have had it drilled into them since the police academy that they will be sent into tough neighborhoods, and that the glory of the profession resides in the plainclothes units of the commissariat engaged in driving out drug dealers and perpetrators of street crime. This is a representation of the profession that is corroborated by the endless reporting of violence in the *banlieues*, especially under Nicolas Sarkozy (2002–2012, first as minister of the interior and then as president of the Republic). New recruits also cannot fail to notice that ordinary policing duties are carried out mainly by officers who did not make it into elite units. Quite rightly, these men and women see their assignments as temporary. Aspiring only to getting back to their home areas, they are little involved in local life. They do not live in the town where they work, they do not use the local facilities or services (if they play football, it is in their own home team), and they return home when they are on leave (enjoying preferential fares for police and military on train travel). If, out of personal conviction or by default, an officer assigned to a *banlieue* wishes to stay there, then the only vague incentive for him or her will be to join a local plainclothes unit. To do so, they will have to prove their ability to demonstrate authority and firmness in their interactions with the public.

All of this contributes to perpetuating a policing tradition that James Q. Wilson classed as the "legalistic style." This operating philosophy privileges law enforcement efforts over peace keeping (de Maillard et al. 2018).

The legalistic style is defined above all by a narrowing of officers' attention to a target population that they consider to be their responsibility. According to them, their clientele exists because figures of authority do not play a role in their lives, or because the youth in question are no longer supported by public institutions such as schools or the job market. Finally, officers fear that the penal system does not do its job properly, releasing offenders instead of keeping them off the streets. Officers' distrust of the population and their definition of the police mandate leads to the frequent, pre-emptive use of force and the adoption of violent operational tactics (Fassin 2013). If these are reported, they rarely prompt an earnest investigation.

The following episode illustrated this process. On 2 February 2017, a police brigade was patrolling in a town in Seine-St-Denis that was marked by intense drug trafficking. The brigade (one of those touted by the minister in 2010, when he explained that he did not want to see any more police officers "in shirtsleeves") stopped and searched some young men, placing them against a wall, hands flat, legs apart. When one of the young men was slapped by an officer, Theo Luhaka, a 21-year old black man, stepped in, causing the other officers to intervene. They pinned him to the ground and one of the police officers proceeded to violate the young man's anus with his extendable baton, causing a ten-centimeter-long internal injury with irreversible medical consequences. The incident was recorded by the town's CCTV cameras and the images were broadcast on the internet. This generated an intense emotional response from the public and brought forward numerous accounts of similar behavior in housing estates in the *banlieues*. As had been the case following insults and sexual violence against the youths in Paris' 12th *arrondissement*, the public realized that not only were police operations in the *banlieues* more aggressive than elsewhere, but they could also be exceptionally humiliating and degrading. This was particularly true among young men from immigrant families, many of whom live in these areas. The police appeared to be perpetuating a tradition of sexualizing altercations, conferring sexual undertones to body searches, frisks, verbal warnings, or acts of aggression, and thus carrying on an entrenched colonial tradition (Blanchard 2008).

In line with past studies (Gorgeon 1994), it is not surprising to see that police officers are involved in discriminatory, racist, and violent behavior. In a recent Eurojustis-France survey, 39% of respondents who were *not* living in social housing answered "yes" to the question, "are the police racist?" The comparable figure for respondents living in housing projects in the *banlieues* north of Paris was 48%. When asked if they thought the police were guilty of carrying out "unwarranted checks on certain persons," the proportions were respectively 25% and 48%. The gap is the same regarding police brutality: half the residents of housing projects in Seine-St-Denis consider police tactics to be "too aggressive," versus 36% of residents of other areas (Roché 2016).

Conclusion

If there is one problem area for the police in France, it is the *banlieue*. These areas are a problem not so much because of the violence and street crime that is more common there, but because of the history of how police are deployed in response. Policing in the *banlieues* is characterized by chronic understaffing and a subsequent resort to a militarized, defensive style of policing which increases the use of pre-emptive violence. So, a self-fulfilling prophecy plays itself out there, against a backdrop of racial segregation and a population which is far poorer and more likely to be from abroad or from French overseas territories. This perpetuates another French tradition: that of violent police control of immigrant populations. In turn, *banlieue* residents are increasingly prone to consider that they are treated like young black men in American ghettos. Although living conditions in US ghettos and French *banlieues* are not really comparable, policing strategies in France have created what researchers consider "subjective ghettos," or images of life there based on the "established conviction that (*banlieue* youths) are treated differently, unjustly, and unequally" (Rey 2017. p. 59).

The structural trends lying behind of this state of affairs remain unchanged. These include budgetary constraints on the French state; geographical segregation (despite some gentrification of the municipalities closest to the cities-proper); and de-industrialization of the economy, which in turn produces a supply of young men with no qualifications who are almost invariably ill-suited for the skilled trades and the service economy. The police in the *banlieues* are called upon to manage the negative externalities generated by these trends, while the rest of the population looks on with varied indifference, concern, and outrage. There has been a visible rise of social protests since 2016, including massive demonstrations against labor law reforms in 2016 and the yellow vest movement of 2018–2019. However, these are unlikely to pacify police operations in the *banlieues*. The kind of police brutality usually seen in the *banlieues* has, in these highly visible cases, targeted French citizens who are neither from these deprived areas nor of migrant descent. Indeed, with officers in high demand for policing large demonstrations in the center of cities, police stations in the *banlieues* are even more scarcely manned than usual, and the forces operating there are often paramilitary units. A greater, and tragically paradoxical, effect of the violence aimed at police officers during the demonstrations is that, in retaliation, this further legitimizes their continued militarization. In turn, this tends will undoubtedly impact the equipment, organization, and tactics being employed in the *banlieues*. Moreover, since voting participation is low among residents, there is ultimately little chance that the political frame of reference that underlies policing strategies in these areas will be reformed any time soon.

Notes

1 For a general overview, see the comparative perspective in Body-Gendrot (2000), and the glossary in; Waddington et al. (2009).
2 The US National Center for Health Statistics reports around 11,000 homicides a year (around 100 times more than in France). As far as police forces are concerned, police firearms cause the death of around ten persons a year in France (around 1,000 in the USA).
3 The last survey was carried out two years before the 2015–2016 terrorist attacks in Paris.
4 Technically speaking, we refer here to the *quartiers prioritaires de la ville* or QPV (high-priority city neighbourhoods), that is the 1,300 neighbourhoods with a population over 1,000 which are poor, both compared to France as a whole and compared to the city in which they are located.
5 In the United States, police per capita in New York City is 1 for 165, in Chicago 1 for 200 and in Los Angeles it is 1 for 310 inhabitants (Federal Bureau of Investigation 2018).
6 Even the city of Paris, though heavily endowed with police officers from the national police, has a sort of municipal police force, the Direction de la prévention, de la sécurité et de la protection, generally entrusted to a commissioner seconded by the *police nationale* and employing around 2,000 officers (de Maillard and Zagrodzki 2017).

References

Blanchard, E. 2008. Le mauvais genre des Algériens. Des hommes sans femme face au virilisme policier dans le Paris d'après-guerre. *Clio. Histoire, Femmes et Sociétés* 27: 209–224.
Body-Gendrot, S. 2000. *The social control of cities*. London: Blackwell.
Cornut-Gentille, F., and Kokouendo, R. 2018. Action de l'État dans ses missions régaliennes en Seine-St-Denis. Paris: Assemblée Nationale, rapport d'information n° 1014.
Cour des comptes. 2011. L'organisation et la gestion des forces de sécurité publique. Paris: Cour des comptes.
Darley, M., and Gauthier, J. 2018. Le travail policier face à la réforme. Une ethnographie de la mise en œuvre des 'Zones de Sécurité Prioritaires'. Politix 124: 59–84.
de Maillard, J., Hunold, D., Roché, S., and Oberwittler, D. 2018. «Different styles of policing: discretionary power in street control in France and Germany», *Policing & Society* 28(2): 175–188.
de Maillard, J., Gayet, C., Roché, S., and Zagrodzki, M. 2020. Les relations polices-populations: dimensions, mesures et explications: Un état des travaux en France. Observatoire national de la politique de la ville, Rapport 2020, Commissariat général à l'égalité des territoires.
de Maillard, J., and Zagrodzki, M. 2017. Plural policing in Paris. Variations and pitfalls of cooperation between national and municipal police forces. *Policing & Society* 27: 53–64.
Dikeç, M. 2007. *Badlands of the republic: Space, politics, and urban policy*. London: Blackwell.
Dilain, C. 2006. *Chronique d'une proche banlieue*. Paris: Stock.

Dufresne, D. 2013. *Maintien de l'ordre*. Paris: Hachette.
Esping-Andersen, G. 1999. *Social foundations of postindustrial* economies. Oxford: Oxford University Press.
Fassin, D. 2013. *Enforcing order. An ethnography of urban policing*. Paris: Seuil.
Federal Bureau of Investigation. 2018. *Uniform crime report*. Washington, DC.
Garland, D. 2019. Penal controls and social controls: Toward a theory of American penal exceptionalism. *Punishment & Society* 40: 1–32.
Gauthier, J. 2010. Esquisse du pouvoir policier discriminant. Une analyse interactionniste des cadres de l'expérience policière. *Déviance et Société* 34: 267–278.
Gauthier, J. and Lévy, R. 2015. Minority police officers in the French Police: The 'Republican tradition' and the Workplace experience of minority officers. *European journal of policing studies* Maklu, 2(4): 405–421.
Gorgeon, C. 1994. Police et public: représentations, recours et attentes. *Le cas français, Déviance et Société* 18: 245–273.
Hargreaves, A. 1996. A deviant construction: The French media and the 'banlieues'. *New Community* 22: 607–618.
Jobard, F. 2005. Le nouveau mandat policier. Faire la police dans les zones dites 'de non-droit'. *Criminologie* 38: 103–121.
Kraska, P. 2007. Militarization and policing. Its relevance to 21st century police. *Policing* 1: 501–513.
Kraska, Peter B. and Kappeler, Victor E. 1997. Militarizing American Police: The Rise and Normalization of Paramilitary Units. *Social Problems* 44(1): 1–18.
Mandraud, I. 2009. Polémique sur les effectifs policiers en Seine-Saint-Denis. *Le Monde*, 29 septembre.
Ocqueteau, Fr. 2017. *Fusionner Police et Gendarmerie nationales?* Sur l'histoire d'un essai non transformé, Guyancourt: CESDIP, Etudes et données pénales series 119.
Pelletier, E. 2019. Suicides, la police meurtrie. *Le Parisien*, 20. August, S. 12.
Pettit, B., and Western, B. 2004. Mass imprisonment and the life course: Race and class inequality in US incarceration. *American Sociological Review* 69: 151–169.
Rémila, N. 2018. Insécurité et victimation: en quartier prioritaire, un sentiment d'insécurité deux fois plus présent que dans les autres quartiers, Observatoire national des politiques de la ville Rapport annuel. Paris: Documentation française.
Rey, H. 2017. Ghettos, banlieues: Is the difference disappearing? *International Social Science Journal* 67: 55–61.
Roché, S. 2016. *De la police en démocratie*. Paris: Grasset.
Wacquant, L. 1993. Urban outcasts: stigma and division in the black American ghetto and in the French urban periphery. *International Journal of Urban and Regional Research* 17: 366–383.
Waddington, D., Jobard, F., and King, M. (Eds.) 2009. *Rioting in the UK and France: A comparative analysis*. Cullompton: Willan.
Zauberman, R., Robert, P., Névanen, S., and Bon, D. 2013. Victimation et insécurité en Île-de-France. Une analyse géosociale. *Revue française de sociologie* 54: 111–153 (available in English at: www.cairn-int.info/article-E_RFS_541_0111–crime-victimisation-and-feeling-unsafe.htm).

Chapter 13

Identity Checks as a Professional Repertoire

Fabien Jobard and Jacques de Maillard

The longest and most striking spate of urban riots in France's contemporary history was sparked by a mere identity check. On 27 October 2005, three children ran from police who wanted to check their IDs, which they didn't happen to be carrying. Two of them never came back from the chase. They were electrocuted by a power transformer that they thought would make a good hideout. "Dead for no reason," said the banners at the many marches and demonstrations that followed, trying to convey the disarray sparked by the degree of brutality that the relationship between urban youth and the police had reached.

In fact, the youths certainly did not run away "for no reason" on that fateful night. ID checks often constitute an opportunity for aggressive behavior on the part of the police, especially towards youths from ethnic minorities – such as Zyed Benna and Bouna Traoré. Since the 1980s, the general public in France has become all too familiar with the phrase "*contrôle au faciès.*" This term is the vernacular equivalent of "racial profiling" that sums up the main argument against this practice, namely its discretionary and discriminatory nature. That stop-and-search is often discriminatory and likely to generate dynamics of defiance has been amply demonstrated by research both in the USA (Paulhamus et al. 2010) and in the UK (Bradford 2017). In France, while social movements began documenting this aspect of police work as early as the 1980s, only in the 2000s did research begin to produce enough quantitative evidence of the extent of the problem that this perennial concern reached the public agenda.

Three dimensions of the problem will be addressed here: describing what the checks are and who is targeted; showing why they are such a cardinal practice for the policing profession in France; and finally reviewing the many heated debates of the last few years to see whether practices have changed as a result – or not.

ID Checks in France

When towns – places where people unknown to each other coexist on a daily basis – started developing in the 19th century, the police officer was

Identity Checks as Professional Repertoire 203

a public agent whose mandate consisted, among other things, in asking passers-by about their social status. This was standard practice even before carrying an official identity card was required by Vichy France (Piazza and Laniel 2008). The tradition only recently found its way into legislation, specifically by way of the "Security and Liberties" law of 2 February 1981. This act gives a precise definition of "administrative" – or "preventive" – stops. They involve no offence or even suspicion thereof and are simply meant to prevent any breach of the peace or public order. These are controversial checks, as "public order" is a vague enough notion to make the domain of police intervention virtually boundless. They grant police colossal freedom when it comes to deciding what public order is or isn't, and monumental discretionary power in choosing to act (Foucault 1981; Napoli 2003).

ID checks are largely regulated by chapter 3 of the Code of Criminal Procedure (Code de procédure pénale, or CPP), i.e. articles 78–1 to 78–6 CPP, established by the law of 1981. Article 78–2 allows administrative or preventive stops whenever a police officer has "plausible cause" to suspect that a person has committed or is about to commit an offence (a rather unspecific formulation already). However, persons might also, and "regardless of their behavior," be stopped to prevent a breach of public order or security. These labels obviously cover an immense realm of possible activities. Preventive stops may also be requested by the public prosecutor for a specific area and time period. There, the *police nationale* and *gendarmes* can perform stops regardless of people's behavior, for the purpose of uncovering explicitly mentioned violations or offences. It is often the case that the offences listed in the public prosecutor's order cover a broad range of possible street offenses, including breaches of immigration laws, which conveniently makes it possible to stop and check just about anyone, and especially anyone appearing to be foreign. These criteria are how most preventive stops are legally justified.

In 1993, the Constitutional Council, whose role consists in ensuring that new legislation is consistent with the French constitution, established that "the practice of sweeping, discretionary ID checks is incompatible with respect for individual freedom" (DC 93–323). In 2017, the Council pointed out that "ID checks must be implemented … exclusively on the basis of criteria that are untinged by discrimination of any kind" (2016-606/607). An earlier decision by the Court of Cassation (France's top civil and criminal court) had already established that the elements used to justify a stop must have nothing to do with who the person stopped is. In particular, their outward appearance – for instance the fact that they look foreign – does not constitute a valid motive for a stop (Ruling, Court of Cassation, 23 April 1985).

However, one peculiarity of French ID checks is that they generate no administrative record. Persons who are stopped are not issued any receipt from the police, and they in turn do not record the stop in any way unless contraband is are found. Simple ID checks leave no trace. What did the Constitutional Council prescribe in 1993 when it posited that ID checks may not be "discretionary"? What concrete measures were contemplated? The Council left these questions up to judges in cases in which a stop is challenged. Then the officer responsible for it must be able to justify it in court. The Constitutional Council could have nullified the bill on the grounds that the police were being granted disproportionate powers, but it did not. As a result, French police officers may check the legality of anyone's status at will, these checks leave no paper trail, and potential claimants – unless they can produce half a dozen reliable witnesses – have no material evidence to support their claims in front of judges, who are the only ones who may protect their rights.

Litigation by the Open Justice Initiative

To challenge the potentially discriminatory consequences of this stop-and-frisk policy, a collective supported by discrimination lawyers and the Open Justice Initiative (OSJI) has brought 13 ID check cases to the civil courts (Hollo 2016). Their claim was that these were not criminal but civil cases, a legal strategy that is much more common in the United States than it is in France. Civil cases may draw upon non-discrimination laws, which largely rest upon European Union legislation that tends to reverse the burden of proof. It is up to the defendant (in this case, the French state) to prove that there was no intention to discriminate against someone who happened to be Black or Arab and has been stopped on the street for no apparent reason.

While the tribunal to which these cases were assigned summarily dismissed all 13 cases (Sayare 2013), two years later the Court of Appeal found unlawful discrimination had been exercised in eight of them. The Court ruled that the French state had failed to justify the stops made by the police officers and, more specifically, to ensure that checks were based on objective grounds rather than based on race or ethnicity. The state appealed to the Court of Cassation, which a few month later confirmed the dismissal of five of the 13 claimants (more on this later) and the fact that eight stops were unlawful (Ruling, Court of Cassation, 9 November 2016). Moreover, the Court of Cassation stated (contrary to the argument of the state) that non-discrimination law *does* apply to police stops. This implied a shifting of the burden of proof to the state and opens further opportunities for potential claimants to seize the initiative. It is now the state's responsibility to prove that a given stop was not founded on a discriminatory decision, if the claimant is able to provide some evidence of the non-objective character of the stop (Dumortier 2015).

Still, concluding that French law has become aligned with American law in this matter would be a stretch. While the Court did quote statistical data suggesting that some forms of police discrimination do exist – including

Jobard et al. (2012) – these data are treated as illustrative rather than evidentiary. Furthermore, witness statements from reliable, neutral third parties are still required. However, in many circumstances (stops performed at night, or in neighborhoods where few outsiders ever transit), these are simply impossible to provide. Finally – and this had a direct impact on the five claimants who were dismissed – the Court argued that in areas "notoriously affected by crime," preventive stops may be allowed. At the end of the day, the requirement of neutral, impartial third-party witnesses on the one hand, and the creation of special territorial exceptions on the other, mean that opportunities for turning to the courts will be few. This is especially true as far as one specific category of people is concerned: youths (often from ethnic minorities) who live in the *banlieues* (suburbs) of major French cities and tend to be stopped either in their own neighborhood or in highly surveilled areas such as railway stations. Thus, in 2016 the Court of Cassation rendered a double-sided ruling. On the one hand, it acknowledged that ID checks may be regulated under non-discrimination law. Also, there was no requirement that a formal complaint had been filed, which was a minor revolution. On the other, the Court concluded that urban areas where policing is already the most discriminatory can be places that continue to justify preventive police stops. In doing so, the Court asserted a general non-discrimination principle while at the same time establishing that police practice can be territorially – and therefore racially and socially – differentiated. They can be law-compliant here, and discriminatory there.

Targeted Populations: Appearance, Gender, and Lifestyle

Over the last few years, studies have been conducted that shed some light on the populations that are targeted by ID checks. As noted earlier, no official records are kept on stops, and as a result, there is no such thing as useful police data. Therefore, the only way to examine targeted populations is to collect independent data, either through observational studies (the least frequent method) or surveys.

A study conducted in Paris in 2007–2008 by Jobard et al. (2012) was the first ever standardized observational study of ID checks. Five characteristics were recorded by the observers stationed in major Paris transit hubs: gender; age (young, older); race (White, Black, North-African, Asian, other); carrying a bag (no bag, bag, big bag); clothes (youth culture, business, casual). These data were collected for 38,000 individuals and compared with the characteristics of the subjects of 525 checks by police that observed at the same locations (see Waddington et al. 2004 for a similar method). Ethnic minorities were found to be vastly over-represented. All other things being equal, the likelihood of being stopped was boosted by a factor of 3.2 to 9.1 for Black people, and 3.6 to 14.5 for North Africans. Other factors highly predictive of a stop included: being a male; being young; not carrying a bag; and wearing clothes identified with "youth culture." Since these variables are mutually correlated – for instance, two-thirds of "youth culture" individuals are Black or North African – determining the exact, independent weight of each variable is a delicate exercise. For example, there is no difference in the likelihood of being stopped between "casually dressed non-white young men" and "youth-culture young white men."

The magnitude of these differences can be seen in Table 13.1. It examines young men of all ethnicities who were wearing typical youth culture clothing and not carrying a bag. The top panel of Table 13.1 describes the frequency of such individuals in the *universe* of travelers observed in six different observation points. They always constituted a small fraction of those passing through these stations. The bottom panel reports the distribution of similar persons who were *stopped* in the same locations. They usually constituted a substantial proportion of all individuals who were observed to have been stopped.

Other studies of persons targeted by stops have used surveys. A survey carried out in 2009 by Beauchemin, Hamel and Simon (2018) involved 22,000 respondents, three-quarters of whom were minorities. Another carried out in 2016 by the French Ombudsman (Défenseur des droits) included

Table 13.1 Stop Rates for Young Men Wearing Typical Youth Culture Clothing and Not Carrying a Bag (All Ethnicities)

Benchmark population	Overall	Target population	Percent of the target in the population
GDN Station	8,008	130	1.6
GDN RER	8,496	352	4.1
GDN Thalys	3,726	4	0.1
Châtelet Station	9,409	303	3.2
Châtelet Innocents	7,687	538	7.0
Stopped population	Overall	Target population	Percent of the target in the population
GDN Station	123	18	14.6
GDN RER	129	55	42.6
GDN Thalys	121	4	3.3
Châtelet Station	68	33	48.5
Châtelet Innocents	83	47	56.6

Source: Prepared by the authors based on data from Jobard et al. 2012.

5,117 respondents and same ratio of minority individuals (Défenseur des droits 2017a). Both studies found that minority populations did *not* differ from the majority in terms of their likelihood of being stopped. Rather, what did set White respondents apart was their smaller risk of experiencing multiple stops. In Beauchemin et al.'s (2018) study, 13% of majority-population respondents recalled being stopped several times over the past year, as contrasted to more than 20% of North African or Turkish second-generation respondents, and 27% among second-generation respondents of African origin. In the Ombudsman's survey, although 23% of male respondents said they had been stopped at least once over the past five years, Black and "Arab" males were six to 11 times as targeted frequently, defined as being stopped more than five times over the past five years.

A survey study carried out with students from the greater Paris area also found no significant difference between Whites and non-Whites in their likelihood of having been stopped at some point over the past year. Again, however, these contrasts were stronger when it came to multiple stops (56% for non-Whites, compared to 41% for Whites) (Jounin 2015). This study highlighted the predictive role played by descriptive and behavioral characteristics of respondents. How they dressed was the key: 76% of those wearing a cap reported having been stopped, versus 42% among those who did not wear one. The difference between hood wearers and non-wearers was also large, 53% versus 42%. Non-Whites were more likely to fall into the cap and hood-wearing categories. An interesting point is that behavioral characteristics seem to counterbalance these effects. White students tend to be found in public spaces, especially festive ones, a lot more often than non-Whites, and as a result, are more exposed to stop-and-search. In addition, they are more likely to be found in possession of cannabis in a public space. A look at gender, clothing, and lifestyle variables further indicates that non-White males are, all other things being equal, the category most targeted by police stops (Jounin 2015).

These findings were corroborated by the "Escapad" survey (Peaucellier et al. 2016) involving 5,432 18-year-old Paris residents. The study found a high frequency of stops among youths (28% recalled they had been stopped), again with significant differences in stop rates among various social groups (41% of males, 47% of school dropouts, and 18% of residents from underprivileged areas). It also highlighted the importance of behavioral variables. Two-thirds of those who had been involved in a brawl reported being stopped during the past year, as well as three-quarters of regular cannabis users. A multivariate statistical analysis revealed that the over-stopped group is made up of two distinct sub-groups. One group was dubbed "Epicureans." They made up 20% of the total sample and consisted of upper-class youths who tend to go out often and consume cannabis and alcohol in much greater amounts than other youths their age. The second high-stop group were "recluses from poorer neighborhoods." They constituted 10% of the total sample, and they tend to live in rough areas, have few friends, usually do not consume any alcohol or cannabis, and rarely go out.

In sum, discriminatory practices do not hinge exclusively on racial characteristics. While race can be said to be a predictive variable indeed, *all other things being equal*, it is certainly not the only relevant feature. Far from it – being a young male is strongly determining as well. However, race seems to be highly predictive as far as repeat stops are concerned, and it often overlaps other risk factors.

The ID Check Process

A police stop may involve only a simple ID check, but also can escalate into a full-blown frisk or search. So-called "safety measures" may occasionally be taken, such as requesting individuals lean against a wall, placing their feet apart, with their back turned to the police and others who may be present. The Ombudsman's study (Défenseur des droits 2017a) offers invaluable information on this aspect of stops. It found that males were 1.5 times more likely to be searched than females, for instance. The same goes for 18–24 year olds versus 25–44 year olds. The risk of being searched redoubles for males who are perceived as Arab or North African, contrasted to all other males. A full 80% of young males perceived as Black or Arab reported having been searched at least once, versus 28% of young males not in that category.

Regarding interactions with the police, studies find great variety in how people are handled by the police. In general, stops tend to be performed courteously, but the targets of stop rarely receive an explanation of why they were stopped. In the observational study conducted in Parisian transit hubs (Jobard and Lévy 2010), three-quarters of the 175 respondents surveyed immediately after having been stopped, reported that the officers had been "neutral" in their demeanor, while 6% considered the police to be "polite" or "respectful." The Ombudsman and Jounin studies yielded similar results. At the other end of the spectrum, the Ombudsman's study noted that 8% of persons stopped reported having been treated brutally during the encounter, 7% said they had been insulted, and 16% were addressed by the familiar pronoun "*tu*" rather than the polite "*vous*." Among males from minorities, these figures are much higher: respectively 24%, 29%, and 32%. In the Jounin study however (which is restricted to a youth sample), race was not a predictor of brutality, but gender and clothing were. Police "brutality" here does not involve (barring some rare exceptions) the use or threatened use of firearms, as opposed to what can happen in the USA (e.g. Skogan 2018), but rather shoving, pressure, and occasionally blows.

The Polis survey, carried out with German and French high school students, makes it possible to compare the respective actions of French and German forces. The German police were reported to give reasons for making stops in 66% of cases involving native Germans and 58% for youths of Turkish origin. Their French colleagues gave reasons for making stops to 54% of natives and about 44% of youths of North African origin (Oberwittler and Roché 2018).

The Consequences of ID Checks

The Ombudsman's survey concurred with other international studies (see for instance Bradford 2017; Epp et al. 2014; Skogan 2018) in finding that stops, especially when lacking justification, are associated with a loss of confidence in the force. In that French study, slightly more than half those who reported having been stopped more than five times over the last five years did not trust the police, contrasted to 18% in the general population.

An aspect of ID checks that differs along social lines is that of the perceptions generated among those who are stopped. In the observational study of persons who had just been stopped, Jobard and Lévy (2010) noted that a vast majority of checks had been considered "neutral, respectful, or polite." But at the same time, 23% of North Africans and 36% of Blacks reported they were "annoyed" or even "very upset" to have been stopped a few minutes earlier. Their rate of annoyance or upset was respectively 1.5 and two times higher than that among Whites (15%). Using Beauchemin et al.'s (2018) data, Mélanie Terrasse (2019) focused on the consequences of stops on self-perception. In this survey, 93 to 97% of migrants born in France said they perceived themselves as being French, but only 63 to 78% of them reported being perceived as French by others. Once the effects of age, occupation, education, and neighborhood were controlled for, multiple (two or more) stops appeared to have a significant (though moderate) impact on how people think they are perceived – 15 to 20%, depending on the groups. In the Ombudsman's study, 46% of respondents who said they had been stopped more than five times over the last five years thought that French citizens are not equal before the law.

In a country such as France that holds citizenship sacred, the topic of police stops can be an emotional one. The process involves checking one's national identity card, which is their statement of citizenship. The ID check is an intensely political gesture for the large proportion of persons stopped who belong to ethnic minorities. They end up losing confidence in the police, they are further persuaded that they are not being perceived as French, and they are more likely than others to be convinced that seeking reparation and justice for unfair stops would be pointless.

ID Checks as a Professional Repertoire

These studies have yielded valuable information regarding the distribution, conduct, and consequences of ID checks. In practice, the legal framework surrounding them is vague enough to permit an extremely wide array of professional practices, which we will now examine in more detail. We then turn to the selection of target populations and conclude by exploring the paradoxical organizational "invisibility" of ID checks.

In practice, how do police officers exercise their discretionary powers? To determine this, we conducted a direct observation study of police officers to understand what contexts prompt them to take the initiative in making preventive stops (de Maillard et al. 2018). It appears that the decision to perform a stop is typically motivated not by the behavior of those concerned, but by entirely different criteria. These include a belief that an individual does not seem to belong to the context, the outward appearance of their vehicle, how they are dressed, and their apparent attitude (as shown by a defiant, sideways glance for example). Our study was carried out in two provincial French towns, and it revealed that more than one in four interactions were discretionary stops initiated by the police. Overall, out of 293 interactions that we observed in the field, 80 featured a stop whose justification we could not find in the behavior of the concerned individual. These percentages differed considerably from those we observed in Germany. Like France (but unlike the United Kingdom), Germany does not systematically document stops, and does not keep statistics on the race of those involved in them.[1] There, however, only 31 stops out of 247 that we observed appeared unjustified.

In France, ID checks are seen as a valuable and, one might say, routine tool for proactively identifying potential offenses. Although an otherwise non-malicious attitude or sustained gaze may not commonly signal any offensive behavior, to the police this might suggest that there is something suspicious going on. Officers can see themselves possessing a personal "flair" for spotting potential troublemakers and may stretch their understanding of the reasonable suspicion that is supposed to guide their decisions to stop people. Besides, since stops largely focus on finding drugs, especially in disadvantaged suburban areas (France is the number one country in Europe for cannabis consumption), ID checks provide an opportunity for searching people and recovering knives or banned substances.

Discretionary stops are also used as a device for asserting police power over housing estate youths. This works along three distinct axes: maintaining a visible presence, instilling respect, and dispensing street justice. When it comes to maintaining their presence, ID checks are a way for the police to take over the area and show the youths "who's boss." Stops perpetuate a relationship of dominance over their "customers" – people who Lee (1981) refers to as "police property" – by reminding them daily that police coercive powers may be exercised against them at will. Stops are usually performed despite the lack of any real security, investigatory, or true identification imperative, and often are imposed on individuals who are perfectly well-known to the officers. In 2013, local associations called upon the Open

Society Justice Initiative to raise public awareness on the case of 15 year olds against whom the police had been ordered to intervene by way of repeated, humiliating, aggressive stops (Boutros 2020). As the area was in the throes of gentrification, these youths (dubbed "unwelcome" in police documents) were expected to "buzz off." The Open Society Justice Initiative's investigation has revealed that the – totally unjustified – stops often gave rise to sexual assaults (batons in trousers, pat-downs of buttocks and testicles, etc.). The ensuing outcry created an opportunity for grown-up men to testify about practices they had been subjected to throughout their childhood.

Stops may also serve the function of commanding respect in situations of defiance or even provocation from the youths. As opposed to the previous case, checks are not routine here, but a response to some specific behaviors perceived as disrespectful. Whereas the bodies of earlier targets were considered "police property" as defined by Lee, in this instance they are "assholes," as described by Van Maanen (1978). One officer we interviewed had this explanation to offer for these stops: "The goal is to command respect, to show we're not afraid of them, you can't let them get away with anything. Then they realize that as long as they leave us alone, we leave them alone too!"

Finally, the last situation can be described as using ID checks as a sanction. Stops can involve a degree of public humiliation, including being forced to lean with one's hands against a wall for several minutes, subjected to a number of questions, or being frisked, all on the street and perhaps in broad daylight. These sanctions are a form of "street justice," which has been described as an important element of routine of policing (Skolnick 1966). Street sanctions can be a fallback when the police lack the evidence to arrest or bring charges against suspects, or when the matter is not serious enough to warrant prosecution. In this type of situation, which was observed in France but not in our German study, stops taken on a "disciplinary rationale" (*rationalité disciplinaire*, Gauthier 2015) were destined to tame those who do not abide by the requirements of the police.

One striking feature of our observations and interviews is that the police consider ID checks as particularly beneficial in terms of their work on the field. They are a mechanism for collecting information, arresting suspects, and asserting their authority. The downsides of stops (such as the public defiance induced by repeat stops) are typically ignored, although this needs to be qualified, depending on both the officers and the units involved. In research carried out in two provincial French towns, four different types of units were observed. This revealed variations in stop routines that were dependent on both the objectives and the methodology of stops (de Maillard and Zagrodzki 2017). Plainclothes units tended to rely on them only marginally, whereas other units focus entirely on "police property." The variations we noticed may derive either from a given squad's remit, whether they work in plainclothes or in uniform, the type and extent of their jurisdiction, or the watch commander's leadership style. In some stop situations, patrol leaders who interacted courteously with the public proved unable to keep their subordinates' aggressiveness in check. Ever since the tenure of Nicolas Sarkozy as minister of the interior in the 2000s, aggressive units tasked with "taking over" and "reconquering territory" (the official terminology of public authorities) have been thriving, resulting in a legitimization of repeat, aggressive, humiliating police stops (de Maillard and Mouhanna 2016).

The Logics Governing Target Selection

It is well known that stops are prompted by proactive cues, based on "shared-recipe" police knowledge about whom to stop for what purpose in particular circumstances (Ericson 1982, p. 86). As elsewhere, the French police act on the basis of "unexamined, implicit and subconscious stereotypes, biases and cultural assumptions" (Bradford 2017, p. 83). Jacques de Maillard et al. (2018) and Gauthier (2015), writing on France, have noted that police classification logics have a complex way of combining dress, behavioral, geographical, and ethnic-racial elements. While no single variable is determining per se, many officers do subscribe to the following syllogism: minority youths are more likely to be delinquents, therefore stopping them is the rational thing to do (this applies in England too; see Quinton 2015).

The immediate context of the situation is also highly relevant. The likelihood that stops may be used in discretionary and humiliating fashion is fueled both by a general feeling of hostility towards the *banlieues* and ongoing tensions with the descendants of immigrants from former French colonies (see among others Jobard 2006; Fassin 2013). Although police officers take refuge behind the code of criminal procedure ("we are merely enforcing the law"), these stops are perceived by ethnic minority youths as part of a de-individuation scheme that tends to assign them to racialized groups (Zauberman and Lévy 2003) and negates their full citizenship (Blanchard 2014).

To policing scholars, these findings will not come as a surprise. Police officers have a wide-ranging conception of suspicion, and exercise implicit bias based on physical and cultural appearance. Such factors reign supreme when it comes to deciding to stop someone. This has been noted elsewhere, in Britain (Delsol and Shiner 2015) and the United States (Epp et al. 2014). Less frequent, however, is the paucity of police data that can be used to monitor stops.

It appears that ID checks seldom require follow-up action. Based on the scattered data available, targets of stops are taken to police stations in less than 15% of cases. Both the *police nationale* and the *gendarmerie* make these estimates sporadically, and they report very low figures. In 1993, the *police nationale* claimed that 3.6% of stops led to arrests, and 25 years later, a *gendarmerie* estimate was a 4% arrest rate (Marc 2016, p. 15). Other than that, the authorities have no administrative tracking of the number of stops and how they are distributed, either among agents and units, or in space and time. Most ID checks are invisible within the police organization itself. The hierarchy does not receive reports about them. In 2014, upon special request from parliament, the *gendarmerie* estimated that 1.5 million people had been stopped by their agents at some point, but they counted only the stops that were made at the request of public prosecutors (Marc 2016, p. 16)!

This lack of transparency hampers any attempt to rationally draw up public policies aiming to regulate, monitor, or guide the use of ID checks. Not that elected representatives seem to be concerned about this. Although a 2016 report from the Senate's Law Commission mentioned that "the Ministry of Interior indicated that no overall statistics were available", the curiosity of French members of parliament was not piqued (Marc 2016, p. 16).

ID Checks as a Political Issue

Racial profiling is mainly referred to in France using the expression "*contrôles au faciès*." This term can be perceived both as a statement of fact and as a call for protest. The phrase has been in use ever since the 1980s, when second-generation immigrants first started to raise their voices regarding police conduct. The study by Jobard et al. (2012), first published in June 2009, provided the first systematic figures ever on stops, and the data were considered at the time as "scientifically indisputable" by the Paris police spokesperson himself (Incyian 2009). A craze of "stactivism" (using statistics for activist means) then seized the nation, as a number of groups and political figures tried to leverage these data to further their own causes (Didier 2018). Interestingly, while statistics are usually perceived as a tool for state control, in this case demands for data resulted from the engagement of many actors who, despite being in a weak position, were hoping to strengthen their case against the state (see more generally Porter 1995).

This had a twofold effect. The first was an agenda-setting one. Presidential candidate François Hollande, who won the election in 2012, promised to fight racial profiling by pushing legislation for "a procedure [that would be] mindful of civil rights." This was universally interpreted at the time as a commitment to introduce a mandatory ethnic monitoring scheme like the one UK forces have been abiding by since 1996 (De Schutter and Ringelheim 2008, p. 379). This measure never saw the light of day (see below). The second, more long-term effect has to do with framing public debate. The lack of any quantitative data on stops has long acted as an enabler of the rhetoric of denial (Satzwich and Shaffir 2009). In fact, police have gone so far as to sue those who dared suggest that discretionary ID checks even existed (Incyian 2009). After 2009, police chiefs and union leaders were relentlessly asked the same question: "everybody knows that police stops are discriminatory; what do you intend to do about it now?" (Jobard and Lévy 2011). The most convincing outcome of research is that the cost of denial has surged dramatically.

A judicial front was also opened, largely supported by the Open Society Justice Initiative – the foundation that had funded the Jobard and Lévy study (Hollo and Neild 2012). This battle was fought in civil courts and culminated in the above-mentioned 2016 ruling by the Court of Cassation. Alongside the judicial battle, the Justice Initiative pressed a legal empowerment strategy fostering the development of leaders from ethnic minorities to champion their cause in France. This resulted, for example, in the creation in 2011 of the "Stop le contrôle au faciès" collective. Their initiatives, included collecting testimonies, posting online videos, and involving rappers and football stars, were supported by the OSJI.[2] The collective gradually joined the rally against discrimination and police brutality, and in support of youths from deprived French *banlieues*. The arbitrariness of police stops ended up being leveraged to cement a cause around which racialized youths may unite.

On 1 June 2012, a few weeks into François Hollande's first and only presidential term, his prime minister announced that the minister of the interior was to spend the summer working on introducing the "*récépissé*," i.e. a receipt issued to stopped individuals in order to avoid racial profiling and minimize repeat stops. By mid-August, the minister announced that the measure would not be implemented, citing the riots that were taking place at the time in the city of Amiens. He announced, "Can you imagine police officers handing out receipts tonight in Amiens?" (14 August 2012, France 2 broadcast). Minister of the Interior Manuel Valls, whose approval rating surpassed that of the prime minister, thus demonstrated how influential he was in the cabinet – until he took over as prime minister a few years later. Police unions voiced their discontent regarding the planned *récépissé* as early as June 2012. One proclaimed, "The public/police rift will not be bridged by making police officers feel the fault is theirs" (SGP trade union, 1 June 2012). They pledged to support the minister of the interior in return for the plan being dropped.

Faced with relentless political and activist pressure, though, the minister introduced two replacement measures that had the potential to significantly impact police practices. The first, revealed in December 2013, was to send messages of trust to the population and consisted of requiring a compulsory police collar number (*matricule*) that was to be worn at all times, even by plainclothes officers. This was actually a reversion to older practice. The requirement that a similar number be worn had been dropped at some point during the 1980s, though no one claimed to know when or how (Béguin 2012). A few years later, the Ombudsman (Défenseur des droits 2017b, p. 47; also Sénécat 2016) pointed out that the collar number was in fact rarely worn by the police, and in 2019, it appeared during the "yellow jackets" protests that many instances of police brutality could not be brought to court because identifying police officers proved impossible! The second measure was introduced by a ministerial order of 25 April 2017. It requires police officers to use body-worn cameras in specific high-security urban areas (*zones de sécurité prioritaire*, or ZSPs). Although these cameras may in principle be triggered at will by the police, they *must* be in use during an ID check.

Although the effects of these measures are hard to assess for the moment, it should be noted that in the context of French policing, the ID check is and remains a totem of sorts. There seems to be no risk that it will be uprooted, and it is not clear how effectively it can be amended.

Conclusion

ID checks are one of the central, and almost definitional, practices of French policing. Not only are they much more frequent than in most other Western European countries (FRA 2010), but studies have consistently shown that they lead to very numerous discriminatory practices, and that they have more to do with asserting order maintenance than advancing peacekeeping. These checks have been in the spotlight for a dozen years or more, owing to the efforts of the Open Justice Initiative. The Initiative has both funded research on the effective practices of police officers and contributed to empowering non-profit organizations by mobilizing the media and political parties around the issue. It has also brought cases before the courts, up to and including the Court of Cassation. In this respect, police forces are currently experiencing levels of pressure that were unknown to them a mere 15 years ago. Does that mean that practices are changing? They are not, or only marginally. The relevant legislation governing stops remains unamended, and the Court of Cassation has reminded everyone that there are indeed in France territories and circumstances that do justify police officers stopping whoever they like. Another aspect to this debate is terrorism. The specter of terrorism has undermined some of the measures that had been taken in response to the debate on ID checks, including new requirements for body-worn cameras and collar numbers.

At the end of the day, discussions over the last decade about ID checks have highlighted several important political features of French policing. The first is the highly centralized nature of policing. Politically, this has turned policing questions into a card to be played on the national political stage. This led to our emphasis on the political ambitions of ministers of the interior and the role played by presidential administrations in police policy. The tenures of both Nicolas Sarkozy (2002–2004, then 2005–2007) and Manuel Valls (2012–2014) have been symptomatic. Second, the debate has revealed the weight of police unions. In contrast to nations in which policing is the responsibility of local government, in France police unions can aim their proposals and protests at one target, namely the minister of the interior. A reform may be ditched for the sole reason that powerful unions do not agree with them. Even legislation that they are unable to prevent can still be killed in practice; witness collar numbers. Third, civil society, which when it manages to get organized (as it did concerning ID checks), still has the power to at least add items to the political agenda and draw support from strong institutions (such as the Ombudsman or political parties). The impasse that political factors have created for reform efforts in France has by-and-large insulated ID checks and related practices from actual change. This has led to an overall increase in political tension around these issues and has added to the urgency of tackling them head on.

Notes

1 In that regard, the idea – often mentioned by American colleagues – that the problem with France lies in the lack of ethnic statistics is misguided. In fact, other than the UK, no Western European country maintains such statistics.
2 See http://stoplecontroleaufacies.fr.

References

Beauchemin, C., Hamel, C., and Simon, P. 2018. *Trajectories and origins: Survey on the diversity of the French population*. Frankfurt: Springer.

Béguin, F. 2012. Le grand retour du matricule dans la police. *Le Monde*, 17 octobre.

Blanchard, E. 2014. Contrôles au faciès : une cérémonie de la dégradation. *Plein Droit*. 103: 11–15.

Boutros, M. 2020. Untitled PhD Dissertation. Evanston: Northwestern University, Department of Sociology.

Bradford, B. 2017. *Stop and search and police legitimacy*. Abingdon: Routledge.

Défenseur des droits. 2017a. *Enquête sur l'accès aux droits*, vol. 1. Paris: Défenseur des droits.

Défenseur des droits. 2017b. *Le maintien de l'ordre au regard des règles de déontologie*. Paris: Défenseur des droits.

Delsol, R., and Shiner, M. (Eds.). 2015. *Stop and search. The anatomy of a police power*. Basingstoke: Palgrave.

de Maillard, J., Hunold, D., Roché, S., and Oberwittler, D. 2018. Different styles of policing: Discretionary power in street controls by the public police in France and Germany. *Policing & Society* 28: 175–188.

de Maillard, J., and Mouhanna, C. 2016. Governing the police by numbers: The French experience. Pp. 273–298 in T. Delpeuch and J. Ross (Eds.) *Comparing the democratic governance of police intelligence: New models of participation and expertise in the United States and Europe*. Cheltenham: Edward Elgar.

de Maillard, J., and Zagrodzki, M. 2017. Styles de police et légitimité policière. La question des contrôles. *Droit et Société* 97: 485–501.

De Schutter, O., and Ringelheim, J. 2008. Ethnic profiling. A rising challenge for European human rights law. *The Modern Law Review* 71: 358–384.

Didier, E. 2018. Globalization of quantitative policing: Between management and statactivism. *Annual Review of Sociology* 44: 515–534.

Dumortier, T. 2015. Les 'contrôles au faciès' saisis par la justice. *Revue des droits de l'homme, Actualités Droits-Libertés.*

Epp, C., Maynard-Moody, S., and Haider-Markel, D. 2014. *Pulled over.* Chicago: University of Chicago Press.

Ericson, R. 1982. *Reproducing order: A study of police patrol work.* Toronto: University of Toronto Press.

Fassin, D. 2013. *Enforcing order. An ethnography of urban policing.* Cambridge: Polity.

Foucault, M. 1981. Omnes et singulatim. Towards a criticism of political reason. Pp. 223–254 in S. McMurrin (Ed.) *The Tanner lectures on human values.* Salt Lake City: The University of Utah Press.

FRA (Fundamental Rights Agency). 2010. *EU-MIDIS: Main results report.* Luxemburg: Publications Office of the European Union.

Gauthier, J. 2015. Origines contrôlées: Polices et minorités en France et en Allemagne. *Sociétés contemporaines* 97: 101–127.

Hollo, L. 2016. A victory in France in the struggle against racial bias in policing. *Open Justice Initiative.* [www.justiceinitiative.org/voices/victory-france-struggle-against-racial-bias-policing.]

Hollo, L., and Neild, R. 2012. Challenging police profiling in France. *Open Justice Initiative.* [www.justiceinitiative.org/voices/challenging-police-profiling-france.]

Incyian, E. 2009. Contrôles au faciès: la réponse de la police. *Mediapart*, 4 juillet.

Jobard, F. 2006. Police, justice et discriminations raciales. Pp. 211–229 in D. Fassin and E. Fassin (Eds.) *De la question sociale à la question raciale?* Paris: La Découverte.

Jobard, F., and Lévy, R. 2010. Identity checks in Paris. *Penal Issues*, January.

Jobard, F., and Lévy, R. 2011. Racial profiling: The Parisian police experience. *Canadian Journal of Criminology and Criminal Policy* 53: 87–93.

Jobard, F., Lévy, R., Lamberth, J., Névanen, S., and Wiles-Portier, E. 2012. Measuring appearance-based discrimination: An analysis of identity checks in Paris. *Population* 67: 349–375.

Jounin, N. 2015. Le faciès du contrôle: Contrôles d'identité, apparence et modes de vie des étudiant(e)s en Île-de-France. *Déviance et Société* 39: 3–29.

Lee, J. 1981. Some structural aspects of police deviance in relation to minority groups. Pp. 49–82 in C. Shearing (Ed.) *Organizational police deviance: Its structure and control.* Scarborough: Butterworth.

Marc, A. 2016. *Rapport fait au nom de la Commission des lois n°598.* Paris: Sénat.

Napoli, P. 2003. *Naissance de la police modern: Pouvoir, normes, société.* Paris: La Découverte.

Oberwittler, D., and Roché, S. 2018. Ethnic disparities in police-initiated contacts of adolescents and attitudes towards the police in France and Germany. Pp. 73–107 in D. Oberwittler and S. Roché (Eds.) *Police-citizen relations across the world: Comparing sources and contexts of trust and legitimacy.* Abingdon: Routledge.

Paulhamus, M., Kane, R., and Piquero, A. 2010. State of the science in racial profiling research: Substantive and methodological considerations. Pp. 239–258 in S. Rice and M. White (Eds.) *Race, ethnicity, and policing: New and essential readings.* New York: New York University Press.

Peaucellier, S., Jobard, F., Lévy, R., and Spilka, S. 2016. Identity checks and youthful Parisians: Analysis of the Paris section of the 2010 ESCAPAD survey. *Penal Issues* 29: 1–4.

Piazza, P., and Laniel, L. 2008. The INES identity card and the politics of national identity assignment in France. Pp. 198–216in C. Bennett and D. Lyon (Eds.) *Playing the identity card: Surveillance, security and identification in global perspective*. London: Routledge.

Porter, T. 1995. *Trust in numbers: The pursuit of objectivity in science and public life*. Princeton: Princeton University Press.

Quinton, P. 2015. Race disproportionality and officer decision-making. Pp. 57–78 in R. Delsol and M. Shiner (Eds.) *Stop and search: The anatomy of a police power*. Basingstoke: Palgrave.

Satzwich, V., and Shaffir, W. 2009. Racism versus professionalism: Claims and counterclaims about racial profiling. *Canadian Journal of Criminology and Criminal Justice* 51: 199–226.

Sayare, S. 2013. France: Court throws out cases claiming racial profiling by police. *New York Times*, Oct. 3, Section A, p. 9.

Sénécat, A. 2016. Oui, le port du matricule est obligatoire pour les policiers et les gendarmes. *Le Monde*, 3 juin.

Skogan, W. 2018. Stop-and-frisk and trust in police in Chicago. Pp. 247–265 in D. Oberwittler and S. Roché (Eds.) *Police-citizen relations across the world: Comparing sources and contexts of trust and legitimacy*. Abingdon: Routledge.

Skolnick, J. 1966. *Justice without trial: Law enforcement in democratic society*. New York: Wiley.

Terrasse, M. 2019. Dimensions of belongings: Relationships between police identity checks and national identity. *Journal of Ethnic and Migration Studies* 46: 1–22.

Van Maanen, J. 1978. The asshole. Pp. 221–237 in P. Manning and J. Van Maanen (Eds.) *Policing: A view from the street*. New York: Random House.

Waddington, P., Stenson, K., and Don, D. 2004. In proportion: Race, and police stop and search. *British Journal of Criminology* 44: 889–914.

Zauberman, R., and Lévy, R. 2003. Police, minorities and the French Republican ideal. *Criminology* 41(4): 1065–1100.

Chapter 14

A Social History of Protest Policing in France

Aurélien Restelli

Protest policing in France has been severely tested in recent years. It can be argued without exaggeration that for the last ten years, every significant social conflict has been followed by a debate over the effectiveness of policing. It has been subjected to two criticisms. On the one hand, protest policing strategies have been accused of being incapable of containing the public disorder that these conflicts engender. Examples of this continue to surface, as the basis of flaws in policing make it possible for demonstrators to attack property or the police themselves. They include the failure of "Opération Cesar," which involved the evacuation of the Notre-Dame-des-Landes airport in 2012 (which we will come back to later); the Necker Hospital attack in Paris; during demonstrations regarding the anti-El-Khomri labor bill in June 2016; and the break-in at the Arc-de-Triomphe during the yellow vest demonstration on 1 December 2018.

On the other hand, French protest policing is accused of embodying a repressive and particularly brutal turn in the handling of social movements and doing so in full public view. The growing number of persons who have been injured in recent demonstrations seems to corroborate this. These two criticisms are of course not raised by the same parties, at the same time, nor in the same political and media circles. But it continues to be the case that police handling of protests has been subject to almost constant critique for some years. At the same time, police action towards crowds is deemed both too harsh and yet equally ineffective in containing the most radical elements among the demonstrators.

Most of the time these criticisms have implied there has been a recent change in policing strategies, and that in the past, protest policing in France was carried out in a reasonable and effective manner. The aim of this sociological study of protest policing is not to call for a return to some golden age, nor conversely to question that there had been such a golden age. Rather, it is to understand the reasons that certain parties put forward when advancing the idea that there has been an important change in the implementation of protest policing in France. Instead this chapter's social history of protest policing therefore focuses on how past events can allow us to understand contemporary actors' representations of it. Or in other words, to identify the "conditions of possibility" (Dewerpe 2006) of the practices and discourse surrounding protest policing today.

Several terms are routinely employed to describe police efforts to uphold public peace. Some authors refer to it as "protest policing" (Della Porta and Reiter 1998), while others refer to "public order policing" (Critcher and Waddington 1996). In French it is quite simple. Most scholars use the expression *maintien de l'ordre* (maintaining order), which is also how the principal actors involved (*police nationale* officers, *gendarmes*, and prefects) describe it as well. To be precise, *maintien de l'ordre* should be distinguished from *rétablissement de l'ordre* (restoring order); only the latter implies active involvement of the police and the use of weapons. Protest policing in this case concerns preventive actions undertaken by the *police* and *gendarmerie*, including crowd filtering barriers, road checks, and searches. Most of the time, though, the expression "protest policing" includes both maintaining order and restoring it. The two are taken together to characterize all the actions taken by police to prevent, contain, and interrupt public disorder caused by protests, popular gatherings, and even recreational events. In this chapter we will refer mainly to all of this as "protest policing." While it is important to give a precise definition – neither too broad nor too narrow – of protest policing, it also should not be isolated from its political and social context. Indeed, one can hardly understand the stakes involved in protest policing without including an analysis of the political environment on the one hand, and the more general relationship between police and the population on the other. Specialized protest policing units form part of the *police* or *gendarmerie*, and as such they are not cut off from debates over delivering security and responding to social disorder more generally. While protest policing is a set of strategies and tactics, these are influenced in part by the policing context in which they fall. One should also add that, insofar as protest policing constitutes a response to the illegitimate actions of crowds in public spaces, attention to the sociology of social movements must not be neglected either. Broad social factors play a role in the dynamics of confrontations between police and demonstrators.

This anchoring of protest policing in a wider policing environment explains some of its characteristics. As with other police activities, there is a division of labor between the *police nationale* and the *gendarmerie nationale*. Thus, a *police nationale* force specialized in protest policing, the Compagnies Républicaines de Sécurité, or CRS (French riot control forces), has co-existed for more than 60 years with a similar unit of the *gendarmerie*, the Escadrons de Gendarmeries Mobiles, or EGM (Mobile Gendarmerie Squadrons).[1] Although these two units are described as relatively equivalent and interchangeable, particularly by the political authorities, they nonetheless respect their differing jurisdictions: *gendarmes* mobile units intervene mainly in rural and semi-urban territories, while the CRS mostly acts in urban areas. The two forces can cooperate if circumstances require. Regardless of the area in which the operation takes place, the units conducting protest policing are subject to strict hierarchical control and depend upon the decisions taken by local administrative authorities, the prefect, or the prefect's representatives. As the representative of the French state in a regional department, the prefect represents the politics of crowd policing. This political dimension to protest policing is most visible in Paris, where the prefect enjoys more power and room for maneuver than elsewhere (Berliere 1996). Political control is a constant in the history of protest policing in France, unquestionably far more so than in other western nations, which can lead to the exploitation of protest policing for political ends (Jobard 2012).

The history of protest policing can be summarized along the following broad lines. There was a long phase of specialization and professionalization in this arena, beginning with the early creation of mobile response units from the 1950s to the 1990s. This was followed by an uncertain time for protest policing in France due to the emergence of increasing urban violence. Finally, there was a return to violent political protests after 2010.

The Professionalization of Protest Policing

As France entered a phase of relative political stability following 1870 and the Franco-Prussian War, the army was still in charge of protest policing. The question of political governance of crowd control was not a central one. In this period the main disruptions to public order centered on social issues. Protest groups gathered, often to defend demands of employees, and if local *gendarmes* were too few the military would be dispatched to maintain order. This posed two problems for the authorities. First, the army was composed of conscripts. There was a risk of fraternizing between soldiers, often of working-class backgrounds themselves, and the protesters they faced. Second, as soldiers were armed only with their rifles, the suppression of these gatherings was sometimes bloody, resulting in numerous casualties.[2] To remedy this, mobile *gendarmerie* platoons were created in 1921. They gradually acquired responsibility for protest policing operations after having proved their worth during social unrest in the 1930s. They were joined, at the end of World War II, by a police force specially dedicated to protest policing, the CRS. In both cases, the state's concern was that these units should be aloof from the social context in which they intervened. For that reason, they were deployed where they were not permanently garrisoned and had the logistic capacity to operate independently.

From the moment these specialized units were created, protest policing was to be characterized as a "process of public violence moderation" (Bruneteaux 1996, p. 89). Despite their often-rudimentary equipment, which was ill adapted to the task of containing sometimes-hostile crowds, these new units managed to develop professional protest policing strategies. Although progress was irregular, a stable and relatively effective set of protest policing approaches emerged in the period between 1930 and the 1960s. These depended upon officers' individual self-control and collective cohesion. Protest policing units delayed making direct contact with crowds as much as possible, instead disrupting demonstrators' confidence with tear gas or water cannons rather than physically accosting them. At the same time, hierarchical control of operations was strengthened, and the CRS and mobile *gendarmes* developed a strong professional identity. In short, between 1920 and 1960, protest policing in France was modernized.

However, while instances of violence during demonstrations were becoming rarer across much of the country, the picture was not so rosy everywhere. In Guadeloupe, during the riots of 26, 27, and 28 May 1967, mobile units opened fire on the crowd, killing eight people. Overall, the pacification of protest policing proceeded most slowly in Paris, for two reasons. First, the capital was both the political seat of authority and had considerable symbolic significance. Mobile forces, when commandeered by Parisians, spoke of their surprise at the violence employed by of local police units. Less well-trained than the CRS and mobile *gendarmes* and encouraged to act very firmly regarding protest (Dewerpe 2006), Parisian police officers occasionally reverted to violent repression. This was dramatically illustrated by a string of bloody incidents that took place there. The list of demonstrations marred by protester deaths is long: 15 killed on 6 February 1934 during a protest of the nationalist leagues; five dead on 16 March 1937 at an antifascist gathering; two dead during the communist demonstration of 28 May 1952 against American General Ridgway (Pigenet 1990); seven dead in the Algerian demonstration of 14 July 1953; several dozen Algerians killed on 17 October 1961; and nine dead at Charonne metro station on 8 February 1962 (Dewerpe 2006). In each case, the victims of police brutality were either communist demonstrators, seen as allies of the USSR, or Algerian freedom fighters who were considered an "enemy within." This persisted until Algeria gained independence in the spring of 1962.

But the fact that these demonstrators were considered a danger to the Republic itself is insufficient to explain these outbursts of violence. Analytically, it is not easy to determine what caused what. Was there violence because the political and social pacification of social movements was so insufficiently advanced that the police were forced into brutal retaliation against the violent action of demonstrators? Or, conversely, was it because the police and *gendarmes* did not show enough self-control or strong enough hierarchical control? This could have contributed to transforming peaceful public protest into a political arena where violence still had a rightful place. It remains that, at the end of the 1960s, the professionalization of protest policing – despite having come a long way – was still a work in progress. The events of May 1968 illustrated this most clearly. Be it on the side of the demonstrators, who denounced the brutality of certain officers, or on the side of the police, who complained of their inadequate equipment and lack of training in protest policing, the protagonists in the clashes of the spring of 1968 highlighted the faults in a still evolving system of protest policing. Changes ensued. Protective gear was reinforced to allow police to hold static barricades for longer periods and resist collective charges against their position. In addition, the CRS and mobile *gendarmes* systematized monitoring protest groups and their plans, in order to anticipate potential disturbances on the ground. Finally, a training camp was set up at Saint-Astier, in south-western France, to simulate real-life situations and improve the training of mobile *gendarmerie* squadrons. Tested in 1969, the National Gendarmerie Training Centre opened on a permanent basis in 1977 (Bruneteaux 1993).

Stabilizing Police Protest Operations

This process of specialization, professionalization, and pacification continued during the 1970s, and resulted in a routinization of crowd policing that became visible in the 1980s. During that period, protest policing could even be considered an integral part of what Pierre Favre labeled the *moment manifestant*. During this "protest moment," protests came to involve familiar stakeholders and routine venues for street demonstrations (Favre 1990). Political violence was waning (Sommier 2008). Even conservative social groups that returned to the streets with the left's rise to power in 1981 were willing to adopt a menu of peaceful protest actions that had been developed by social movements following World War II. During this period, units responsible for protest policing could encounter groups that were difficult (such as workers or peasants) or turbulent (such as students), but all of them recognized the legitimacy of the police to oversee their demonstrations and put down any violence that broke out. They even acknowledged the police as representatives with whom they might establish a dialog, in contrast to the anti-establishment groups on the far left and the far right of the political spectrum, who were very active in the 1970s. Protest police had once regularly intervened to avoid bloody clashes between these hostile groups. For example, on 21 June 1973, police responsible for ensuring security at the meeting of the neo-fascist group Ordre Nouveau in Paris' Latin Quarter clearly failed when they were attacked by leftist commandos seeking to disrupt the meeting. Numbering barely a few hundred, the leftist group injured more than 70 police officers. Now they were now free to concentrate on the supervision of increasingly peaceful movements, with demonstrators whom they considered as temporary adversaries, not enduring enemies (Monjardet 1996).

It was at this time that specialized forces finally secured a virtual monopoly on protest policing. Following a steelworkers' protest on

23 March 1979, plainclothes officers who had been in charge of gathering information and making arrests were side-lined after one of them was mistaken for an undercover agitator from the security service of the CGT (Confédération Général du Travail, i.e. General Confederation of Labor) trade union (Monet 1990). The next to go were the Pelotons de Voltigeurs Motoportés. These squads consisted of two motorcycle policemen whose role was to charge and disperse, often violently, protesters lagging at the end of a demonstration. They were abolished following the death of Malik Oussekine on the night of 6 December 1986, on the side-lines of a student protest. From that date on, all major demonstrations were policed exclusively by the CRS and mobile *gendarmes* and by officers of the Compagnies d'Intervention of the Prefecture of Paris. The prefect's rapid intervention teams were better screened and better trained than in the 1970s and 1990s (Fillieule 1997b). They were practically the only forces sent into the streets to police crowds, and they demonstrated their know-how. Their operations fell under what was called the "hierarchical continuity" within a company or squadron. Hierarchical control of these units was very strong, group action was highly coordinated, and individual initiative was discouraged (Monjardet 1996, p. 129). Protest policing may indeed have been removed from the military domain, but it was entrusted to units whose operation was based on a disciplinary framework closely resembling that of the military. But the result was a reduction of incidents of brutality by individual officers.

This concentration of protest policing ground operations in the hands of specialized units was also made possible by the fact that protesters had accepted the idea of a "trend toward the pacification of conflicts" (Fillieule and Tartakowsky 2013, p. 149). Indeed, they were fully a part of it. Far-left parties and trade unions that had sought confrontations with police during the 1950s and 1960s now actively cooperated with them to ensure that demonstrations were peaceful and orderly (Sommier 1993). This cooperation also facilitated the work of the intelligence services, who gained to a wealth of useful information that helped to protect marches and better prevent outburst of violence. The prefectures and police services had willing allies in the trade unions' security services, who were anxious to promote a positive image of their movement. As a result, French police rarely intervened in protests using weapons or physical force. Rather, they were involved in prediction, negotiation, and control, in concert with protesters (Fillieule 1997b, p. 271). A handful of blunders, such as the violent steelworkers' demonstration of 23 March 1979,[3] or tragedies like the death of Vital Michalon during an anti-nuclear protest at Creys-Malville in 1977, were not enough to undermine the routinization of protest policing that had been underway since the 1970s. The French philosophy of protest policing allows for a degree of relative disorder, so long as its intensity is limited in time and space, and the police show a certain tolerance toward event virulent protesters. This is what Olivier Fillieule refers to as the "patrimonialist management of social conflicts" (Fillieule 1997b, p. 352).

Protest Policing in the *Banlieues*

Certain areas did not enjoy this pacification of conflicts, however. These were working-class neighborhoods that were home to peoples from the former colonies. Inhabited mainly by immigrants from the Maghreb and sub-Saharan Africa, these neighborhoods were often located on the periphery of urban centers. They are widely referred to as *banlieues*. These areas feature a concentration of economic and social problems, including high rates of poverty and unemployment, poor public transport connections, and racial discrimination in access to employment. The relationship between residents and the police has long been deteriorating as well. It is not unusual for police interventions there to result in fatalities among young males – often black and Arab – and thus to provoke angry reactions from the community. Urban riots posing the police against local youths began in municipalities in the Lyon region in the 1980s, and they would become a major challenge to French protest policing. Full-scale riots, which had been an occasional occurrence in the 1970s and 1980s, became more frequent in the 1990s after local youths died as a result of police brutality (Motta 2016). Although the topography of these new areas of protest was quite different from that of the large avenues where the trade unions traditionally march, protest policing could be conducted in the same way, using containment and ensuring that clashes did not spread to surrounding neighborhoods. The rioters' *modus operandi* was not so different to that seen in the far-left demonstrations in the 1970s, involving as they did damage to public and private property, looting of businesses, and assaults on police officers. What did change was the difficulty police faced in dispersing groups or directly confronting them, since the very layout of dense urban cores and the agile mobility of rioters hindered the collective efforts of the CRS and *gendarmerie* units. Most of the time, therefore, the police would simply wait until their opponents got tired and had nothing left to destroy before moving back into an area.

This could be observed until the autumn of 2005. Then, rioting spread to many *banlieues*. Following the death of two teenagers in an electricity substation, where they had been hiding from police during a chase in Clichy-sous-Bois, France fell into a three-week period of urban violence. While under normal circumstances there were enough police to hold out for some time and wait for the rioters to run out of steam, the intensity of these simultaneous clashes forced politicians to consider calling in the army (Dufresne 2007). One characteristic of this episode was the considerable importance of politics in the management of policing operations (Kokoreff 2006). In a sense, the 2005 riots made it clear how protest policing in France is as much a political issue as it is a technical one. This could be seen in particular in the Ministry of the Interior's insistence that arrests were made, and in its defense of a judicialization of protest policing. The strategy was to actively seek out and arrest demonstrators committing offences, then bringing them to court to be judged for their actions. Though it is not easy to pinpoint when this judicialization of crowd policing first appeared, its beginnings can be identified at the start of the millennium. At that time, a results-based policy began to be implemented within the *police nationale* and then the *gendarmerie*. The main principles of protest policing were not challenged, but during police operations officers were encouraged to judicialize the public and facilitate the prosecution of arrestees.[4] This results-based approach, implemented during the November 2005 riots, was to be adopted again during the student protests against the Contrat Première Embauche (a labor law regarding contracts for young first-time employees) the following spring, as well as against future social movements.

The traditional organization of street protest policing units, being by their nature collaborative and centralized, did not easily allow for this type of action. It became necessary to introduce tactical changes to protest policing by adding units better suited to springing from police ranks to make arrests. These included the Brigades Anti-Criminalité (anti-crime squads, or the BAC) and the Compagnies de Sécurisation et d'Intervention Security and intervention squads. Also, divisions of existing units specialize in making arrests at demonstrations. These include the Équipes Légères d'Intervention (rapid response teams within the mobile *gendarmerie*) and the Sections de Protection et d'Intervention (protection and intervention teams, within the CRS) (Jobard 2015). Emphasizing arrests in this way was not risk-free for the police forces or the protesters. It almost guaranteed there would be increased hands-on contact between them that could lead to exchanges of blows and the risk of injury. It should be noted, however, that arresting demonstrators was not a phenomenon that appeared at the turn of the millennium; it was always done in the past by *police* and *gendarmes* in protest policing. What changed was the public show made of these arrests. The prefectures and the Ministry of the Interior made sure they were recognized for their successful crowd policing strategy.[5]

New legislation creating additional offenses was passed in order to facilitate the judicialization of protest policing. For example, the offence of "participating in an assembly with a view to preparing willful acts of violence" was introduced in 2010. As it has been applied, any protester within range of a group displaying violent behavior or which one might suspect of violence, can be prosecuted. In a less direct intervention, it is not unusual for the minister of justice to issue a circular to prosecutors, who will carry out any criminal investigations, informing them of offences for which arrestees might be charged.

This "individualization of crowd policing" (Lippens 2016) did not happen only at the legal level. It also took shape through the adoption by crowd policing units of new non-lethal weapons. First came the flashball riot gun at the end of the 1990s, then the LBD 40, its more powerful and more accurate brother, in 2007. Both the flashball and the LBD 40 belong to the class of so-called "sub-lethal" weapons.[6] With them, officers can target protesters individually, and no longer must confront an entire crowd. These weapons are supposed to be used in situations of legitimate self-defense, but recent use of the LBD 40 has shown that they are also used to punish protest leaders. They also enable police to single out protesters whom they believe will be difficult to arrest, or to push static protesters to disperse without having to resort to a baton charge (Lippens 2016). One of the consequences of the introduction of the LBD 40 into crowd policing has been to help maintain physical distance between police and demonstrators. However, these weapons can also cause irreversible injuries or mutilation, as opposed to the effects of often incapacitating but non-injurious agents such as tear gas (Lippens 2016).

Weapons like the flashball and LBD riot guns illustrate how the boundaries of protest policing have been blurred by the introduction of the specter "urban violence" into protest dynamics. This newly introduced term was first used to designate episodes of rioting in working-class neighborhoods, but its use eventually spread to other protest locations. Consequently, protest control principles such as proportionality of response, action only in self-defense, and reactivity to events have become rather fuzzy in their application. This blurring of boundaries can also be seen in two related phenomena that date back to the 1980s. For one, security duties were added to the traditional duties of specialized crowd policing units. They were also assigned to patrol neighborhoods thought likely to foster criminal activity, in order to prevent delinquency. This territorial assignment meant a loss of mobility for these squads. On the other hand, new units – the Compagnies d'Intervention (intervention squads) – were created in many counties.[7] These enabled leaders to send ready-formed units into the field without waiting for the CRS or mobile *gendarmes* to arrive.[8] They were intended, therefore, to replace specialized forces in certain areas.

This continued use of units other than CRS and mobile *gendarmes* for protest policing thus responded to tactical necessity. Officers specialized in public order stressed the importance of their mobility and initiative, while specialized units were sometimes described as too large or cumbersome, or insufficiently reactive. The resulting growth in the variety of actors involved in crowd policing was the result of deliberate strategic choices. Nevertheless, it appears also that budget cuts and limited leeway in terms of available manpower – intensified by the General Review of Public Policies in 2007 – played a role in imposing this hybrid model of policing upon policy makers.

Recent Challenges to Protest Policing

Urban violence during the 1990s and 2000s may have reshaped some aspects of protest policing in France but it did not redefine its underlying framework. More importantly, while major events in crowd policing occurred during this period, they were not followed by significant debates in the political and media fields. The opposite was true for three events during the 2010s.

The Failed Evacuation of the Notre-Dame-des-Landes Zone in 2012

In the autumn of 2012, the newly elected government of François Hollande planned to evacuate an area located in the Nantes countryside, in order to begin construction of a new airport. Radical green activists were already legally (and illegally) settled there and had developed a model of society based on environmental sustainability and direct democracy. The police-led operation, codenamed "César," was a dismal failure. The CRS and *gendarmes* progressed very slowly through wooded areas and hedgerows, and there were numerous injuries among both the police and the activists (called "zadists"). After a few days, the government put an end to the operation. They had underestimated the endurance and tenacity of their opponents. They had not understood that a *Zone à Défendre* (ZAD) was also a *Zone de vie* (Zone-to-live-in) (Jobard 2014) and was not merely an area people just passed through. At Notre-Dame-des-Landes (and the same was to happen at Sivens[9] or at Bure) the police were not dispersing a crowd or putting an end to a violent episode, but rather they were reconquering territory that was resisting the sovereignty of the French state. They were holding their own ground and uprooting them would require more manpower and expense. In 2018, more militarized units were used to dislodge the activists and destroy their homes. This time the operation was organized in quasi-military fashion and required almost a year of preparation. The government involved 2,000 *gendarmes* and consumed an impressive amount of ammunition. Over 16,000 grenades were launched by *gendarmes* in the space of a few weeks, and one protester had his hand ripped off by one of those grenades.

Cortège de tête Challenges the Principles of Demonstrations

In the spring of 2016, protests against El-Khomri legislation (concerning labor matters) took a rather particular turn. Whereas during previous confrontations damage to property and clashes with the police typically occurred at the end of a march or during the dispersal of demonstrators, a new phenomenon appeared. This was labeled the *cortège de tête*, or "head of the demonstration." In a new tactic, several thousand demonstrators marched in front of the trade unions that had registered the demonstration at the prefecture. In the lead, they directly sought a confrontation with the police. They were a heterogeneous group. The *cortège de tête* included both radical protesters dressed in black and peaceful supporters of labor, as well as curious passers-by. In Paris, but also in Nantes and Lyon, this new protest configuration posed a major problem for the police. It was not easy for them to act, differentiating "good" demonstrators from "bad." The use of tear gas, baton charges, and other tactics aimed at sectioning off the violent group from the rest of the procession, was not effective. All of the demonstrators were impact indiscriminately, which raised tensions between them and the police. Further, this new crowd configuration appeared jointly with a new strategy involving political violence by far-left militants and the spread of anti-police sentiment – embodied by the slogan "Everybody hates the police" – to large sections of the protesting public. In sum, the spring of 2016 provided a real challenge to past practices around protest demonstrations.

The Gilets Jaunes: A coup de grace to French Protest Policing?

Ultimately it was the *gilets jaunes* (yellow vests) movement that would most severely shake the police world regarding protest policing. A long and divisive period in French history was characterized by intense clashes between protesters and police. Stemming from demands driven by the falling real incomes of lower-income people, it soon became a global outcry against the French economic and political system. Beginning in mid-November 2018, a great number of French towns experienced weekly demonstrations. Protesters wearing high-visibility yellow vests that drivers must have in their cars, gathered and attempted to reach seats of power (ministries or prefectures) or symbolic places (like the Champs-Elysées). On several occasions the *police nationale* and *gendarmerie* were overcome by the sheer numbers and energy of the protesters. They vandalized the Arc de Triomphe, set fire to the prefecture of the Haute Loire (on 1 December 2018), and looted stores on the Champs-Elysées (on 16 March 2019). The movement brought together individuals who were unfamiliar with demonstrations or the trade union culture, yet the *gilets jaunes* movement challenged the French doctrine of protest policing. Indeed, the protesters often refused to negotiate with the authorities. This made it extremely complicated for police to engage in dialog with them. On the contrary, the clashes remained very violent and resulted in hundreds of injuries on both sides, including most notably 24 *gilets jaunes* who were partially blinded and five who had their hands blown off by grenades. To this must be added the death of a woman in Marseille in December, following the firing of a tear gas canister into her apartment by the CRS. There was utterly unprecedented use by police of the ammunition at their disposal. For example, in just one day on 1 December 2018, more than 10,000 grenades of all types were used by *police* and *gendarmes*.

The absence of designated spokespersons to represent demonstrators, the difficulty in anticipating unrest due to the disorganization of the intelligence services, the absence of reliable specialized mobile forces trained for protest policing, and a lack of crowd control training for many officers were the main reasons advanced to explain why policing was so chaotic during the *gilets jaunes* period. In a way, all of these shortcomings had already been identified in the spring 2015 in parliamentary report taking stock of the state of protest policing (Mamere and Popelin 2015). The underlying problems it discussed were exposed by the *gilets jaunes* movement, because of its unpredictability and long duration. The movement threatened to deal a fatal blow to the French-style approach to protest policing, which was already weakened. To repress the unrest caused by the *gilets jaunes*, the authorities had to put forward a new approach to protest policing. It was based on reactivity rather than simple aggression and granted greater autonomy for units on the ground. The latter contrasted with a hierarchical style that had prevailed in protest policing for several decades. Above all, the government and prefects began to resort to political and legal mechanisms, not just policing tactics. They prohibited demonstrations in certain parts of cities, including Paris, Lyon, Toulouse, Nantes, and even Rouen. They set up preventive checkpoints on the street, at train and underground stations, and sometimes even at the foot of buildings that housed well-known activists. The police were backed completely by administrative controls of public spaces. This led to an increase in the number of arrests each Saturday, making the trend toward the judicialization of protest policing even more conspicuous.

In the end, these three episodes reignited public debate about protest policing. They opened questions that seemed to have been resolved for decades. Among the concerns were the disfunction of certain units due to a lack of training, a worrying number of civilian injuries in a nation that claims to be democratic, and the overly visible political control of operations. The fact that protest policing became a political issue and the subject of public debate seems to be a consequence. Ultimately, this is surely not so much a crisis of protest policing, but rather it reflects uncertainty regarding what protest policing is in France today, and what it should be. A once-relatively balanced approach to protest policing has given way to a profoundly uncertain situation in which each operation threatens to give rise to scandal or extended enquiries into what occurred and what should have been done. It is in this sense that we speak of a "challenge." The police have not yet managed to formulate appropriate strategies for controlling newer social movements that have evolved in recent years and for their tactics of refusing negotiation and occupying more defensible areas.

Could France Look Elsewhere?

Without a doubt, protest policing in France has once again become an issue. On closer inspection, this should have been predictable. In a broad review published in 1997, Olivier Fillieule (1997a) warned against the temptation to consider the secular process of pacification of social conflicts as something that must persist. The events of the last 20 years (including the growth of urban crime, the return of political violence, and the refusal of protesters to comply with legislation governing the right to demonstrate) have shattered the ultimately fragile framework guiding French protest policing. But if debates surrounding protest policing have taken on such great significance, this is certainly also linked to the fact that, in other European countries, the pacification process has continued. Indeed, several countries neighboring France have been looking at some depth into the adoption of "de-escalation" techniques in policing. This has been encouraged by a new model of crowd psychology embodied by the "KFCD model." This acronym – *Knowledge, Facilitation, Communication, Differentiation* – indicates that the aim for decision-makers should be first and foremost to protect and support demonstrators, and to maintain dialog with them for as long as possible (Fillieule et al. 2016, p. 14). Being relatively impervious to practical and theoretical progress along these lines, France has also not taken part in the GODIAC (Good Practice for Dialogue and Communication as Strategic Principles for Policing Political Manifestations in Europe) project. This discussion brought together representatives of 12 European countries between 2010 and 2013, with the aim of synthesizing and unifying the principles of de-escalation. French protest policing could once have been viewed as a brilliantly exportable model. Now it remains isolated from broader discussions of policing. The repeated failures of policing efforts in recent years, and the handling of the *gilets jaunes* movement, have given foreign police forces the impression that France is now years behind in terms of its public order maintenance philosophy.

There is nothing irreversible about this fall from grace. French protest policing has weathered numerous crises, and many officers in the *police nationale* and *gendarmerie* realize that their doctrine must evolve to facilitate dialog with demonstrators and de-escalation at the front line. The biggest obstacle to this is likely to be political, where guidelines governing labor relations and decisions to repress protest movements are decided upon. In order to better understand how protest policing works in France, it is necessary to reverse course and rework Dominique Monjardet's definition: if protest policing is a *technique* (more or less guided by a *doctrine*), materialized by a set of *practices* which that technique is supposed to foster, it is *also* and *above all* a policy in the sense that it is a choice made within the framework of a government strategy.[10]

Notes

1 By a semantic shortcut, an officer who is part of a *police nationale* CRS company is known as "a CRS." This term is not applied to the mobile *gendarmes*.

2 The most famous event is the shooting at Fourmies, on 1 May 1891, during which troops opened fire to disperse a demonstration and killed nine people, including women and children. This was not an isolated incident: Patrick Bruneteaux counted 30 such victims killed by army fire during protest marches, between 1900 and 1908 (Bruneteaux 1996, pp. 39–40).
3 During a demonstration of steelworkers organized by the CGT on 23 March 1979 in Paris, far-left autonomous activists, taking advantage of flaws in the police apparatus, looted and destroyed many luxury goods stores in the center of Paris.
4 This can take the form of an arrest at the site of the demonstration, or later with the help of increasingly available video footage of the event, which can be used to identify the perpetrators of crimes.
5 Thus, Nicolas Sarkozy, then minister of the interior, was able to trumpet the news of over 5,200 arrests made, following the 2005 riots, proving beyond a doubt that the police had come out of the events victorious.
6 The makers of these products have come to be very cautious with their semantics, describing them as "sub-lethal" or "less lethal" weapons.
7 A number of these units were to become Compagnies de Sécurité et d'Intervention (security and intervention squads) in the 2000s, at Nicolas Sarkozy's request.
8 This is discussed in more detail in Jobard (2015).
9 Sivens is another Zone to Defend which appeared in south-western France in 2013. Eco-protester Rémi Fraisse was killed there by a concussion grenade launched by a mobile *gendarme* on 25 October 2014: this was the first casualty at a protest since the 1980s.
10 The original quote from Monjardet is: "if protest policing is a *policy* in the sense of 'a choice made within the framework of a government strategy', it is also a *technique* (more or less guided by a *doctrine*), materialized by a set of *practices* which that technique is supposed to engender and regulate" (Monjardet 1990, pp. 207–208)

References

Berliere, J. M. 1996. *Le Monde des polices en France: XIXème-XXème siècles*. Bruxelles: Complexe.

Bruneteaux, P. 1993. Cigaville: quand le maintien de l'ordre devient un métier d'expert. *Cultures et conflits* 9–10: printemps-été. https://journals.openedition.org/conflits/223

Bruneteaux, P. 1996. *Maintenir l'ordre: Les transformations de la violence d'Etat en régime démocratique*. Paris: Presses de la Fondation Nationale des Sciences Politique.

Critcher, C., and Waddington, D. 1996. *Policing public order: Theoretical and practical issues*. Aldershot: Avebury.

Della Porta, D., and Reiter, H. 1998. *Policing protest: The control of mass demonstrations in western democracies*. Minneapolis: University of Minnesota Press.

Dewerpe, A. 2006. *Charonne, 8 février 1962: Anthropologie historique d'un massacre d'Etat*. Paris: Gallimard.

Dufresne, D. 2007. *Maintien de l'ordre: enquête*. Paris: Hachette.

Favre, P. 1990. Introduction. Pp. 11–65 in P. Favre (Ed.) *La Manifestation*. Paris: Presses de la Fondation Nationale des Sciences Politiques.

Fillieule, O. 1997a. Du pouvoir d'injonction au pouvoir d'influence? Les limites de l'institutionnalisation. *Les Cahiers de la sécurité intérieure* 27: 101–125.

Fillieule, O. 1997b. *Stratégies de la rue. Les manifestations en France*. Paris: Presses de Sciences Po.

Fillieule, O., and Tartakowsky, D. 2013. *La Manifestation*. Paris: Presses de Sciences Po.

Fillieule, O., Viot, P., and Descloux, G. 2016. Vers un modèle européen de gestion policière des foules protestataire? *Revue Française de Science Politique* 66: 295–310.

Jobard, F. 2012. Le spectacle de la police des foules: les opérations policières durant la protestation contre le CPE à Paris. *European Journal of Turkish Studies* 15 [Online].

Jobard, F. 2014. Mort de Rémi Fraisse: l'Etat à l'épreuve, entretien accordé à. *La Vie des Idées*. [Online: https://laviedesidees.fr/Mort-de-Remi-Fraisse-l-Etat-a-l.html]

Jobard, F. 2015. La police en banlieue après les émeutes de 2005. *Mouvements* n° 83: 75–86.

Kokoreff, M. 2006. Sociologie de l'émeute: Les dimensions de l'action en question. *Déviance et Société* 30: 521–533.

Lippens, B. 2016. *Vers une individualisation des la gestion des foules? L'influence des violences urbaines et des lanceurs de balles de défense sur le maintien de l'ordre. Mémoire de Science Politique*. Paris: Université Paris 1 Panthéon-Sorbonne.

Mamere, N., and Popelin, P. 2015. *Rapport n°2794*. Enregistré à la Présidence de l'Assemblée Nationale le 21 mai 2015.

Monet, J. C. 1990. Maintien de l'ordre ou création du désordre? Les conclusions de l'enquête administrative sur la manifestation du 23 mars 1979. Pp. 229–244 in P. Favre (Ed.) *La Manifestation*. Paris: Presses de la Fondation Nationale des Sciences Politiques.

Monjardet, D. 1990. La manifestation du côté du maintien de l'ordre. Pp. 207–228 in P. Favre (Ed.) *La Manifestation*. Paris: Presses de la Fondation Nationale des Sciences Politiques.

Monjardet, D. 1996. *Ce que fait la police: Sociologie de la force publique*. Paris: La Découverte.

Motta, A. 2016. La bavure et l'émeute. Genèse d'un signe déclencheur type dans le Rhône (1979–2000). *Revue Française de Science Politique* 66: 937–961.

Pigenet, M. 1990. La 'manifestation Ridgway' du 28 mai 1952: De la démonstration 'dure' à l'affrontement physique. Pp. 245–268 in P. Favre (Ed.) *La Manifestation*. Paris: Presses de la Fondation Nationale des Sciences Politiques.

Sommier, I. 1993. La CGT: du service d'ordre au service d'accueil. *Genèses* 12: 69–88.

Sommier, I. 2008. *La Violence politique et son deuil. L'après 68 en France et en Italie*. Rennes: Presses Universitaires de Rennes.

Chapter 15

Domestic Intelligence and Counterterrorism in France

Laurent Bonelli

Since the early 1960s, France has been hit by regular outbursts of political violence. The November 2015 attacks in Paris and Saint-Denis that killed 130 persons and wounded more than 400 were among the most internationally visible episodes of violent terror, but the list of these events is a long one. The first line of defense against terrorism and other forms of political violence in France remains firmly in the hands of the police. Unlike Germany and the United Kingdom, domestic intelligence and counterterror operations are the exclusive concern of specialized police units. Further, each major terrorist attack has been treated as an opportunity for police to reassess their actions, identify their shortcomings, and make organizational, regulatory, and legislative changes. Many of these adaptations to the changing world of political violence are documented in this chapter. Finally, because the urgency and trauma resulting from political violence tends to overshadow other activities – including even political surveillance and counterespionage – police practices end up being justified first and foremost by their effectiveness at counterterrorism. This chapter offers readers an introduction to French domestic intelligence agencies and shines some light on the transformations they have gone through since the late 2000s. The chapter complements earlier works on the subject, especially Shapiro and Suzan (2003) and Bonelli (2008).

This chapter is based on a long-term study of domestic intelligence. From 1999 to 2019, interviews were carried out with some 60 members of intelligence services at various levels, from directors to rank-and-file officers through middle managers, and repeated at regular intervals with key informants in order to keep track of ongoing developments. These interviews were complemented by a review of the available "gray" literature (briefings, reports), as well as the many published memoirs of former or current intelligence practitioners. I have also monitored interviews they have given, journalistic investigations (which are of varying quality), and the hearings of parliamentary committees of inquiry.

Restructuring Domestic Intelligence Services

The "Merah Affair" provides a good entry point into making sense of recent developments in domestic intelligence operations. In March 2012, Mohammed Merah carried out three attacks against French military personnel and a Jewish school in the cities of Toulouse and Montauban. He killed seven people, including three children, and caused outrage throughout the country. This event occurred well before the well-known attacks of 2015, and the death toll was the heaviest since violent attacks in 1995.[1] As often happens in such cases, questions were raised about the effectiveness of the intelligence services. Politicians, journalists, and victims' families were swift to emphasize the failures of the Central Directorate for Domestic Intelligence (Direction centrale du renseignement intérieur – DCRI), which, though aware of the young man's dangerousness, was unable to stop him.

Soon after the events of 2012 – a process that was probably made quicker by changes in political leadership – three administrative and parliamentary inquiries were launched. Following the election of François Hollande in May 2012, the new minister of interior, Manuel Valls, commissioned a report on the Merah affair from two high-ranking *police nationale* officials. The report was publicly released in October and pointed at "objective failures" as well as "management and organizational issues" (Leonnet and Desprats 2012). Turnover at the presidential level also made it possible to create two parliamentary committees of inquiry (Cavard and Urvoas 2013; Urvoas and Verchère 2013). Both parliamentary reports launched scathing attacks on the previous administration's counterterrorist strategy ("led by a masquerading agency whose territorial architecture has failed") and pleaded in favor of rebuilding a domestic intelligence *continuum* to fight terrorism.

A Brief History of Domestic Intelligence Agencies

All these reports concurred on heavy criticism of the reform of 27 June 2008, which had restructured police intelligence and was perceived as having unexpectedly led to the Merah affair. Before the reform – described below – two main domestic intelligence agencies coexisted, namely the Direction centrale des renseignements généraux (DCRG) and the Direction de la surveillance du territoire (DST).

The DCRG was the product of a merger between the special railway police (created in 1855) and the Brigade de renseignements généraux de police administrative de la Sûreté (founded in 1911) (Berlière 1996). Since 1942 the DCRG had been responsible for "collecting and centralizing the political, social, and economic intelligence required to keep the government informed."[2] This general-purpose agency had a strong local presence around the country. It conducted rather comprehensive surveillance of political, union, civil association, and religious groups, for the purpose of anticipating and uncovering potentially subversive threats to the established social and political order. As of 2008, it boasted slightly more than 4,000 agents, 700 of whom belonged to the Renseignements généraux de la préfecture de police (RGPP). This Parisian unit stood apart because of the special status of the capital city, a locus of both power and protest. It enjoyed substantial autonomy from the rest of the DCRG. Intelligence was mostly collected in open fashion; officers did not hide their position from the many informants they rubbed elbows with, and in fact forged strong links with them. They built trust in this fashion in order to be in the know about what was going on in the country. Reflecting their reputation, the socialist minister of interior in 1949, Jules Moch dubbed them the "meteorologists of French political, social, and economic life."

Anglo-Saxon eyebrows might rise in response to this extensive, yet open, surveillance of a significant portion of the French population. However, it was perfectly legitimate in the eyes of French elites who, although they periodically agreed to adjust and even scrap some types of missions altogether (such as the surveillance of mainstream political parties and election forecasting in the late 1990s), seem reluctant to relinquish this tool.

The second main intelligence unit, the DST, was created in 1944. It was tasked with "looking for and preventing, on the territory of the French Republic, activities inspired, engaged, or supported by foreign powers that may threaten the country's security, and generally fight such activities."[3] Initially, it was clearly a counterespionage agency. Prior to its collapse, the USSR had been the focus of most of its energy. After, the DST refocused on economic intelligence, nuclear proliferation, biological, chemical, and ballistic weapons, and – most importantly – the fight against terrorism. This new concern had been gathering momentum since the early 1980s. In 2006, DST head Pierre Bousquet de Florian indicated that counterterrorism made up 50% of the agency's activities, with counterespionage accounting for 25%, and protecting the country's economic and scientific heritage the remaining 25%. The DST looked more compact (1,700 staff in 2008), more Parisian, and more specialized than the DCRG. Since its agents were worked in secrecy and enjoyed some judicial powers, they were more likely to resort to covert surveillance methods (including wiretapping and surveillance) than their colleagues in the DCRG.

These differences between the two intelligence branches anchored their strong and distinct institutional identities, and very few staff ever transferred from one to the other. The 2008 reform, however, suddenly disrupted the rather stable division of intelligence tasks between the two organizations.

The 2008 Reform

In 2008, the DCRG and DST were reshuffled. This was just one of several reorganizations to come, so Figure 15.1 summarizes the main lines of their

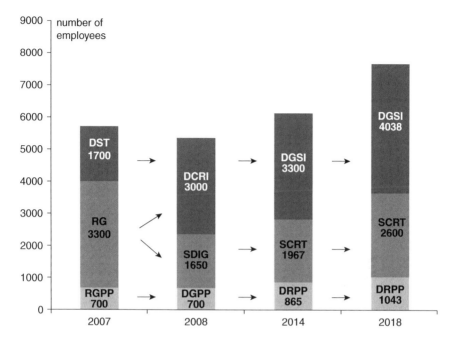

Figure 15.1 The Evolution of France's Domestic Intelligence Agencies.
Source: prepared by the author.

DST: Direction de la surveillance du territoire
RG: Renseignements généraux
RGPP: Renseignements généraux de la préfecture de police de Paris
DCRI: Direction centrale du renseignement intérieur
SDIG: Sous direction de l'information générale
DRPP: Direction du renseignement de la préfecture de police de Paris
DGSI: Direction générale de la sécurité intérieure
SCRT: Service central du renseignement territorial

evolution between 2007 and 2018. Two new agencies were created, the Direction centrale du renseignement intérieur (DCRI) and the Sous-direction de l'information générale (SDIG). The DCRI took on all DST's former personnel, and in addition the violent protest and research sections of the DCRG. These additions were not always well accepted by their colleagues.[4] The SDIG was essentially the intelligence division of the Direction centrale de la sécurité publique (DCSP). The RGPP, however, evaded the reform, simply changing its name to become the Direction du renseignement de la Préfecture de police de Paris (DRPP), with no change whatsoever to their organization or missions.

These new organizational arrangements created a significantly unbalanced relation between the DCRI and the SDIG. While the DCRI replicated the DST's organizational approaches and operational logics, the SDIG had to be content with those who stayed. To make matters worse, they found themselves under the supervision of public safety units (i.e. urban police forces), which were notoriously unsympathetic, if not downright hostile, to the work of the DCRG.

All the most prestigious intelligence tasks (counterterrorism and counter-espionage in particular) as well as the bulk of staff (about 3,000) and material resources thus fell under the monopoly of the DCRI. This "French-style FBI," as it was (perhaps a bit hastily) dubbed by some zealots, aroused significant enthusiasm from politicians and the media. However, it was also criticized by many police officers. They resented its lack of inclusiveness and were worried by the unmitigated triumph of the DST's methods, especially as far as counterterrorism was concerned. One particular bone of contention was what these officers considered to be an artificial division in the field of surveillance. The DCRI paid no attention to movements and organizations (as opposed to what the RG used to do) and focused instead exclusively on "individuals likely to – or having already – become involved in violence."[5]

Rationales for Reform

Sorting through the reasons behind a reform reveals the influence of many different conflicting interests – from internal squabbling to wider disputes at the national level and within the bureaucratic system – and weighing them all is no easy task.

To begin with, the intensification of international cooperation in matters of counterterrorism, which began in 2001, convinced many intelligence bosses that the existing RG/DST split was incomprehensible to foreign agencies, especially in the English-speaking world. It seemed that France would be well-advised to build one single large, secretive domestic agency, if it wanted to hold its own in exchanges with other nations' services. In this respect, the DST happened to be a better candidate than the RG to organize around.

But this move only contributed to internal frictions at the RG, pitting the advocates of an operational (i.e. action-oriented) brand of intelligence against those oriented toward a more traditional, information-gathering model. The latter, who had seen their influence gradually wane ever since the early 1990s, appeared to have been sidelined during pre-reform negotiations.

The importance of purely internal factors is nothing new among intelligence agencies. A merger of intelligence units had already been attempted in 1990 under the aegis of Jacques Fournet, who had run both agencies at some point. The main stumbling block had been a political one. The then-president of the Republic, François Mitterrand, was resolutely hostile to such a reorganization, as was his successor Jacques Chirac. Both were reluctant to grant too much power to a single entity, preferring instead to be able to turn to one or the other, depending on the circumstances. In 2008, Nicolas Sarkozy took the opposite stance. A staunch advocate of the merger, he became the driving force that made it happen. As a former minister of interior (2002–2004 and

2005–2007), he had both the resources and supporters needed to make it work. His motives were two-pronged. First, Sarkozy himself had earlier been affected by the political use of both the RG and the DST. This occurred during internal struggles that shook up his political party, the UMP (Union pour la majorité présidentielle). It was the majority party in the build-up to the 2007 presidential election. Prior to this, Sarkozy had been implicated in the "Clearstream" scandal. He had also made political mistakes during the 2005 riots, and news of his investigation of an advisor to the socialist candidate had leaked. These setbacks convinced him that the existing system of dual intelligence services was politically impossible to control. As an alternative, a single organization could be controlled, if it was headed by a loyal follower. Bernard Squarcini, head of the DCRI from 2008 to 2012, was one of those. Later, the French press ended up calling him "the President's spy" (Recasens et al. 2012). There were structural motives behind the reorganization as well. Intelligence fell victim to budgetary streamlining that was initiated by the president, not to mention by his larger ambition to redefine the form and mission of the state (Bonelli and Pelletier 2010). As an intelligence officer told us in August 2007, "reforming consists in doing more or better with less money. But in this case, they found a rhetorical sledgehammer, terrorism. Terror simply blows up the last remaining psychological or administrative sociology barriers [to reform]."

Criticizing the 2008 Reform, Implementing a 2014 Reorganization

The criticism voiced by several intelligence officers regarding the unbalanced consequences of the reform was not lost on Jean-Jacques Urvoas. He was a member of parliament for the *département* of Finistère, and he had been national secretary of the Socialist Party (PS) in charge of security issues (i.e. basically the shadow home secretary) since May 2009. In this capacity, he had a great many contacts with the police and became a genuine expert in these matters. This was evidenced by his subsequent book (Urvoas 2012a) and several memos for the Jean Jaurès foundation, the Socialist Party's main think-tank, two of which dealt with intelligence agencies (Urvoas and Vadillo 2011; Urvoas 2012b). In these papers, Urvoas voiced his concerns regarding the SDIG's deterioration. Dismissing the "scorned stooge of our national security apparatus" (Urvoas 2012b, p. 21) noted that "former RGs were being rejected" (p. 13) from the DCRI and made a plea for a better balance between domestic intelligence and information gathering. After being re-elected in 2012, he became president of the Commission des lois constitutionnelles, de la législation et de l'administration générale de la République (Law Commission). There he was a member (and, from 2014, the head) of the Délégation parlementaire au renseignement (Parliamentary Intelligence Committee). Crucially, he was involved in the two parliamentary committees of inquiry set up in the wake of the Merah affair – respectively as president and reporter of the first inquiry (Urvoas and Verchère 2013) and reporter of the second (Cavard and Urvoas 2013). Both investigations came to conclusions that were in line with his long-standing stance on such matters.

Along with others, Urvoas contributed to making the socialist political and administrative elite question the DCRI's monopoly on counterterrorism. While (almost) no one denied that the DCRI was the best agency to deal with individuals identified as potentially violent, some argued that it could not continue to have sole responsibility for the early detection of terrorist threats, a claim the agency had been making since its creation.

Mounting criticism, both internal and external, of the DCRI's counterterrorism approach, which was magnified by the Merah incident of 2012, led on 9 May 2014 to another reform of the intelligence services. It was to partially restore a balance between the DCRI and the SDIG. The former became the Direction générale de la sécurité intérieure (DGSI), and it escaped falling under the Direction générale de la police nationale (DGPN). Instead, it reported directly to the minister of interior. The reorganization also brought new financial independence to the DCRI, along with more options for recruiting non-police staff members with linguistic or technological skills, and new secrecy requirements regarding its activities. As for the SDIG, it became the Service central du renseignement territorial (SCRT). It gained some independence from the police *Sécurité publique*, as well as more prestigious missions, especially in the area of local intelligence emphasizing radical Islamism.

The 2015 Attacks and their Aftermath

While the terrorist attacks of January and November 2015[6] did nothing to alter this redistribution of responsibilities, they triggered a massive recruitment campaign that enlarged the DGSI's headcount from 3,300 to more than 4,000 by 2018. The SCRT grew from less than 2,000 to 2,600 staff members, and DRPP's from 865 to 1,043 members. In accordance with the July 2018 Plan d'action contre le terrorisme, or PACT, no less than 1,900 additional counterterrorism officers are to be hired by 2023.

The DGSI was confirmed as the operational leader for the prevention and suppression of domestic terrorism. The agency became responsible for individuals "at the top of the spectrum," i.e., those deemed most likely to take violent action. For its part, the SCRT was charged with monitoring those showing signs of radicalization but were deemed to not being quite as seriously involved. At the local level, the agencies combine their efforts as members of prefect-led "local assessment groups" (Groupes d'évaluation départementaux, or GED). These bodies acts as clearinghouses for locally reported cases of radicalization, whether from institutions (mostly schools and social workers) or private individuals (via a dedicated hotline managed by the counterterrorism coordination unit, UCLAT – Unité de coordination de la lutte antiterroriste). It is at this point that targeted individuals are classified, sorted, assigned a threat level, and passed along to the relevant agency.

From 2014 to 2019, the SCRT became increasingly involved in "radicalization," a theme that helped the agency regain some of the influence it had lost since the reform of 2008. However, the *gilets jaunes* ("yellow vests") crisis of winter 2018–2019 became the episode that cemented its position in the world of intelligence. Political leaders and policing agencies had been caught unawares by the magnitude, violent disposition, and determination of the movement. Not having anticipated the situation, they were at a loss as to strategies for keeping the movement in check. They also felt the effects of losing their older links to specific communities, something that had gotten lost in the reorganizations. Social and economic information gathering, which was also sacrificed on the altar of reform, appears to have been crucially missed during this crisis. The new National Intelligence Strategy, adopted in July 2019 noted that:

> for state policies to be implemented, it is essential to know what movements are agitating in social life, and even more what trends are flowing through our society. From this perspective, being familiar with local life and able to connect with its players (elected officials, voluntary sector, and the media) are major issues for the competent intelligence services.
> (CNRLT 2019, p. 4)

The DCRG's traditional missions, which had been entirely removed from the previous strategic plan in 2014, were brought back to life.

This detailed description of the evolution of France's main domestic intelligence services was a necessity, given how diverse and little-known their structures and missions are. This does not, however, exhaust the subject of counterterrorism. Other police agencies have roles to play this area as well. One in particular is the Sous-direction antiterroriste (SDAT) of the Direction centrale de la police judiciaire (DCPJ). It has a counterpart in the Paris prefecture of police called the Section antiterroriste (SAT). There are also investigation units of the *gendarmerie nationale* which are particularly active in the Basque country and Corsica. These mostly intervene at the request of the judicial authorities, and not to routinely gather intelligence.

Another actor is the Direction générale de la sécurité extérieure (DGSE). It is theoretically involved only in foreign intelligence, but its technical capabilities in the data realm also support domestic terrorism investigations. Mention should also be made of the Direction nationale du renseignement et des enquêtes douanières (DNRED), a customs intelligence and investigations unit, and the financial investigation unit called Traitement du renseignement et de l'action contre les circuits financiers clandestins (TRACFIN). Both are attached to the Ministry of the Economy and combat the financing of terrorism. Finally, the military is engaged as well, through the Direction du renseignement et de la sécurité de la Défense (DRSD) and the Direction du Renseignement militaire (DRM). The Ministry of

Justice additionally has an intelligence unit called Service national du renseignement pénitentiaire (SNRP). It is tasked with monitoring radicalized prison inmates. This complex assemblage of agencies is coordinated by such entities as the État-major permanent (EmaP) and the Coordination nationale du renseignement et de la lutte contre le terrorisme (CNRLT). However, the domestic intelligence services – the DGSI in particular – stand out as the lead agencies in terms of both expertise and resources (by way of comparison, the SDAT boasted just a little over 200 staff in 2018).

While introducing the reader to recent developments in the organization of French domestic intelligence was important, a review of what they do in practice is needed as well.

Intelligence in Action

Contrary to the image presented by spy films and novels, intelligence involves first and foremost analysis and writing. Only then can intelligence be used to hinder or neutralize targeted groups or individuals.

Fact Sheets, Notes, and Dossiers

From the inception of intelligence gathering, reports, notes, and lists of suspects have piled up in police offices. The secret services – along with surveyors and demographers – are among the greatest producers of the gigantic mounds of information that characterize the modern nation state (Bourdieu 2012, p.336). Starting in the 19th century (and during the Second French Empire especially), intelligence-gathering activity began to be routine. The services became better organized and increasingly standardized the manner in which they collected and classified information. They were driven by a quest for accuracy, consistency, and clarity, and their reports had to be consistent, transferable, and indexable (Dewerpe 1994 p. 144).

A key element in this trend was the creation of individual records. Every encounter with a source – a contact from the political world, unions, the voluntary sector, religious organizations, and the like – is usually recorded in writing. In the case of a meeting with an informant, these records become full-fledged contact notes, complete with comments and analysis by the agent involved. Notes can then be combined with other documents, such as internal material from an organization, articles from the media, wiretap and surveillance reports, and diverse other sources, in order to create – and later update – dossiers of individuals and organizations whose role is deemed significant.

These records may be complemented by information transmitted from other police agencies, either on their own initiative – when someone is arrested in possession of "subversive" documents or equipment, for instance – or via databases such as the wanted persons system (Fichier des personnes recherchées – FPR). In this database, intelligence services may create an "S" record ("S" for threat to the state's safety). They will be informed whenever a listed individual crosses a border, is stop-and-searched, or even subjected to a routine traffic stop, both in France and throughout the Schengen area.[7]

The dossier is one of the building blocks of intelligence work. However, each agency has its own, slightly idiosyncratic ways of building and using them. Agencies with an RG-oriented tradition mainly rely on "open" intelligence collection. In curious fashion, they entertain mutually beneficial relationships with activists, the voluntary sector, religious personalities, local authorities, and even journalists and scholars, many of whom are quite willing to help or supply information on a given topic. Political adversaries, rival organizations, and others with conflicting interests may also exchange data that may be useful to them.

Of course, this does not preclude the use of covert techniques (*techniques de milieu fermé*, i.e. infiltrated informants, wiretapping, personal and electronic surveillance, and other sources of information) especially in environments that make it difficult to establish more transparent relationships with information providers. Blackmail (in particular, using the threat of deportation in the case of illegal immigrants), coercion, and financial rewards are also used on a regular basis.

Given their long history of counterespionage efforts, the creation of dossiers differed slightly at the DST, and still does at the DGSI. To begin with, their dossiers are classified, as are their operations and the identities of their staff. Without delving too deeply into the DST's historical relationship with secrecy, until the early 1990s the agency was mostly pitted against its foreign counterparts. This was a fight of spy vs. counterspy in which everyone else's information was coveted. While this remains a major aspect of the DGSI's work, secrecy also appears to be used as a convenient way of keeping all the activities of the agency out of sight, including out of police sight.

The importance of the counterespionage function also explains the primacy of covert operations. Following people, wiretapping, using safe houses owned by the agency to hold covert meetings with useful contacts, bugging private premises, and the like, are routine activities for DST and DGSI agents. Today, digital interception is of course central to their work. Building diagrams of relationships from phone contacts, monitoring social network exchanges, and exploiting browser history and location data, are now routine ways of collecting information about individuals (Bigo and Bonelli 2019).

Another key asset is their special judicial status. Whereas the RG and its successors had to submit a file to the judicial police when a case was deemed to be prosecutable, some DST (then DGSI) officers are actually *officiers de police judiciaire* (OPJ), i.e. they possess the ability to take a case directly to a magistrate (or the other way around). This is known as the "J" (J for *judiciaire*) activity of the DGSI. It makes it possible for them use more aggressive investigative techniques, especially in intercepting communications.

The role of foreign agencies is another unique characteristic of DGSI dossiers. This unit has long been engaged in trusting collaborations with other intelligence services, either on a bilateral basis or in the context of such forums as the

Club de Berne (Bigo 1996). These collaborations first formed with their counterparts from the Western bloc, and later with those from the Maghreb and the Middle East. The latter services are particularly able to warn of the arrival of identified activists and transmit information about their own nationals.

Briefings and Reports

Intelligence briefings (white for the RG/SCRT, on blue paper for the DST/DGSI) combine information originally scattered over a wide variety of sources and are meant to raise awareness among political – or even judicial – administrative authorities about specific investigations or events. Information that is disseminated from the intelligence services to external recipients goes through a series of successive filters, at various levels of the hierarchy depending on their importance. These briefings make up both the agency's written legacy – internal knowledge that will be passed on to new staff – and an institutional façade, since its activities will be judged on the basis of these reports. Specific skills and the utmost attention to detail are required to write them. Training is provided on report writing, and intelligence products are carefully reviewed and edited. As a superintendent (*commissaire*) from the RG put it,

> We had designed a proofreading system and those of our senior staff that were ... very good at this managed the youngsters. Pretty soon, everyone's writing had become OK and, in any case, I proofread everything myself before it was sent out. Not that I was necessarily such a good writer myself, but when I noticed that something was wrong, I had two potential editors to rewrite a paper and make it palatable to someone like the prime minister or the Ministry of Interior.
>
> (Interview, February 2013)

Similar consideration is given to summary reports (*synthèses*) written by police officers. These documents review a particular topic and can be as long as 50 pages. They are mainly based on briefings from local and central units, but also general media sources (occasionally) or academic publications (very rarely). The police in charge of the report may ask local services to quantify and qualify the phenomenon in their jurisdiction. The whole point of these reports is to provide, as a *commissaire* put it, a "quantified picture" of a given phenomenon.

These reports are highly valuable to political and administrative leaders, as well as journalists. They typically provide information that is both quantitative (counting "Salafist" mosques, "Black Bloc Anarchists," or the number militants in a violent far-right organization) and qualitative (with concrete examples, anecdotes, timelines, and biographical sketches of the main leaders), and they present them in a confidential format. The combination of the legitimacy of the statistics (intelligence agencies do their own counting and thus have a monopoly on statistics pertaining to the issues they work on) and the authority of the intelligence services, gives these reports considerable symbolic force when it comes to explaining societal developments.

Of course, criticism is rife throughout administrative and governmental services of such bits of "police" analysis, which many simply ignore. Even within agencies, doubt is not uncommon. At the DST, for instance, several – non-police – directors voiced reservations when interviewed about their subordinates' analyses. As one of them told us,

> The way I validated all this human, or even technical, intelligence that was brought to me from within the house was with huge amounts of reading and frequent, systematic contacts with scholars and diplomats … I was almost as focused on non-confidential intelligence, i.e. high-quality media studies and open sources, because when you send a blue briefing for signature, to make sure you're not saying anything stupid, you have to know the text itself inside out to begin with, and then you must put your team's analysis in a broader perspective.
> (Interview, June 2010)

The nature and content of these briefings and reports raises the concern that they mix the general perspectives and political concerns of the police with their factual analyses. Sociologist Peter K. Manning has observed that "suspicion is a police posture to the world" (Manning 2003, p.11). Research has long documented that generalized suspicion is a worldview that is firmly rooted in the ordinary activity and professional socialization of the police (for an overview see Jobard and de Maillard 2015, pp. 98–110). Specific forms of this can be seen in intelligence agencies. While their colleagues from urban forces are primarily concerned with public order, intelligence officers are engaged in defending the social and political order. This involves focusing specifically on groups that may threaten it – especially those that get organized to do so. DCRG Commissaire Lucienne Bui Trong warned that Islamic preaching may only bring about a few conversions here and there, yet "small active minorities may assume a major role in history" (Bui-Trong 2003, p. 161). DST Director Jean Rochet depicted the events of May 1968 as a form of manipulation of the discontent of French youths by "ringleaders acting upon orders from abroad [who] took things in their hands with the avowed objective of overthrowing the regime" (Rochet 1985, p.73).

These kinds of suspicions certainly may not be baseless. Conspiracies do happen and groups plotting to overthrow governments, or more prosaically hoping to alter the course of history, do exist. Still, by focusing exclusively on these, one may be led to overestimate their role, or even consider them to be organized and structured in a way that they are not, ultimately imputing all forms of unrest and social development to their hidden influence. This point of view is also reflective of institutional constraints. One reason why an intelligence officer will be looking for a conspiracy – where a sociologist might see but a process – is that it is their job to identify wrongdoers and take countermeasures. This imperative toward action can structure the descriptive narrative that will eventually become a report on the event, one that fits the clue-based approach to conspiracies described by Carlo Ginzburg, i.e. connecting scattered elements to offer some plausible account of the facts (Bonelli and Ragazzi 2014).

Briefings and reports also compete for attention at every level of the hierarchy, straining to gain credit or honors, or simply to gain an attentive ear. "You have to lay it on a bit thick if you want to get the message across," an officer from the RG told us about his briefings. It is, moreover, a way of lowering the risk of a major event happening without having been anticipated. Overestimating danger in their briefings and reports is often how intelligence services guard themselves against criticism should a terrorist attack occur, or, more prosaically, should a demonstration be better-attended or more violent than anticipated. Being able to say "I told you so" but "I haven't been heard" can be a good defense. One strategy for re-legitimizing the agencies caught up in such crisis situations is opportunistically disseminating (i.e., "leaking") written evidence of their prior concern through friendly journalists.

The wealth of information accumulated in their dossiers therefore constitutes the foundation of the work of domestic intelligence services. However, once shaped into briefings or reports, this information may be used to neutralize suspects before they act. The translation of intelligence into operational knowledge can take two forms: administrative and judicial.

Administrative Actions

Administrative interventions (*l'entrave administrative*) include deportation, even in the case of legally resident foreign nationals. Another measure is a ban on entering French territory (*interdiction du territoire français*, or ITF) which is handed down by a court following criminal sentencing. However, intelligence services more often resort to ministerial deportation orders (*arrêtés ministériels d'expulsion*, or AME). This is a frequently used device aimed at so-called "preachers of hate." Any foreign national exhibiting behaviors deemed likely to "violate the fundamental interests of the state, or linked to terrorist activities, or deemed to constitute explicit and deliberate acts inciting discrimination, hatred, or violence against a specific individual or group" may be deported.

According to the Ministry of Interior, during 2015 about 80 individuals were subjected to such measures. This device is convenient in practice, as orders only include minimal information motivating the deportation decision. Only in the case of a potential (non-suspensive) appeal does the government have to provide evidence of the potential threat – in the form of intelligence reports, for instance. These reports, however, are anonymous, in order to protect sources. This makes it very difficult to actually reverse the burden of proof, putting it on the government. According to Human Rights

Watch, "as a rule, administrative deportation orders target individuals the government cannot or would rather not prosecute" (Human Rights Watch 2007, p. 21 and 28).

Individuals that may not be deported because their life might be at risk in their country of origin are placed under house arrest. They are usually placed in a rural area as far removed as possible from major urban centers, which prevents them from pursuing their activities. Resettlement is also extremely burdensome. Arrestees are required to sign a registry at the local *gendarmerie* up to four times a day for as long as they refuse to be deported or remain unable to find a country willing to accept them. Because intelligence services in potentially host countries will ask their French counterparts for a briefing about candidates for expulsion, this can be difficult. The state of emergency declared in the aftermath of the attacks of 13 November 2015 (which lasted until 1 November 2017) broadened the scope of these practices. Of the 754 house arrest orders that were handed down, most went to activists categorized as being part of "radical Islamism" or a far-left protest movement (Hennette-Vauchez et al. 2018).

Finally, beginning in 2009, France inaugurated a procedure for freezing terrorist assets (*dispositif national de gel terroriste*). It may be triggered by an order from the minister of economy against any individual suspected by intelligence services who aims to "commit or try to commit acts of terrorism, take part in them, or fund them." Their assets can be frozen for an indefinitely renewable period of six months. Suspects are left a sum of money to cover household expenses (clothing, food), while fixed expenses (rent, telephone, electricity, taxes, loans) are paid directly to their creditors. The number of asset-freezing orders rose from 44 in 2012 to 187 in 2018 (Boyer and Krimi 2019, p. 77). As a police officer from the DCRI once told us, "it's not going to de-salafise the Salafists, but at least it helps contain the problem and prevent any expansion" (Interview, November 2012).

Other disruptive mechanisms are available to security agencies as well, including involving agencies that regulate food and veterinary medicine and investigate tax issues. They can close venues housing radical activities (proselytism, funding, propaganda). For instance, a halal butcher's shop may be shuttered for not complying with food hygiene regulations, a house of worship for lack of compliance with safety rules, and a cybercafe or streetwear shop for tax reasons. "They will open new ones", an officer pointed out, "but it will cost them time, energy, and money" (author's notes, November 2012).

Judicial Actions

In matters of counterterrorism, intelligence services may also turn to judicial measures to interrupt targeted activities. As mentioned before, a number of DGSI agents actually are judicial police officers, which means they have the authority to ask for an order from a specialized court. One of the devices they rely most upon is the charge of "criminal conspiracy in connection with a terrorist enterprise" (in French, "AMT"). The charge could involve taking part, or attempting to take part, "in a group assembled or an alliance formed with a view to preparing, as evidenced by one or several material facts." Earlier, an act of terrorism was punishable by ten years in prison, but the potential sentence was extended to 20 years in 2006, and to 30 years in 2015. This wide-ranging criminal charge lies at the core of the French counterterrorist system. It makes it possible for the authorities to take preventive action before an attack has been perpetrated (Alix 2010). As indicated by a top intelligence official,

> Even though they have been identified as part of some violent action or planned violent action, sometimes we can't manage to convict them when reaching the trial phase. That's when the charge of AMT comes in handy, making it possible to judge them for *the entirety of their activity*. We're not convicting them for an attack, nor for an assassination either, but still we are able to put them on trial for belonging to a terrorist organization or group.
>
> (author's notes, June 2013)

The AMT is known as an "obstacle offence" (*infraction obstacle*) and it became the spearhead of counterterrorism in France. As described by Pierre Bousquet de Florian, head of the DST from 2002 to 2007, the AMT is part of a doctrine known as "preventive judicial neutralization." A compendium of sentences involving AMT reveals that it was the main offense (i.e. no other criminal offence was associated with it) 50% of the time, and as much as 80% in some years (Bonelli 2008, p. 184). Its application accelerated when French nationals began travelling to the Iraq-Syria area, but establishing specific legal infractions implicated in this proved difficult. Now, the mere willingness to join what is considered a terrorist group is an actual offence, whether one actually does so or not (Mégie 2019). Up to 2 January 2017, 385 AMT cases involving 1,214 individuals (348 of whom were indicted) had been referred to the Paris public prosecutor. In 2015–2016, 114 individuals were sentenced on that count.

Further, the DGSI's role as both an intelligence agency and a judicial authority makes it possible for them to use the AMT in non-judicial contexts. It can be used to obtain information or even implement what practitioners call a "fishing net" strategy (also referred to as "kicking the anthill"). This involves in rounding up many individuals who may have some kind of tie to a radical network in order to destabilize the group by disrupting their logistics. Although praised by some police officers, use of the AMT has attracted heavy criticism from both magistrates and civil liberties advocates (Blisson 2017).

Conclusion

This chapter has provided an overview of the organization and activities of the French domestic intelligence services. The review has raised more general issues as well. Many of these are raised in the distinction between "high" and "low" policing. In a set of categories introduced by policing scholar Jean-Paul Brodeur (1983), "high policing" protects the interests of the state (and in practice, those who run it) rather than individuals or local communities. High police are empowered with special authority and routinely use advanced technologies, wide-ranging telephone and internet tapping, secrecy, deceit, and perhaps even extralegal policing tactics. Low policing, by contrast, is concerned with protecting the general public and maintaining community peace. Traditionally, most low policing is reactive. Investigations are largely initiated by calls from victims, and the core mission of responding officers is to make individual arrests that lead to convictions via open legal processes.

High and low policing activities are traditionally considered to be distinct, operating in different realms. This gap is accentuated in the Anglo-Saxon world by the organization of policing. There, responsibility for individually victimizing crime is entrusted to local police forces operating under local laws, while combatting violent subversion (as well as some organized crime) is a national policing priority (Bayley and Weisburd 2009). In France, by contrast, the domestic intelligence services are an integral part of the national policing apparatus. Their officers graduate from the same schools as their colleagues from main-line forces and the judicial police. Transferring from one agency to another is not uncommon, especially when it involves a promotion. The responsibilities of the various forces are of course different (Monjardet 1996), and require different skill sets and social aptitudes. Yet, these agencies are not independent from one another. Quite the opposite, they are in competition for resources (funding, staff, equipment) and jostle for recognition (honors and prestige). Policing thus appears to be a field – as Pierre Bourdieu (1994) labeled it – in which everyone is trying to maintain their role and their own guiding principles in the same task environment (Goffman 1991)

Differences between the two emerge when they are contrasted to one another. While many features of low policing are well documented by decades of research, high policing now deserves more attention. Existing research on high policing frequently consider it to be a tool for political decision makers. In this view, their missions, organization, and operations are a by-product of government priorities, which in turn are partly influenced by the threat environment and in part by other concerns. However, just as studies of urban police forces show that their role is not limited to fighting crime, but that they also contribute to defining the margins of the social order, field studies demonstrate that domestic intelligence services do more than just fight terrorism. They serve as a form of *gatekeeper of the political order*, allowing some social movements to play a role in it, and disqualifying others (Keller 1989; Gill 1994). They are responsible for weakening, neutralizing, and controlling social forces that might disrupt the political order. In that sense, intelligence agencies are in engaged in defining and redefining the boundaries of what is the acceptable degree of system change the state will tolerate.

They are of course not the only bodies involved in maintain this boundary, and their relationship with professional politicians may take a confrontational turn at times. Yet these confrontations should not detract from the issues that really matter. Within the array of state institutions, the intelligence agents enjoy authority which is guaranteed both by the secrecy surrounding their activities and their quasi-monopoly over the tools they use to enumerate and neutralize what they define as threats. This ensures that they maintain a strong position in the bureaucratic game. Their positioning grants them autonomy that is lent by government officials, who will defer to them on a day-to-day basis if they "get the job done." The intelligence services are given what Jean-Paul Brodeur (1983) called a "grey check." In the long-term relationship between the intelligence and political worlds, their role is that of a go-between bridging the gap between the establishment and potentially subversive groups. The negotiation, prevention, disruption, neutralization work they accomplish holds up their end of the bargain (Sentas 2016; Innes, Roberts and Lowe 2017).

Intelligence officers thus occupy a strategic position at the heart of democratic regimes. They play a sometimes-autonomous role in exercising state violence, while by gathering and assessing intelligence they also take part in the closure of the political game. In the future, a joint analysis of both high and low policing would help us assess how policing taken as a whole defines as well as maintains the social and political order.

Notes

1 Between July and October 1995, France was rocked by a series of terrorist attacks perpetrated by members of the GIA (Armed Islamic Group). Targeting the transport system, they killed ten and injured more than 200.
2 As per the ordinances of 17 November 1951 and 14 March 1967.
3 Ordinance of 22 December 1982.
4 As mentioned by the members of parliament, "In practice, personnel from the former DCRG were often perceived by their colleagues from the 'ST' as 'peasants attacking the castle, about to corrupt the blue blood of pure intelligence practitioners' ... Not only have the feuds of old not dissipated, but here and there, they continue unabated within one and the same department" (Urvoas and Verchère 2013, p. 127).
5 Memo to zonal directors, PN/DRI/N°6384, 8 July 2008.
6 On 7 January, the Kouachi brothers targeted the Paris office of *Charlie Hebdo* newspaper, killing 12. On 8 January, Amedy Coulibaly killed a female local police officer in the neighboring town of Montrouge, and on the next day, took hostages in a kosher supermarket in Paris, killing four. On 13 November, three commandos indiscriminately shot at cafe terraces and the Bataclan concert hall in Paris, while three bombs were detonated at the crowded Stadium de France in Saint-Denis, killing 130 and injuring 413.
7 The FPR is part of SIS II, which covers the entire Schengen area.

References

Alix, J. 2010. *Terrorisme et droit pénal: Étude critique des incriminations terroristes*. Paris: Dalloz.

Bayley, D. H., and Weisburd, D. 2009. Cops and spooks: The role of police in counterterrorism. Pp. 81–100 in D. Weisburd, T. Feucht, I. Hakimi, L. Mock, and S. Perry (Eds.) *To protect and to serve*. New York: Springer.

Berlière, J. M. 1996. *Le monde des polices en France*. Bruxelles: Complexe.

Bigo, D. 1996. *Polices en reseaux: L'expérience européenne*. Paris: Presses de Sciences-Po.

Bigo, D., and Bonelli, L. 2019. Digital data and the transnational intelligence space. Pp. 100–122 in D. Bigo, E. F. Isin, and E. Ruppert (Eds.) *Data politics: Worlds, subjects, Rights*. London: Routledge.

Blisson, L. 2017. Risques et périls de l'association de malfaiteurs terroriste. *Délibérée* 2: 16–20.

Bonelli, L. 2008. Les caractéristiques de l'antiterrorisme français: Parer les coups plutôt que panser les plaies. Pp. 168–187 in D. Bigo, L. Bonelli et T. Deltombe (Eds.) *Au nom du 11 September: Les démocraties occidentales à l'épreuve de l'antiterrorisme*. Paris: La Découverte.

Bonelli, L., and Pelletier, W. (Eds.). 2010. *L'Etat démantelé. Enquête sur une révolution silencieuse*. Paris: La Découverte.

Bonelli, L., and Ragazzi, F. 2014. Low-tech security: Files, notes, and memos as technologies of anticipation. *Security Dialogue* 45: 476–493.

Bourdieu, P. 1994. *Raisons pratiques: Sur la théorie de l'action*. Paris: Seuil.

Bourdieu, P. 2012. *Sur l'Etat: Cours au Collège de France (1989–1992)*. Paris: Seuil.

Boyer, V., and Krimi, S. 2019. *Rapport d'information sur la lutte contre le financement du terrorisme international*. Paris: Assemblée nationale, n° 1833.

Brodeur, J. P. 1983. High policing and low policing: Remarks about the policing of political activities. *Social Problems* 30: 507–520.

Bui-Trong, L. 2003. *Les racines de la violence: De l'émeute au communautarisme*. Paris: Audibert.

Cavard, C., and Urvoas, J. J. 2013. *Rapport sur le fonctionnement des services de renseignement français dans le suivi et la surveillance des mouvements radicaux armés*. Paris: Assemblée nationale.

CNRLT. 2019. *La stratégie nationale du renseignement*. Paris: Présidence de la république.

Dewerpe, A. 1994. *Espion: Une anthropologie historique du secret d'Etat contemporain*. Paris: Gallimard.

Gill, P. 1994. *Policing politics: Security intelligence and the liberal democratic state*. London: Frank Cass.

Goffman, E. 1991. *Les Cadres de l'expérience*. Paris: Editions de Minuit.

Hennette-Vauchez, S., Kalogirou, M., Klausser, N., Roulhac, C., Slama, S., and Souty, V. 2018. Ce que le contentieux administratif révèle de l'état d'urgence. *Cultures & Conflits* 112: 35–74.

Human Rights Watch. 2007. *Au nom de la prevention: Des garanties insuffisantes concernant les éloignements pour des raisons de sécurité nationale*, 19: 3D.

Innes, M., Roberts, C., and Lowe, T. 2017. A disruptive influence? "Preventing" problems and countering violent extremism policy in practice. *Law & Society Review* 51: 252–281.

Jobard, F., and de Maillard, J. 2015. *Sociologie de la police: Politiques, organisations, réformes*. Paris: Armand Colin.

Keller, W. 1989. *The liberals and J. Edgar Hoover: Rise and fall of a domestic intelligence state*. Princeton: Princeton University Press.

Leonnet, J., and Desprats, G. 2012. *Affaire Merah: Réflexions et propositions*. Paris: Ministère de l'Intérieur.

Manning, P. 2003. *Policing contingencies*. Chicago: University of Chicago Press.

Mégie, A. 2019. Le contentieux judiciaire antiterroriste depuis 2015: "Massification", spécialisation et politization. Pp. 187–206 in R. Seze (Ed.) *Les Etats européens face aux militantismes violents*. Paris: Riveneuve.

Monjardet, D. 1996. *Ce que fait la police: Sociologie de la force publique*. Paris: La Découverte.

Recasens, O., Hassoux, D., and Labbé, C. 2012. *L'espion du président: Au cœur de la police politique de Sarkozy*. Paris: Robert Laffont.

Rochet, J. 1985. *5 ans à la tête de la DST*. Paris: Plon.

Sentas, V. 2016. Policing the diaspora: Kurdish Londoners, Mi5 and the proscription of terrorist organizations in the United Kingdom. *British Journal of Criminology* 56: 898–918.

Shapiro, J., and Suzan, B. 2003. The French experience of counterterrorism. *Survival, Global Politics and Strategy* 45: 67–98.

Urvoas, J. J. 2012a. *11 propositions choc pour rétablir la sécurité*. Paris: Fayard.

Urvoas, J. J. 2012b. Les RG, la SDIG et après? Rebâtir le renseignement de proximité. *Note de la Fondation Jean Jaurès*, n°115.

Urvoas, J.J. et Vadillo, F. 2011. Réformer les services de renseignement français. *Note de la Fondation Jean Jaurès*.

Urvoas, J. J., and Verchère, P. 2013. *Rapport d'information en conclusion des travaux d'une mission d'information sur l'évaluation du cadre juridique applicable aux services de renseignement*. Paris: Assemblée nationale.

Chapter 16

Border Policing in France

Sara Casella Colombeau

Border policing has not been a focus of research on policing in France, but the topic has been addressed by numerous authors with a specialist interest in border controls and immigration policies. This chapter reviews the development of border policing in France by examining the operational practices involved and the organizations that are responsible for implementing them. The aim is to illustrate how scholars from wide-ranging disciplinary traditions have approached these questions. The chapter is divided into two complementary parts: research that examines the main themes and underlying rationales for border policing in France, and a report of ethnographic field research that focuses on street-level interactions between police and those whose identities they investigate.

State Control over Individual Mobility

The earliest studies of border policing focused on the question of state control over individual mobility. In parallel with the questions raised by John Torpey (2000) regarding the construction of a state monopoly over mobility control, Gérard Noiriel examined the way in which a transition from local to national control of movement accompanied a broader political transformation, that of the nationalization of society (Noiriel 2005). As the volume of individual movements within France grew, local face-to-face mechanisms for social control that existed under the Ancien Régime were called into question. In the 18th and, above all, the 19th centuries, the growth of the central government led to the emergence of new techniques and technologies for controlling individuals from a distance. To the end of the 19th century, these controls concerned French nationals who moved outside their local circle of social acquaintances. Then the state began to control the movement of foreigners, in addition to their traditional surveillance of "vagabonds" and other itinerant populations.

The French policing system progressively adapted in response to this growing priority on mobility control (Blanc-Chaléard et al. 2001; Napoli

2003; Berlière and Lévy 2011). This not only involved a restructuring of police forces, but also the development of new procedures and technologies, notably in the field of identity control.

The *gendarmerie*, a centralized military corps responsible for policing in rural areas, was traditionally in charge of controlling the movements of individuals and itinerant populations. This task was radically transformed in the 19th century by the emergence and development of new modes of transport, notably railways. It was at this time (in 1854) that the Special Railway Police (Police spéciale des chemins de fer) was set up as a branch of the general security forces (Sûreté générale). They were responsible for monitoring foreigners and dealing with crime on the railway lines, in trains and at stations (Berlière 1987). Their jurisdiction was soon extended to include population surveillance in ports and in the French *départements* with a foreign border. Their special police stations operated across the entire railway network and in all border regions. Control of vagrancy was also entrusted to the regional mobile brigades of the judicial police, another branch of the national police force with nation-wide jurisdiction. These police services were both national and centralized, at a time when most policing activities were organized at municipal level (and remained so until 1941). Thus, the "institutionalization of the police was largely the product of efforts to combat vagrancy and mobility" (Jobard 2010, p. 96). These police forces were under the direct authority of prefects (representatives of the state in the *départements*), not town mayors. The Special Railway Police became the Police spéciale in 1911, and in 1937 took the name of Direction des renseignements généraux (General Intelligence Division), the French domestic intelligence agency.

The importance attached by the police to detecting false identities and ensuring that people had a unique, verified identity was a direct response to the acceleration of mobility beyond the reach of local acquaintance networks that characterized social control in an earlier era. The development of modern practices for population control contributed to the professionalization and institutionalization of police services in France (About 2004, 2007; Crettiez and Piazza 2006; About and Denis 2010; Piazza 2011). A specialized service for surveillance of foreigners was set up in the Paris police headquarters (Préfecture de police) in the late 19th century, and a system of police records was tested there as early as the 1870s. The aim was to find systematic methods to both codify configurations of the human body and to keep on file the records of individuals arrested by the police. Known criminals were not the only people recorded in these police files; their use was very rapidly expanded to include foreigners (About 2004) and also "nomads" (Kaluszynski 1987) and political opponents (About 2007). These new identification technologies were adopted by the general security forces and the Special Railway Police. During the 1920s, it was general practice to keep files on foreigners, as they were required to register with the police for legal residence in the country. Surveillance of foreigners thus became part of an increasingly bureaucratized policing function. The formalization of police categories and their de facto association, via the filing techniques applied, produced an implicit link between criminality and migration, between interior enemy and foreigner, and contributed to an ethnicization of these categories.

The conflation of foreigners, criminals, and undesirables was particularly marked in the late 1930s. There was a general tightening of immigration laws and the creation of internment centers where foreigners were imprisoned "due to their criminal record and their activity judged to be 'a *danger to national security*'" (Clochard et al. 2004, p. 5). The first such center, set up in the region of Mende in January 1939, served to detain foreigners that the administration wished to expel, but lacked the means to do so (Fischer 2004). Internment became a major border policing practice when it became necessary to deal with Spanish republican refugees. Between January and April 1939, the French authorities constructed camps to detain the large numbers of refugees crossing the border between Spain and France; most were detained in these camps immediately upon their arrival (Peschanski 2002). Similar policies were applied to citizens of Algeria, a French colony at that time, who were also placed in detention centers. In the latter case, the aim was to repatriate them to *départements* in Algeria. Unlike the earlier period, when Algerians were to be treated as French nationals, their internment instead became common practice beginning in 1957 (Blanchard 2011). This infringement of their freedom of movement was characteristic of their status as "paradoxical citizens" and was applied widely during the Algerian War of independence.

In short, research on border policing in France also documents that it was not limited solely to controls at border crossing points. The policing of mobility and foreigners has structured the development of the French national police force and influenced the emergence of central police practices and techniques, such as identification and record systems. In addition, mobility control involving the cataloging of people in administrative categories, and centralizing police records contributed to the institutionalization of boundaries between French people and foreigners, between nomadic and settled populations, and between colonial subjects and full citizens, within France itself.

A History of the French Border Police

From the 1930s, despite the wide range of actors involved in border policing in France, a form of specialization began to emerge within the national police force, resulting in the creation of the Air, Border and Railway Police (Police de l'air, des frontières et des chemins de fer) (Casella Colombeau

2013). The development of the French border police took place in three stages.

First, from the 1950s to 1970s, border policing was structured for the specific purpose of policing the French frontier. Following a merger of the border section of the Renseignements généraux (RG) and the Air Police (created in 1929), the resulting agency changed its name many times and will be referred to here under its current title of Police aux frontières, or PAF. The PAF had mainly administrative and intelligence functions. In the early days, the work of its officers resembled that of other RG units across France, the only difference being their deployment at border points, stations, ports, and airports. Border policing thus corresponded above all to intelligence gathering on the political activities of travelers, and on labor unrest in ports, airports, and international railways stations. An amalgamation of various existing structures, the PAF had little internal cohesion. Its specific identity as a force operating at the French borders emerged progressively in the 1950s and 1960s. Thanks to their presence at border points, PAF officers had privileged access to information on travelers via the identity documents they were required to show before crossing the border. Their main tasks were thus to consult central police files and enter new data, notably on wanted individuals and known offenders. The type of information gathered and produced was operational, i.e. used in police inquiries or searches for suspects or convicted criminals.

However, while foreigners were implicitly associated with criminality or political discontent, it was not the PAF's role to limit the number of immigrants entering France. It was not until the second stage of the PAF's development, in the mid-1970s, that the role of border policing in France became that of enforcing restrictive immigration policies. This new function was in line with the reorientation of immigration policy that took place in France and other European countries at that time. In 1972, the government adopted the Marcellin-Fontanet circulars, named after the ministers of the interior and of employment, which made granting of a residence permit conditional upon obtaining a work permit before arrival in France. Until then, most immigrant workers had regularized their status after reaching the country. In July 1974, French President Valery Giscard d'Estaing officially put an end to labor migration.

Border policing was also strengthened. As the responsibilities of the PAF were reoriented towards controlling cross-border migration, it gained new powers, new resources, and more staff. In 1969, 820 law enforcement officers in junior and supervisory positions joined its ranks, along with 20 middle-ranking officers. Personnel numbers increased steadily, rising from 385 in 1955 to 2,818 in 1975.[1] Most of the new recruits were uniformed law enforcement officers, working most notably in the mobile border brigades created in 1974. These brigades patrolled between border posts, taking over the work previously entrusted to the riot police, the Compagnies républicaines de sécurité (CRS). The PAF's professional identity and mission, formerly limited to border posts and to administrative rather than operational policing, was thus transformed. Its border presence was strengthened, with the broadening of its scope of intervention to include patrolling along all national borders.[2]

In addition to checking identity documents, officers were responsible for identifying foreigners supposedly entering France for a short visit but actually seeking to live and work there. The aim was to combat clandestine immigration by targeting "false tourists," now a prime target of the border police. In 1974, the PAF became a central division, independent of the RG, much like the judicial police division. This reform marked a turning point, signaling a much stronger institutional anchoring of the PAF in the French law enforcement landscape. From then on, the air and border police force expanded steadily, both in scope and in size.[3]

In the 1980s, PAF officers were given the task of manning the detention centers for irregular immigrants present in France and awaiting expulsion. Initially set up on an informal basis, these centers were officialized as *centres de rétention administrative* (administrative retention centers) in 1981 (Fischer 2017). Additional detention centers were opened on the French borders in the 1990s, the largest one at Roissy-Charles-de-Gaulle airport outside Paris (Makaremi 2008, 2009a). The work of the PAF thus became more diversified, although certain centers were managed by the *gendarmerie*, by public security police officers, or by the Paris region police headquarters.

The third stage in the development of the PAF in France is linked to the European Union, and especially the creation of the Schengen Area allowing the free movement of individuals within its borders. The Schengen Agreement was signed in 1985, but it was the Schengen Convention implementing the Schengen Agreement signed between France, Germany, Belgium, Luxembourg, and the Netherlands in 1990 that transformed the role of the PAF. Under this Convention, systematic border checks at the internal borders of the Schengen Area, i.e. between two signatory states, were abolished. As many of these internal borders are along the frontiers of France, the creation of the Schengen Area threatened to transform the daily activities of PAF officers and their geographical distribution. Yet staffing levels did not fall because of this dramatic change in border policy, suggesting that officers were redeployed to new missions and new postings elsewhere in the country. Didier Bigo (1994) has shown that the involvement of civil servants from the French interior and justice ministries in the Schengen Agreement negotiations contributed to a de facto association between questions of security and immigration at European level. From the late 1980s, senior PAF personnel took part in the technical working groups that negotiated the Schengen Convention, and thus helped to define the conditions for lifting border checks at European internal borders. But a large-scale reorganization of the PAF was also initiated at a senior level, involving three main dimensions.

First, the PAF continued to operate at the internal borders, despite the closure of large numbers of border posts. In 1990 the PAF manned 68 fixed posts. It was present at 38 permanent checkpoints at the end of 1992. The PAF maintained its presence by transferring personnel to the mobile border patrols operating between border posts. To ensure the legality of any continuing identity controls, the French code of criminal procedure was modified in 1993 (even before the Schengen Convention came into force). Henceforth, in the Schengen Area, delimited by a line drawn 20 kilometers from the physical border, the rules applying to identity controls on the French territory were modified to allow police officers to make identity checks within them without prior justification. Hence, in a context of national border opening, identity checks were legitimated for reasons of proximity to the national border, and as such, they were little different from traditional border controls (Casella Colombeau 2017b). Bilateral agreements were also signed with neighboring Schengen Area members to create Police and Customs Cooperation Centers (PCCCs). These brought together all the bodies responsible for maintaining security on either side of the border (Maguer 2002). The agreements also included readmission clauses enabling PAF police officers to expel irregular immigrants back into neighboring countries from which they had arrived. These legislative and organizational changes allowed for continuity of border policing in a context of free circulation of persons following the creation of the Schengen Area. Such procedures were conducted at other border points as well, notably between Austria and the Czech Republic (Darley 2008a). The "reintroduction" of border controls during the European migrant crisis in 2015 was thus a less radical measure than it might seem, given that they had never actually been abolished (Casella Colombeau 2019).

The second dimension of this reorganization was a restructuring of the PAF's activities inside France. Between 1994 and 1999, the Police de l'air et des frontières symbolically changed its name to DICCILEC – Direction centrale du contrôle de l'immigration et de la lutte contre l'emploi de clandestins (Central Division for Control of Immigration and Illegal Employment). The term *frontière* (border) disappeared, and the division's resources were devoted entirely to fighting irregular immigration. New services were set up in French *départements* with large immigrant populations, and their officers conducted criminal investigations, focusing on illegal activities linked to migration. This change in the organization and responsibilities of the PAF is similar to that experienced by the French customs services (Domingo 2007). The aim was no longer to simply apprehend individuals who broke the immigration laws, but also to investigate the criminal networks and organizations that were behind this immigration, including smugglers, producers of false passports and identity documents, and employers of irregular immigrants. To carry out this mission, the PAF cooperated with other administrative bodies including URSSAF (the agency responsible for collecting social insurance contributions), the labor inspectorate in charge of combating the employment of foreigners without work permits, and municipal registry offices (to track down "marriages of convenience"). Immigration was now recognized as a new sector of international criminal activity. The existence of a continuous link between small-scale local criminality and highly organized transnational criminal networks (Casella Colombeau 2017c) gave rise in 1996 to the creation of the Office central de répression de l'immigration et des étrangers sans titre (Central Office for the Fight Against Illegal Immigration, or OCRIEST). OCRIEST, the first agency to operate under the authority of the PAF, was a sign of the importance attached to this issue by the national police authorities; central offices are elite services whose role is to coordinate investigations at national, European, and international levels.

The third dimension of this reorganization was a reinforcement of border controls for individuals arriving from outside the European Union, both inside France (mainly at airports) but also at the external borders of the Schengen Area in other member states. The PAF thus contributed to the organization of cooperation between European countries. In the 1990s, the European Commission funded a series of working groups that brought together officers from the border police and border guard services of its member states. This initial networking between national police forces served as a basis for setting up specialized, ad hoc centers hosted by different member states. These served as coordination points for the control of sea, air, or land borders and to harmonize training for police officers operating at European borders. These centers were later merged to create Frontex, the European Agency for the Management of Operational Cooperation at the External Borders. It was created in 2004 to reinforce border policing in countries facing by large numbers of migrants seeking to enter the European Union. To address this problem, Frontex sent preselected officers (including PAF officers) on short-term missions to provide back-up at these borders. This European cooperation did not radically modify the deployment of PAF officers, but it influenced certain practices, such as the recording of information obtained at border posts. These data are transmitted to Frontex for so-called "risk analysis" (Casella Colombeau 2017a). A set of instruments has been developed in the framework of European cooperation, reflecting an approach to border policing based on prevention and management of migration risk.

Since the 1990s, PAF has thus evolved in much the same way as other border police forces across Europe. Its work has been affected, for example, by the development of new identification technologies (biometry) and the multiplication of data files (Bigo 2001; Bonditti 2005; Bigo et al. 2013). Cooperation in border policing through Frontex (Ottavy and Clochard

2015) is not limited to EU members. From the 1990s, efforts were made to involve neighboring countries in the policing of EU external borders. The negotiations for a readmission agreement between Morocco and the European Union studied by Nora El Qadim (2015) are a case in point. Responsibility for border policing has also been delegated to the private sector, primarily airline companies (Guiraudon 2002), ferry operators (Clochard 2015; Maquet 2015), and road transport companies (Guenebeaud 2019). They can now be fined for transporting passengers who do not have valid documentation. Visa applications are also partly processed by private companies in countries of origin (Infantino 2019).

Border Protection at the Street Level

Research on recent changes in French border policing is based largely on ethnographic studies that address the question from the point of view of staff in the field and focus above all on border areas and control measures that are currently in place. Police organizations and border policing bodies are just some of the many actors involved. It is precisely by exploring the interactions between these various actors, and notably the people whose identities are investigated, that the literature sheds light on the recent transformations in border policing in France.

Expanding the Territorial Scope of Border Policing

Studies on the border between France and the United Kingdom at Calais have evidenced a widening of the border policing intervention zone. With the tightening of border controls, migrants seeking to enter Britain illegally are forced to find temporary shelter at the town periphery or in informal camps (Agier 2008). Since the 1980s, the policing of migrants in the Calais region has been characterized by a series of contradictory measures designed either to disperse these populations and limit their visibility by destroying their informal settlements or, conversely, to concentrate them in isolated peripheral areas, as illustrated by the Calais shantytown that sprang up in the spring of 2105. In both cases, the aim is to force the migrants to leave spontaneously by "making their life impossible" (Guenebeaud 2016), doing so through multiple arrests without charges, destruction of their property and food, and other harassment techniques. These dispersion strategies (Babels et al. 2019) are not limited to the local area. Since the early 2000s, authorities in Calais have implemented programs to disperse migrants across France by sending them to accommodation centers far from border regions. Even though most ultimately return to the Calais area, these dispersal efforts continue. The role of the border police thus involves not only confining individuals, but also forcing them to move on a regular basis so that large, visible populations do not have time to form.

Be it via house arrest, reception centers, or detention, the use of confinement to control mobility has increased very sharply since the 1990s (Darley et al. 2013; Lemaire 2014; Michalon 2015). This has transformed the very nature of the national border. It is now a place where rules about foreigners are enforced and, above all, where their expulsion is arranged. Contrary to the traditional idea of a border as a linear barrier, Olivier Clochard (2010) uses the term "reticular border" in order to highlight the connections and circulation between these control points, which are spread across the country.

Moreover, with the tightening of legislation on foreigners' rights of residence in France since the 1990s, public security police responsible for policing criminal activities in urban areas has focused their attention on undocumented foreigners. Numerical police targets for this type of offense were imposed in the mid-2000s (Le Courant 2010). This has led to an upsurge in identity checks to detect foreigners present in the country illegally. Examining the effects of this policing on foreigners' avoidance and survival strategies (Veron 2013; Le Courant 2015), the literature reveals that numerous police services across France have specific objectives for the surveillance and control of foreigners.

Exercising Physical Restraint and the Effects of Border Policing

Chowra Makaremi has examined expulsions of migrants held in detention centers at national borders, places officially called "waiting zones." People are sometimes expelled under escort. They are handcuffed and guarded by several police officers in the plane that takes them from France (Makaremi 2009b). In the 1990s, following the death of a detainee during his expulsion, the use of force by PAF officers was standardized and professional intervention techniques were devised to physically restrain individuals without harming them (Makaremi 2009b, p. 48). This "technification of force" led to the creation of UNESI, a specialized PAF unit for expulsion under escort, in 1999. This codification of physical restraint techniques modifies the power relations between police officer and subject, the aim being to weaken his or her capacity to resist.

Research has revealed the wide variety of actors involved in border policing. They come from the legal system, private organizations responsible for receiving migrants and supervising their detention (Tassin 2016), workers in the voluntary sector (Fischer 2017), and so on. Their involvement in the policing of borders and migrants is often self-contradictory. Volunteers and activists, for example, are generally hostile to the objectives of border policing, but they are obliged to adopt criteria for selecting foreigners to assist that give them a good chance of avoiding expulsion (Pette 2014).

Many scholars of border policing in France have sought to identify the effects of the interaction between the investigators and their targets on the production of statistical or administrative categories that give rise to new ways of characterizing subjects. The existence of policing practices that threaten migrants' physical well-being testifies to the construction of a radical migrant "otherness," one that is manifested notably through physical control over their bodies (Babels et al. 2019; Tyszler 2019). The effects of gender attribution and racialized representations of individual migrants are especially visible in detention centers (Michalon 2015). These studies tie in with the classic questions raised by sociologists of the police, but focus more on the effects of categorization than on the techniques, uncertainties, and rationalization of police targeting practices (Gauthier 2010). This literature places emphasis on the way in which the police use, reinforce, and transform the categories that serve to define a frontier between "them" and "us."

New Perspectives in Research on Border Policing

The overview presented above describes the broad scope and depth of research on border policing. In the past, however, this research has had little connection to other strands of policing studies. However, new series of studies with a more direct approach to the practices, representation, and techniques of the public and private security forces in charge of border policing have recently emerged. These projects look more closely at organizational (Pillant 2015; Tassin 2016; Guenebeaud 2017), professional (Bigo 2014; Casella Colombeau 2017c), and institutional matters. Studying the division of tasks in a retention center, Louise Tassin (2016) took particular interest in the informal mediation services provided by the staff – mostly immigrant women – of a private company operating in the center. Their personal backgrounds were seen as a useful resource in mediating between detainees and those in control. Her research, which demonstrates the effects of ethnic categories stemming from the division of labor in these detention centers, also sheds light on links between the construction of the boundaries of French society and barriers internal to society.

Professional rationales are also an explanatory factor in border policing practice. Boredom, geographical isolation, and the routine nature of border policing activities make the job unattractive to many (Darley 2008b). Performance incentives and career advancement schemes also influence policing practices. In Calais, CRS policing units usually responsible for riot policing are temporarily assigned to border policing tasks (Guenebeaud 2017). An exceptional performance bonus plan introduced in 2004 encourages these officers to make as many arrests as possible during their mission in Calais. Work on routine border control tasks sheds light on the practical realities of the assignment. Research on face-to-face interaction during border controls has made it possible to look beyond discourses on the increased technicality and intangibility of these controls (Darley 2008b).

More broadly, analysis of the discourse around police reliance on their instincts and experience in targeting individuals during border controls has revived a central question in sociology of the police, that of racially targeted identity checks (Darley 2008a). While identity checks at national borders are supposed to be performed in a uniform manner for all travelers, the border police have latitude to adjust their thoroughness (Crosby and Rea 2016). In other words, selection and filtering processes are applied at all borders. Officers find themselves in a bind, that of ensuring strict control over immigration without hindering the inflow of people who will contribute to the country's economic growth. At the French–Italian border, and likewise at the border between Austria and the Czech Republic inside the Schengen Area (Casella Colombeau and Darley 2019), the choices of the border police are especially visible. There, most travelers cross the border without hindrance, in accordance with the principle of the free movement of persons. The way in which the police there select people to be investigated – or not – based upon immediately visible criteria reflect deeper representations involving people's ethno-racial categories, gender, type of clothing and luggage, and means of transport. The stereotypical representations used to establish a typical traveler profile are defined and communicated between colleagues. These informal rules are highly localized, varying from one border area to another according to the economic activities of the region concerned.

Conclusion

Policing in France was initially organized around the control of internal migrants and foreigners. From the 1950s, a new specialized police force, the PAF, was set up to monitor the nation's borders, but it was not until the 1970s that the PAF was given responsibility for immigration control. From the 1990s, in response to the political developments linked to European construction, the PAF extended its scope of action to include internal and external borders, and those located within French territory. The resulting border policing described in this chapter is not unique to France. French research on this topic is highly internationalized and its scope extends well beyond France alone. Comparative studies, such as the collective publication *La police des migrants* (Babels et al. 2019) that includes contributions by several of the authors cited here, have revealed the similarities between border policing practices in diverse geographical and political contexts (in France, Greece, or Morocco). The research examines filtering at the border, harassment of migrants to chase them away from border regions, and confinement and expulsion. In these varied contexts, the question of migration – a phenomenon built upon complex social, political, and economic dynamics – is perceived primarily as an issue of border policing and control of foreigners.

Notes

1 Document d'information sur le Service Central de la PAF [Information document on the PAF central services], October 1975.
2 Plan de la conférence de Monsieur André Dierickx, chef du Service central de la Police de l'air et des frontières à la 31e promotion des commissaires de police [Summary of the address by André Dierickx, head of central air and border police services, to the 31st graduation class of police superintendants], 10 October 1979, E.N.S.P.
3 Officer numbers rose from 4,241 in 1983 to 5,500 in 1993. Sources: CAC 1995 0073 – Art. 4 and CAC 1994 03368- Art.1.

References

About, I. 2004. Les Fondations d'un Système National d'identification Policière En France (1893–1914) [The foundations of the national system of police identification in France (1893–1914) Anthropometry, Reports and Files]. *Genèses* 54: 28–52.

About, I. 2007. Identifier les étrangers: genèse d'une police bureaucratique de l'immigration dans la France de l'entre-deux-guerres [Identifying the foreigners: Origin of a bureaucratic policing of immigration in the interwar period]. Pp. 125–160 in G. Noiriel (Ed.) *L'identification: genèse d'un travail d'État [Identification: Genesis of a State work]*. Paris: Belin.

About, I., and Denis, V. 2010. *Histoire de l'identification des personnes [History of persons identification]*. Repères. Paris: La Découverte.

Agier, M. 2008. *Gérer Les Indésirables: Des Champs de Réfugiés Au Gouvernement Humanitaire [Managing the undesirables: Refugee camps and humanitarian government]*. Paris: Flammarion.

Babels, B. S., Casella Colombeau, S., Gardesse, C., Guenebeaud, C., and Le Courant, S. (Eds.) 2019. *La Police Des Migrants. Filtrer, Disperser, Harceler [Migrants policing: Filtering, dispersing, harassing] Bibliothèque Des Frontières*. Paris: Le Passager Clandestin.

Berlière, J.M. 1987. La Professionnalisation de La Police En France: Un Phénomène Nouveau Au Début du XXe Siècle [Police professionalisation in France: A new phenomenon in the early 20th century]. *Déviance et Société* 11: 67–104.

Berlière, J. M., and Lévy, R. 2011. *Histoire des polices en France: de l'Ancien régime à nos jours [History of police forces in France: From Ancien régime to nowadays]*. Paris: Nouveau Monde éditions.

Bigo, D. 1994. The European internal security field: Stakes and rivalries in a newly developing area of police intervention. Pp. 161–173 in M. Anderson and M. den Boer (Eds.) *Policing across national boundaries*. New York: Pinter Publishers.

Bigo, D. 2001. The möbius ribbon of internal and external security. Pp. 91–116 in M. Albert, D. Jacobson, and Y. Lapid (Eds.) *Identities, borders orders: Rethinking international relations theory*. Minneapolis: University of Minnesota Press.

Bigo, D. 2014. The (in)securitization practices of the three universes of EU border control: Military/navy – Border guards/police – Database analysts. *Security Dialogue* 45: 209–225.

Bigo, D., Carrera, S., Hernanz, N., Jeandesboz, J., Parkin, J., Ragazzi, F., and Scherrer, A. 2013. *Mass surveillance of personal data by EU member states and its compatibility with EU law*. Rochester, NY: Social Science Research Network.

Blanc-Chaléard, M. C., Douki, C., Dyonet, N., and Milliot, V. 2001. *Police et Migrants: France, 1667–1939 [Police and migrants: France, 1667–1939].* Rennes: Presses Universitaires de Rennes.

Blanchard, E. 2011. *La Police Parisienne et Les Algériens: 1944–1962 [Parisian police and the Algerians: 1944–1962].* Paris: Nouveau Monde éd.

Bonditti, P. 2005. Biométrie et maîtrise des flux: vers une 'géo-technopolis' du vivant-en-mobilité? [Exploring the political issues behind the use of biometrics and new technologies in state monitoring of individual mobility]. *Cultures & Conflits* 58: 131–154.

Casella Colombeau, S. 2013. *Surveiller Les Personnes, Garder Les Frontières, Définir Le Territoire La Police Aux Frontières Après La Création de l'espace Schengen (1953-2004) [Watching the persons, guarding the borders, defining the territory: The Police Aux Frontières after the creation of the Schengen territory (1953–2004)].* Paris: Institut d'Etudes Politiques de Paris.

Casella Colombeau, S. 2017a. National origins of Frontex risk analysis: The French border police's fight against Filières. Pp. 101–115 in J. Mackert and B. Turner (Eds.) *The transformation of citizenship: Boundaries of inclusion and exclusion.* London: Routledge.

Casella Colombeau, S. 2017b. Policing the internal Schengen borders: Managing the double bind between free movement and migration control. *Policing & Society* 27: 480–493.

Casella Colombeau, S. 2017c. Des 'faux touristes' aux 'filières': la reformulation de la cible des contrôles par la police aux frontières (1953–2004) [From "false tourists" to "smugglers": The French border police and the redefinition of its targets (1953–2004)]. *Cultures & Conflits* 105–106: 163–188.

Casella Colombeau, S. 2019. Crisis of Schengen? The transformation of border police practices at the Schengen internal borders in Ventimiglia in 2011 and 2015. *Journal of Ethnic and Migration Studies* [www.tandfonline.com/doi/abs/10.1080/1369183X.2019.1596787?journalCode=cjms20].

Casella Colombeau, S., and Darley, M. 2019. Définir La Cible Du Contrôle Migratoire [Defining the target of migration control]. Pp. 21–50 in Babels, B.S., Casella Colombeau,S., Gardesse, C., Guenebeaud, C., and Le Courant S. (Eds.) *La Police Des Migrants: Filtrer, Disperser, Harceler [Migrants policing. Filtering, dispersing, harassing].* Paris: Le Passager Clandestin.

Clochard, O. 2010. Le contrôle des flux migratoires aux frontières de l'Union européenne s'oriente vers une disposition de plus en plus réticulaire [The control of migration flows at the EU borders is evolving towards a reticular border]. *Carnets de géographes* no. 1, online.

Clochard, O. 2015. Enfermés à Bord Des Navires de La Marine Marchande [Confined in merchant ships]. *Annales de Géographie* 2: 185–207.

Clochard, O., Gastaut, Y., and Schor, R. 2004. Les camps d'étrangers depuis 1938: continuité et adaptations [Internment camps for foreigners since 1938 as continuity and adaptation from the French model to construction of the Schengen space]. *Revue européenne des migrations internationales* 20: 57–87.

Crettiez, X., and Piazza, P. 2006. Introduction. Pp. 11–26 in *Du papier à la biométrie identifier les individus [From paper to biometry, how to identify individuals]. Collection académique.* Paris: les Presses Sciences Po.

Crosby, A., and Rea, A. 2016. La fabrique des indésirables: Pratiques de contrôle aux frontières dans un aéroport européen [Producing undesirables at the border]. *Cultures & Conflits* 103–104: 63–90.

Darley, M. 2008a. *Frontière, Asile et Détention Des Étrangers. Le Contrôle Étatique de l'immigration et Son Contournement En Autriche et En République Tchèque [Border, asylum and aliens' detention: State migration control and its circumvention in Austria and the Czech Republic].* Paris: Institut d'Etudes Politiques de Paris.

Darley, M. 2008b. Le Contrôle Migratoire Aux Frontières Schengen: Pratiques et Représentations Des Polices Sur La Ligne Tchéco-Autrichienne [Migration control at Schengen borders: Police practices and representations on the Czech-Austrian border]. *Cultures & Conflits* 71: 13–29.

Darley, M., Lancelevée, C., and Michalon, B. 2013. Où sont les murs? Penser l'enfermement en sciences sociales [Where are the walls? Thoughts on detention in social sciences]. *Cultures & Conflits* 90: 7–20.

Domingo, B. 2007. La Douane, Un Instrument Oublié Dans La Mise En Oeuvre d'un Espace de Liberté, de Sécurité et de Justice Européen? [Customs: The forgotten instrument of the implementation of Europe's freedom, security, and justice area]. *Politique Européenne* 23: 37–55.

El Qadim, N. 2015. *Le Gouvernement Asymétrique: Des Migrations: Maroc/Union Européenne [Asymetrical government of migration. Morocco/European Union].* Paris: Dalloz.

Fischer, N. 2004. Les expulsés inexpulsables. Recompositions du contrôle des étrangers dans la France des années 1930 [The undeportable deportees: Revisiting the control of foreigners in France in the 1930s]. *Cultures & Conflits* 53: 25–41.

Fischer, N. 2017. *Le territoire de l'expulsion. La rétention administrative des étrangers et l'État de droit en France: Gouvernement en question(s).* Lyon: ENS Éditions.

Gauthier, J. 2010. Esquisse Du Pouvoir Policier Discriminant [An outline of discriminatory police power: An interactionalist analysis of the experience of policing]. *Déviance et Société* 34: 267–278.

Guenebeaud, C. 2016. Le corps face à la frontière: Étude de la répression des migrants' sans-papiers à la frontière franco-britannique. *Corps* 14: 31–39.

Guenebeaud, C. 2017. Dans La Frontière : Migrants et Luttes Des Places Dans La Ville de Calais [In the border: Migrants and struggles for places in Calais]. *Géographie*. Lille: Thèse de doctorat, Université Lille 1.

Guenebeaud, C. 2019. Nous Ne Sommes Pas des Passeurs de Migrants: Le Rôle Des Transporteurs Routiers et Maritimes Dans La Mise En Œuvre Des Contrôles à La Frontière Franco-Britannique. *Lien Social et Politiques* 83: 103–122.

Guiraudon, V. 2002. Logiques et pratiques de l'Etat délégateur: les compagnies de transport dans le contrôle migratoire à distance. Partie 1 et 2 [Logics and practices of the delegating state: Transport companies in the remote control of migration. Part 1&2]. *Cultures & Conflits* 45: 51–113.

Infantino, F. 2019. *Schengen visa implementation and transnational policymaking: Bordering Europe.* London: Palgrave Macmillan.

Jobard, F. 2010. Le gibier de police immuable ou changeant. *Archives de politique criminelle* 32: 93–105.

Kaluszynski, M. 1987. Alphonse Bertillon et l'anthropométrie. Pp. 269–286 in P. Vigier (Ed.) *Maintien de l'ordre et polices en France et en Europe au XIXe siècle.* Paris: Creaphis Editions.

Le Courant, S. 2010. De l'étranger menotté au clandestin. Ce que fait la politique de contrôle de l'immigration [From handcuffed to illegal alien: The effect of policing on immigration control]. *Champ pénal/Penal field* 12 [DOI: 10.4000/champpenal.7889]

Le Courant, S. 2015. Le poids de la menace. L'évaluation quotidienne du risque d'expulsion par les étrangers en situation irrégulière [The burden of threat: How do undocumented migrants evaluate their everyday risk of being deported?]. *Ethnologie française* 45: 123–133.

Lemaire, L. 2014. Islands and a carceral environment: Maltese policy in terms of irregular migration. *Journal of Immigrant & Refugee Studies* 12: 143–160.

Maguer, A. 2002. La Coopération Policière Transfrontalière, Moteur de Transformations Dans l'appareil de Sécurité Français [Cross-border police cooperation: Vector of transformations in the French security system]. *Cultures & Conflits* 48: 33–56.

Makaremi, C. 2008. Pénalisation de la circulation et reconfigurations de la frontière: le maintien des étrangers en 'zone d'attente' [Penalizing movement, reframing borders: Alien detention in the French waiting zone]. *Cultures & Conflits* 71: 55–73.

Makaremi, C. 2009a. Governing borders in France: From extraterritorial to humanitarian confinement. *Canadian Journal of Law and Society* 24: 411–432.

Makaremi, C. 2009b. Violence et Refoulement Dans La Zone d'attente de Roissy [Violence and push back in the Roissy "waiting zone"]. Pp. 41–62 in C. Kobelinsky and C. Makaremi (Eds.) *Enfermés Dehors [Shut out]*. Broissieux: Éditions du Croquant.

Maquet, P. 2015. Passer le port? La gestion des passagers clandestins au Pirée [Getting into and through the harbor: Managing stowaways in Piraeus]. *Cultures & Conflits* 99–100: 57–74.

Michalon, B. 2015. L'espace intérieur de la rétention. Policiers et retenus: travailler et habiter dans un lieu d'enfermement des étrangers en Roumanie [The inner space of detention: Policemen and detainees working and living in detention centers in Romania]. *Annales de geographie* 702-703: 208–230.

Napoli, P. 2003. *Naissance de la police moderne: pouvoir, normes, société [Birth of the modern police: power, norms, society]*. Paris: la Découverte.

Noiriel, G. 2005. *État, nation et immigration: vers une histoire du pouvoir [State, nation and immigration: Towards an history of power]*. Collection Folio/Histoire. Paris: Gallimard.

Ottavy, E., and Clochard, O. 2015. Franchir les dispositifs établis par Frontex. Coopérations policières transfrontalières et refoulements en mer Égée [Getting around Frontex controls: Cross-border police cooperation and forcible return in the Aegean]. *Revue européenne des migrations internationales* 30: 137–156.

Peschanski, D. 2002. *La France Des Camps: L'internement (1938–46) [Camps in France: Internement policies (1938–46)]*. Paris: Gallimard.

Pette, M. 2014. Associations: les nouveaux guichets de l'immigration? Du travail militant en préfecture [Are non-profit organizations the new offices of immigration services? Activists' work in a local administration]. *Sociologie* 5: 405–421.

Piazza, P. 2011. *Aux origines de la police scientifique: Alphonse Bertillon, précurseur de la science du crime [Origins of the scientific police: Alphonse Bertillon, pioneer in science of crime]*. Paris: Karthala.

Pillant, L. 2015. Les conséquences socio-spatiales des nouvelles modalités du contrôle migratoire à la frontière gréco-turque [Changes of the migratory control at the

Greek-Turkish border and their socio-spatial consequences]. *L'Espace Politique: Revue en ligne de géographie politique et de géopolitique* no. 25 [DOI: 10.1186/s40878-019-0128-4]

Tassin, L. 2016. Les frontières de la rétention : genre et ethnicité dans le contrôle des étrangers en instance d'expulsion [The frontiers of detention: Gender and ethnicity in the supervision of foreigners awaiting expulsion]. *Critique Internationale* 3: 35–52.

Torpey, J. 2000. *The invention of the passport: Surveillance, citizenship and the state*. Cambridge: Cambridge University Press.

Tyszler, E. 2019. From controlling mobilities to control over women's bodies: Gendered effects of EU border externalization in Morocco. *Comparative Migration Studies* 7: 25–35.

Veron, D. 2013. Cartographie de la frontière et topographie clandestine: [Mapping the border and clandestine topography]. *Hommes & Migrations* 1304: 19–25.

Chapter 17

Police and the Public in France

Sebastian Roché

How should we best analyze citizens' judgment of the police and the dynamics of those assessments in France? The first part of this chapter examines the current state of research in France on the complex question of police–public relations. This section describes what may be learned from general studies on the topic, focusing specifically on the distinction between support to an organization's missions (diffuse support) and an organization's actions (specific support). Next, I discuss studies that have rethought the approach to attitudes towards the police. These studies examine the conceptualization of police–public relations based on measurements of satisfaction, trust, and legitimacy. Research suggests that insofar as the public is concerned, the French police rank lower than most European Union countries. In addition, national studies, monographic works, and quantitative reports have also examined the wide range of variation in assessments of the police, and the effects that residential location and ethno-religious identity have on citizen judgments of the police. The chapter also looks at popular evaluations of the use of violence in neglected suburbs and for purposes of riot control, the latter being an emerging topic that may continue to grow in importance as climate-related protests proliferate.

The second section of this chapter focuses on the two main results of this research review, the low levels of trust and legitimacy of French police, and the importance of ethnic and social divisions in these issues. It examines police reforms and how they have addressed those. While some limited progress has been made, most reforms that were envisaged have not yet been realized. We suggest, finally, that the two main research results may be explained by the absence of policing policy designed to build trust and legitimacy, and to correct the practices that undermine support for the police.

The Dynamics of Police–Public Relations in France

French research on police–public relations developed belatedly. For example, tensions between young people and the police were not studied until recently, as evidenced by Renouard (1993), who cites no studies prior to

1992. Though empirical research developed much earlier in the United Kingdom and the United States, the field's weak theoretical structure was not specific to France, as Brown and Benedict's (2002) international literature review documented. The term "attitudes towards the police," which was used to describe any public perception of the police by the public, functioned as a catch-all that was commonly used in research reports. This situation, however, gradually changed.

Three factors reinvigorated French research from the 1990s onward, and particularly during the 2000s. First, Europe-wide research projects sought to operationalize the concepts of trust and legitimacy and improve the quality of measurement. The Eurojustis-France project, European Social Survey (ESS) 2010, the Police Youth Relations in Multi-Ethnic Cities (POLIS) project, and the Understanding and Preventing Youth Crime (UPYC) project are paradigmatic in this regard. Second, qualitative studies of ethnic identity and spatial segregation, and their effects on relations with the police and on identity checks, were conducted by the Open Society Foundation and the Centre de Recherche sur le Droit et les Institutions Pénales. Finally, new surveys carried out by human rights defense organizations such as the French Défenseur des droits and the European Fundamental Rights Agency (FRA), as well by the Observatoire National de la Délinquance et des Réponses Pénales (ONDRP) and Institut National de la Statistique (INSEE), all have contributed to enriching French research in the field.

Image and Trust in National Studies: What Is Being Measured?

The first quantitative studies, whose questions would be repeated several times in later surveys, were carried out in November 1975 by the polling institute, Institut français d'opinion publique (IFOP). These studies dealt with perceptions of "police efficiency." Peyrefitte's 1977 report, which focused on perceptions of violence in society, asked respondents to judge whether police actions were too limited or too far-reaching, and for example asked whether officers should carry firearms (Peyrefitte 1977, annexes, vol. 1, p. 71). The question of relations with the police was not raised. Beginning in the mid-1980s, the theme of trust in the police appeared.[1] The polling institute, CSA, asked the now-classic question about "trust in the following institutions," and, since the late 1990s, IFOP has asked the French "what do you spontaneously think of the police?" and includes "trust" among the potential responses. "Trust" received 53% of votes in 1999, 44% in 2012, 47% in 2015, 50% in 2019, and 43% in 2020. The trust question was not differentiated from questions measuring "police image" and "police opinion." All those questions were single, non-contextualized judgments of the police as an institution. Such questions became more frequent in media surveys conducted in the 2000s for political science units, and for the *Cadre de Vie et Sécurité* or CVS studies by ONDRP (a national yearly study by the Observatoire National de la Délinquance or National Delinquency Watch, a body connected to the Institut des hautes études de la sécurité intérieure), and INSEE.

Figure 17.1 gathers all existing longitudinal data from various French sources between 2005 and 2020. Four questions have been used consistently over that time period. Two ask the respondent whether they "trust" the police (IPSOS, an opinion poll company and the Centre d'Etudes de la vie Politique Française, CEVIPOF, which is an academic research unit). Two ask the public about their "opinion" about the "action" of police (ONDRP-INSEE) and about their "satisfaction for the action" (Delouvrier, a think-tank that commissions polls). This allows us to observe levels of positive evaluation of the police with different question wording, and also to track any possible correspondence between major security incidents and public assessments of police.

Figure 17.1 also indicates that the French terrorist attacks of late 2015 correspond to a strong upward tick in the two indicators containing a reference

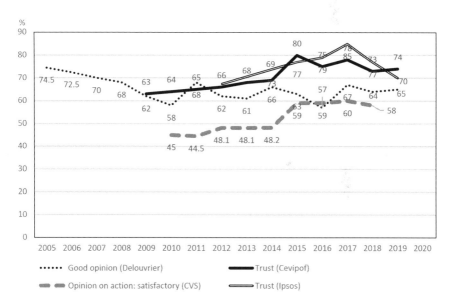

Figure 17.1 Trends in General Assessments of Police.

Source: "Do you have a good opinion, a rather good opinion, a rather bad opinion, or a very bad opinion of the action of the state insofar as…" (source: Delouvrier 2019); "In general, regarding police or gendarmerie action in today's French society, would you personally say that it is…" (satisfactory), CVS (D'Arbois de Jubainville 2019),/"Do you trust a lot, rather trust, rather distrust or distrust a lot" "the police" (% trust a lot, rather trust) (source: CEVIPOF 2019); Do you trust a lot, rather trust, rather distrust or distrust a lot each of the following organizations? "the police" (% trust a lot, rather trust). The missing value for 2018 is replaced by the average of 2017 and 2019 scores (source: Ipsos). Figure prepared by the author.

to trust in general, or even to action, but not on the indicator of "a good opinion" (Delouvrier 2019). The uptick in "trust" in 2015 was measured by a CEVIPOF study that was conducted *after* the Bataclan attack that took place in November of that year (CEVIPOF 2019; IPSOS 2019). However, one may wonder: why should police failure to prevent the attacks cause a surge in citizen "trust" in the police? Shouldn't failure to prevent the attacks have resulted in a loss of faith? What is the underlying psychological mechanism at work here? There seems to be a rise in the normative belief that police have a useful function in society. Interestingly, it occurs despite the fact that police could not detect the plans of the terrorist groups, and despite the chaotic action taken by police during the *Charlie Hebdo* and the Bataclan 2015 attacks. Such a belief is probably derived from the fact that they neutralized or caught terrorists in action or just after, and fueled by expectations of a need for protection due to the uncertainty created by a new threat. The findings suggest that two-thirds of respondents will answer positively as long as the question is formulated generally, and this ratio increases to three-quarters in the wake of an attack. However, only about half of respondents remain positive when a specific action is mentioned (although this ratio increases to two-thirds after an attack). The deficit in this case ranges from 15 to 19 points; this can be seen in the difference between the CEVIPOF barometer and the national CVS survey.

It is important to examine carefully the meaning of these one-question opinion indicators, which may not be as intuitive as appears at first glance. Those questions are not theoretically founded measures of the concept of "trust." In all likelihood, surveys which do include the word "trust" do so without providing context, and do not measure trust in the sociological sense of trust of A in B for undertaking C in a relevant way at a relevant time (Harding 1993; Robbins 2016). Opinion surveys suggest that as soon as the term is further contextualized or made more specific, trust levels fall. Figure 17.2 considers opinion questions more specifically focused on police action "against crime," and compares them to opinions about police effectiveness to limit the risk of burglary. The first, specific formulation was used by a CVS poll (Rizk 2011). In this context, policing not in general but *against crime* was considered 46% "effective" and "very effective," averaged from 2007 to 2011. Moreover, the share of "very effective" responses was only 3.4% (see Figure 17.2). More detailed analysis of the data (not shown) demonstrates that there are effects of victimization on survey responses: if a household member was a crime victim near their home, the level of trust in police effectiveness against crime drops to 34.7% and of high effectiveness to 2.3% ("very effective").

The left side of Figure 17.2 reports responses to two other contextualized questions about comparative trust in effectiveness asking, "who do you trust to limit the risk of burglary?" and "who do you trust for improving the situation in your neighborhood?" These surveys offered alternatives to the

Police and the Public in France 273

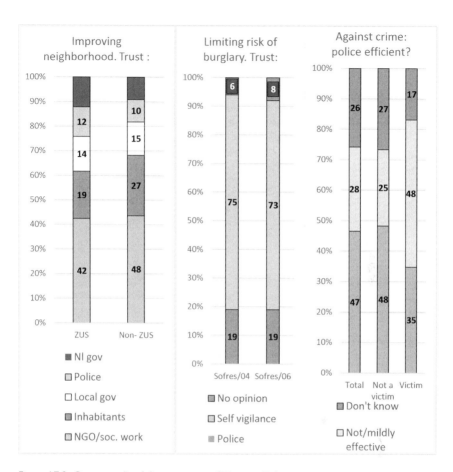

Figure 17.2 Contextualized Assessments of Trust in Police.
Source: For improving the situation in your neighborhood, do you trust" (the national government, inhabitants of the neighborhood, the locally elected leaders, the national police, NGOs, social workers or mediators), source: DIV (2006); "Who do you trust most to limit the risk of a burglary?" ("your personal vigilance and your home protection system", "police supervision in your neighborhood", "no opinion"), 2004 and 2005, national representative sample (SOFRES 2006). SOFRES is an opinion poll company. "Is police action against crime..." (very effective and effective/not very effective and not effective at all/don't know) 2007 to 2011, source: CVS (Rizk 2015). Figure prepared by the author.

police as someone to trust. In the first case, the alternative was "your personal vigilance and your home protection system." In two surveys, self-protection was preferred by about 75% of respondents, contrasted to 19% who trusted "police supervision in your neighborhood." In the second case, the alternatives were "the national government," "local government" (the mayor), "inhabitants of the neighborhood," or "NGOs [non-governmental organizations], social workers or mediators." Only 10–12% in deprived neighborhoods (called ZUS for sensitive urban areas) or outside them respectively selected the national police. Responses like this are very far from the general support levels indicated by responses to general opinion questions. For example, in Figure 17.1, support during 2005 stood at almost 75%.

More generally, it seems conceptually necessary to make a distinction between non-contextualized general trust and contextualized trust that is linked to performance. The first dimension refers to what David Easton (1965) dubbed "diffuse support" of public institutions, and the second to his idea of "specific support" for their actual performance. This distinction makes it possible to understand the differences in levels of support between questions tapping general attitudes (single, global judgments, often connoted in value) and contextual ones that refer to performance by the police (on specific issues, and by comparison with other players). It also makes it possible to understand why general attitude indicators remain stable over time: they are relatively insensitive to context because they refer to a judgment of the recognition of the mission entrusted to the organization.

Cross-country Studies of Police Performance: Victim Satisfaction and Police Effectiveness

A useful focus for studies of opinions of the police concerns their value, not for an abstract "society in general," but rather for services the police render locally or to crime victims. These projects focus on assessing local police performance rather than its image or general reputation. In addition, these new studies make it possible to compare judgments between police in different countries, for the police in many nations share a common set of responsibilities. Before the advent of the European Social Survey 2010, police image was often judged in comparison to other societal actors, such as churches, political parties, or the media. One common approach was to ask how much "confidence" people had in each of these institutions. Given the differences in services rendered by each profession, such an approach is methodologically questionable. Differences between popular judgments of each distinct institution had no particular meaning. It is not clear that one percentage point of trust in the police is equivalent in any meaningful way to one percentage point of trust in, for example, the media. The assumed universality of the metric used is highly uncertain. Comparing police forces at the national is a more appropriate approach, especially within the European Union. Despite wealth differences among countries, common standards and exchanges between countries are developing. Within the European Union police missions as defined by law are generally similar. We cannot deny that there are differences in the way they are carried out and perceived by the public, but this can be measured by empirical studies.

France first participated in a major comparative survey in 1989, when they joined the ongoing International Crime Victim Survey, or ICVS. Since then, France has participated into each new round of the survey. Among its many publications, see a report by van Dijk et al. (2007). New questions about local police performance were devised for this project, such as "do your local police do a good job?" Given the survey's focus, there were also questions regarding crime victims' satisfaction after reporting incidents to the police. Questions like this had never before been used in public debate. The latest available ICVS placed France at a modest level in Europe in terms of satisfaction with reporting a crime to police. It fell somewhere between Poland and Portugal. Figure 17.3 presents results of the 2005 round of the ICVS. On the left it ranks nations by the percentage of respondents who reported that police were doing "a good job" in controlling crime in the local area. On this measure, respondents placed France above Greece and Spain, and below Sweden and Luxembourg. They were far from Finland and Denmark, which score at the top of both league tables in Figure 17.3. It is likely that the lack of a strong police culture of servicing the public explains France's mediocre result. When crime victims were quizzed about how satisfied they were with police performance, France was sandwiched between Portugal and Poland. When some countries fare poorly on one indicator in Figure 17.3, they manage to "make up for it" on the other, while other nations such as France remain stuck near the bottom.

Regarding opinion measures that set judgments of the police in a specific service context, there is evidence that negative experiences affect judgments of the police more than positive experiences improve people's views. This "asymmetry" in the impact of experience seems to reflect a general human bias toward negativity, or one that makes the effects of "bad" experiences stronger than the effects of "good" experiences (Skogan 2006). However, questions about the links between satisfaction and the services delivered (called "responsive police contacts"), or their effect on trust in the police, have hardly been raised in France. The effects of exposure to identity checks are clearly negative (see Chapter 13 in this volume), but no research results are available on the positive effects of good quality services that are rendered.

It was not until the CVS survey of 2007 (Cadre de Vie et Sécurité, by ONDRP and INSEE) that an aspect of police–population relations, judgments of the quality of service provided while filing a police report, was integrated into an ongoing national survey. However, these data were not analyzed until 2019, unveiling the weak interest in them on the part of the French Ministry of the Interior. Indeed, unlike in the United Kingdom, police–public relationships are seemingly not a priority for French national authorities. A recent publication documented that, in the two years preceding the 2018 round of the survey, crime victims felt that their reporting "went well" in 85% of cases of theft without violence and in 78% of instances of physical violence not motivated by theft. Satisfaction with advice provided by the police hit 71% for victims of

276 Sebastian Roché

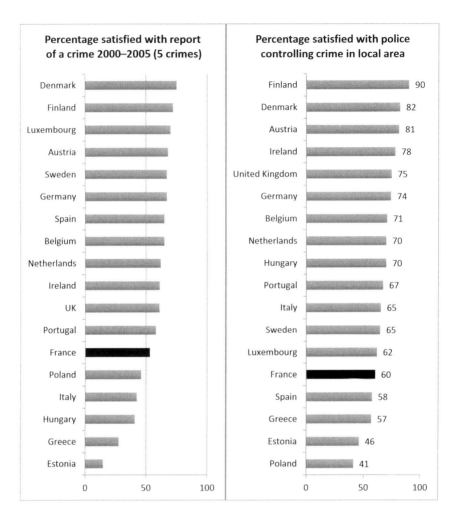

Figure 17.3 Performance of Local Policing.
Source: Police are police doing a good job in controlling crime in the local area; Victims' satisfaction when reporting a crime to police (victim of one of the five most frequent crimes). Source: (ICVS 2005; van Dijk et al. 2007). Figure prepared by the author.

non-violent theft and 65% for victims of violent crime. In cases of sexual violence outside and inside the household, satisfaction with advice provided by police officers (or *gendarmes*) was 56% and 65%, respectively (D'Arbois de Jubainville 2019).

The results of the CVS survey showed generally more positive judgments about the police than were documented in the ICVS, though to a lesser extent for the quality of advice offered by officers. However, declaring that the reporting of a crime "went well" (CVS wording) does not equate with respondents' "satisfaction" with the police.[2] According to the CVS, 40% of the people who said they were dissatisfied with the time and attention allotted to their case still reported that the filing process went "well." Reaching "satisfaction" with reporting a crime is more demanding of police than obtaining a "went well" in various steps in the process of reporting it. Positive evaluation of the procedure is not enough to forge satisfaction with a service. Perhaps complainants managed to leave the police station with the form they desired in hand, which was often their main aim. The distinct phrasing of the questions also likely explains some of the discrepancies between the results of the ICVS and the CVS. The satisfaction level measured in the Eurojustis-France survey[3] (on a four-category scale ranging from "quite" to "not at all") are close to those reported in the CVS survey for all of France, but are lower than for the disadvantaged area of Seine-Saint-Denis in the area of greater Paris (see the next section). Contrasting the two, 81% in France as a whole, but only 67% in Seine-Saint-Denis, were satisfied with police station visits. When they called stations, 81% of the national sample and 64% in Seine-Saint-Denis reported being satisfied. For roadside checks, the comparable figures were 72% in France and 70% in Seine-Saint-Denis, and for identity checks it was 62% for the country as a whole and 54% in Seine-Saint-Denis.

Comparative Studies of Trust and Legitimacy

Max Weber's discussion of the concept of authority places great emphasis on a people's subjective recognition of their ruler's prestige. Leaders who have this form of recognition find it necessary to use force less often. In line with Weber, social psychologists (see Tyler 1990) focus on public trust in the police and their perceived legitimacy and examine the links between them. Among the disputed questions one is: does the recognition of prestige create trust? Or rather does trust engender legitimacy, as Hough et al. (2014) suggest? The emphasis on "fair personal treatment" and "quality of decision making" (the two main pillars of "procedural justice") is a new way of interpreting existing research on public opinion. This includes reports of citizen attitudes about the way police treat people, the use of force, tensions arising during identity checks, and ethnic discrimination by the police. I recently proposed an analysis of this conceptual evolution (Roché 2017). We are not interested here in the validity of the theory, but rather in its effects on how the relationship between citizens and the police is measured in surveys, and on the results that concern France within the European Union.

The most important survey that attempted to operationalize measures of fairness and procedural justice by the police is the European Social Survey 2010 (ESS), which included an entire module on the topic. In particular, the survey measured legitimacy as a combination of three elements: consent (public recognition of the moral right enjoyed by an organization to be obeyed); sharing of moral ends (or values) between those in power and those who are subject to it; and the feeling that legality is respected. In the author's model, trust fuels legitimacy (Hough et al. 2014). Various aspects of trust, defined as the anticipation by A (respondent) of B (the police) carrying out C (a given action) in a desirable manner, are spelled out (Harding 1993). This approach separates so-called instrumental trust (for example, rapid police arrival times) from other aspects of trust judgments. These include, for example, distributive trust (belief in the equal treatment of all social groups) and trust in the respectful and impartial treatment of citizens (or procedural fairness).

Figure 17.4 presents two aspects of the relation of police with the public. In terms of decision making, the French police is attributed a level of

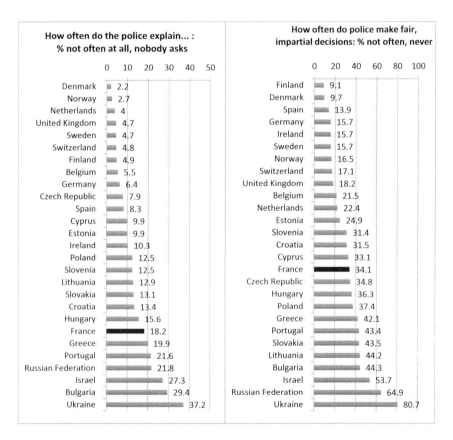

Figure 17.4 Trust in Police Fairness.

Source: "How often do police explain their decisions/actions when asked" (% no: not often at all + nobody asks), "How often do police make fair, impartial decisions" (% rarely: not often + never); source: ESS 2010. Figure prepared by the author.

unfairness (34%) that is close to the median of EU countries, midway between Finland (9%) and Ukraine (81%). In the eyes of the public, this measure of police unfairness placed them between Cyprus and the Czech Republic. This left France at a significant distance from Germany (16%), the other major continental country, or even Spain (14%), a recent democracy. Regarding police inability or anticipated unwillingness to justify their action, the ranking

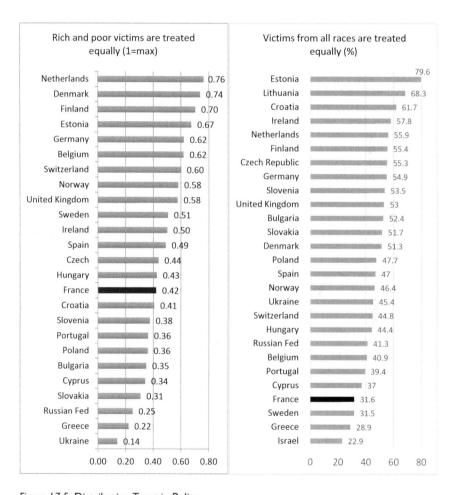

Figure 17.5 Distributive Trust in Police.
Source: "When victims report crimes, do you think the police treat"…"People of a different race …. worse, same race worse, or from all races equally" (% different race treated equally), "rich people worse, poor people worse, or are rich and poor treated equally" (rich and poor treated equally, score from 0=never to 1=always); source: ESS 2010. Figure prepared by the author.

of the French police is even lower. Fully 18% of the public stated that the police do not explain their actions during encounters with the public, putting them in the lower third of the EU and standing between Hungary and Greece. Overall, perceptions of police procedural justice are low in France.

Figure 17.5 examines two aspects of distributive justice: the beliefs that minority groups are being treated the same as others in society, and that the rich and poor are treated equally. France's score for distributive justice varies from one indicator to another. In terms of equal treatment of the rich and poor, the French police lie in the bottom 40% of nations, nestled between Hungary and Croatia. When it comes to equality of treatment by race, French police do not occupy an enviable position among EU countries. A plausible explanation could be that the service delivered to poor sections of cities and to ethnic minority is weaker than for the better off, and that on top of this there exists disparities in stop-and-search which are greatly resented by low-income neighborhood residents and ethnic minority groups. The next section will provide additional examples of the contrasts in policing between social groups and urban neighborhoods.

Other findings of the European Social Survey (not shown here) were also revealing. Compared to other European nations, French police did not score highly in terms of their legitimacy, or in the belief that people have a moral obligation to obey them under all circumstances. Here France fell again in the lower third of 27 countries of the European Union (see Hough et al. 2014).[4] On the dimension of instrumental trust in the police, measured by their perceived effectiveness against delinquency, France was about average (Hough et al. 2014, p. 256). Another significant element of public opinion of the police – but one that is not explicitly part of procedural justice theory – is that of police integrity. Police integrity is recognized in international research as a central element defining the quality of a state. In the 2010 ESS, police integrity was measured by the opinion that police accept bribes. Respondents rated their police on a scale of 1 (never) to 10 (always). France's score of 4.55 was mediocre, falling between Cyprus (4.55) and Portugal (4.96), and slightly closer to Russia (6.70) than Denmark (1.61).

Police Quality, Local Contexts, and the Public

International research focuses a great deal of attention on the consequences of ethnic divisions and residential poverty for crime and justice. Minority group identities are routinely taken into consideration by European scholars interested in attitudes towards the police. In Great Britain, perceptions of the police vary greatly by social identity, both by minority and majority groups (Bradford 2014). In turn, how the police are perceived affects the process of minority identification (Millings 2013). Often, research sets out not to observe aggregate opinions at the national level, but rather how they are distributed across more or less disadvantaged groups and in specific contexts. Less is known in France about general support for the police than about the dynamics of people's expectations and dissatisfactions.

Experiences with the police, the effects of neighborhood context, and the dynamics of race and ethnicity have hardly been examined quantitatively through surveys in France. This is in contrast to the growing number ethnographic studies in poor neighborhoods, which focus on these issues. This research is reviewed in Roux and Roché (2016), in a summary of relations between police, minorities, and disadvantaged neighborhoods. Some research monographs on marginalized suburban communities suggest that the police as an organization has been not been exempt from racism (for example, Boucher 2010, or Fassin 2011). In this view, suburban minorities feel they were being targeting as members of a "race" or "ethnicity." We have observed, however, that this line of research does not consider identity in reference to disadvantaged urban areas. Other monographic works reveal that not everything in the negative relation with police can be understood just in terms of ethnic discrimination. In housing projects, the police are perceived as an opponent of the deprived neighborhood or groups of young people (Lapeyronnie 2008). This research assumes the existence of a uniform ethnic identity in a neighborhood; rather, we have found divisions within minority groups, such as North Africans and sub-Saharan Africans (Roux and Roché 2016). Another division pits adults against youth "from the streets," who are held responsible for various problems. Through investigations using focus groups, we have shown in the same research the importance of an ethno-territorial composite identity among young people that is built on opposition to the police. It seems to us that, in France, neighborhood identification emerges strongly and mixes with ethnic identification, especially among young people, and together these structure their judgments of the police. Consequently, the type of neighborhood is a predictor of tense police–citizen relations.

A quantitative survey has been conducted to describe and evaluate relationships between citizens and the police (Roux et al. 2011; Roché and Roux 2017). The Eurojustis-France metropolitan sample consists of a national component plus a booster sample that was interviewed in a disadvantaged suburb of Paris: the Seine-Saint-Denis *département*. This *département*, home to the riots of 2005, has one of the highest poverty rates in France. The booster sample is used to account for socio-economic conditions as well as ethnic origin. The study considers various channels for public contact with police (face-to-face contact, telephone calls), their judgments regarding police actions (handling requests, making aggressive raids, checking identity cards, or inspecting motor vehicles), and attitudes about individual treatment (respect, racism). Over a two-year reference period, in France overall, 19% of 18–29 year olds and 8% of 20–40 year olds were stopped by police at least once. But in Seine-Saint-Denis those numbers jumped to 39% and 20% respectively, more than twice as high. The survey also measured respondents' judgments about various aspects of the quality of police work (identity checks and police raids, for example), and the trust placed in the police.

In Figure 17.6, people's most negative judgments concerned disrespectful and ethnically differential treatment: although criticisms are higher in Seine-Saint-Denis, both residents of metropolitan France and of Seine-Saint-Denis often estimate that people are "not treated respectfully"(40.4–48.7%), that persons of foreign origin are treated "worse" (45.8–56.2%), and that the police are often "racist" (39.1–41.9%). A second aspect concerns police capacity to meet people's expectations, and use of force. Several aspects of police operations were tested (aggressive raids, abusive identity checks), as well as police responses when they are contacted (not showing up when called, not being present when needed, how they deal with disorders). In the French sub-sample, those aspects are, on the whole, less criticized. However, in Seine-Saint Denis, infectiveness in dealing with crime, lack of presence when needed, and abuse of ID checks are as disappointing to citizens as the lack of respect. When calculating two scores of difference (number of points, difference as a percentage) between answers in the two samples, citizen judgment of modes of action proves the most contrasted. Judgments are always more negative in Seine-Saint-Denis than in France overall, and much more so when they concern modes of action and weak police mobilization to solve the local problems. The difference measured

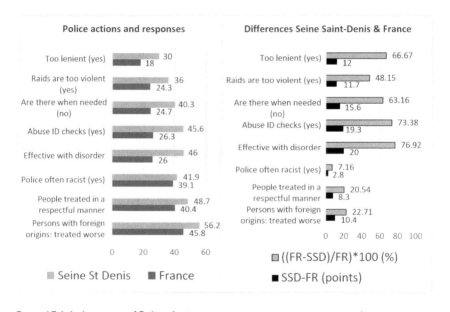

Figure 17.6 Judgements of Police Actions.

Source: Chart presents difference between France and the region of Seine-Saint-Denis, Source: (Eurojustis-France 2011; Roché 2016, p. 117); Left-hand chart presents survey results, right-hand chart presents two measures of differences between the two surveys. Figure prepared by the author.

in number of percentage points shows that dissatisfaction is superior in Seine-Saint-Denis when compared to France by at minimum 2.8 points (for racism) and at maximum for abuse of ID checks (19.3 points). The difference measured as a proportion (the gap between the percentage found in Seine-Saint-Denis and France divided by the percentage found in France and multiplied by 100) indicates that in Seine-Saint-Denis the inhabitants are 76.9% more likely than in France to think that the police do not deal well with problems, and 73.4% more likely to think that the police abuse identity checks. We learn from EU-wide comparative surveys that French police score low on quality of treatment. However, more than police ethnic discrimination or bad treatment during interactions, the greatest contrast of Seine-Saint-Denis versus metropolitan France regards the lack of basic and peaceful policing services.

The survey included more questions probing the link between perceptions of the police and social identities. Ethnic groups were defined based on the geographic origins of respondent's parents, and religion was directly reported. People's experiences and judgments appear to be sensitive to their ethnic or religious group, which is in accordance with the findings of research carried out in other European Union nations. In the survey (results not presented here), respondents were asked if they had ever seen a police officer or *gendarme* treat someone disrespectfully: 22% of non-practicing Muslims and 33% of practicing Muslims responded that they had, while only 8% of practicing Christians and 5% of non-practicing Christians responded in the positive. Among those identifying themselves as "without a religion" (the majority population in France), 10% reported they had observed instances of disrespectful treatment. Similarly, practicing Muslims were more likely to think that "the police miss everything" and that foreigners are given poorer treatment (Roché 2016, p. 137 and 145). Statistically, minority ethnic origin has the same negative effect as religion on judgments of the police (Roché and Roux 2017), as the two groups largely overlap.

These ethno-religious differences in police–public relations in France have been confirmed by other studies, including the UPYC survey of middle school students (Roux 2018) and the EU-Midis European survey comparing majority and minority groups in France and other European countries (FRA 2010) and others (Gauthier et al. 2019). Youth groups are another population evidencing a poor relationship with the police, as a summary of existing research by René Lévy shows (Lévy 2016). Several other surveys based on representative samples confirm these results (Tiberj and Simon 2010; Défenseur des Droits 2017).

Use of Force by Police: Identity Checks, Police Raids, and Crowd Control

The use of physical and verbal violence by police has not been addressed by many scientific investigations, and the absence of questions about police violence in European surveys is striking. But repeated violent confrontations during law enforcement operations and violence arising out of daily interventions by the police deserve more attention. We provide two illustrations here.

According to the Eurojustis-France survey, residing in highly disadvantaged areas – housing projects called "HLMs" in France – reinforces negative views of police activities. The case of aggressive police raids illustrates this, and the findings are summarized in Figure 17.7. Persons who do not reside in housing projects witness violence during police raids less often. Among residents of HLMs in France, 36% of respondents witnessed police interventions and criticized them as too violent, while in Seine-Saint-Denis this figure was 51%. This is 2.5 times more frequent than for respondents of the metropolitan French sample living outside HLM areas. Similarly, respondents in housing projects in Seine-Saint-Denis declare that they have witnessed more disrespectful behavior than any other category, and especially residents of non-housing projects in the French sample. Another European study, POLIS, found that French police stopped adolescents more frequently than did the German police (de Maillard et al. 2016), and that stops in France resulted in more police violence (physical and sexual) than they did in Germany (Oberwittler and Roché 2018). Among young people aged 13 to 19 who were of North African origin, 34% reported that French police displayed violent behavior during stops, compared to 10% of young people of French origin. In Germany, on the other hand, only 9% of young people of Turkish origin and 4% of German origin felt the same way about stops carried out by the police (Roché 2016, p. 22).

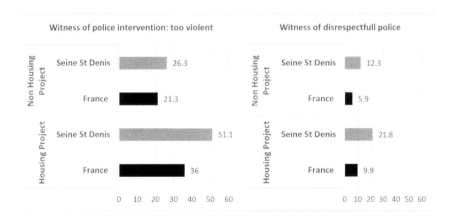

Figure 17.7 Witnesses of Negative Police Behavior.

Source: "Police officer disrespectful" (number of times, % more than once); "Police raids are too violent" (% yes, base: respondents with police raids around their homes); Housing projects and Non-Housing projects areas in metropolitan France and Seine-Saint-Denis. (Eurojustis-France 2011). Figure prepared by the author.

Regarding law enforcement, a series of police interventions made national news, either because of the scale of the events or because of the fatalities involved: during the evacuation of the Sivens dam site in 2014 (one death); in Notre-Dame-des-Landes during nearly four years of conflict over a proposed airport project (2014 to 2018); during the yellow vests movement (one year, tens of thousands of participants, two killed, and nearly 30 injured during police action); and during the annual national "Fête de la musique" festivities in Nantes in 2019 (one participant killed). We have only fragmented information about public judgments of police behavior on these occasions. We can, however, make three observations. First, polls show that the French have little appetite for violence, whether by police or by demonstrators: 10–12% of respondents reported that "Police violence against the yellow vests" is "justified," and 8% said "Violence shown or demonstrated by yellow vests" is "justified." Approval of the police after police violence was exposed by social media and the press decreased by eight points to 66% in 2020 (see Figure 17.1). Second, these polls show that partisan proximity orients the way acts of police violence are interpreted. Speaking through the president of the Republic, the prime minister, or the minister of the interior, the government denies the existence of police violence and questions the relevance of the term as far as the policing of the yellow vests movement is concerned. By contrast, 31% of ruling party supporters (Macron's La République en Marche, or LREM) felt that police violence is "justified." Only 1–2% of supporters of political parties on the left agreed, compared with 25% of the supporters of right-wing political parties and 20% of Front National supporters.[5] It appears that it is party affect, not any socio-economic category, that accounts for levels of support for police violence. Police use of force is rarely considered excessive among supporters of the party in power. According to a survey conducted in April 2019, only 14% of respondents who were supporters of LREM rated the police violent, compared to 39% overall, 21% on the right, 54% on the left, and 49% among Front National supporters (ELABE 2019). A comparison of studies of different law enforcement operations reveals a similar pattern. Notre-Dame-des-Landes is a second example: only 23% of LREM supporters condemned police evacuation of a contested area, compared with 59% of respondents on the left, 32% on the right, and 38% from the Front National (ODOXA 2018). Proximity to the party in power led, in both cases, to a favorable assessment of the use of force to achieve government goals.

Finally, although this point has not been examined in depth, it may be that it is violence that shapes diffuse public support for the police. It has been noted that the exposure of citizens and police officers to terrorism has been accompanied by an increase in support for police in several survey measures collected in 2015. (This was addressed in the discussion around Figure 17.1 above.) Also, because police violence against criminals and terrorists is probably perceived as a bulwark against proven threats to the public, this may engender support for police use of violence. Conversely, criticism of police violence during demonstrations may have contributed to a general decline in trust in the police since 2019, as the public tends to identify with victims, and there is evidence that direct exposure to police violence during the yellow vest movement is correlated with anger against the police (Mahfud and Adam-Troian 2019).

Police–Public Relations as Political Questions

To understand the results of empirical research in France, it is useful to understand the politicization of issues surrounding the police and the long-term trends that drive policing policies. These include questions of police–public relations, and of police practices that are known to negatively affect citizen's judgments. Indeed, low public satisfaction and weak trust in the police in France when compared to many EU countries – plus the even lower satisfaction, trust, and legitimacy accorded the police in disadvantaged neighborhoods and among minority groups – illustrate a failure to treat problems that had been diagnosed in the late 1970s but not successfully addressed by government since then.

Initial Diagnosis of the Need to Change Police–Public Relations

From the early 1970s onward, as a result of increasing property crime rates during the economic boom of the "Trente Glorieuses," the issue of public insecurity and fear of crime came center stage in national policy debates in many European countries. In France in the early 1970s, homicide levels were close to those of its continental European neighbors, and they were much lower than in the United States. However, the rise in property crime rates and the government's realization that public insecurity was mounting raised questions about what responses could be made to these issues. These were provided in the "Peyrefitte report" dated July 1977, named after the future minister of justice. Police were described as undermanned in housing projects and in the "new urban zones" on the outskirts of cities. In response, the creation of "small neighborhood outposts" was recommended, rather than opening new large police stations, and use of the so-called "*îlotage*" (beat policing) methods was supported. Having noted that "citizens do not collaborate easily with their police," a proposal was made to "improve relations between citizens and the police." The commission envisioned this as a tool for improving efficiency. As a result, it was necessary to "deepen the professional and civic training of police officers; to privilege the key tenets of their mission of providing safety; and in improving their attitudes vis-à-vis the public" (Peyrefitte report 1977, p. 173).

The solutions discussed in the Peyrefitte report were taken up by subsequent governments following the victory of socialist leader François Mitterrand in the May 1981 presidential election. The same summer, car joyriding and riots in the suburbs of Lyon inaugurated a tradition of clashes with the police. The government's response was a program called the "*anti-été chaud*" ("anti-hot summer"). In partnership with local communities, the program sought to occupy youth during the school holidays. Police participation took the form of "*centres loisirs jeunes*" (youth leisure centers, or CLJ), which were operated seasonally by "the everyday police" (police who are not in charge of investigating serious crimes). In parallel, the minister of the interior commissioned a new report from Socialist Party deputy J-M. Belorgey. Completed in 1982, the report (entitled "*La police au rapport*," or "Accountable Policing") was rejected by the minister who commissioned it, most likely because it was judged to be too progressive. Indeed, the report was the first of its kind to officially assert the need for police transparency and accountability to citizens. It also introduced the idea of the police being mindful of their legitimacy, though the term was not explicitly used. According to the report, the police must be a "public service," not a "force." The report's three principals were, first, "sectorization." This is the idea that the police can be particularly useful when assigned at the neighborhood level, especially for effective prevention, and this suggested that local police outposts should be opened. The second principle, that of "territorial loyalty," meant that maintaining a stable group of police officers in neighborhood precincts allowed familiarity to develop between the police and the local population. "Versatility," the third principle advanced by the Belorgey plan, noted it was preferable for "uniformed police officers to be vested … with some of the powers of the judicial police …" (Belorgey 1991, p. 12) so that minor affairs may be handled and possibly resolved locally. Broadly speaking, this 1982 proposal revisited the main concerns of the Peyrefitte report of 1977. It restated the need for police coverage at the neighborhood level and more effectiveness in judicial work, plus it added stronger democratic requirements, such as transparency and accountability.

The main thrusts of the 1982 report provided a roadmap for the community policing reform begun by Prime Minister Lionel Jospin in 1997, 15 years later. The three principles guiding this reform effort were: (1) "Security is first and foremost a responsibility of the state; (2) Security must be equal for all; and (3) Security depends to a large extent on the relationship of trust established between security services and the population" (Ministère de l'Intérieur 1997, p. 92). Note in particular the reference to "trust." The policy of "*îlotage*," or foot patrol (1997–2002), focused on correcting geographical inequalities of access to police services and improvements in local investigations of petty crimes. Its reception by the public proved positive on several points according to a survey commissioned by the Ministry of the Interior in December 2001 and which compared opinions of the respondents in the areas where policy was not implemented to those where the experiment took place since March 1999. A reanalysis of the data showed that visibility of the police on foot in their neighborhood, which guarantees citizen contact with police officers, clearly is superior (with 38% saying it had increased, compared to 19%), and so is perceived effectiveness (with 58% saying it had increased compared to 39%) in test zones where the reform was implemented by comparison with control zones (Roché 2005).

The Late and Partial Politicization of Discrimination and Police Violence

Poor police–youth relationships in the French suburbs at the end of the 1970s have not been analyzed as a political issue. This is probably because of their contrast with the student movements of 1968–1972, and because of police clashes with the more radical fringes of that movement between 1976 and 1978 (Renouard 1993). Discrimination did not quickly become a political issue despite mounting activity by associations formed to deal with the subject (for example the CRAN, a federation of associations for the advancement of Black rights[6]), and this remained true even after the riots of 2005, the most serious in France to date. The issue of discrimination entered the political arena only in the presidential election of 2012. Then, the candidate François Hollande promised to introduce receipts that would be delivered following identity checks in order to better track police stops, and also to monitor racial and ethnic profiling and discrimination. His minister of the interior, Manuel Valls, promptly abandoned the promise during the first few months of Hollande's five-year term. However, the issue of discrimination and violence against minorities and residents of disadvantaged neighborhoods – where the problem is concentrated – was dealt with thoroughly in a 2006 study of discrimination in Paris (this project is described in Chapter 2 of this volume). It was differently addressed during citizen groups' 2016 prosecution of the state in the civil courts for discrimination. These legal proceedings went against the state, for the first time in France. Emmanuel Macron took up the question of ethnic inequality in policing during his 2017 presidential campaign. But, once again lacking real eagerness to grapple with the issue once in power, ministers of the interior in Macron's administration have not, as of this writing, chosen to take concrete action on these matters. Ethnic discrimination is currently not viewed as a problem requiring corrective action by the Ministry of the Interior, either through new police policies or via new practices. Suburban police violence also has not appeared on the platforms of political parties during significant elections.

Based on all of this, it is not surprising that research findings point to the existence of confrontational policing in underprivileged neighborhoods, identity checks that discriminate against minorities, and low trust in police in poor areas. The studies cited here document that judgments of the police grow worse when there is direct contact with police officers. Regarding their tactics, a multivariate analysis of available data showed that more aggressive police actions (increased identity checks and confrontations with the public) have negative effects on judgments that the police are "fair" (Roché and Roux 2017). Both identity checks and what is judged to be too-aggressive policing undermine trust and legitimacy.

Finally, during the period under review, the question of disproportionate use of force by the police has emerged in political debates about certain high-visibility cases. These included, for example, the death of the environmental activist Rémi Fraisse in 2014 at the Sivens dam site. The issue of police violence was also at the heart of the debate surrounding the yellow vest movement (November 2018–September 2019), as many videos attest. The database established by the journalist David Dufresne records nearly 30 permanent injuries and thousands of persons wounded during yellow vest episodes. The police inspectorate (IGPN) itself documented their impressively frequent use of rubber bullets (19,071 fired in 2018 compared to 6,357 the previous year) and sting-ball grenades (5,420 in 2018 compared to 1,367 in 2017).[7] It should be noted that Nordic countries, where trust and legitimacy levels are the highest in the EU, proscribe the use of less-lethal weapons such as rubber bullet guns and grenades. In fact, there is strong correspondence between public authorities' decision to authorize these weapons in law enforcement and the level of democracy measured by various indexes (Roché 2019). These instances of violence have been judged harshly by a large segment of the French public, but these judgments are mainly a function of respondents' stance toward the ruling party and do not necessarily reflect a general political conservatism. Supporters of rather centrist parties such as LREM are more favorable to police violence than the main right-wing party, the Front National (recently renamed Rassemblement National). Explanations of attitudes regarding police action during public demonstrations therefore seem different from those usually used in the context of other police missions. It would be useful for scholars to pursue this distinction, especially in a context where leaderless movements and civil disobedience in the name of environmentalism are emerging in various countries.

Police use of violence does not strongly resonate in public opinion as long as it remains confined to neglected suburbs, where ethnic minorities and the poorest families are overrepresented. Neither the use of violence by the police in poor suburbs nor (more surprisingly) the yellow vest movement led to formal investigations or commissions of inquiry by the Assemblée Nationale, unlike responses to parallel situations in the United Kingdom. Echoing the English historian of the French police Clive Emsley's analysis, one could interpret this state of affairs as the consequence of the widely held idea that the state has the right to do whatever it needs to defend itself. This view makes it almost impossible to place blame on "an official who has acted in the name of the legitimate defense of the State, whatever the abuses or excesses committed" (Emsley 1989, p. 28).

Conclusion: Police–Public Relations and Public Policy

Citizens' views of their relationship with the police are determined by several sets of factors. On the one hand, the way public authorities conceive of the police–public relationship is central. Is it an issue for the government? What are ideal police–public relations? A government's policies on public safety and police practices result largely from the answers to these questions, which evolve with time. People's judgments, in turn, may be understood as reactions to these practices ("policy feedback"), either because they observe them or because they experience them directly (they are stopped by police for an identity check, they report a crime, or they are victims of police violence, or protected by police actions). However, between 1977 and 2020, the politicization of questions of insecurity led to policing policies that do not directly address the goals of increasing trust and legitimacy. The main measures taken have been on emphasizing foot patrols, adding specific training modules for officers, and holding workshops geared toward young people, including police visits to schools (Wuilleumier 2014). The creation of local police outposts, which was implemented between 1998 and 2002 in the context of community policing, was quickly shut down. Finally, in neglected suburbs, living conditions, ethnic and territorial identities, and exposure to repeated police stops and aggressive police action, are the main determinants of diminished trust in the police. Such police modes of action have remained unquestioned by government.

On the other hand, police–public relations are also influenced by political tensions or crises during which citizens confront the police (criminals in the case of terrorism, or protesters in demonstrations). France's exposure to terrorism has increased support for the police among all segments of the public; violence against terrorist attackers appears necessary. However, public approval of violent policing behavior during protests is highly contingent on who supports the governing party.

Forty years after the first official diagnoses of the state of police–public relations appeared, quantitative studies show there have been few variations in public assessment of daily police work. They also suggest that the police in France enjoy less support than in many other European Union countries, when it comes to integrity, distributive trust, fair treatment, and legitimacy. The lack of reform moving police toward greater local accountability, the disproportionate use of violence against poor neighborhoods or more recently against demonstrations, and an absence of programs aimed at improving the quality of police services or highlighting the importance of trustworthiness as a goal for policing, are the likely causes. Warnings from human rights organizations such as the Contrôleur général des lieux de privation de liberté and the Défenseur des droits (two French ombudsmen) have not been much heeded. Embracing these reforms would imply a transformation of police culture and the culture of the French Ministry of the Interior to which they report.

Notes

1 An article by Gorgeon (1994) summarizes various survey questions dating from the late 1980s and early 1990s.
2 Note the important difference in the way the two survey groups measure the same concept. This frustrates the systematic use of polling data to monitor police performance.

3 The Eurojustis research project, funded by the European Commission, seeks to develop indicators of trust and legitimacy with regards to police and the law. Its French branch is working on a pilot study.
4 However, other aspects were more positive. For example, in France, respondents said that there was a good rate of correspondence between the values attributed to the police and those attributed to society. In procedural justice theory this is known as "moral alignment." In France, police are believed to share with respondents the same conception of good and evil in approximately three-quarters of cases. This was the equivalent of Denmark in the survey. This placed the French police at the top of the rankings regarding moral alignment, so it was not that the police and the people share different views of right and wrong that accounts for low legitimacy.
5 IPSOS/Sopra Steria, surveys conducted on January 11–12, 2019, and August 30-September 3, 2019.
6 The association, a federation of associations for the advancement of Blacks' rights, commissioned a poll by the Institut CSA on identity checks in the general population and among "visible minorities."
7 Press conference held on June 13, 2019. The figures on the use of non-lethal weapons concern essentially November and December 2018, and therefore exclude the months of 2019 during which demonstrations continued.

References

Belorgey, J. M. 1991. *La police au rapport*. Nancy: Presses Universitaires de Nancy.
Boucher, M. 2010. *Les internés du ghetto: Ethnographie des confrontations violentes dans une cité impopulaire*. Paris: L'Harmattan.
Bradford, B. 2014. Policing and social identity: Procedural justice, inclusion and cooperation between police and public. *Policing & Society* 24: 22–43.
Brown, B. and Benedict, W. 2002. Perceptions of the police: Past findings, methodological issues, conceptual issues, and policy implications. *Policing*, 25: 543–580.
CEVIPOF. 2019. En quoi les Français ont-ils confiance aujourd'hui? Baromètre de la confiance politique, Paris, SciencesPo-CEVIPOF, sweep 9. [a yearly report is published online] [www.sciencespo.fr/cevipof/sites/sciencespo.fr.cevipof/files/CEVIPOF_confiance_vague10-1.pdf].
D'Arbois de Jubainville, H. 2019. La satisfaction ressentie par les victimes lors du déplacement à la police ou à la gendarmerie. *La Note de l'ONDP* n°36, juillet.
Défenseur des Droits. 2017. Relations police- population: le cas des contrôles d'identité, vol. 1: Enquête sur l'accès aux droits. Paris. [https://bit.ly/2LUSvGF].
Delouvrier. 2019. *Baromètre de l'Institut Paul Delouvrier, Les services publics vus par les Français et les usagers*. Paris. [a yearly report is published online] [www.slideshare.net/Kantar-Public-France/les-services-publics-vus-par-les-franais-et-les-usagers-dition-2019?from_action=save].
de Maillard, J., Hunold, D., Roché, S., Oberwittler, D. et Zagrodzki, M. 2016. Les logiques professionnelles et politiques du contrôle: Des styles de police différents en France et en Allemagne. *Revue française de science politique* 66: 271–293.
Easton, D. 1965. *A systems analysis of political life*. New York: John Wiley & Sons.
ELABE. 2019. *Les Français et la police* ("The French and the police"). April 5 [opinion poll report].
Emsley, C. 1989. La légitimité de la police anglaise: une perspective historique Comparée. *Déviance et société* 13: 23–34.

ESS. 2010. European Social Survey, results based on the author's use of the online analysis of the data. [www.europeansocialsurvey.org/data/download.html?r=5].
Fassin, D. 2011. *La force de l'ordre: Une anthropologie de la police des quartiers*. Paris: Seuil.
FRA: EU-MIDIS. 2010. *Données en bref: Contrôles de police et minorités*. Luxembourg: Publications Office of the European Union.
Gauthier, J., de Maillard, J. and Peaucellier, S. 2019. Représentations et expériences de la police: Une enquête auprès des étudiants. *Questions pénales* 32: 1–6.
Gorgeon, C. 1994. Police et public: représentations, recours et attentes; le cas français. *Déviance et société* 18: 245–273.
Harding, R. 1993. The street-level epistemology of trust. *Politics & Society* 21: 505–529.
Hough, M., Jackson, J. and Bradford, B. 2014. Trust in justice and the legitimacy of legal authorities: Topline findings from a European comparative study. Pp. 243–265 in M. Hough, K. Kerezsi, Lévy, R. and Snacken, S. (Eds.) *Routledge handbook of European criminology*. London and New York: Routledge.
IPSOS. 2019. Fractures Françaises, Paris, Ipsos/Sopra Steria for Le Monde, la Fondation Jean Jaurès et l'Institut Montaigne. [a yearly report is published online] [www.ipsos.com/sites/default/files/ct/news/documents/2019-09/fractures_francaises_2019.pdf].
Lapeyronnie, D. 2008. *Ghetto urbain: Ségrégation, violence, pauvreté en France aujourd'hui*. Paris: Robert Laffont.
Lévy, R. 2016. La police française à la lumière de la théorie de la justice procédurale. Déviance et Société 40: 139–164.
Mahfud, Y. and Adam-Troian, J. 2019. "Macron demission!": Loss of significance generates violent extremism for the Yellow Vests through feelings of anomia. *Group Processes and Intergroup Relations*: 1–17. DOI:101.71177/71/31636884433002219880954.
Millings, M. 2013. Policing British Asian identities: The enduring role of the police in young British Asian men's situated negotiation of identity and belonging. *British Journal of Criminology* 53: 1075–1092.
Ministère de l'Intérieur. 1997. Des villes sûres pour des citoyens libres ("Safe cities for free citizens"). *proceedings from Villepinte Conference*, October 24–25.
Oberwittler, D. and Roché, S. (Eds.) 2018. *Police citizen relations around the world: Comparing sources and contexts of trust and legitimacy*. London: Routledge.
ODOXA. 2018. *Gérard Collomb et l'évacuation de la ZAD de Notre-Dame des Landes*. survey conducted on January 4. [www.odoxa.fr/sondage/gerard-collomb-largement-inconnu-francais-patit-dun-niveau-de-popularite-tres-moyen/].
Peyrefitte, A. 1977. *Réponses à la violence*. Paris: Presses Pocket, 2 vol.
Renouard, J. M. 1993. Les relations entre la police et les jeunes: la recherche en question. *Déviance et société* 17: 419–438.
Rizk, C. 2011. Opinion sur l'efficacité de l'action de la police et la gendarmerie. *Grand Angle n°28*. Paris: ONDRP-IHNES.
Robbins, B. 2016. What is trust? A multidisciplinary review, critique, and synthesis. *Sociology Compass* 10/10: 972–986.
Roché, S. 2005. *Police de proximité*. Paris: Le Seuil.
Roché, S. 2016. *De la police en démocratie*. Paris: Grasset.
Roché, S. 2017. Trois concepts clés pour analyser la relation police-population: confiance, légitimité et justice procédurale. *Cahiers de la sécurité et de la justice* 40: 103–111.
Roché, S. 2019. Le LBD ou le chaos. *Esprit* (Avril): 9–14.

Roché, S. and Roux, G. 2017. The "silver bullet" to good policing: a mirage: An analysis of the effects of political ideology and ethnic identity on procedural justice. *Policing: An International Journal* 40: 514–528.

Roux, G. 2018. Perception of police unfairness amongst stigmatized groups: The impact of ethnicity, Islamic affiliation and neighborhood. Pp. 193–218 in S. Roché and M. Hough (Eds.) *Minority youth integration*. New York: Springer.

Roux, G. and Roché, S. 2016. Police et phénomènes identitaires dans les banlieues: entre ethnicité et territoire, une étude par focus groups. *Revue française de science politique* 66: 729–750.

Roux, G., Roché, S. and Astor, S. 2011. Final report based on the two French opinion polls. Minorities and trust in the criminal justice. French case study. analyse des données françaises de l'enquête européenne Eurojustis.

Skogan, W. 2006. Asymmetry in the impact of encounters with police. *Policing & Society* 16: 99–126.

SOFRES. 2006. Observatoire de la sécurité 2006. [opinion poll for ASSA-ABLOY] online [www.tns-sofres.com/publications/observatoire-de-la-securite-2006].

Tiberj, V. and Simon, P. 2010. Vie citoyenne et participation politique. Pp. 109–115 in C. Beauchemin, C. Hamel et P. Simon (Dirs.) *Enquête sur la diversité des populations en France: Premiers résultats*. Paris: INED [Institut National des Etudes Démographiques].

Tyler, T. 1990. *Why people obey the law*. New Haven: Yale University Press.

van Dijk, J., van Kesteren, J. and Smit, P. 2007. *Criminal victimization in international perspective: Key findings from the 2004–2005 ICVS and EU ICS*. Tilburg: Tilburg University.

Wuilleumier, A. 2014. L'enseignement du juste en école de police et de gendarmerie: Quelles stratégies pédagogiques? *Les Cahiers de la Sécurité Intérieure* 27–28: 242–255.

Chapter 18

Community Policing Initiatives in France

Jacques de Maillard and Mathieu Zagrodzki

Scholars working on the question of community policing may be tempted to view the French model of policing as incompatible with the concept. Rather, both the *police nationale* and the *gendarmerie nationale* are seen first and foremost as accountable not to the public, but to the government. One staple of policing studies is a traditional dichotomy anchored by the image of a rather brutal, centralized, high (e.g. oriented toward national security) French style of policing model that is devoted to performing political surveillance and protecting the interests of the state. This is contrasted with the decentralized (though highly bureaucratic), low (street) policing of the British system that focuses on everyday criminality and maintaining peace while remaining mindful that the foundation of its legitimacy is public consent (see Brodeur 2010, p. 64). One obvious trap of dichotomizing is oversimplification, which in this case may lead us to lose sight of the complexity of each nation's approach. It is true that French police have an ambivalent relationship to community policing initiatives, to say the least. France is no stranger to the police–public relationship problems that have plagued other Western countries, particularly in urban settings. The constant tension between youths and the police in some neighborhoods (epitomized by occasional outbursts of rioting), the growth of insecurity among the public at large, and inadequate police performance are issues that have been under scrutiny since the late 1970s. The 1980s and 1990s saw the rise of alternate themes, such as proximity to the public, or a more supportive relationship between police forces and underprivileged areas. Partnerships emerged involving the police and local bodies, especially municipalities. These developments culminated in a community policing reform effort in the late 1990s. During the 2000s, however, progress stalled. Both new management trends and the politicization of security issues led to a reconsideration of the suitability of community policing as a reform strategy. This chapter examines the stages by which community policing advanced and then retreated on the reform agenda during this period.

Before proceeding, an important semantic point needs to be made. French terminology – like that in several other European countries, whether Latin, such as Spain and Italy, or Nordic, such as Denmark and Sweden – refers to such initiatives as *police de proximité*, i.e. "proximity policing." Other possible

French translations of "community policing" would be "*police de communauté*" or "*police Communautaire*." However, the concept is not quite in accord with how most elected officials and police managers envision the role of policing in the French society. The Republic is, in fact, supposed to be the exact antithesis of "community." In the French language, the word "*communauté*" has come to be closely associated with "ethnic communities" (see de Maillard 2008) and is thus laden with a meaning that contradicts the inclusiveness of the English term. Beyond these semantics, the three defining features of community policing put forward by Wesley Skogan (2006) remain quite helpful for the purpose of highlighting features of the reforms implemented in France. One is that police officers should be assigned to specific areas, and responsibilities should be decentralized within the police organization. Rather than driving through extended areas, they ought to patrol smaller territories on foot, or riding bicycles or possibly horses. Territorial units are headed by managers who are in charge, among other things, of defining objectives and allocating resources for their assigned territory. Rank-and-file officers are encouraged to identify local issues and find collaborative solutions with the public. This in turns leads to the second feature of community policing, namely a significant degree of involvement by the public in safety matters. This might be achieved through public meetings aiming to help the police gather information on local needs and problems, raise awareness on their own working conditions and constraints, but also make it possible for the public to offer a direct critique of police action and/or transmit information that may help investigations. Some forces even promoted programs supporting self-protection initiatives. The third dimension has to do with broadening the scope of the police mission. Community policing agencies typically expand beyond their traditional, primarily reactive stance toward recorded crime, in addition, shifting toward a broader, more proactive intervention model that involves prevention programs and broad, problem-solving efforts.

These three dimensions highlight some distinctive features of French community policing initiatives. Here we do this chronologically, with the turn of the 21st century providing a key change in its direction. At first, community policing was seen as an experiment; then it became a seemingly central priority in policing; but it was finally symbolically and practically relegated to backstage. This is where it has remained since the 2000s. Although a new community policing initiative was launched in 2017–2018, it soon seemed to be facing another reversal. Remaining elements of this brief relaunch can still be observed, but skepticism about their future seems called for.

From Early Experiments to "*Police de Proximité*"

The operations of urban French police forces were considerably affected during the second half of the 20th century by two radical societal shifts (Monjardet 1996, 1999). The first swept through all Western countries, in the form of as improved technology (radio, telephone, cars) that made it possible for police to intervene more quickly and easily when they were called. However, this technology-led move toward reactive policing also contributed to cutting the police off from the ordinary routines of public life. It is well-established that the police car window acts as a barrier to communication. The second societal shift was more specifically French. Its effect on policing came via the 1941 nationalization of the police by Vichy France during the German occupation of World War II. This completely changed the way police officers related to their organizational hierarchy, which became a national one. The *commissaire de police* (superintendent/district commander) now reported to the prefect, one link in a chain of command that culminated with the minister of the interior. In this system, mayors were suddenly shunted aside. Police officers were recruited on a national basis, resulting in their being less familiar with and knowledgeable about the specific areas they were assigned to. From this point onward, the Paris Prefecture of police became in part a police academy, as most officers who were newly recruited in the provinces spent their formative years there, before transferring back toward home. This was the police system that was to be questioned in the 1970s.

The French Model: Criticized but Not Challenged

Crime-fighting was not much of a political issue throughout the 1950–1960s. Ministers of the interior were primarily concerned with protecting the state's interests, which involved the political surveillance of any movement likely to threaten the Republic. They also did a fair amount of crowd policing, particularly in the context of struggles over decolonization (see Chapter 3 in this volume). The situation was to change during the 1970s – so much so that, characteristically, in 1974, the minister of the interior defined his job as "being the minister of the security of the French." Security and crime issues suddenly appeared on the political agenda. This was more of a comeback for these concerns. They had featured prominently in political discourse throughout the 19th century, because of a sharp rise in volume crime (thefts grew 11-fold between 1950 and 1984) that paralleled similar trends across Western nations. Such was the overall situation when a series of reports appeared that questioned the prevailing policing system.

One report, for example, was that of the Working Committee on Violence, Serious and Petty Crime (aka the Peyrefitte report). This was submitted to the prime minister in 1977. It recommended rebalancing the distribution of police resources, especially toward newly urbanized areas where their absence was seriously felt. The report also called for creating small neighborhood police stations with a focus on beat patrols and providing training courses to improve police–public relationships. In the early 1980s especially, a series of reports published as part of the decentralization efforts launched in 1982 (the Dubedout report on deteriorated neighborhoods, the Schwartz report on youth integration, and particularly the Bonnemaison report on crime prevention) called for some radical change in local policing. These reports favored a more territorial approach (at town or neighborhood level), with more partnerships with other organizations and the increased involvement of the public. Regarding prevention and security, the Bonnemaison report (1982) led to the creation of municipal crime prevention boards. These were co-chaired by mayors and prefects, and included police representation.

Within the Ministry of the Interior itself, the *police nationale*'s relationship with urban areas started being reappraised with a rather critical eye. In the early 1980s, a report commissioned by the ministry documented, based on a wide-ranging survey, that police officers were out of touch with local communities (Ministère de l'intérieur et de la décentralisation 1983). The report emphasized, among other things, that

> although the police are expected to multi-task, they are not necessarily multi-skilled; ... the techniques and methods of prevention are imprecise and little-known; ... there is a lack of understanding between the police and the public; the police lack the tools to get a proper grasp of their environment ....
> (Ministère de l'intérieur et de la décentralisation 1983, pp. 135–136)

Although not immediately effective in terms of fostering training initiatives, this report indicated that some initial diagnosis of these issues had already been undertaken, including how difficult it was to act in the domain of public security. In the late 1980s, the Institut des Hautes études de la sécurité intérieure (later renamed Institut national des hautes études sur la sécurité et la justice, and now attached to the prime minister's office) was created. For a while it constituted, if a bit intermittently (see Ocqueteau and Monjardet 2005), a forum where reform-minded police officers, senior civil servants, and policing scholars were able to exchange views. The Institute was particularly useful in promoting exchanges with the international academic community, thereby fostering the circulation of knowledge and introduction of reformist ideas from abroad.

Once the gulf separating police from their communities had been recognized, proposals for reforming police practices began to emerge. In 1976, for instance, an ordinance required that prevention-oriented beat patrols must be implemented. They were to focus on limited areas, so that it would be possible for the police and the public to actually develop a relationship. However, these initiatives never really took off, mostly because they were systematically understaffed. This was especially true of the *îlotage* (beat patrols). These units were in fact well-known to be staffed by officers who were not being assigned to general duties, such as top athletes.[1] In case of emergency, though, these units were the first to be mobilized. Such innovations were viewed with a complete lack of interest by police officers, and they constituted a priority. Monjardet (1996) identified three structural barriers to reform: institutional (top-down demands always prioritize public order); organizational (information flows among services are difficult to measure and assess); and professional (arrests are perceived as the most prestigious way of exercising policing powers).

To some extent practices developed by the *gendarmerie*, although never formally labelled as such, had a great deal of overlap with community policing. The *gendarmerie* has always fostered a force with a strong sense of belonging to the rural and semi-urban territories it is responsible for. Given it huge geographical reach – they cover 95% of the national territory and police 50% of the population – the *gendarmerie* needed to maintain an extensive network of informants throughout the country. In return, they could be counted upon to provide a number of informal services (Mouhanna 2001). However, this policing model also had its shortcomings. By the late 1980s it was questioned from within, as the *gendarmes* – who lived in barracks with their families – were seeking a better work–life balance and were not attracted by institutional living. By the end of the 1990s, due in part to the physically immense territory covered by the *gendarmerie* but also because of internal tensions stemming from ever-increasing pressure for internal accountability, demands for institutional change mounted.

However, although the *gendarmerie* experienced difficulties, most of the toughest issues in policing cropped up in urban areas, which were under the jurisdiction of the *police nationale*. Elected officials and the police were at cross purposes, as:

> [Elected officials] were demanding some conspicuous, constant, dissuasive police presence, whereas [the police] were developing the BAC, the anti-crime squads whose main objective was to keep the lowest possible profile in order to catch criminals in the act. The former wanted uniformed beat patrols, considered by the latter to be utterly inefficient from a repressive – and therefore policing – point of view.
>
> (Monjardet 1999, p. 19)

The Hard-to-Implement 1997–2002 *"Police de Proximité"* Reform

As a result, in the mid-1990s, the situation did not appear to favor the development of community policing initiatives in France. Still, the idea was gaining ground within the Ministry of the Interior and it could even be considered a non-partisan issue. On both ends of the political spectrum, closer proximity to the community and improved police–public relationships were felt to matter. In 1993, the minister of the interior was Charles Pasqua, a member of the right-wing Gaullist party (Rassemblement pour la République) who could hardly be suspected of being unsympathetic to the force (he was nicknamed "France's #1 cop" at the time). However, he drew a somewhat critical picture of the French model of public security:

Out of the three missions of domestic security – protecting the institutions, fighting crime, and ensuring the day-to-day safety of people and goods – the French model has for a very long time been more mindful of protecting the State than meeting the people's needs ... Though ours must remain a national police and isn't expected to give up on any of its prerogatives, the force today should be anchored in city life, and make daily security and the citizens' expectations a major concern. There can be no such thing as a truly preventive, dissuasive, repressive, and efficient police force without support from the people.
(Charles Pasqua, IHESI conference, 1993, quoted in Monjardet and Ocqueteau 2004, p. 59)

The "proximity" aspect, fueled as it was by the popularity of partnership-based approaches, appeared to be a common concern. The Security Framework Act of 1995 (Loi d'orientation et de programmation pour la sécurité), which was passed by a center-right majority, explicitly refers to the concept of "proximity security." The 1997 political upheaval only accentuated these dynamics, as the new left-wing coalition administration made security one of its top priorities, second only to unemployment. Two types of reforms were considered: implementing so-called "local security contracts" between the state and local governments, and reforming urban police forces in order to enable some form of community policing.

Reform was announced with great pomp during a colloquium in Villepinte in 1997. It was in many ways very much akin to what other Western countries labeled "community policing." First, it aimed at redefining the police officer's job, putting the officer at the center of the system. While the theoretical content itself was only defined later (in 1999), it did meet the standards of community policing legislation. The plan specified three policing objectives: anticipating and preventing obstacles; knowing one's area of jurisdiction and being known by the residents; and meeting people's needs through constant dialog and attentive listening. It recommended five "modes of action." These were neighborhood-based coverage of the area; permanent contact with residents; versatile police action including prevention, repression, and dissuasion; territorial empowerment and accountability; and delivery of high-quality services. Finally, seven operational protocols were to be followed. These included collecting demands for security; management by objective; problem-solving management; developing teamwork; internal and external communication; results-based performance appraisal; and a spirit of public service.

Next, as far as methodology was concerned, the reform was to begin with an experimental and appraisal phase, and only later was to proceed to the general deployment of the scheme. The detailed plan described several implementation phases. There was to be an experiment involving five pilot sites, followed by a gradual deployment over 63 wards at first, then 180, and finally the program was to be initiated in all 468 public security wards (*circonscriptions de sécurité publique*).

Another facet of "proximity policing" was the idea of contract agreements between the state and local government institutions. These were called "local security contracts." These contracts enabled prefects (the state's representatives in the *départements*), *commissaires*, public prosecutors, and local government institutions to commit to shared public safety goals.

Still, the implementation of the reform was marred by many difficulties and setbacks. First, the Paris Prefecture of Police, although part and parcel of the general directorate of the *police nationale*, only did the bare minimum to implement the reform. Paris did not fundamentally alter its functioning in any way. The creation of neighborhood security squads (*Brigades de sécurité de quartiers*, or BSQs) notwithstanding, the brand of community policing implemented in Paris, completely aside from the rest of the general directorate of the national police, mainly consisted in merging its two types of police stations – the *commissariats de police judiciaire* and *commissariats de sécurité publique*, i.e. the criminal police and public safety units respectively. This unified the capital's policing system and aligned it with the rest of the country, but without modifying the basic doctrine driving field operations.

Most importantly, the bulk of the reform, which was supposed to apply to the entire staff of the central directorate of public security, was in fact more complex than expected. This is made very clear by Sebastian Roché (2005). He reports that the project may not have received full backing from all political decision-makers. Although Minister of the Interior Jean-Pierre Chevènement oversaw its design and implementation, he was not convinced himself by a reform that was mainly the brainchild of Prime Minister Lionel Jospin. In fact, the service-oriented reform did not quite match J.-P. Chevènement's idea of the "republican" police.[2]

Second, resources matter enormously. Community policing involves an ability to deploy a lot of personnel in the public arena. However, except for the *adjoints de sécurité* (police community support officers hired on a contract basis), the Ministry of the Interior was not really able to secure significant extra funds to support community policing. No effort was made to reduce the headcount of the *compagnies républicaines de sécurité*, i.e. the crowd control units, even though these could have been overstaffed, with 15,000 men when the entire central directorate of public security only boasted 65,000 officers.

Third, to conduct the reform, the Ministry needed support, both internal (from police practitioners and representative organizations) and external (from local government organizations). However, police unions, feeling that the reform had suffered from insufficient negotiations with them, grew increasingly skeptical, if not downright critical. As for local governments, as mentioned above, many mayors were keen to have a police force with an improved ability to meet their residents' security needs. But the reform did not involve much dialog and was often not understood by mayors, who were mostly interested in putting more officers on the beat – but these never materialized.

Fourth, timing was a decisive factor. After the project had been plagued by multiple delays, the government (in this case the prime minister and minister of the interior) decided that the reform had to be fully implemented by the time the 2002 presidential election came. The whole plan and its various stages of deployment was structured in response to this deadline, and implementation of a detailed reform package became driven by a political time frame. This triggered a sense of urgency that led the various actors to trade mutual accusations of proceeding too fast, and this then hampered the overall success of the reform. This hurry-up approach made it difficult to win the hearts and minds of working officers. The reform was even more difficult to steer because those in charge of designing and implementing it at the central directorate of public security were too few in number to reach out and involve field practitioners. Reformers insisted on forcing everything into one mold, using standardized criteria throughout the country in order to geographically identify neighborhoods and assign personnel. At the local level, indiscriminate application of one framework everywhere was perceived as yet another example of excessive Paris centralism. The reform was indeed steered from Paris and imposed on localities, relying on their obedience as opposed to their buy-in (Roché 2005, pp. 163–192).

In addition, training was a neglected facet of the reform. Officers were not prepared at the time for this new way of doing police work. Dominique Monjardet is quite critical of this lack of know-how. He noted,

> if [the police] have no other available resource, to make contact with a group of youths, than stop-and-search (usually illegal to boot), it is doubtful that their action will be productive at all. In this immense enterprise consisting of improving the skills and know-how of a police force that must be visible in the public space, almost nothing was done.
> (Monjardet 2002, p. 550)

Finally, even though the original plan called for an ongoing appraisal of the program with a view toward making necessary adjustments along the way, the body overseeing it (Inspection générale de la police nationale) produced only four reports. They were all clearly biased against reform and contained very little information pertaining to an appraisal of the program (for a scathing review see Roché 2005).

At the end of the day, the whole reform process was turned into a forced march, as many at the Ministry did not believe in it and its proponents were not able to secure the reliable ongoing assessments that were needed to build an effective program. Its deployment was extremely dependent on – and its pace was defined by – the political calendar. The inner logic of the reform was a highly centralized one. It was to be implemented locally, but matters were decided centrally. There is something strikingly paradoxical about a reform that preached organizational decentralization yet was carried out in a most centralized fashion. One might have thought that over time, some flexibility would spread through this centralized framework, as the dynamics of the reform and specifically the idea of empowering local echelons got the better of it. But as it turned out – with a little help from yet another political upheaval in 2002 – a completely different logic ultimately prevailed.

Sarkozy, Community Policing, and a "Results Oriented" Culture

The 2000s saw a sharp decline of police–public rapprochement initiatives in favor of managerial approaches focused on the repressive activities of the police, as France's conservatives returned to power. François Hollande's later five-year term did not alter this trend, and in any case, after the 2015 terror attacks in Paris the fight against terror became first priority. While the current president's (Emmanuel Macron) election platform did mention day-to-day security policing, the effects of his administration's priorities are not yet clear.

Even while debates over community policing were going on, the 1990s also saw the rise of a harsher stance on security in French political discourse and media depictions of society. The concept of "zero-tolerance" policing quickly gained traction in politicians' speeches. It became the trend of the moment, fueled by a drop in crime that was billed as the "New York Miracle." In 1998, Minister of the Interior Jean-Pierre Chevènement sent a delegation to New York to meet New York Police Department officials, in order to learn what practices might be imported to France.

Although ultimately New York magic could only be exported to a very limited extent (de Maillard and Le Goff 2009), the trend toward more aggressive policing continued through 2001–2002, as it became clear that security issues would dominate the April 2002 presidential election campaign. Anything related to insecurity was sure to feature prominently in the media, which prompted conservatives to zoom in on this issue during the mayoral and presidential elections of 2001 and 2002, respectively. On 14 July 2001, during Bastille Day celebrations, Jacques Chirac (quoted in Zagrodzki 2017) declared,

> There is no such thing as inevitable insecurity. There is, however, such a thing as a lack of authority from the state, and a lack of political will. What I am saying is that this growing, heightening insecurity – this wave of insecurity – is unacceptable, the exact opposite of the spirit of human rights, and it needs to stop.

On 16 October 2001, two police officers were killed during a burglary in Le Plessis-Trévise, near Paris. This tragic event sparked a total of seven demonstrations by police officers between 23 October and 14 December. In response, the government released €350 million to shore up the police budget, but footage of policemen demonstrating on the streets had a disastrous, long-lasting impact on the government's image (Monjardet 2002). On 3 March 2002, in the middle of the presidential election campaign, the sitting prime minister and presidential candidate Lionel Jospin admitted that he had failed as far as security was concerned. He admitted during a TV evening news interview on TF1 that he had "sinned by naivety" when it came to crime. This failure was one of the factors that led him lose an election in which the number one issue had been security in the eyes of French voters. Polls revealed that 60% of voters said it was their priority issue, on the day before the vote (Roché 2005, pp. 259–264). Jospin was eliminated in the first round of balloting, capturing barely more than 16% of the vote.

The re-election instead of Jacques Chirac and the victory of the conservatives at the subsequent parliamentary election, led to a new cabinet being appointed. Nicolas Sarkozy – former mayor of Neuilly-sur-Seine and one of a group of self-styled "uninhibited conservatives" – became minister of the interior. Sarkozy immediately embarked on a vigorous campaign promoting a results-oriented culture of policing. The police, particularly the *commissaires*, were to be evaluated – and compensated – based on their numbers. Pitting this new, data-based approach to policing against community policing, which he deemed soft, inefficient, and excessively "social," he decided to backtrack on most of what had been done by the left in matters of security. His ministerial order of 24 October 2002 (Sarkozy 2002) aimed at reorienting police efforts against urban violence and crime. The order laid down three principles. The first spoke to "granting territorial managers a modicum of autonomy in how to organize their department, especially in terms of dividing up community policing sectors, of which there are too many and is labor-intensive and clearly tends to dilute the effectiveness of operational action." He noted a need to increase staffing levels during peak crime hours, especially at night. Finally, he called for a better operational balance leaning toward procedural judicial activity and law and order maintenance.

Reading between the lines of this order, one understands that local police managers (i.e. the *commissaires*) would see that they were now able to simply disregard the fundamental tenets of community policing, including the division of their territories into sectors and confidence-building activities with the public. Emphasizing judicial and law-and-order maintenance activities meant that patrolling and making arrests were instead to be prioritized. This was community policing's fate, after three years of debate. Instead, security policies suddenly took a sharp repressive turn. This policy emphasis was in accordance with the strategy of a minister who wanted was to focus more sharply on this particular aspect of the job of minister of justice (Roché 2005, pp. 232–233). He saw this policy role as neglected by the previous cabinet. Community policing became political, associated in rhetoric with "nice guy" policing.

Finally, the domestic security law of 18 March 2003 created a series of new offences and associated sanctions. The law targeted prostitution, begging, itinerant relocation from place to place, squatting, loitering, and intimidation. Other targets included begging using children or disabled people, and the illegal occupation of property by traveling migrants from Eastern Europe. The logic was one of aggressive order maintenance, a far cry from the spirit of community policing.

As noted earlier, the new minister of the interior wanted policing to be managed by performance measures. The effectiveness of *police nationale* and *gendarmerie* services was to be assessed on the basis of crime and arrest rates, in particular. This excessive reliance on, and unwanted consequences of, a results-oriented culture in France has been highlighted by the parliamentary opposition, some police unions, and several scholars (Matelly and Mouhanna 2007; Douillet et al. 2014). The evidence shows that the pressure to meet numerical quotas led some in the force to manipulate statistics in order to meet their targets. The issues included serious offences being reclassified as misdemeanors; victims being discouraged from filing a complaint when showing up at the police station; and easier-to-solve cases being prioritized over those that might require thorough investigative work. As examples of the latter, Laurent Mucchielli (2008) notes that over the 2002–2006 period there was a sharp increase in the number of cases of clandestine illegal entry (up 52%) and drug-related offences (up 40%). Both offenses basically only need to be officially recorded in order for them to be put in the cleared-up category as well. As the officers themselves put it, you must "nurture your stats."

This repressive, arrest-and-restraint-based approach has tended to exacerbate the issue of police–public relationships by inducing a highly aggressive policing style in which proactive stop-and-search is central (de Maillard and Zagrodzki 2017). Fabien Jobard and Marta Zimolag (2005), in their study of complaints against officials in a position of authority judged at the Tribunal de grande instance in Melun, showed that the number of such cases doubled over 2000–2003 as compared to the 1995–1999 period, and even quadrupled against the 1975–1994 period in that very same jurisdiction. Mucchielli (2008) notes that these offences rose by 15% nationally between 2002 and 2006. While the number of convictions in this type of case has remained stable and even slightly decreased after these studies (16,139 in 2010 vs. 15,254 in 2015),[3] these figures nevertheless do point at a persistently difficult relationship between the police and part of the population, as do the frequent clashes between the force and the youths in a number of sensitive areas (Mohammed and Mucchielli 2007).

In April 2008, special neighborhood squads were created, the *unités territoriales de quartier*, or UTEQ. Later they became the *brigades spécialisées de terrain* or BSTs. They were active in several sensitive pilot areas in suburban Paris, and later expanded were to encompass a total of 45 neighborhoods throughout the country. These were left in place under the next alternative administration, as the left maintained these units when they came into power. They were intended to rekindle a trust relationship between the police and the public, according to Prime Minister François Fillon. This could be taken to suggest that community policing was somehow becoming fashionable again. This impression, though, needs to be quite seriously qualified. For one, the initiative was highly targeted, focused on several specific areas. It was not a national policy aimed at reforming the police mission. The reform had a limited character. This was not least because of budget constraints that plagued all public agencies at the time, and a decrease in staffing levels experienced by the *police nationale* at the same moment. Most importantly, when Minister of the Interior Brice Hortefeux turned the UTEQs into the BSTs, he insisted that the officers involved would be neither "atmosphere officers or social educators." Nor would they be "elder brothers in short-sleeved shirts merging into the background."[4] His text clearly indicates that the chosen approach for these units was still a decidedly repressive one (see below). Assigned as they were to sensitive areas with the expectation of providing visible police presence, they patrolled both in cars and on foot. They were equipped on a day-to-day basis with riot-control equipment, such as 40 mm rubber-bullet less-lethal launchers and tactical vests. The imagery projected by these units was clear. Ultimately, they were but one more instance of the general tendency of the French police to lean on the side of proactive units with an offensive mandate (de Maillard and Zagrodzki 2017; Darley and Gauthier 2018).

Hollande, Tentative Reform, and the Challenge of Terrorism

The election of François Hollande seemed to point to a brighter future for advocates of less aggressive policing methods. One of the main points of his electoral platform in the domain of security was the creation of better-funded Priority Safety Zones (Zones de Sécurité Prioritaires, or ZSPs). Their objectives were to include a more local approach to policing; targeting high-crime areas; improving police–public relationships; and fostering partnerships with local actors. The scheme was indeed implemented with gusto at the beginning of Holland's five-year term. Fifteen target areas were designated as early as the summer of 2012, and the effort reached a total of 80 areas between late 2012 and late 2013. An assessment of the project that was conducted in Marseilles produced mixed reviews (Mucchielli 2015). In particular, drug trafficking, which was a key point of the local strategy, was not affected for long. Still, the opportunity for initiating a genuine, partnership-based dynamic was not lost, as both national authorities and local bodies teamed up to improve quality of life in the areas. However, this effort stopped in its tracks when a new minister of the interior was appointed in early 2014. Then came a wave of terrorist attacks during 2015. In any case, changes mostly occurred in terms of the coordination of institutional actors, as opposed to policing methods, which remained largely untouched.

More generally, police–public relationships and day-to-day safety issues were put on the backburner from 2015 onwards, because the fight against terrorism was prioritized. Although a wave of solidarity with the police was observed after the attacks of January 2015, their image was tarnished by several ensuing incidents (Roché 2016). The many successive extensions of the state of emergency, strong-armed crowd control during demonstrations against the "*loi travail*," disproportionate repression and restrictions against football fans,[5] as well as the death of young men (Rémi Fraisse and Adama Traoré) during encounters with the *gendarmerie* were among the factors that contributed to disappoint François Hollande's voters.

Racial profiling, however, is the issue that generated the most criticism against the president of the Republic, and it came to epitomize the dashed hopes of many of his supporters. Then Minister of the Interior Manuel Valls shelved the idea of the *récépissé de contrôle d'identité* as early as 2012. The government had made a campaign electoral promise to ask *police nationale* and *gendarmes* to deliver a receipt to persons being stopped and searched. Among other things, this could provide evidence to prove that they were being repeatedly targeted and thus discriminated against. Alternative measures were put in place. Uniformed officers had to visibly display their force identification number. A new Ethics Code was put in place. Patrol units received body cameras. However, the issue of racial profiling remains contested, so much so that, following a complaint lodged by 13 people of African and North African origin, the state was condemned by the Cour de Cassation on 9 November 2016 for ID checks that were considered discriminatory. This ruling raised a more general question regarding the overuse of stop-and-search identity checks by the French police. It had, in fact, become their primary point of contact with the public (de Maillard et al. 2018).

As is often the case, it took two tragedies for the discussion about police–public relationships to return to the political and media spotlight. One incident took place in Viry-Châtillon, where two officers suffered very serious injuries as their car was fire-bombed. The second was in Aulnay-sous-Bois, where a young man was severely injured by the BST during his arrest.[6] One of the major consequences of this affair was a change in the rules pertaining to body cameras, which the police and *gendarmes* had been using since 2014. There had been no systematic appraisal of body cameras. When their use was made permanent by a law of 3 June 2016, the decision was based on positive feedback received from beat police officers, and not on any scientific research. It was only on 27 April 2017 that an ordinance experimentally required all officers in 31 ZSPs to systematically record all stops.[7] The effects of this experiment were officially evaluated, albeit by the Ministry itself and not by an independent assessor.

Macron and Policing as "Sécurité du Quotidien"

While security concerns were not a central theme of Emmanuel Macron's electoral platform, he did advance the concept of "day-to-day" (*quotidien*) security policing. It involved a number of ideas that clearly reflected the spirit of community policing. These included the police mixing with residents in sensitive areas, the development of local partnerships, conflict management and dialog training courses, officer empowerment, and decentralized decision-making. These ideas are featured under the rubric of the "Police de Sécurité du Quotidien" (PSQ). Translated as the "day-to-day security policing," this reform was announced in February 2018.[8] Although it is too early to assess either its implementation or its effectiveness, the PSQ already appears to have prompted a number of initiatives. Given how flexible the whole concept is, these new efforts have varied considerably in shape and scope, depending on local needs, unit size, the social and security context, available resources, and the degree of personal involvement by local *police nationale* and *gendarmerie* managers. In some cases, the PSQ label was simply attached to existing initiatives, such as the *gendarmerie*'s *brigades de contact*. In others, it did create actual windows of opportunity for innovative local police managers to foster new approaches, such as creating local police–public steering committees. Still, at the national level, in the absence of any coordination and monitoring body, the project does not seem to benefit from a massive amount of support.

Conclusion

The stop and start character of policy innovation described in this chapter illustrates how difficult it is to reform police organization and practice in France. Three characteristics of the French model of policing are apparent in this process. First, the model is a highly centralized one. The nation's two national forces are steered from Paris by the Ministry of the Interior. Scant autonomy is afforded to local executives, which makes it difficult for them to respond to local needs. Second, a traditional model of policing based on interventions and arrests is favored within the force. Efforts at improving relations with the public or seeking advice from outside the institution tend to induce a degree of defiance, skepticism, or even downright hostility from a corps that perceives itself as unfairly out of favor. Finally, and as a direct consequence of the previous point, order maintenance services are organized in such a way as to encourage specialization. Key units with a strongly interventionist mandate – epitomized by the *brigades anti-criminalité*, the BACs, are first and foremost expected to deliver measurably aggressive results.

The political and administrative context if policing also does not allow for in-depth, carefully thought-out reforms. Reform thinking and organizational change are usually monopolized by the powerful police hierarchy and allied civil administration elites. They face ministers who come and go, and often are not strong enough to push for ambitious change.[9] In addition, unions matter in the French political environment, and about 70% of all police personnel are union members. Union demands mostly pertain to staffing levels, equipment and remuneration, however, and they have never been known for being on the cutting edge of thinking about police–public relationships. To the contrary, they tend to consider that such initiatives cast doubt upon their professionalism.

Yet local initiatives have emerged here and there. The PSQ did help some *police nationale* department heads push for increased involvement of the public in safety policies, and it did help advance problem-solving policing. The *gendarmerie* has built a reputation for greater proximity with the public. One of the most visible elements of this are the *brigades territoriales de contact*. These were launched in early 2018, tasked with meeting directly with residents and local elected officials. However, while community policing continues to appeal to a number of managers and field practitioners, it would be too optimistic to conclude that this movement is receiving full institutional support from top political and administrative echelons.

Notes

1 In France, top athletes in amateur sports may receive state support in the form of an (almost) "no-show" civil servant job.
2 In the French political space, J.-P. Chevènement might be called a "full-fledged republican." Coming from a leftwing background, he gradually came to take positions that leaned on the side of defending the unity of the Republic against decentralization.
3 Source: Ministry of Justice.
4 "*Hortefeux renomme sa police de proximité*", Le Monde, 18 August 2010.
5 According to a count made by the Association Nationale des Supporters (see www.association-nationale-supporters.fr/arretes/), travel bans were ordered against visiting fans in 45 League 1 games over the 2016/17 season.
6 It should be noted that the officers involved in this case (known as the "Théo case"), in which a young man was seriously injured, were from the Aulnay-sous-Bois BST. The national outcry was fierce enough to prompt President Hollande to visit Théo in hospital.
7 The decision of recording these interactions was left to the officers' discretion, and still is, except for the areas specifically mentioned in the ordinance.
8 "*Lancement de la Police de Sécurité du Quotidien*", ministère de l'Intérieur, 8 February 2018.
9 France has had seven different ministers of the interior since 2012.

References

Brodeur, J. P. 2010. *The policing web*. Oxford: Oxford University Press.
Darley, M., and Gauthier, J. 2018. Le travail policier face à la réforme: Une ethnographie de la mise en œuvre des Zones de Sécurité Prioritaires. *Politix* 124: 59–84.
de Maillard, J. 2008. Activating civil society: Differentiated citizen involvement in France and the United Kingdom. Pp. 133–150 in B. Jobert and B. Kohler-Koch (Eds.) *Changing images of civil society. From protest to governance*. London: Routledge.
de Maillard, J., Hunold, D., Roché, S., and Oberwittler, D. 2018. Different styles of policing: Discretionary power in street control in France and Germany. *Policing & Society* 28: 175–188.

de Maillard, J., and Le Goff, T. 2009. La tolérance zéro en France: Succès d'un slogan, illusion d'un transfert. *Revue française de science politique* 58: 655–679.

de Maillard, J., and Zagrodzki, M. 2017. Styles de police et légitimité policière: La question des contrôles. *Droit et Société* 97: 485–501.

Douillet, A. C., de Maillard, J., and Zagrodzki, M. 2014. Une centralisation renforcée par le chiffre? Les effets contradictoires des indicateurs chiffrés dans la police nationale en France. *Politiques et management public* 31: 421–442.

Jobard, F., and Zimolag, M. 2005. *Quand les policiers vont au tribunal:* Analyse d'un échantillon de jugements rendus en matière d'infractions à personnes dépositaires de l'autorité publique dans un TGI parisien (1965–2003). Paris: Cesdip Études et Données Pénales n° 97.

Matelly, J. H., and Mouhanna, C. 2007. *Police: des chiffres et des doutes.* Paris: Michalon.

Ministère de l'intérieur et de la decentralization. 1983. *Les policiers, leurs métiers, leur formation.* Paris: La Documentation Française.

Mohammed, M., and Mucchielli, L. 2007. La police dans les 'quartiers sensibles': Un malaise profond. Pp. 98–119 in L. Mucchielli (Ed.) *Quand les banlieues brûlent. Retour sur les émeutes de novembre 2005.* Paris: La Découverte.

Monjardet, D. 1996. *Ce que fait la police: Sociologie de la force publique.* Paris: La Découverte.

Monjardet, D. 1999. Réinventer la police urbaine. *Les Annales de la recherche urbaine* n°83–84: 14–22.

Monjardet, D. 2002. L'insécurité publique: Police et sécurité dans l'arène électorale. *Sociologie du travail* 44: 543–555.

Monjardet, D., and Ocqueteau, F. 2004. La police: une réalité plurielle. *Problèmes politiques et sociaux* n° 905. Paris: La Documentation Française.

Mouhanna, C. 2001. Faire le gendarme: de la souplesse informelle à la rigueur bureaucratique. *Revue française de sociologie* 42: 31–55.

Mucchielli, L. 2008. Le "nouveau management de la sécurité" à l'épreuve: délinquance et activité policière sous le ministère Sarkozy (2002–2007). *Champ pénal*, vol. V.

Mucchielli, L. 2015. Evaluation de la méthode globale (Zones de sécurité prioritaires). *Les rapports de recherche de l'ORDCS* n°6.

Ocqueteau, F., and Monjardet, D. 2005. Insupportable et indispensable, la recherche au ministère de l'Intérieur. Pp. 229–247 in P. Bezes, M. Chauvière, J. Chevallier, N. de Montricher, and F. Ocqueteau (Eds.) *L'État à l'épreuve des sciences sociales: La fonction recherche dans les administrations sous la Ve République.* Paris: La Découverte.

Roché, S. 2005. *Police de proximité.* Paris: Seuil.

Roché, S. 2016. *De la police en démocratie.* Paris: Grasset.

Sarkozy, N. 2002. *Circulaire du 24 octobre 2002 relative à l'adaptation de l'action des services territoriaux de la sécurité publique au renforcement de la lutte contre les violences urbaines et la délinquance.* Paris: Ministère de l'Intérieur.

Skogan, W. G. 2006. *Police and community in Chicago: A tale of three cities.* New York: Oxford University Press.

Zagrodzki, M. 2017. *Que fait la police? Le rôle du policier dans la société.* La Tour d'Aigues: éditions de l'Aube.

Chapter 19

Policing and Gender in France

Mathilde Darley and Jérémie Gauthier

The 1983 film *Faits divers*, directed by French documentary film-maker Raymond Depardon, unveiled the daily life of a police station of the 5th *arrondissement* in Paris. It was an exclusively male professional environment, organized around virile sociability, in which women, when they did appear, could only aspire to victim status.[1] In the early 1980s, policing in France was still "a man's job" and the recent and modest opening up of the profession to women had not yet disturbed this male monopoly. However, as the rhetoric of state "modernization" developed, profound transformations, including the feminization of the workforce, were under way in a certain number of public organizations. Over the following decades, goals of gender equality and the spread of egalitarian norms – inspired by the UK- and US-led "diversity" framework (Bereni and Jacquemart 2018) and associated with the paradigm of the "fight against discriminations" (Fassin 2002) – became an issue of legitimacy for a number of public and private organizations. The police institution, having already undergone numerous attempts at transformation (Jobard and de Maillard 2015), was a prime candidate for this reforming trend.

Nonetheless, the police were generally described in studies as particularly resistant to change, due to a so-called "police culture" uniting its members. In particular, it was said to possess, as other organizations, a uniquely "gendered substructure" (Acker 1990), where the "cult of masculinity" (Reiner 2000) was a pillar of police identity (Fielding 1994; Heidensohn 1992; Hunt 1990; Waddington 1999). Indeed, as of the 1990s, a number of studies of policing highlighted that the police organization was not "gender neutral" (Acker 1990), because the police culture and the exclusively male community it promoted had substantially encouraged and justified the exclusion of women (Westmarland 2001, p. 8). Described as "naturally" more vulnerable, physically and psychologically, than their male colleagues, women were supposedly incompatible per se with police work involving danger and "macho culture" (Heidensohn 2008). The development of the fields of law and public order seems thus to have greatly contributed to "preserving masculinity" and to slowing women's access to the policing profession, but also the ability of the police to accept and work with gender (Brown 2007).

The opening of law enforcement careers to women in most Western countries as of the 1970s therefore constitutes an "unprecedented anthropological event" (Pruvost 2008). It was a response to the demands of certain feminist groups, but also to a legitimacy crisis within the institution, which, it was hoped, could be alleviated at least in part by the feminization of the workforce. However, this opening was soon marred by the numerous reports pointing to discrimination against women having entered the police force (Silvestri 2003, p. 30). Those findings encouraged British and American social scientists to question the effects of the cult of masculinity on internal relations among police officers (Burke 1993), but also on the relationship between police officers and the public. For a long time, however, French studies on the police paid only marginal attention to gender as "a bi-categorization system based on a hierarchy between sexes (men/women) and between the values and representations associated with them (masculine/feminine)" (Bereni et al. 2008, p. 7). A parallel can be drawn between this observation and two other conditions. First, the long invisibility of gender in French social sciences (Le Feuvre et al. 2013) – particularly in the sociology of policing – and French organizations, especially public ones (Marry et al. 2017). Second, the policing model prevalent in France is based on a hierarchical view of power relationships that glorifies authority. It is marked in addition by the singular importance given to tasks that are perceived as "virile," because they require the use of force in the fight against crime. This is to the detriment of administrative or preventive duties, which are stigmatized as "social work" (Darley and Gauthier 2014).

The gender division found in police work being partly mirrored in sociological work, research on the French police remained, until the mid-2000s, an almost exclusively male field. This probably accounts for the "gender blindness" of the research it produced. The male domination prevailing in the police world seems to have long been taken for granted, without being the subject of specific questioning by the male ethnographers of the institution. And yet, the late and unprecedented feminization of the institution, and the gender bias observable in the selection of police targets (and subsequently reflected in all branches of the criminal justice system), might well have attracted the attention of researchers. Not until the end of that decade did the first women-led field studies in different police units begin to flourish (Lemaire 2008; Mainsant 2008; Proteau and Pruvost 2008; Pruvost 2007a, 2007b; and more recently: Guenot 2018; Morelle 2017; Pérona 2017). These studies were conducted mainly within the street policing and criminal investigation departments. A number of these studies helped bring to light the impact of sex and gender on policing, be it in "the gendered allocation of patrols ... or the disruption of the power relations between (majority) male and (usually minority) female colleagues" (Pruvost 2007b, p. 142). Research also revealed the gendered division of labor that excludes women from the most noble aspects of police work (Boussard et al. 2007; Mainsant 2014). There was research on their interactions with target populations and the handling of so-called "gender" violence (Pérona 2017;

Mainsant 2012), and on the effects of police stereotyping regarding colonized populations (Blanchard 2008, 2012). The feminization of research into the police thus seems to have been, at least in part, a necessary condition for documenting gender norms in the policing world.

In line with these studies, this chapter documents that gender norms play a key role in strategies for establishing one's professional identity in the police force. Additionally, it illustrates that an ethnographic study carried out by a two-person male/female research team, conducted precisely within an institution where "norms, procedures and organizational culture are [particularly] marked by gender bias" (Bereni et al. 2008, p. 140), is able, by observing "gender in action" (Westmarland 2001, p. 12), to make its impact particularly salient. This unique research relationship seems to have facilitated the identification of situations revealing how gender is implicit in police work. This made it possible to then question the inclusion of dominant gender norms on a continuum that shapes police sociability, the relationships between police officers and citizens, and also the gendered aspect of the relationship between the ethnographers and the subjects of their study. Thus, we intend to contribute to showing how, despite the feminization of the institution, the "gender system" (Rubin 1975) constructed within the police institution rests on the reiteration of stereotypes that confirm virile masculinity as the dominant professional reference point.

To do this, we will first consider in parallel the gendered structure of the policing profession and the order of the interactions between police officers and the public. The resistance to the feminization of police units can be linked to police officers' gendered representations of the populations they deal with. We will then attempt to articulate these gender norms and sexual norms, showing how the dominant gender in the institution is rooted in the supremacy of masculine heterosexuality. Finally, we call into question models of "normal sexuality" that are promoted in the police institution in general, and in units in charge of sexual offenses in particular.

Policing: It's a "Man's Job"[2]

> You shouldn't bring too many women in, one or two is enough: it's handy in some cases, like in surveillance operations, a bloke is less careful when he's being followed by a woman, or when some people only want to talk to a woman. But if we got to 50% of women, we'd lose some of our image. I'm aware that's misogynous, but we're not social workers: when we intervene, it's got to be ship-shape and when it's got to hurt, it's got to hurt. If you ask me, we have to keep that, the big cars, the tough guys, all that. In the end it's the arrest we're after, whether it's caught in the act or whatever, so there needs to be that fear; we're hunters, in a way.
>
> (Male officer, crime squad, 3 July 2014)

Most of the men we interviewed in units specializing in the use of force (such as the Brigades Spécialisées de Terrain,[3] the Compagnies de Sécurisation,[4] and the Brigades Anti-Criminalité[5]) were also opposed to the feminization of their units, which was said to threaten the credibility of officers whose professional legitimacy is in large part founded on their ability to use physical force. The gradual entry of women into the police from the mid-1970s (Pruvost 2008) has not, then, succeeded in reversing the tendency for this to be a primarily male world. The modest feminization of the workforce that has occurred has, for the most part, come in units in which the potential use of force is not an issue. In 2017, women made up 79% of the workforce in the administrative branch of the police, 61% in the scientific branch, but only 22% of field operatives. In this last group, women made up 27% of the *commissaires* (or superintendents) and 25% of the commanding officers, but only 20% of police constables (Ministry of the Interior 2017). This discrepancy can be attributed in equal measure to the scarcity of female candidates for constabulary-level entry tests and the higher "entrance fee" demanded by recruiters, who value candidates who can demonstrate their ability to "conform to the rules of a virile model that remains dominant within the institution" (Gautier 2018, p. 164). The proportion of women in riot police units (such as the CRS – Compagnie Républicaine de Sécurité) barely exceeded 3% in 2018, excluding administrative staff.[6]

In the police station where we carried out our research, we also found that it was in the crime-fighting divisions[7] – where the use of physical force is considered most likely and an inherent part of what defines the mission and prestige of the department – that the fewest women were to be found.[8] These division departments are further characterized by their promotion of a hegemonic model of masculinity, one associated with the ability to demonstrate one's physical strength and aggressiveness (Connell 1987). This legitimizes the warrior-male, "rogue-hunter" type as the dominant professional identity.

> You've got to be tough, you can't lose eye contact, or you lose ground. Back when we had a monopoly in the poor neighborhoods, we had to be feared. When we turned up, we wanted the guys to be shitting themselves. You've got to feed that cowboy image a bit, even if it is a bit of a caricature. The tough guys from the crime squad, that has a psychological impact. We play on that; we know we're putting on a front. People on the outside say, "those crime squad cowboys, they're so full of themselves …"
>
> (Male officer, crime squad, 3 July 2014)

It follows that men working within units specialized in the use of force are more inclined to accept women colleagues who opt for a virilization of their behavior – those they can "consider as blokes" because "they've got brawn" (Male officer, crime squad, 2 July 2014). To avoid "blurring genders," however, those women are also expected to uphold certain attributes traditionally associated with femininity. Consequently, women police officers, whose place within the institution depends first and foremost on being appreciated (including in a sexual sense) by their male colleagues, have a delicate part to play in embodying their gender. They must be neither precious nor pretentious nor, worse still, "tomboys" or "lesbians" (Field journal, Compagnie de Sécurisation, December 2013). Above all, "women colleagues," if they want to "make a place for themselves" (in the words of one of our informants), must not introduce any fundamental changes to the gender order prevalent within the police institution. The rare women who have entered units specialized in the use of force therefore put in place strategies to distinguish themselves from their female colleagues, whose absolute physical and psychological alleged incompatibility with police work they reiterate. In so doing, they take up one of the main assertions of the hegemonic masculinity model, legitimizing the exclusion of women from the police profession because of their alleged lack of physical strength which makes them more vulnerable to "danger" (Silvestri 2003, p. 34).

> I don't stand back and wait for the job to get done, I'm more of a leader, I try to be there and keep tempers down. You've got to have a strong personality and be in good shape. If you have to run, you've got to be able to run. I get on really well with the boys, I like that they speak frankly, women are much more underhand ... We can't start patrolling with two girls and one guy, you've got to be reasonable, we don't have the same physical abilities, or even the confidence, sometimes ..."
> (Woman officer, crime squad, 20 November 2013)

To "play their part" in the police and, *a fortiori*, within units specializing in the use of force, women officers themselves actually contribute to reiterating gender stereotypes. By naturalizing differentiated female abilities, they justify the ineluctably subordinate position of women officers in the fight against delinquency and thereby, their own status as "outsiders" in the institution (Brown and Heidensohn 2000). Professional stereotypes associated with the female gender have to do not only with appearance,[9] but also with women's supposed predisposition to take on certain tasks, such as "vice and juveniles" (Field journal, Compagnie de Sécurisation, 16 November 2013), because of the "emotional involvement" they imply (Pierce 2003). Pre-empting this, women police officers generally try to distance themselves from such gendered assignments, to set themselves apart from the "social worker," a figure unanimously rejected within the police institution. In so doing, they reproduce the gender stereotypes at work within the institution. Thus, women confirm this gendered organization of police tasks that, by opposing "social work" and "crime-fighting," contributes to define the codes of the profession and to confine women to the "feminine" construct of the administrative and emotional worlds, while their male counterparts, on the contrary, maneuver in a world of action and danger (Hunt 1990, p. 15).

Sexist Machos: The Targets of Police Action[10]

Recent debates in France around issues of police profiling focused mainly on the racial biases in police checks (DDD 2017; Fassin 2011; Jobard et al. 2012; see also Chapter 13 in this volume). However, statistically, the greatest disproportion is not in the race of those stopped but their gender. At the start of the decade, a survey carried out by questionnaire in Grenoble and Lyons on a sample population of 13,500 adolescents showed that 31% of boys had already been stopped by police, versus only 14% of girls (Astor and Roché 2013, p. 102). Paralleling this, an observational study carried out in several Paris metro and train stations showed that, all other things being equal, a young white woman was between three and seven times less likely (depending on the location) than a young white man to be stopped by police (Jobard et al. 2012). More recently, a questionnaire-based survey confirmed, in 2016, that men were stopped more often than women (23% of men versus 10% of women had been stopped in the previous five years (DDD 2017, p. 12)). While a 2017 study of a representative sample of the French mainland population revealed that 38% of the men surveyed had been stopped once or more in the two years preceding the study, versus only 24% of women.[11] Gender therefore acts as a filter for the populations to be targeted by the police. In turn, this leads to an under-representation of women among those people arrested. Indeed, a quantitative two-year study at a police station in a so-called "sensitive" Parisian *banlieue* showed that women made up little more than 7% of all those brought in to the station (Gauthier 2012, p. 193). These statistics confirm that the police client base, especially in the case of police-initiated contacts with police (i.e. checks and arrests) as opposed to contact initiated by the public (in the form of complaints or calls for help), is predominantly male.

Our ethnographic study reveals certain statistically proven aspects of this gendered selection, while situating it in the broader professional context in which it occurs. Indeed, in "crime-fighting" work, police focus their attention almost exclusively on men, and in particular on the supposedly dangerous figure of the "*banlieue* youth." His supposed "origin," deduced from his physical appearance and compounded by the stigma of residence is a *banlieues*, is associated with an increased likelihood to commit acts of delinquency – and so justifies frequent checks (DDD 2017; Fassin 2011; Jobard et al. 2012; Chapter 13 in this volume). As one officer noted to us, "In some cultures, women don't occupy a very good position and we see those cultures more in the rough neighborhoods than elsewhere" (Woman officer, crime squad, 3 July 2014).

The characteristics assigned to "*banlieue* youths" by police officers are therefore grounded on overlapping stereotypes of class ("rough neighborhood"), race ("in some cultures," generally referring indiscriminately to North Africans and Muslims), and also gender ("women don't occupy a very good position"). Those social and racial attributions are indeed associated with a particular gender identity.

From these stem a discourse indicating that street policing is a "man's job," which rests for the main part on the emphasis put on the supposed machoism of young men from working-class neighborhoods and on the virile confrontation which is consequently inherent in any interaction with them.

RESEARCHER: Are you allowed to frisk men?
POLICEWOMAN: Yes. But my Sarge doesn't want me to, he says it's just not done. But in reality, when we stop and search 15 guys and there are only five of us, I'm not going to stand there looking at them, so I'll frisk one or two. That said, all the North African guys, they really don't like being frisked by a woman, mind. They don't even look you in the eye, they don't want to talk to a woman, most of them, it's pretty crazy, they don't like it one bit … So, in those cases, I'm careful with the North African guys, because it can lead to clashes because they get so pissed off that they get angry and it can cock up the whole operation. So, I avoid frisking men as much as possible, unless it really can't be helped.
(Woman officer, crime squad, 17 April 2004)

In conflictual interactions, sexism can be used as a resource by people that police officers try to submit to forced procedures, such as ID checks, searches, and frisks. This in-situ questioning of the legitimacy of woman police officers by their clients, and the fact that their presence alone can be a hindrance to police imposing their authority, leads to a weakening of their position relative to their male colleagues while also preventing them from carrying out certain tasks which are particularly common in crime-fighting units (such as a frisk or an ID check). These observations illustrate how the marginalization of women in the policing world and in the street culture of the working-class neighborhoods (Mohammed 2009) mirrors the virile constructs inherent to both those spaces. The glorification of the "real power struggle with the guys in the rough neighborhoods" (Male officer, Compagnie de Sécurisation, 16 November 2013) thus leads officers to favor male targets. Indeed, the inability to use (or threaten to use) force on "girls" seems to rob crime squads of one of their main status symbols:

RESEARCHER: Is it unthinkable for a male officer to slap a girl? Policeman: Oh, yeah, utterly unthinkable. A female colleague can get physical, get close up. With blokes, if I get up close, I'm going to follow through and I might slap him if needs be, whereas, with a girl, if I move in on her … Well, it's not to back right off again!
(Interview, male officer, crime squad, 2 July 2014)

In other words, the lesser legitimacy of women conducting certain police jobs, particularly in units emphasizing the use of force, is explained not so much by the norms, values, or professional practices of those units. Rather, it is occasioned by the personal characteristics not only of the women themselves, but also of the targets of police action. These are the "sexist machos" who "naturally" offer less resistance to male officers.

Sexuality as the Organizing Principle for Gender Order

Our focus on the gendered structure of policing led us also to note the importance of norms associated with sexuality in the construction of the gender identities prevailing in the institution. First, while the supremacy of heterosexuality contributes to maintaining gender order in relationships between colleagues, the growing visibility of homosexuality among personnel contributes, at least in part, to eroding that order. Second, the analysis of police tasks specifically dedicated to policing sexual offences at first also seems to lead to the observation that gender norms hinging on the virile male stereotype have been partially challenged. Nevertheless, it ultimately confirms the role of sexuality as one of the main instruments for reaffirming a hegemonic heterosexual masculinity within the police institution.

Hierarchies of Intimacy in Police Sociability

The preservation of a gender order within policing rests not only on the perpetuation of a masculine identity which glorifies physical strength, but also on a hierarchy of sexes and sexualities that is reflected in the many references to officers' marital relations. Jokes are often made about male officers living with a partner, and they tend to highlight the incompatibility between the professional identity and job demands of being a police officer and any kind of commitment to domestic life. Wives or partners are represented as posing a threat to the officer's masculinity, through their attempts to drag him to into home and family:

> You've been bloody had, you didn't want to move in, you moved in, you didn't want to buy the flat, you bought the flat, you didn't want the civil partnership, you got the civil partnership, you don't want kids … just you wait and see, you'll be done for!
> (Field journal, crime squad, 4 July 2013)

Such reminders of gender order, which make the world of policing an almost perfect illustration of hegemonic masculinity (Fielding 1994), also reaffirm differentiated gender roles. They imply, in a very traditional sense, the need for men to demonstrate their "heterosexual desire" and for women, their "sexual reserve" (Clair 2013, p. 113).

RESEARCHER: There's a lot of talk about "rubbing elbows" with friends in other divisions to exchange info. Do you have your own little network of colleagues, too?

POLICEWOMAN: No, no. I value my colleagues in the department, but I avoid being too friendly, on the other hand, precisely because I'm a woman and there's a certain distance that I want to keep. I'm not going to go and rub elbows elsewhere to get into such-and-such a department ... I wouldn't want people thinking that I'm using my charms for any network. I wouldn't want it to be seen as seduction, so I just avoid it. I am actually super reserved as far as that goes.

(Interview, woman police officer, Police rescue, 22 May 2013)

Networking among staff is frequently described as essential for the exchange of information related to investigations, as well as for promotion to more highly valued divisions (Darley and Gauthier 2014; Mainsant 2014). But we can see here that gender, as one aspect of organizational structure, shapes officers' experience by "imposing different normative expectations for male and female workers" (Pierce 2003, p. 57) and, more importantly, by "setting limits on women's behavior" (Pierce 2003, p. 66). These calls to order are all the more significant because they occur in a professional context which is already marked by the over-sexualization of sociability, where sexual or sexist jokes and bragging about one's (hetero)sexual performance are considered essential attributes for displaying police masculinity. Thus, sexuality appears to continue to function within the police institution as an organizing principle of a heterosexual hierarchy, one that "institutes what is normal [and] classifies social actors", but also "disqualifies ... deviants" (Clair 2016, p. 53).

One might suppose that the dominance of heterosexuality in police sociability and in the definition of police target groups would begin to wear thin in the contemporary context, which is one of the "softening of social and legal obligations having long weighed on homosexual minorities" (Giraud 2016). Indeed, since homosexuality was decriminalized in the early 1980s, homosexuals are no longer targeted groups (Gauthier and Schlagdenhauffen 2019a; Jaouen 2017; Tamagne 2000). The mobilization of the gay community and the introduction of anti-discrimination legislation have contributed to transforming the role of the police and the law regarding the LGBTQ population. Opposition to homosexuality has gradually given way to rejection of homophobic discrimination and violence. In parallel, there has been a mobilization of LGBTQ police officers since the 2000s, in line with what can be seen in US- and UK-based organizations. This gives visibility to gay, lesbian, bi- and transsexual police officers, and allows them to denounce homophobia in their profession and claim the same rights as their heterosexual colleagues. The sustained effects of these changes on the "heterosexual hierarchy" are not yet clear. However, the first results of investigative interviews carried out between 2015 and 2019 with police officers describing themselves as gay, lesbian, or bisexual, indicate that conforming to heterosexual norms continues to be a condition for establishing a legitimate professional identity (Gauthier and Schlagdenhauffen 2019b).

Policing Sexual Offenses: A Gendered Job

Sexuality appears to be one of the main instruments confirming hegemonic heterosexual masculinity within the police institution. Consequently, it is interesting to test these observations within divisions dedicated to policing matters related to sexuality. These include the Brigade des mœurs (or Vice Squad) and the Brigade des mineurs (or Juvenile Crime Squad), units that deal with sexual violence against adults and young people.[12] Indeed, sexual norms within divisions whose core work involves the handling of sexual offences do seem to differ from those prevailing within policing generally. The *mœurs* and *mineurs* units provide valuable insights in this respect. Use of force by members of these units is almost nonexistent, and the typical street policing identity – defined by the unspoken link between "physical strength" and "being male" – is not the prevalent model.

> I'm more intellectual than manual, and I prefer to work in an office than be chasing people around. I only go to the firing range because I have to, it's not my cup of tea ... In here, you need to have a more psychological approach to people.
> (Male officer, Brigade des mœurs, 12 February 2014)

The *mœurs* and *mineurs* units occupy a unique position in the hierarchy of police jobs. Officers from other teams often spontaneously bring up the work carried out by those police officers as being poles apart from their own. They can't imagine working there because of the "special nature" of the matters these units handle. They involve intimacy and sex, making it difficult to maintain the crucial divide between the private and the professional spheres. Although sex and intimacy are omnipresent in the everyday relations between officers – particularly in those units specializing in the use of force – they are only mentioned in jest and contribute to asserting officers' virile masculinity. For the officers who work in the *mœurs* and *mineurs* units, on the contrary, it is precisely the special nature of their work that legitimizes them and provides a space to assert unique professional skills such as listening and empathy with victims. Yet these are precisely the skills which are discredited in most other divisions, particularly because they provide no scope for the display of masculinity and are therefore relegated to the female end of policing activity.

> You won't find more humane people than the officers in this team ... They know how to listen, how to change their tone of voice ... It's one of those jobs where psychology is really important.
> (Deputy chief sergeant, Brigade des mœurs, 18 July 2013)

This quote illustrates how gender norms guiding street policing, as described earlier, are set aside or even challenged by the teams who specialize in the handling of sexual offenses. Indeed, in those teams, social and psychological skills (in particular with regard to the "rape victim," an archetypal figure regularly mentioned by officers of all divisions) are considered part of their professional know-how, one that transcends gender roles. It follows that the positions occupied by victims and perpetrators in the work culture are significantly different from those held by so-called "crime-fighting" teams. While the latter focus on the "perpetrator," actual or alleged, the former defines the usefulness of their mission by the support they provide to victims. In their work, quality listening, psychological support, and respect for due process are as important as obtaining criminal sanctions for the perpetrator.

> When we work on real cases, we are really useful to victims and it's so nice when you get a call, months after a case, from parents or children who call to say thank you, or who send a card. It's really important, that feeling that you're helping people to rebuild their lives, it's truly satisfying.
> (Male officer, Brigade des mœurs, 02 July 2014)

In other words, emotions and feelings that are shunned in other divisions, are elevated to the rank of policing skills by the officers in these units. This is true not only in their relations with victims, but also in their interactions with suspects.[13] Their relations with suspects do not revolve around the virile confrontations that are so dear to street policing units. Rather, they focus on a form of emotional work centered on empathy. Units handling sexual violence combine concern for victims and the importance of women, which, in street policing, are characteristically side-lined. However, this amounts to reproducing rather than challenging gender stereotypes that differentiate and essentialize "masculinity" and "femininity." This was confirmed by observations of the daily activities of those units. We saw in interviews with male suspects in sexual offence cases the prevalence of moral norms rooted in a heteronormative gender order. This called for responses by officers who see themselves tasked with the "educational correction" of suspects.

> You know what, when you get out of here, you're going to remember my face and you're going to do me a favor, when you next meet a girl who's coming onto you, you're going to be a man. You've got to be smart enough to know if she wants it or not. It doesn't mean she's going to give you a blowjob after ten minutes.
> (Male officer interviewing a 14-year-old suspected of sexual assault on a 17-year-old minor, Brigade des mineurs, 11 February 2014)

Though the aim is to impart in "sexual deviants" values that place respect for women at the heart of the educational process, the message underlying these warnings reaffirms a differentiated attitude of men and women toward sexuality. It is women's presumed taste for seduction as well as their characteristic inconsistency that makes it difficult for men to control their sexual desires:

> That's what girls are like. They'll say yes five times and no the sixth, you've just got to know how to listen ...
> (Debriefing after questioning, Brigade des mineurs, 11 February 2014)

Conclusion

This ethnographic study by a two-person male/female team heavily underscores the prevalence of gender norms in professional hierarchies. These are apparent in subordinate relationships within the institution, in the organization of professional skills, and as a principle for ranking target populations. Despite the historic process of the institution's feminization, gender dictates and taboos remain strongly rooted in policing. Women maneuver in an institution where the dominant gender identity is that of the virile male. As illustrated by examples of the teams specialized in crime-fighting and in sexual offences, this gendered norm can fluctuate within the institution. Gender, nevertheless, acts as an organizing principle which contributes to the creation of hierarchies inside the policing profession, and to their selection of suspects and assignments (Mainsant 2012). From the broader perspective of public prosecution, it would seem that this "sexually differentiated nature of the handling of illegal activities" (Cardi 2009, p. 1) by the policing institution could shed light on other fields of study, such as the under-representation of women in the criminal justice system more generally (Vuattoux 2014). Most importantly, the forms of masculinity conveyed by the institution and the virile reputation of the policing profession could be studied in light of the difficulty the French police are having in evolving beyond their basic function of repression. The relatively recent incursion of French social scientists into the study of the gendered realities of police work thus lays the groundwork for future research. This research should further question the performative effects of gendered attributions, in parallel with other forms of hierarchy – particularly sexual, social, and ethno-racial – that shape both police handling of the public and the professional codes in force within the organization.

Notes

1 This status can nevertheless be questioned, as we see in a shocking scene where an investigator asks a young woman to apologise to her alleged rapist for the trouble she caused in reporting him.
2 Interview, male officer, Compagnie de sécurisation, 16 November 2013.
3 In 2010, the Brigades Spécialisées de Terrain (BST) took the place of the Unités territoriales de quartier (Uteq) or Neighbourhood Territorial Units, which were created in 2008. As of 2012, they were sent specifically into the *zones de sécurité*

prioritaires, or high priority security areas, created under the socialist government in neighborhoods said to be sensitive. See Darley and Gauthier (2018).
4 The Compagnies de sécurisation (CS), created in 2003, are specialized urban crime-fighting units. Reintroduced in 2008 in order to strengthen security in the capital and in the sensitive neighborhoods, their remit is to intervene firstly in high-risk events or instances of urban violence.
5 The Brigades Anti-Criminalité (BAC) first appeared in the early 1970s in Paris, before spreading to other medium and large towns in the 1990s. Crime squad officers usually operate in plain clothes, in unmarked vehicles and specialize in high-risk operations in urban areas, in particular in those neighborhoods said to be "sensitive" because of the concentration of delinquent behavior there. See Fassin (2011).
6 Ministry of the Interior 2017. This report compares professional equality between men and women.
7 These are the Brigade anti-criminalité (BAC), Brigade spécialisée de terrain (BST), and Compagnie de sécurisation (CS).
8 At the time of this study of the Compagnies de Sécurisation, women accounted for three out of 50 officers, in the crime squad two out of 42, and in the BST three out of 30.
9 Quite significantly, the women we interviewed within departments specialised in the use of force all presented different characteristics typically associated with femininity (long hair, make-up, jewellery).
10 Field journal, Compagnie de Sécurisation.
11 ELIPSS/PREFACE survey carried out in 2017 on a sample of 2,900 people in mainland France, within the framework of the PROFET ("Ordinary Practices and Representations in the Face of the State") program, funded by the national research agency and coordinated by Alexis Spire (CNRS-IRIS).
12 The Brigade des mineurs also handles sexual assaults on adults who were minors at the time of the assault.
13 A recent study shows that police empathy can vary depending on the status of the victims, however; see Pérona (2017).

References

Acker, J. 1990. Hierarchies, jobs, bodies: A theory of gendered organizations. *Gender and Society* 4: 139–158.
Astor, S., and Roché, S. 2013. *Enquête 'POLIS-autorité' Premiers résultats: Rapport à l'attention de l'Éducation Nationale.* Grenoble: PACTE – Laboratoire de sciences sociales.
Bereni, L., Chauvin, S., Jaunait, A., and Revillard, A. 2008. *Introduction aux études sur le genre.* Bruxelles: De Boeck.
Bereni, L., and Jacquemart, A. 2018. Diriger comme un homme moderne: Les élites masculines de l'administration française face à la norme d'égalité des sexes. *Actes de la recherche en sciences sociales* 223: 72–87.
Blanchard, E. 2008. Le mauvais genre des Algériens: des hommes sans femme face au virilisme policier dans le Paris d'après-guerre. *Clio: histoire, femmes et sociétés* 27: 209–224.
Blanchard, E. 2012. Des Algériens dans le 'Paris Gay': Frontières raciales et sexualités entre hommes sous le regard policier. Pp. 157–174 in P. Rygiel (Dir.) *Politique et administration du genre en migration. Mondes Atlantiques, XIXe-XXe siècles.* Paris: AHI/Publibook.
Boussard, V., Loriol, M., and Caroly, S. 2007. Une féminisation sur fonds de segmentation professionnelle genrée: le cas des policières en commissariat. *Sociologies pratiques* 1: 75–88.

Brown, J. 2007. From cult of masculinity to smart macho: Gender perspectives on police occupational culture. *Sociology of Crime Law and Deviance* 8: 205–226.
Brown, J., and Heidensohn, F. 2000. *Gender and policing: Comparative perspectives*. Basingstoke: Macmillan.
Burke, M. 1993. *Coming out of the blue: British police officers talk about their lives in "the job" as lesbians, gays and bisexuals*. New York: Cassell Publishing.
Cardi, C. 2009. Le féminin maternel ou la question du traitement pénal des femmes. *Pouvoirs* 1: 75–86.
Clair, I. 2013. Pourquoi penser la sexualité pour penser le genre en sociologie? Retour sur quarante ans de réticences. *Cahiers du Genre* 1: 93–120.
Clair, I. 2016. La sexualité dans la relation d'enquête: Décryptage d'un tabou méthodologique. *Revue française de sociologie* 57: 45–70.
Connell, R.W. 1987. *Gender and power: Society, the person, and sexual politics*. Stanford: Stanford University Press.
Darley, M., and Gauthier, J. 2014. Une virilité interpellée? En quête de genre au commissariat. *Genèses* 4: 67–86.
Darley, M., and Gauthier, J. 2018. Le travail policier face à la réforme: Une ethnographie de la mise en œuvre des 'Zones de Sécurité Prioritaires'. *Politix* 4: 59–84.
Défenseur des droits. 2017. *Enquête sur l'accès aux droits. Volume 1–Relations police/populations: le cas des contrôles d'identité*. Paris: Défenseur des droits. www.defenseurdesdroits.fr/sites/default/files/atoms/files/enquete-relations-police-population-final2-11012017.pdf
Fassin, D. 2002. L'invention française de la discrimination. *Revue française de science politique* 52: 403–423.
Fassin, D. 2011. *La force de l'ordre: Une anthropologie de la police des quartiers*. Paris: Seuil.
Fielding, N. 1994. Cop canteen culture. Pp. 46–63 in T. Newburn and E. Stanko (Eds.) *Just boys doing the business: Men, masculinity and crime*. London: Routledge.
Gauthier, J. 2012. *Origines contrôlées: La police à l'épreuve de la question minoritaire à Paris et à Berlin*. Thèse de sociologie à l'Université de Versailles-Saint-Quentin-en-Yvelines.
Gauthier, J., and Schlagdenhauffen, R. 2019a. Les sexualités 'contre-nature' face à la justice pénale: Une analyse des condamnations pour 'homosexualité' en France (1945–1982). *Déviance et société* 43: 421–459.
Gauthier, J., and Schlagdenhauffen, R. 2019b. Facing normative heterosexuality: The case of LGBT police officers in France. Paper presented at the international conference *Police, justice et homosexualités. Regards sociologiques, historiques et comparatifs*. Paris: Ecole des Hautes Etudes en Sciences Sociales.
Gautier, F. 2018. Une 'résistible' féminisation? Le recrutement des gardiennes de la paix. *Travail, genre et sociétés* 1: 159–173.
Giraud, C. 2016. La vie homosexuelle à l'écart de la visibilité urbaine. Ethnographie d'une minorité sexuelle masculine dans la Drôme. *Tracés: Revue de Sciences Humaines* 30: 79–102.
Guenot, M. 2018. *Le crime ne paie pas: Les Groupes d'intervention Régionaux de la Police judiciaire. Sociologie politique de la construction d'une institution au succès improbable*. Paris: Thèse de doctorat, Université Paris 8.
Heidensohn, F. 1992. *Women in control? The role of women in law enforcement*. Oxford: Oxford University Press.

Heidensohn, F. 2008. Gender and policing. Pp. 642–665 in T. Newburn (Ed.) *Handbook of policing*. Cullompton: Willan.

Hunt, J. 1990. The logic of sexism among police. *Women & Criminal Justice* 1: 3–30.

Jaouen, R. 2017. *L'inspecteur et l'inverti: La police face aux sexualités masculines à Paris 1919–1940*. Rennes: Presses Universitaires de Rennes.

Jobard, F., and de Maillard, J. 2015. *Sociologie de la police: Politiques, organisations, réformes*. Paris: Armand Colin.

Jobard, F., Lévy, R., Lamberth, J., and Névanen, S. 2012. Mesurer les discriminations selon l'apparence: Une analyse des contrôles d'identité à Paris. *Population* 67: 423–451.

Le Feuvre, N., Bataille, P., and Morend, L. 2013. La visibilité du genre dans des revues de sociologie du travail: Comparaisons France et Grande-Bretagne (1987–2012). *Cahiers du Genre* 1: 121–150.

Lemaire, É. 2008. Spécialisation et distinction dans un commissariat de police: Ethnographie d'une institution segmentaire. *Sociétés contemporaines* 72: 59–79.

Mainsant, G. 2008. L'Etat en action: classements et hiérarchies dans les investigations policières en matière de proxénétisme. *Sociétés contemporaines* 4: 37–57.

Mainsant, G. 2012. *L'État et les illégalismes sexuels. Ethnographie et sociohistoire du contrôle policier de la prostitution à Paris*. Paris: Thèse de doctorat, Ecole des Hautes Etudes en Sciences Sociales.

Mainsant, G. 2014. Comment la 'Mondaine' construit-elle ses populations cibles? Le genre des pratiques policières et la gestion des illégalismes sexuels. *Genèses* 4: 8–25.

Marry, C., Bereni, L., Jacquemart, A., Pochic, S., and Revillard, A. 2017. *Le plafond de verre et l'État. La construction des inégalités de genre dans la fonction publique*. Paris: Armand Colin.

Ministère de l'Intérieur. 2017. *Bilan social 2017: Rapport de situation comparée relatif à l'égalité professionnelle entre les femmes et les hommes*. Paris: Ministère de l'Intérieur.

Mohammed, M. 2009. Les affrontements entre bandes : virilité, honneur et réputation. *Déviance et Société* 33: 173–204.

Morelle, M. 2017. La fabrique de territoires policiers: Des pratiques professionnelles en débat dans une commune francilienne. *Droit et Société* 3: 469–484.

Pérona, O. 2017. La difficile mise en œuvre d'une politique du genre par l'institution policière: le cas des viols conjugaux. *Champ pénal/Penal field* 14. [https://journals.openedition.org/champpenal/9546]

Pierce, J. L. 2003. Les émotions au travail: le cas des assistantes juridiques. *Travailler* 1: 51–72.

Proteau, L., and Pruvost, G. 2008. Se distinguer dans les métiers d'ordre (armée, police, prison, sécurité privée). *Sociétés contemporaines* 4: 7–13.

Pruvost, G. 2007a. *Profession: policier, Sexe: féminin*. Paris: Maison des Sciences de l'Homme.

Pruvost, G. 2007b. Enquêter sur les policiers: Entre devoir de réserve, héroïsation et accès au monde privé. *Terrain* 48: 130–148.

Pruvost, G. 2008. *De la 'sergote' à la femme flic: Une autre histoire de l'institution policière, 1935-2005*. Paris: La Découverte.

Reiner, R. 2000. *The politics of police*. Oxford: Oxford University Press.

Rubin, G. 1975. The traffic in women: Notes on the "political economy" of sex. Pp. 157–210 in R. Reiter (Ed.) *Toward an anthropology of women*. New York: Monthly Review Press.

Silvestri, M. 2003. *Women in charge: Policing, gender and leadership*. Cullompton: Willan Publishing.
Tamagne, F. 2000. *Histoire de l'homosexualité en Europe: Berlin, Londres, Paris*. Paris: Seuil.
Vuattoux, A. 2014. Adolescents, adolescentes face à la justice pénale. *Genèses* 4: 47–66.
Waddington, P. A. 1999. Police (canteen) sub-culture: An appreciation. *British Journal of Criminology* 39: 287–309.
Westmarland, L. 2001. *Gender and policing*. Cullompton: Willan Publishing.

Chapter 20

The Police and Sexual Violence

Océane Perona

Feminists in France have been denoucing police officers' behavior towards victims of sexual violence since the 1970s (Mossuz-Lavau 2002). Police were accused of trying to dissuade women from filing complaints, of showing hostility towards, them and of systematically questioning their testimony. Studies elsewhere find that police officers are more or less inclined to take charge of female complainants, depending on their degree of specialization in sexual offences, and that they see certain cases of rape as a consequence of victims' recklessness (Smeets 2012). Police officers prioritize rape victims according to the victim's proximity to their attacker (Maier 2014). They are likely to adopt a role as guarantors of moral order in dealing with complainants and defendants (De Man and Van Praet 2012). Research in the social psychology and criminology fields explains the treatment of rape by the judicial system through the existence of gender stereotypes among those actors. They identify "rape myths" that hinder the processing of cases (Lonsway and Fitzgerald 1994). The term "myth" refers to the fact that common representations of rape do not correspond to the reality of this form of violence.

Some of these myths relate to rape victims, who may be liars, women with bad reputations because of their sexual behavior, or women who may bear responsibility for their own victimization (Stewart et al. 1996). On the latter point, the first criminological research on rape in the 1960s made it a crime "precipitated by the victim" and analyzed aggression as the product of both the victim's and the aggressor's behavior (Amir 1967). Other myths concern patterns of sexual violence, which are allegedly committed by a man unknown to the victim in the public space, with great brutality, accompanied by physical resistance on the part of the victim, leaving her physically injured. This scenario is described as "real rape" in the literature (Estrich 1987). This work underlines that the proximity of the aggression to this scenario favors both the denunciation of the case to the police services (Du Mont et al. 2003), the favorable reception of the complainants by the police (Sleath and Bull 2017) and the defandant's conviction by the courts (Chennells 2009). Victims assaulted by former companions, those who flirted with the defendant before the assault, as well as those who were drunk, are blamed for their behavior and receive little sympathy (Temkin and Krahé 2008).

Other studies place the response to rape by different professionals in the context of the organizations to which they belong. This is the perspective adopted by Patricia Yancey-Martin (Yancey-Martin 2005). She offers an analysis of the care of rape victims in the United States. According to Yancey-Martin, the judicial treatment of victims has changed little since the 1970s for organizational rather than cognitive reasons. Her analysis pays attention to the relationships between the different institutions dealing with victims: Rape crisis centers, the police, the prosecutor's office, and the hospitals that conduct the complainants' forensic examinations. She argues that the mistreatment of victims is the product of the constraints of organizations, despite the empathy that workers may individually feel for complainants. For example, if police officers are particularly inquisitive when questioning complainants, it is first and foremost because they are required to investigate both the prosecution and the defence. They must demonstrate that the story is true and that the rape is characterized as such. Such a perspective is more organizational than structural. It leads the author not to interpret the harshness of professionals towards complainants as a sign of hostility or suspicion towards women reporting rape.

These studies allow us to question police work on sexual violence in the French context. From Yancey-Martin's perspective (2005), we assume that it is not reducible to the sexism of the actors but that it is shaped by professional logics specific to the police field, themselves more or less permeable to gender representations. The sociology of police work will then be brought into dialog with the work on the myths of rape. More specifically, we will focus on the hierarchies that police officers operate between cases, which seem to reveal the logic of internal valuation of the work of investigators and allow us to nuance the cognitive hypothesis of sexism among legal professionals. Several studies conducted within different police services point out that official hierarchies and organizational charts are far from being the only criterion for distinction within the police institution. They highlight the importance of elements such as targeted populations (Mainsant 2008); the type of offences prosecuted (Lemaire 2008) or activities carried out behind the scenes (Pruvost 2008b); and in prestige rankings between actors in the different segments (Bucher and Strauss 1961) of the police institution. Other recent studies have shown that "real police work" is assessed according to whether or not it allows actors to stage manly qualities valued in the institution, such as physical strength or courage in the face of male and dangerous target populations (Barbier 2016; Darley and Gauthier 2014). But this logic of valuing cases according to the possibility that they give police officers the opportunity to demonstrate their virile qualities does not work when we are interested in actors who perform office work and investigate sexual offences.

In investigations dealing with sexual violence against adults or minors, the "value" of cases for officers is determined by the skill they require (which is determined by the complexity of the investigation), by characteristics of suspects (their dangerousness), and by the stigma attached to different kinds of sexual offences by society (Monjardet 2002). In France, criticism of how the public is received by police station staff is long-standing. Since the 1970s, police have recognized that citizens are not always treated well when they arrive (Pruvost 2008a). Since the 1980s, there has been political support for improving the treatment of victims through the criminal justice system. This desire is reflected, among other things, in the creation of victim support offices in 1982, attached to the Ministry of Justice. The law of 15 June 2000 requires police and *gendarmerie* services to consider all complaints that they receive. This law also allows victims to file complaints throughout the country. In 2003, the police and *gendarmerie* services adopted a public reception charter. Since 2003, police and *gendarmerie* services have been incorporating social workers, in order to improve how citizens are received. This was extended to all areas of the country in 2006. The presence of psychologists in police stations has been common since 2011.

These measures are not specific to the reception of victims of sexual violence. Since the late 1980s, various public reports regarding violence against women have mentioned the need to train police officers and improve the reception of victims, without this being reflected in the systematic creation of units dedicated to the treatment of sexual offences by the police. Finally, there are local initiatives to improve the reception of victims. In Paris, the commission to combat violence against women in the prefecture of the department has set up a sub-commission dedicated to the reception of rape victims in police stations. This commission brings together police officers, magistrates, doctors, and victim support associations. It is chaired by the commissioner who heads Judicial Police District A.

This chapter sets out the criteria for how officers classify violence and prioritize different cases, in order to distinguish more broadly between what is considered to be "real work" and "dirty work" in sexual violence investigations (Hughes 1962, p. 5). This will clarify the features that give cases high value in the eyes of investigators and will highlight tensions that may emerge between many of the sexual violence cases that are handled by officers and violence as they would ideally construct it. This will help explain the character of the sexual violence investigations that they routinely conduct.

How Investigations Proceed

In France, the investigative work is carried out by police and judicial police officers. Judicial police officers are police officers or *gendarmes* who have passed an examination giving them a special qualification. They have extensive powers to conduct their own investigations. They can take a suspect into custody or conduct searches. Judicial police officers are *police nationale* or *gendarmes* who are empowered to record offences and collect evidence for investigations. The Code of Criminal Procedure (Code de procédure pénale) provides that officers and agents of the judicial police are responsible for "recording offences under criminal law, gathering evidence and seeking the perpetrators" (Code of Criminal Procedure, article 14 et seq.). They investigate under the control, supervision, and direction of the public prosecutor. They are in contact daily with magistrates of the public prosecutor's office (*parquetiers*). Neither the commissioners nor the officers (*lieutenant, capitaine, major*) conduct investigations. The *gardiens de la paix* and *gradés* (*brigadier-chef* and *brigadier-major*) conduct investigations and work in plainclothes. The investigation work may be carried out by specialized units within the Departmental Public Security Directorates (Direction départementale de la sécurité publique) or by specialized units within the Central Directorate of the Judicial Police (Direction centrale de la police judiciaire). In the case of sexual violence, investigations may be entrusted to the minors squads (*brigades des mineurs*) of the Departmental Public Security Departments when the victim is under 18 years of age and to the *brigades des mœurs* (vice squads) of these same departments when the victim is an adult. In Paris, it is the criminal affairs groups (named crime groups) of the Local Direction of Judicial Police of the Police Prefecture of Paris (Direction régionale de la police judiciare de la préfecture de police de Paris) that conduct investigations on the rape and sexual assault of adult victims.

These are considered elite services, not open to young police officers as they graduate from the police academy. The officers who work in these units are in plainclothes, unlike their colleagues in non-specialized services in local commissariats. When sexual violence is reported to law enforcement institutions, investigations are carried out as follows. When the attacks have been reported to the police or *gendarmerie* (for rural territories), they notify a magistrate of the public prosecutor's office, who will oversee the conduct of the investigation. The magistrate then refers the matter to the competent police department for investigation. Throughout the investigation, police officers report the results of their investigations to the prosecutor. At the end of this investigation phase, the police officers forward to the magistrate the file consisting of a set of disparate documents (minutes, medical certificates, photographs, psychological reports, results of telephone analyses, emails, etc.). The latter may then decide to prosecute or close the case.

This Research

The data for this chapter were collected as part of doctoral thesis research in political science. They come from a ten-month ethnography in a Parisian judicial police service and 20 interviews with investigators from three minors squads. The ethnography was combined with the creation of a database of 477 cases processed by the Parisian judicial police service between 2011 and 2014.

Within the Directorate of the Judicial Police of the Paris Police Prefecture, it is the units in charge of criminal offences that deal with sexual violence on adults. The unit consists of two units, nicknamed "crime groups" by investigators. Each is headed by a commander, supported by an assistant with the rank of captain. The two crime groups each have five investigators from the supervisory and enforcement corps. In total, the department has ten investigators and four officers. Most police officers are between 35 and 50 years of age, although one was 28 years old. All had at least five years' experience in the force when they had joined their crime group. The gender distribution of the workforce was highly unbalanced: of the 14 staff members in the service, only two were women. All investigators were white. The composition of the service is thus relatively homogeneous in terms of age, gender, family situation, and ethno-racial affiliation. In addition to this ethnography in a unit specialized in sexual violence against adults, I conducted 20 interviews with police officers from three minors squads. The interviews were always conducted in the offices of the agents. As with the officers of the judicial police, the investigators of the minors squads were between 30 and 50 years old. However, in contrast to the crime groups of the judicial police, half of the staff were women.

All the police officers interviewed, as well as the persons subject to investigation, were anonymized with fictitious first names. In addition, identifyers for the reported cases examined here were changed in order to guarantee the confidentiality of litigants (Béliard and Eideliman 2008).

Based on these data, this chapter highlights three different rationales for police action in cases of sexual violence. We will first look at factors involved in the degree of police interest in an investigation, and then move to their assessment of the dangerousness of suspects. Here they focus on three issues: maintenance of public order, protection against further violence, and the defense of children and families. Finally, we examine the impact of another decisive factor: how the case will be received by the judicial system.

Complex Cases and Mysteries are Valued

> So, we've already had an investigation work done, it didn't fall into our lap. It required findings, sampling, cross-checking. Police work, you know, investigative work, intellectual work. Which made it possible to identify, question the individual, perhaps to obtain evidence. That's a great case. A big deal is not the guy who's going to kill someone on the street and leave his ID card. It's not a big case. Anyway, as a policeman, it's not "ah, I'm going to kill her," he drops his ID card, with the victim's blood on it, to prove that it's the right one, with his

DNA, to prove that it's the right one. No, that's not a good case, that's just a case. The big case is [when you] work.

(Paul B., 51 years old, group leader, minors squad)

Paul B.'s comments clarify the criteria that contribute to the investment of more investigative effort by police officers in the studied services. Highly valued cases are those that allow investigators to prove their skill by resolving an enigma, that of the identity of the perpetrator, and to attribute responsibility for the act to the perpetrator based on evidence that they uncover. It is not so much a confrontation with physical danger as their uncovering a *mystery* that characterizes a highly valued case. In investigative services, "good cases" are those in which police officers can demonstrate their investigative skills, their innovative spirit, their intuition, and their ability to deduce solid conclusions (Dedieu 2010). The same is true for the investigation services that are higher in the prestige hierarchy within the institution: it is the performance of the police officers that determines the value of investigations. The case of Souleymane D., that Victor L. (34 years old, investigator, crime group) and Joël C. (50 years old, group leader, crime group) describe as "the biggest case in the group's history," is exemplary of the way investigations are valued according to the performance of investigators.

The case began with the attack in Paris on a young white woman with ginger hair and green eyes by a black man who forced her to withdraw money from an ATM by threatening her. He then forced her to return to her apartment, where he seized a kitchen knife with which he stabbed her 15 times before raping her. She managed to alert the paramedics before she fainted. The matter was referred to the Direction de la police judiciaire de la préfecture de police de Paris. Three days later, another very similar young white woman was raped in Paris in her room by a man wearing a sweater over his face. Finally, five days after the first attack, a 15-year-old white girl was raped in Foresty, in her room, by a black man who stabbed her four times with a boxcutter. Police connected the cases because of the physical similarity of the victims and the perpetrator's *modus operandi*. The public prosecutor entrusted them with the Foresty investigation because of similarities with the Parisian case.

The police first attempted to identify the assailant through the distribution of a sketch by one of the victims, then decided to search for him in Foresty. There, they contacted the officers at the police station, explaining that they were looking for a man who was probably from Mali. Indeed, one of the victims reported that her attacker had scarifications on his temples, identified by the police as characteristic of Fulanis. Foresty police officers told them that many African immigrants work in the bus transport company. Victor L. and Michel D., another investigator from "Crim'2," found the Foresty transport company manager, who explaind that his employees will not confide in him, but that he employs a mediator as a link with the African community who would be able to assist them. However, the police officers did not obtain any information from the mediator and returned to Paris empty-handed. But two days after their visit to Foresty, the judicial police and the Foresty police station received an anonymous letter stating that the individual they were looking for was named Souleymane D. and that he had left France for the Netherlands. A search of the files revealed to Victor L. and Michel D. that Souleymane D. was implicated when he was a minor in 1997 for stabbing and raping a 17-year-old white girl with ginger with green eyes. But the investigators wanted to be sure that their suspect and Souleymane D. were one and the same person and for that, they needed to compare the DNA found on the complainants to that of Souleymane D. Victor L. had the idea of consulting the archives of the 1997 proceedings, in the hope of recovering contact DNA from sealed objects or from a report. It is possible to retrieve an individual's DNA from an object they have touched. Michel D. then proposed to send the files containing Souleymane D.'s fingerprints for analysis, arguing that only the respondent's DNA was likely to appear at the precise location where the fingerprints were taken. The comparison of the two DNAs revealed that Souleymane D.'s DNA was identical to the DNA that was recovered as evidence, thanks to the traces of semen left by the aggressor. Souleymane D. was finally arrested by the Dutch police for violent robbery and incarcerated in the Netherlands before being extradited to France to be directly heard by an investigating judge. Following this case, Michel D. received a letter of congratulations from his superiors for thinking of consulting fingerprints in the old file.

The police account of the Souleymane D. case places great emphasis on the intellectual skills of the investigators and on their understanding of the crossovers and connections between elements of theis cases. It favors the technical dimension of the work, to the detriment of relationships with the population (Mucchielli 2006). The principle of action in criminal investigations remains individual prowess (Monjardet 2002), which is confirmed by the congratulatory letter received by Michel D. Yet it was because of an anonymous informant that they initially obtained the identity of the suspect, as well as his location. It was the contact with Foresty's mediator that opened up the case, not the discovery of DNA in an old file.

It should be noted that in specialized sexual violence investigations, most of the comments emphasizing the technical aspect of investigations were made by male police officers. On this point, it is interesting to draw a parallel with the work on the entry of men into predominantly female professions (Angeloff and Arborio 2002). The sociology of the police has indeed shown that welcoming victims (Mainsant 2014) and carrying out emotional work (Hochschild 2003) are tasks that are devalued because they are female. However, these activities constitute an important part of the investigations carried out by the services studied. Therefore, insisting on the most scientific and technical points of investigations can be understood as a way of deviating from the most "feminine" aspects of police work. In addition to the technical nature of the investigations, and the mystery surrounding the suspect's identity, the prestige of the Souleymane D. case among investigators is also explained by the nature of the acts committed by the accused, which determines his dangerousness in the eyes of the police.

Assessing Suspect Dangerousness

The complexity of an investigation alone is not enough to make a "big case"; those allow police officers to confront dangerous suspects. Here we observe a mechanism described by Dominique Monjardet (2002): in investigative policing, the value of the officer is measured by the value of the suspect he arrests. But what is a "valuable" suspect in the investigations before us? How do police officers assess the dangerousness of a respondent, and what does this say about their perceptions of the legitimacy of their actions? The dangerousness of suspects is judged along three dimensions: those of public order, protection against further violence, and defense of children and the family.

Protecting Public Order

Police officers prioritize cases that provide them with the opportunity to display advanced investigative techniques. However, these techniques vary depending on whether or not the offender is known when it is reported. When victims do not know their attacker, the investigation conducted by the police must identify, locate, and arrest the accused. These cases enable investigators to demonstrate their skills. On the other hand, when the offender is known to the victim, particularly if it is a spouse or ex-spouse, it is presumed that little effort is required to truly identify and locate them. This has a significant influence on officers' assessment of those cases. The valuation of cases is therefore very strongly dependent on the relationship between the victim and offender. This is a factor which often differentiates incidents based on the locations where violence occurs. In the proceedings of the crime group of the Local Direction of Judicial Police of the Police Prefecture of Paris, while 53% of attacks committed by strangers took place in the public space, this is the case for only 6% of marital rape cases. Barbara G., a criminal investigation officer, stated that she preferred to investigate "a hand up her ass in a lobby" rather than a marital rape, on the grounds that in the latter case, "the added value of the criminal investigation police is zero." In other words, a sexual assault committed by a stranger in public space is considered to fall more within the jurisdiction of the judicial police than a rape committed by a spouse, even though both are crimes. This is in turn linked to the greater propensity of investigators to place a suspect in police custody when the assault took place in the public space. As a consequence, the aggressiveness of police repression of sexual offences depends on the level of public disorder they threaten. In this respect, sexual violence can be compared to prostitution, since it is the threat to public order that determines police actions towards prostitutes (Mainsant 2013), a norm reinforced by the law that defines the offence of solicitation. On the other hand, the law does not differentiate sexual violence according to the location in which it is committed. Moreover, the private dimension of such violence constitutes an aggravating circumstance during sentencing, when the perpetrator is a spouse or a close acquaintence. Despite this, police officers are reluctant to intervene in the private sphere, and place little value on cases of rape between spouses.

Attackers who attack people unknown to them are a potential threat to all women in public spaces. Conversely, spousal rapists only rape their spouses, which reduces their dangerousness in the eyes of the police and reduces the value of these cases in their eyes. In the end, the differential valuation of cases according to the place in which sexual violence takes place is linked to the actions police take in response. This values cases more on the basis of the number of people potentially affected than on the gravity of the harm done to the victim.

Preventing Further Violence

The use of physical violence is decisive in police assessment of an aggressor's dangerousness, to the point of taking precedence over the sexual dimension of the case being built against him. Take the case of the complaint of Hua W., a 50-year-old undocumented Chinese prostitute, who claimed to have been raped by a client, Jean-Marc L. He was 40 years old and a financial analyst. Hua told police investigators that a client gave her an appointment to perform a blowjob in a hotel, but instead of going to the hotel he drove her home, where he offered to drink wine with her, which she accepted. He then asked her for a blowjob, to which she replied that she wanted to see if he had the money. As he did not, she refused to perform oral sex, which triggered the anger of her attacker, who pulled her by the hair, hit her, and bit her to the point of making her arm bleed.

Jérôme P., one of the investigators of the crime group, considered Jean-Marc L. dangerous because he hit and bit the complainant hard enough for her to bear the marks of the violence she suffered. At the end of the investigation, rape charges were dropped by the prosecutor. However, Jérôme P. considered that Jean-Marc L. "will kill a woman next time," which marks him a target worthy of police action. He similarly described the attacker of a 62-year-old homeless Chinese woman who beat up his victim on the street before trying to undress her and then escape. Jérôme P.'s opinion was shared by the other officials in the group, who considered the accused a "swine," and he was arrested "before he could kill a woman." The fact that it was an attempted crime was secondary to their judgment.

The goal of preventing further violence further distinguished between cases and has an impact on police efforts. In 82% of cases where the suspect used physical violence, he was placed in police custody. This proportion dropped to 61% in the absence of physical violence. The prioritization of preventing further violence is common in the field of sexual violence and prostitution enforcement (Mainsant 2008). It may be related to the general decline in tolerance of bodily harm in contemporary societies (Mucchielli 2011), which in this case is left to the police to reinforce.

Protecting Children and Families

Police perceptions of the dangerousness of suspects in cases involving minors follow a somewhat different logic from that applied to assailants of adult victims. Sexual violence against minors that is reported to the police is more often committed in private spaces (Pérona 2017). Moreover, it is *less* often accompanied by other physical violence. The intensity of the violence committed is not essential in defining a "big case" for investigators when it comes to children. Cases valued by the police are those where their action has prevented the act of violence or has reduced the extent of the violence that does occur.

Even without going as far as violence, physical contact between the accused and the minor victims is not essential in order to make the "big case." In the account of Samia M. and Francis C., both of whom work in the unit dedicated to child pornography offences attached to one of the Ile-de-France minors squads, a suspect's occupation can be involved in his being labeled as dangerous by the police. The fact that a suspect works in a profession that is in contact with many children puts him in a position to victimize many of them, and therefore to represent a danger. Samia M. and Francis C. apply a similar reasoning to the possessors of child pornography material, when it comes to revealing or not to those around them the nature of the offence they have committed:

> When there is no child, and you see that it is not the big pervert in quotation marks, you try to minimize so as not to destroy the family unit. Because the goal of the game is not to destroy the person, it's not our goal. That justice will take care of it. But our job is to make him understand what he did. And when there are no children in the family, we try not to overdo it ...
> (Francis C., 45 years old, investigator in minors squad, child pornography unit)

> Then, when there are children, or when there is a risk, when you feel that it is really dangerous, then you have to alert the family. Because it's actually going to be the only way to protect society. Since they are alerted, they will be able to report to the police if there is a problem.
> (Samia M., 40 years old, investigator in minors squad, child pornography unit)

Possessors of child pornography are not the only dangerous suspects for officers serving in the minors squads. Perpetrators of intra-family rape are also labelled as target populations worthy of police action, not because of the number of potential victims nvolved, but because of the nature of the relationship between them and their victims:

> The cases that are close to my heart, because I feel useful in these types of offences, are the offences of rape and sexual assault that are intra-family and we also have a lot of them. We have an important role to play in protecting children, and we can have a rather thankless role sometimes in this kind of procedure, because children are not aware that for them ... they are not aware that they are in danger and that in fact what we do to them is wrong, because they think they are receiving love in these kinds of situations. So when we explain to them that it's not normal, that what Dad, or Grandpa, or Uncle, or the cousin are doing, is not normal, they realize that maybe in our office, maybe months after, maybe weeks after, or even years after, that what they have been victims of is still quite serious. And we are faced with perpetrators, on this type of offence, who can be dangerous, because they have reached their family circle, they have gone looking for the easy way out, and as a result they have destroyed an entire family system that could be structured and is no longer structured overnight.
> (Caroline S., 34 years old, investigator, minors squad)

Their abuse of a position of authority, whether due to a suspect's profession (e.g. doctors, teachers, bosses) or to the existence of a family relationship between the victim and offender, allows the police to assess the dangerousness of the individual, which appears to be closely linked to the stigma attached to the offences committed.

Finally, it should be noted that these dimensions of suspect dangerousness are not racialized. Unlike the police officers of the anti-procuring brigade, who rank their target populations according to their geographical origin (Mainsant 2014), officers of the judicial police and the juvenile brigades do not link an individual's dangerousness to his or her ethno-racial affiliation. It is the suspect's behaviour and the characteristics of the assault that are at the core of the police action, and not the social background of the individual.

In summary, the involvement of young victims reorganizes the hierarchy of police prestige across investigations, since assaults committed in the private sphere, and particularly within the family, are considered worthy of police attention and can claim to be important cases. It is in the name of child and family protection that police officers consider their intervention in the private sphere to be legitimate. Conversely, incidents sheltered by marital relationships are still an area where police officers are reluctant to act. Finally, the valuation of suspects by the minors squads and the crime groups do not completely overlap. While both groups refer to them as "predators," defining their dangerousness, this category is assessed very differently depending on whether the victim is an adult woman or a child. Thus, for police officers working in crime groups, the ideal predator is a violent street rapist who threatens any passer-by. On the other hand, the ideal predator for the minors squads is embodied by the incestuous father who attacks his daughters or by a teacher who puts many children in danger. These different images of the predator refer to different but not exclusive bases for police action: the need to protect public order, prevent further violence, and defend children and the family. The final criterion determining police responses to sexual violence, that of a case's potential for judicial punishment, remains to be examined.

Potential for Judicial Action

> And there are very often criminal responses in the offences we deal with. And that's nice too. Because, for example, colleagues in narcotics units, they can work day and night on a case and have much less criminal response. Because the business we're dealing with is shocking. At the trial, of course, a juror is shocked by the comments made by the victim, by the comments made by the defendant, it is shocking. And when we are witnesses and have to appear at the trial, our words are very important, because jurors drink our words.
>
> (Caroline S., 34 years old, investigator, minors squad)

Caroline S.'s comments reveal that the potential decisions of judges are seen by officers as another criteria shaping their response to cases. To paraphrase Dominique Monjardet (2002), it is not only "the arrest of suspect number 1 who makes the first cop in France," but also the officer's appearance before a court and his or her conviction rate. The prestige of cases for police officers serving in the juvenile brigades, but also for those working in crime groups, is indexed by the toughness of the response provided by magistrates. In addition, tough judicial responses are considered generally satisfactory by officers of the minors squads and the judicial police. Contrary to many reports by sociologists of the police, the officers I interviewed do not consider "their action to be hindered by a judicial system biased by the judges' leniency towards criminals" (Jobard and de Maillard 2015, p. 102). For them, the sanctions that are imposed express their repulsion against sexual violence. This point deserves to be highlighted, as it goes against the view that police routinely denounce "judicial laxity" (Jobard 2016). This has been reported in studies of other investigative services, for example among narcotics squads (Barbier 2016). A quick look at law enforcement statistics reveals differences in judicial responses to offences handled by minors and drug brigades. In 2014, the police and *gendarmerie* reported 11 times more drug-related offences than rape and sexual assault of minors (Ministry of Interior 2015). However, the proportion of people sentenced to prison for drug offences is only twice as high as that of those sentenced for sexual violence against minors. The former represents 14% of all people sentenced to prison in 2014, the latter 8% (Ministry of Justice 2015).

This tougher judicial response to sexual violence is associated with a sense of the effectiveness of police action among investigators in the juvenile brigades, who regularly compare their work with that of drug squads:

> In some brigades, you have the same guy 50 times in front of you. It's unbearable. Here, I've never had a recurrence. Never. I've never had the same person twice. In fact, really characterized and all that, I never had a recurrence. So, I think I'm useful for something. I loved working in the narcotics, you have an adrenaline, hiding places, perquisites, you have a very strong field side. On the other hand, you arrest a drug dealer, a pot dealer, we agree, within ten minutes he is replaced. So, there are a lot of sword blows in the water. Whereas here, I have the impression that even if the guy doesn't eat, once again the idea is not to say I'm going to put a guy in jail for 20 years, but really to put a situation to rest.
>
> (Martine R., 49, investigator, minors squad)

Martine R.'s comments testify to the coexistence of different hierarchies of prestige between different segments of the police institution (Lemaire 2008). While working in the drug brigade allows actors to get closer to the model of masculine warefare, work among minors is valued because it has visible effects outside the institution. It responds to a social demand for child protection, and has consequences that are visible to police officers, as they regularly lead to criminal penalties.

This commitment to repression has an impact on policing. In the criminal brigades of the judicial police, officers constantly anticipate the decision that the magistrate will take at the end of the investigation, assessing from the moment a complaint is received whether a case will "hold," and whether it will "give something." This assessment is based on the characteristics of the assault, mainly the relationship between the victim and the aggressor, as well as on the location of the assault and the length of time it took to be reported. Sexual violence committed by a stranger in a public place and promptly reported is more frequently identified as "good business" by investigators and leads to more frequent police apprehension of a suspect. These cases are also the ones which judges are most likely to prosecute (Pérona 2017).

Conclusion

By focusing on the rankings that police officers grant different investigations, we have seen how different factors affect the investigative efforts of police working sexual violence cases. Their priorities echo what social psychology has identified as "rape myths," or common representations of sexual violence.

For investigators assigned to crime groups, it is the proximity of the case to a mythical scenario describing violent street rape that contributes to its prestige within the organization. Big cases are those that fit the police imagination regarding "real rape." One factor that shapes police intervention is the speed with which rapes are reported by victims, since three-quarters of rapes attributed to strangers are reported within 24 hours, half the average for all rapes. We have seen how the value of the case is also based on the demands it places on the professional skills of investigators.

We have also seen that references to the dangerousness of offenders affects the classification and prioritization of investigations, even aside from whether the case reflects a stereotypical vision of what is rape and what is not. Thus, police officers do not simply consider marital rape less serious than street rape.

The first dimension of dangerousness is the threat that a case presents to public order and is linked to the preventive dimension of police action. The second dimension on which cases are rated is the prevention of further violence. However, unlike other services, sexual assault cases are not prestigious because they allow police officers to perform difficult physical feats and demonstrate their courage in the face of suspects. Instead, what makes police officers value an investigation is that it is consistent with their mandate to protect women and children from male physical violence. It is through the victims that police officers confront the violence of the respondents. It is therefore not surprising that police officers take respondents who have used physical violence into police custody more often than others. Finally, the third dimension of the dangerousness of the respondents is that of the risk to children and families. This supports the legitimacy of interventions by police officers of the minors brigades in the private sphere.

These points highlight the convergence of specialized sexual offence investigations with other parts of the police institution. The logic of protecting public order and repressing crime, as well as the value placed on the violence of suspects, is not specific to the services studied. These goals can be observed elsewhere in public security (Darley and Gauthier 2014), and in other investigative services such as the repression of prostitution (Mainsant 2014). However, the motives of the police officers we met do not fully correspond to the virile model dominant in the institution. They are oriented towards protecting the physical safety of individuals, more than on fighting "real bad guys."

Finally, these bases for police action mean that the investigators' valued cases are those closest to the "real rape" scenario identified by social psychology, with the notable exception of incestuous rape. However, these hierarchies are not based on hostile discourse towards victims, nor on distinctions in the harm suffered by victims based on their relationship with their aggressor.

References

Amir, M. 1967. Victim-precipitated forcible rape. *The Journal of Criminal Law, Criminology, and Police Science* 58: 493–502.

Angeloff, T., and Arborio, A. M. 2002. Des hommes dans des 'métiers de femmes': Mixité au travail et espaces professionnels dévalorisés. *Sociologia del lavoro* 85: 123–135.

Barbier, K. 2016. *Accessoires. L'invisibilisation des femmes dans les procédures pénales en matière de stupéfiants*. Thèse de Sociologie, Université Versailles Saint-Quentin en Yvelines, Guyancourt.

Béliard, A., and Eideliman, J. S. 2008. Au-delà de la déontologie. Pp. 123–141 in D. Fassin and A. Bensa (Eds.) *Les politiques de l'enquête*. Paris: La Découverte.

Bucher, R., and Strauss, A. 1961. Professions in process. *American Journal of Sociology* 66: 325–334.

Chennells, R. 2009. Sentencing: The 'real rape' myth. *Agenda: Empowering Women for Gender Equity* 82: 23–38.

Darley, M., and Gauthier, J. 2014. Une virilité interpellée? En quête de genre au commissariat. *Genèses* 97: 67–86.

Dedieu, F. 2010. La course aux 'belles affaires,' la congruence d'intérêts professionnels et organisationnels dans la police judiciaire. *Déviance et société* 34: 347–379.

De Man, C., et Van Praet, S. 2012. Des atteintes sexuelles commises par des mineurs: Une analyse de dossiers du parquet de la jeunesse. Pp. 109–163 in C. Adam, D. De Fraene, P. Mary, C. Nagels, and S. Smeets (Eds.) *Sexe et normes*. Bruxelles: Bruylant.

Du Mont, J., Miller, K.-L., and Myhr, T. L. 2003. The role of "real rape" and "real victim" stereotypes in the police reporting practices of sexually assaulted women. *Violence against Women* 9: 466–486.

Estrich, S. 1987. *Real rape*. Cambridge: Harvard University Press.

Hochschild, A. R. 2003. Travail émotionnel, règles de sentiments et structure sociale. *Travailler* 9: 19–49.

Hughes, E. 1962. Good people and dirty work. *Social Problems* 10: 3–11.

Jobard, F. 2016. Colères policières. *Esprit* Mars-Avril: 64-73.

Jobard, F., and de Maillard, J. 2015. *Sociologie de la police: politiques, organisations, réformes*. Paris: Armand Colin.

Lemaire, É. 2008. Spécialisation et distinction dans un commissariat de police. *Sociétés contemporaines* 72: 59–79.

Lonsway, K., and Fitzgerald, L. 1994. Rape myths in review. *Psychology of Women Quarterly* 18: 133–164.

Maier, S. L. 2014. *Rape, victims, and investigations: Experiences and perceptions of law enforcement officers responding to reported rapes*. New York: Routledge.

Mainsant, G. 2008. L'Etat en action: Classements et hiérarchies dans les investigations policières en matière de proxénétisme. *Sociétés contemporaines* 72: 37–57.

Mainsant, G. 2013. Gérer les contradictions du droit 'par le bas'. *Actes de la recherche en sciences sociales* 198: 23–34.

Mainsant, G. 2014. Comment la 'Mondaine' construit-elle ses populations cibles? *Genèses* 97: 8–25.

Ministère de la Justice. 2015. *Les condamnations – Année 2014*.

Ministry of Interior. 2015. Annuaire des crimes et des délits par dé, partement, années 2009 à 2014. Paris: Minsitry of Interior.

Monjardet, D. 2002. Les policiers. Pp. 265–274 in L. Mucchielli and P. Robert (Eds.) *Crime et sécurité: l'état des savoirs*. Paris: La Découverte.

Mossuz-Lavau. 2002. *Les lois de l'amour* (2e éd.). Paris: Payot & Rivages.

Mucchielli, L. 2006. L'élucidation des homicides: de l'enchantement technologique à l'analyse du travail des enquêteurs de police judiciaire. *Déviance et société* 30: 91–119.

Mucchielli, L. 2011. *L'invention de la violence*. Paris: Fayard.

Pérona, O. 2017. *Le consentement sexuel saisi par les institutions pénales: Policiers, médecins légistes et procureurs face aux violences sexuelles*. Thèse de Science Politique. Paris: Saclay.

Pruvost, G. 2008a. *De la « sergote » à la femme flic. Une autre histoire de l'institution policière (1935–2005)*. Paris: La Découverte.

Pruvost, G. 2008b. Ordre et désordre dans les coulisses d'une profession. *Sociétés contemporaines* 72: 81–101.

Sleath, E., and Bull, R. 2017. Police perceptions of rape victims and the impact on case decision making: A systematic review. *Aggression and Violent Behavior* 34: 102–112.

Smeets, S. 2012. Corps de police et corps délictueux: la réaction policière à la 'déviance sexuelle'. Pp. 187–226 in C. Adam, D. De Fraene, P. Mary, C. Nagels, and S. Smeets (Eds.) *Sexe et normes*. Bruxelles: Bruylant.

Stewart, M. W., Dobbin, S. A., and Gatowski, S. I. 1996. "Real rapes" and "real victims": The shared reliance on common cultural definitions of rape. *Feminist Legal Studies* 4: 159–177.

Temkin, J., and Krahé, B. 2008. *Sexual assault and the justice gap: A question of attitude*. Oxford: Hart Publishing.

Yancey-Martin, P. 2005. *Rape work*. New York: Routledge.

Index

aggressive police style 13, 40, 47, 302, 304; police raids 281–282, 284, 288–290, 304; stops 202, 211–212
Algerian war 45–48
arrests: number of 103, 108, 150–151; power of 14, 25, 61, 150, 154, 158; stops and 212–214

banlieues policing: command centralization 194–195; crime and fear 187–190, 195; immigrant conditions 188; officer assignment 192–192, 197; police militarization 192–197; policing styles 49, 190, 197–198, 199; protest policing in 225; public opinion of 198; social trends in 188–189
border policing: history of 12, 254–255; organization of 256–260; origins of 253–254; practices 261–263; Schengen regulations 258; scope of policing 260–261
British contrasts 21, 44–45, 83, 294

career development 105–107
centralization 97–98; efficiencies of 73–74; hierarchy 77–79; history of 4, 5, 23–25, 28–30, 71; logic of 71–72, 147–148; problems of 61–64, 77, 82–83
civilians in policing 96–97
colonial period 39–40, 41–45; legacy of 13–14, 41–45
community policing 16, 79–82; Emmanuel Macron 306–307; François Hollande 305–306; by gendarmerie 298; history of 302; implementation of 298–302; meaning in France 295, 299; metrics driven 304; Nicolas Sarkozy 303–305; organization of 307–308; Paris 300; politics of 302–305; racial profiling 306; terrorism 305–306; zero tolerance 302
coproduction of security 147, 153, 157–160
corruption 119
criminal intelligence: crime pattern analysis 86–87; history of 100–102, 104; organization of 91–95, 97, 100, 102, 107–108, 110–111; procedures 86, 88, 90, 98; reform of 89, 91

De Gaulle period 34–35
discrimination: against gays 318; against women 311; mobilization against 122, 197, 203–205; racial/ethnic 39, 41, 43, 46, 205–208, 225, 277, 281
dual policing system 1, 4, 21–22, 54–55, 58–61, 64–65, 66–67

external oversight 116, 121–123, 126–127

gendarmerie: history of 3, 30–32, 55–61; organization of 73, 87–88
gender issues: encounters with police 315–317; feminization trends 313; LGBTQ issues 318; masculinity 310; police research on 311–312; roles in policing 15; in sex crimes units 319–321; sexual hierarchy 317–318; stereotypes 314
Governance 9–10, 155–157, 178–180

housing police 151, 152–153

identify checks (police stops) 12–13; history of 203–204; impact on community 209; legal status 204–205, 214; politics of 213–216; practice 208, 210–213; racial profiling 202, 205–208

insecurity: in the banlieues 187–190; politicization of 302; public insecurity 286, 290, 294
intelligence-led policing *see* criminal intelligence
interactions: and ID checks 208–210; gendered 312, 316; 320; police officers and public 79, 197, 283

management: culture 81, 104–105, 108–110; new public 101, 304
militarization of police 39–40, 189, 192–197
municipal police 8, 10, 30, 148–151, 154

Napoleonic system 23–26

oversight of policing: internal 118–121, 125–126; judicial 110–118; legislative 116–118; media 123–125; political 6, 7; professional 118–119, 126–127; public 123–124

Paris policing 26–28, 33, 34, 300
partnerships 9; collaboration 170–172, 175–177; governance of 169, 174–176; history of 165–168; obstacles to 170–173; police 172, 173–174, 177–178; public involvement 174; schools 173–174; scope of 168–169, 173; trends in 164–165, 173, 179–181
performance management 101–102, 112–113, 302–305
plural policing 7, 8, 9, 10, 147, 153; governance of 155–159; trends in 147–148,157–159, 160
police nationale: history of 3, 33–35, 55; organization of 73–74, 87–88
police research 1, 42–43, 97
police style alternative 157–160; French 13, 40, 49, 304; legalistic 197–198; protest policing 230
political role of police 10, 11, 76–77
private security 8, 133, 148; arming of 139–143, 154–155; functions 136, 143–144; growth of 133–135; oversight of 137–139; personnel 135
protest policing 11–12; in banlieues 225–226; case studies 228–230; criticisms of 219; European models 230–231; history of 221–223; jurisdiction 221, 224; scope of 220; tactics and strategy 226–227
public opinion 14, 15–16; history of research 270; measurement issues 269, 272, 274 277; national rankings 276, 278, 279; police effectiveness 274, 276–277; and policy 287; and politics 285–290; race and ethnicity 280–283, 284; trust in police 270–274, 278, 280; use of force 283–284; victim satisfaction 2, 279
public–police relations 79–80, 269–290

racialized policing 13, 40–41
recruitment 74–76, 80

sexual violence: children 335–336, 339; investigation of 328–331; legal issues 327, 329; myths about 326; organization of police 330; prestige of cases 327–328, 339; prosecution 337–338; suspect dangerousness 333, 339; violence level 334, 339
specialization of police 5–6, 89–90, 106, 107, 112
stops, searches *see* identity checks
Sûreté générale 32

terrorism policing 11; 2015 attacks 240–242; conduct of 242–246; expansion of 236–237; fate of suspects 246–247; high policing 249; judicial system 247–248; organization of 235, 237–238; reform of 238–240
transport police 151–152

Vichy period 33–35
violence: domestic 112, 178, 181; judicial control of police violence 118, 121, 125–126; police 13, 61, 41, 45, 48, 116, 121, 124, 138, 193, 198–199, 250, 269–270, 284–286, 288–290; political 11, 223, 228–229, 231, 234, 238; politicization of 288–290; sexual 14, 167, 173–174, 318–322, 326–339; urban 188, 191, 195, 197, 225, 227, 303